A CERTAIN SCIENTIFIC RAILGUN

Astral* Buddy

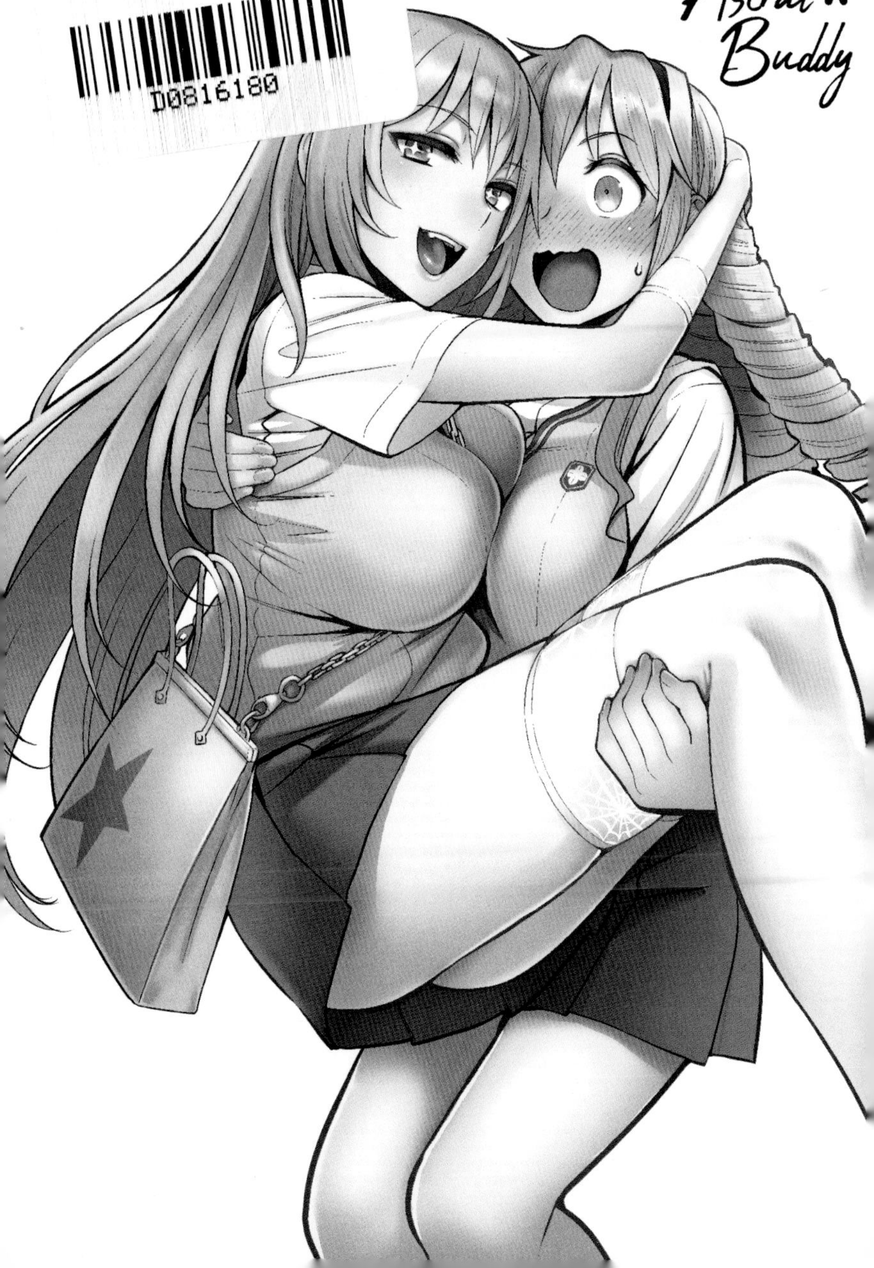

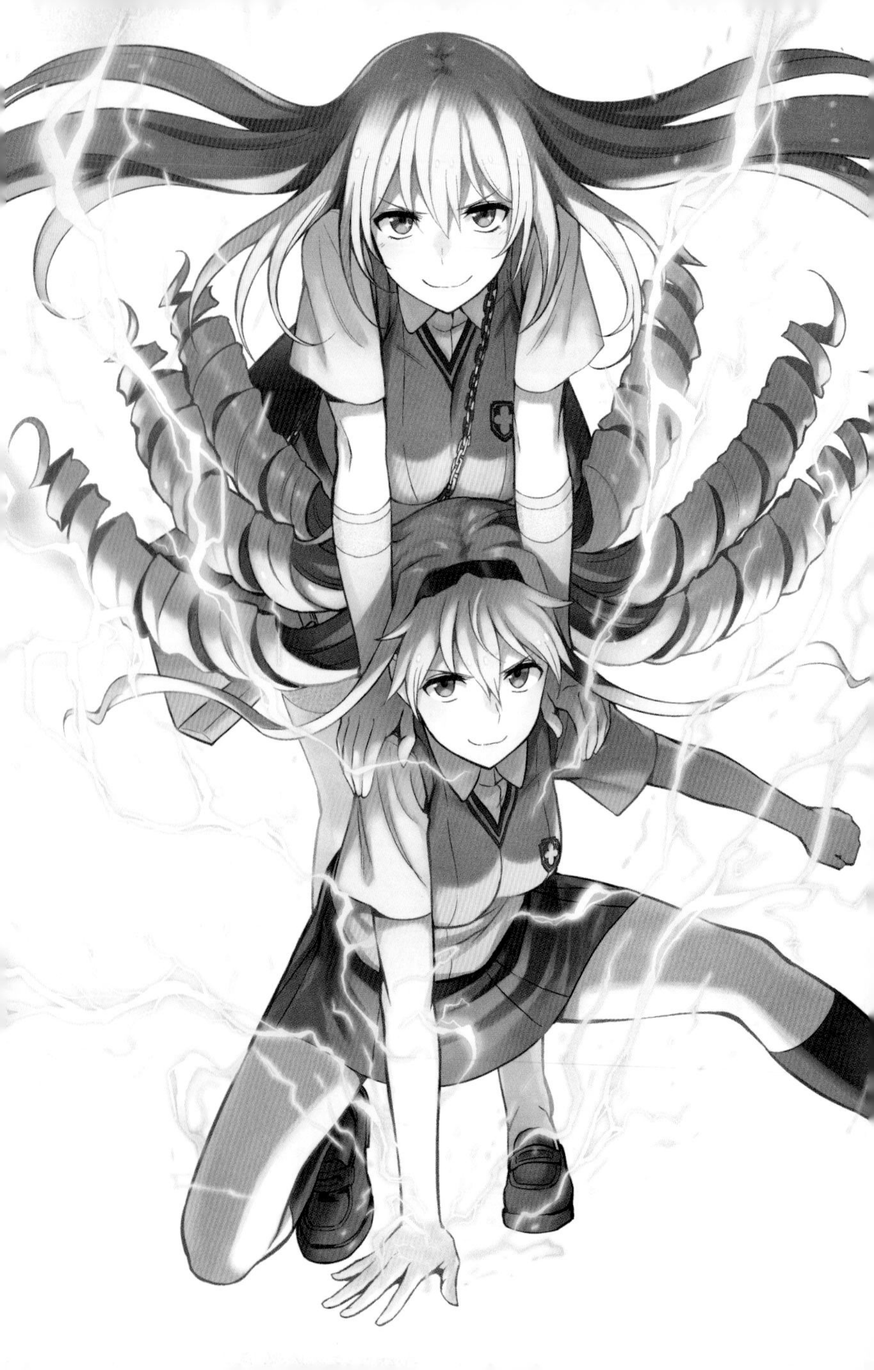

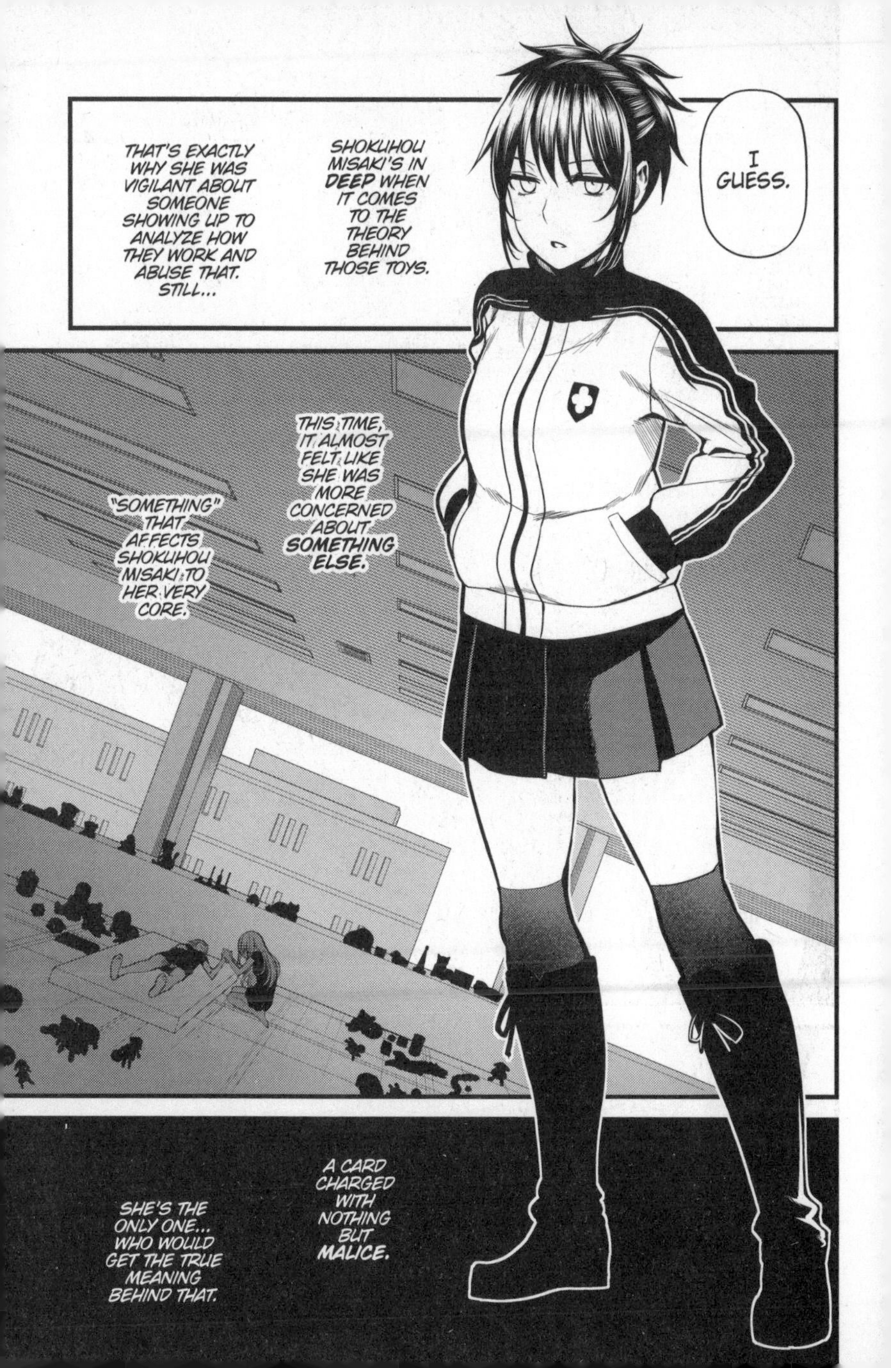
I GUESS.
SHOKUHOU MISAKI'S IN DEEP WHEN IT COMES TO THE THEORY BEHIND THOSE TOYS.
THAT'S EXACTLY WHY SHE WAS VIGILANT ABOUT SOMEONE SHOWING UP TO ANALYZE HOW THEY WORK AND ABUSE THAT. STILL...
THIS TIME, IT ALMOST FELT LIKE SHE WAS MORE CONCERNED ABOUT SOMETHING ELSE.
"SOMETHING" THAT AFFECTS SHOKUHOU MISAKI TO HER VERY CORE.
A CARD CHARGED WITH NOTHING BUT MALICE.
SHE'S THE ONLY ONE... WHO WOULD GET THE TRUE MEANING BEHIND THAT.

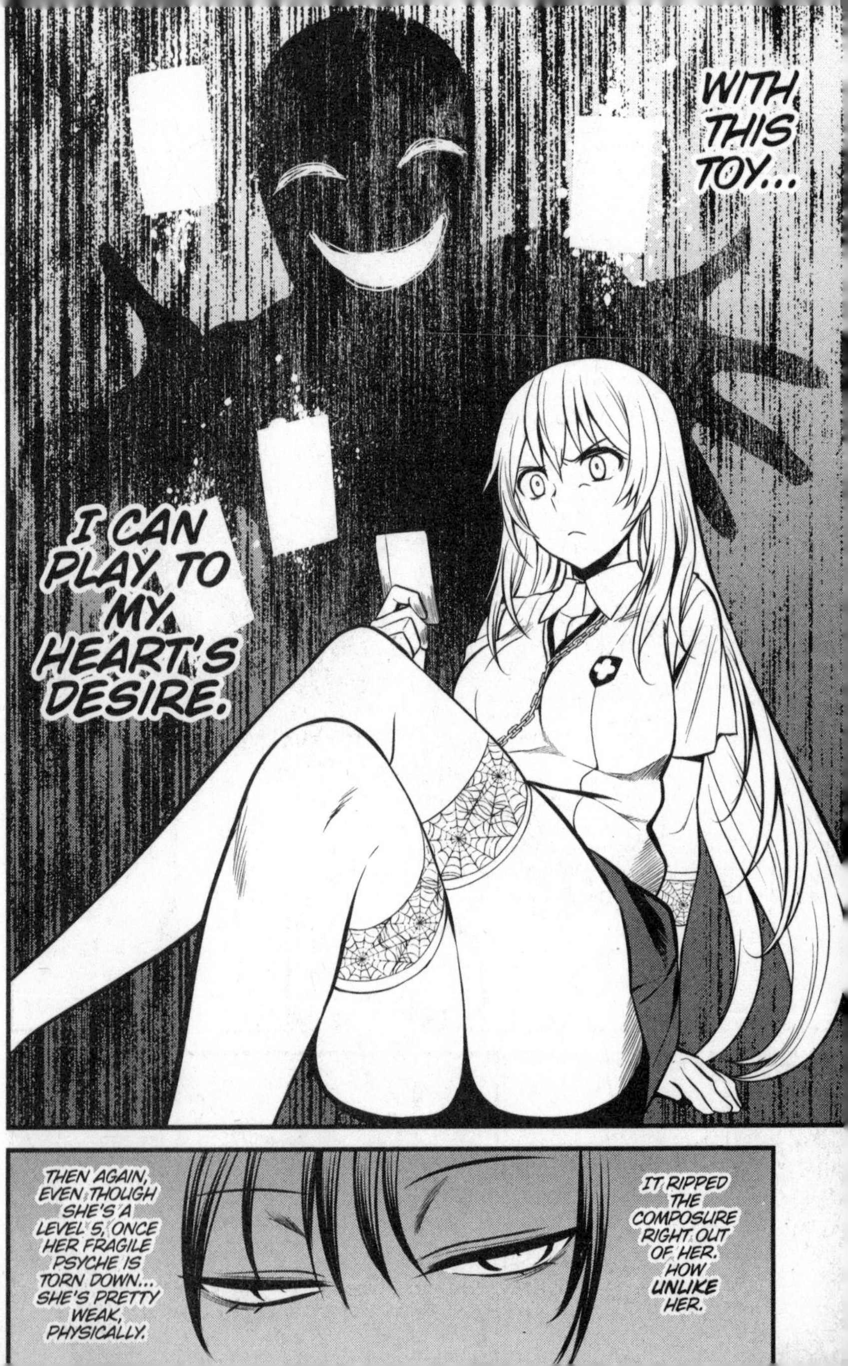
WITH THIS TOY...
I CAN PLAY TO MY HEART'S DESIRE.
IT RIPPED THE COMPOSURE RIGHT OUT OF HER. HOW UNLIKE HER.
THEN AGAIN, EVEN THOUGH SHE'S A LEVEL 5, ONCE HER FRAGILE PSYCHE IS TORN DOWN... SHE'S PRETTY WEAK, PHYSICALLY.

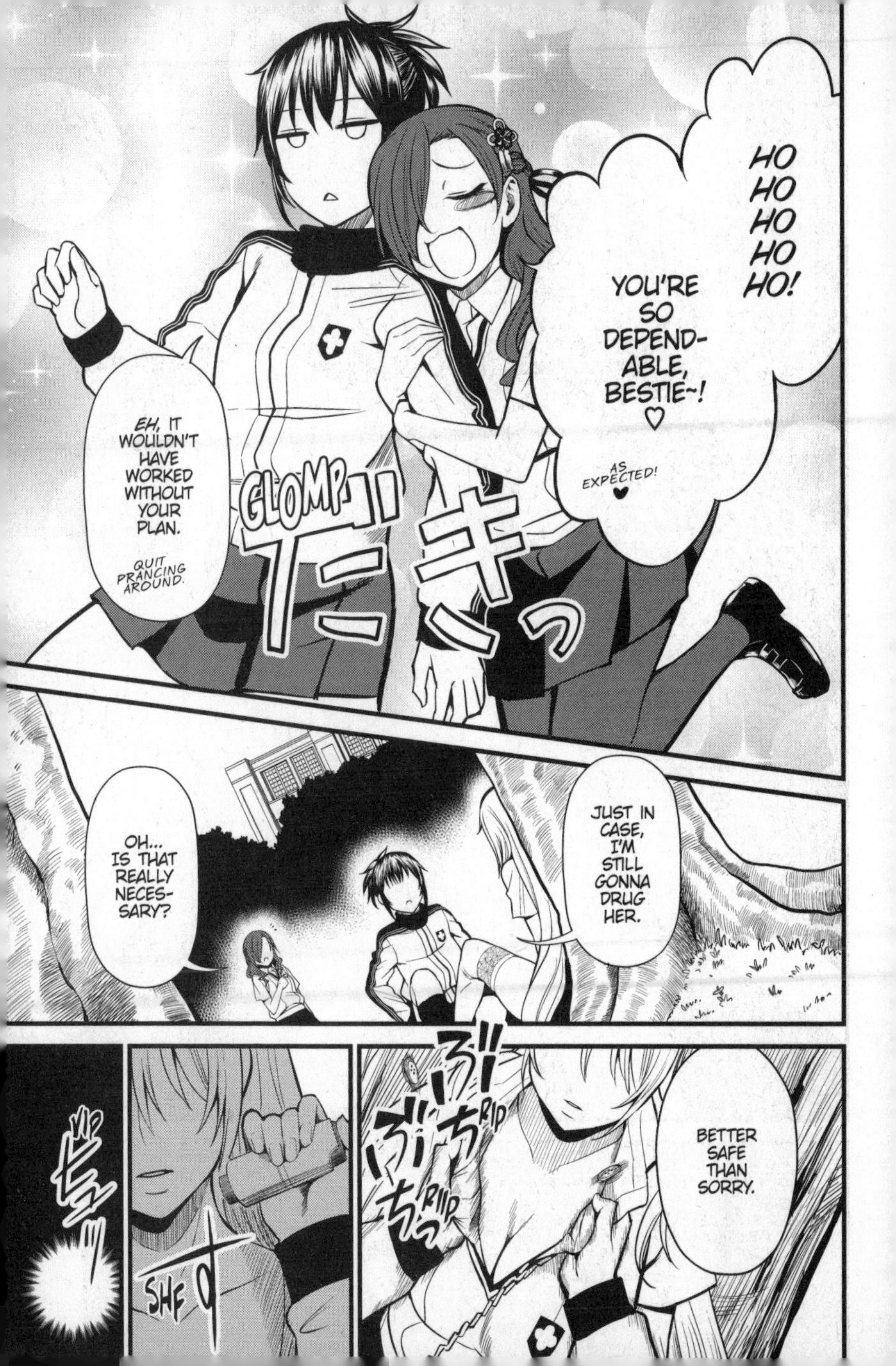
HO HO HO HO HO!
YOU'RE SO DEPENDABLE, BESTIE~! ♡
AS EXPECTED! ♥
GLOMP
EH, IT WOULDN'T HAVE WORKED WITHOUT YOUR PLAN.
QUIT PRANCING AROUND.
JUST IN CASE, I'M STILL GONNA DRUG HER.
OH... IS THAT REALLY NECES-SARY?
BETTER SAFE THAN SORRY.
RIP
RIIP
SHF

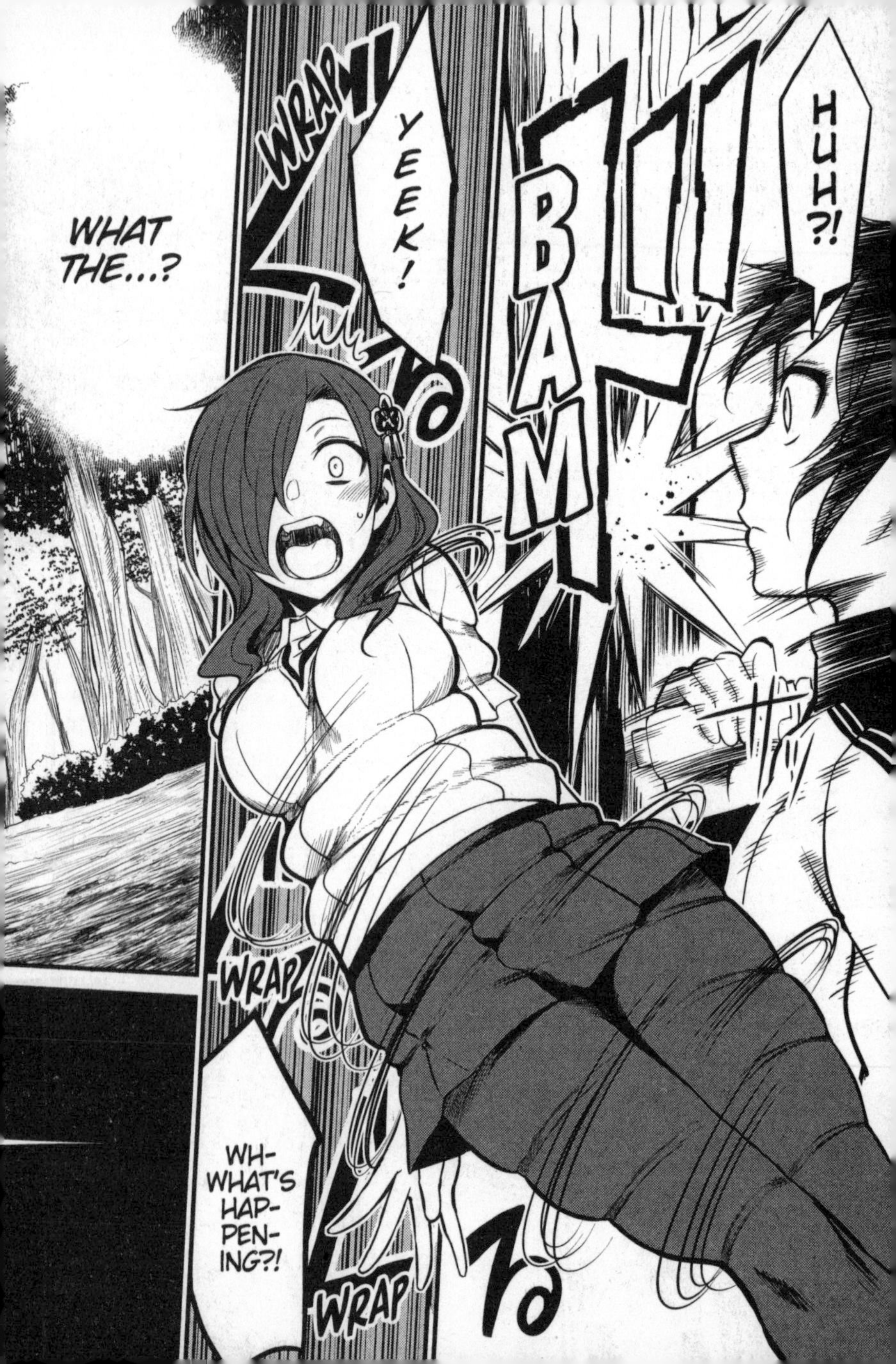
HUH?!
BAM
YEEK!
WRAP!
WRAP
WH-WHAT'S HAP-PEN-ING?!
WRAP
WHAT THE...?

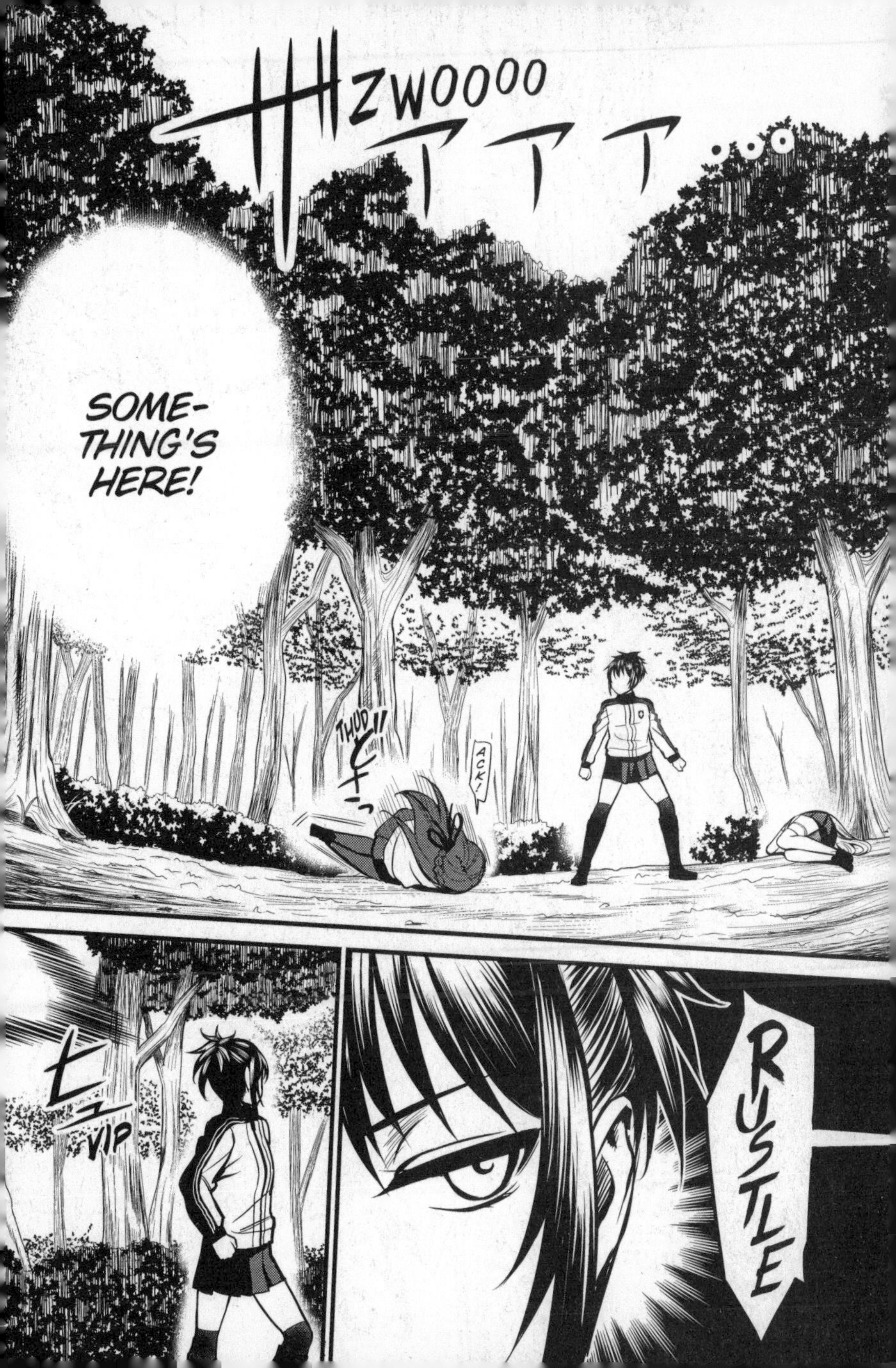
ZWOOOO
SOME-
THING'S
HERE!
ACK!
THUD!!
RUSTLE
ヒュ
VIP

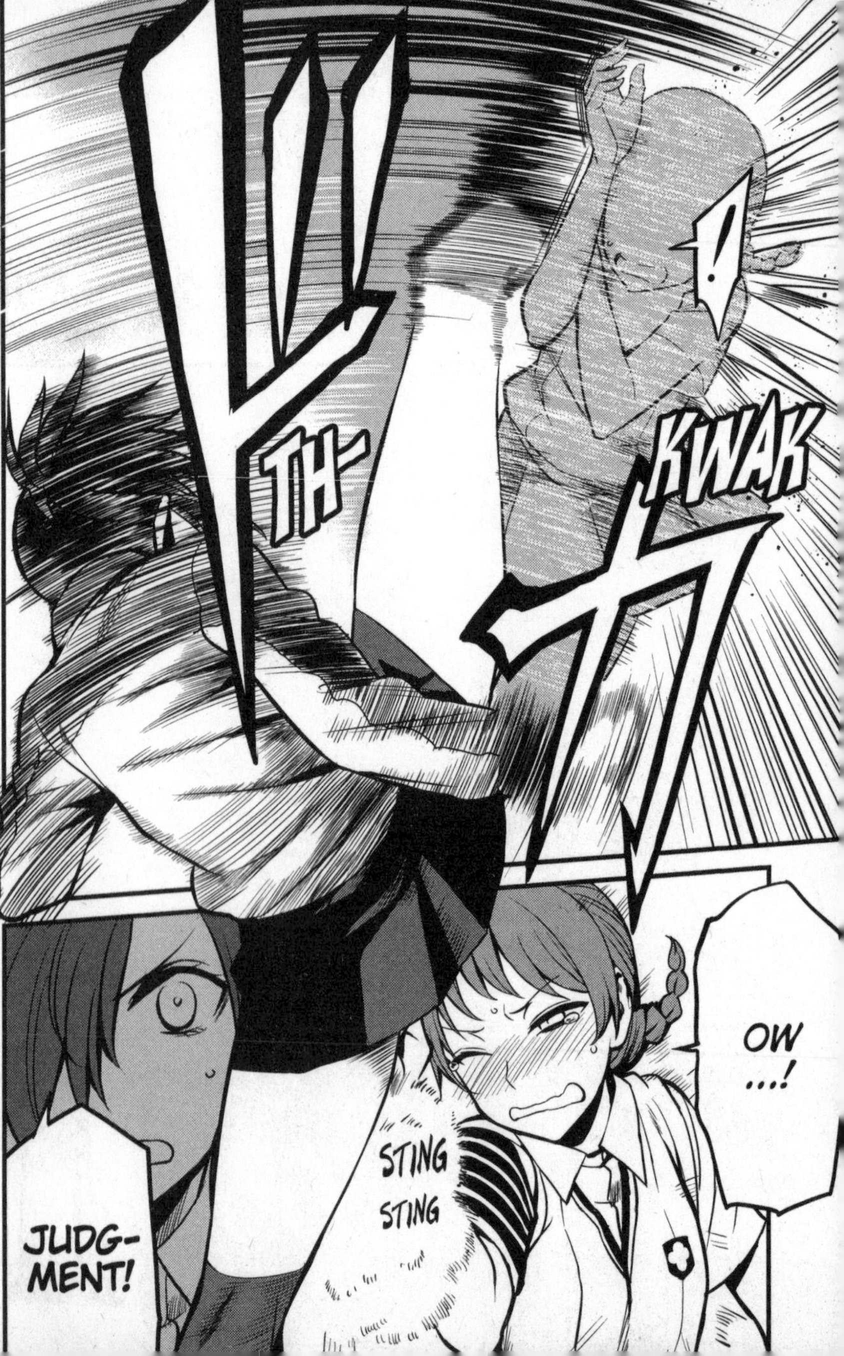
!
TH-
KWAK
OW ...!
STING
STING
JUDG-
MENT!

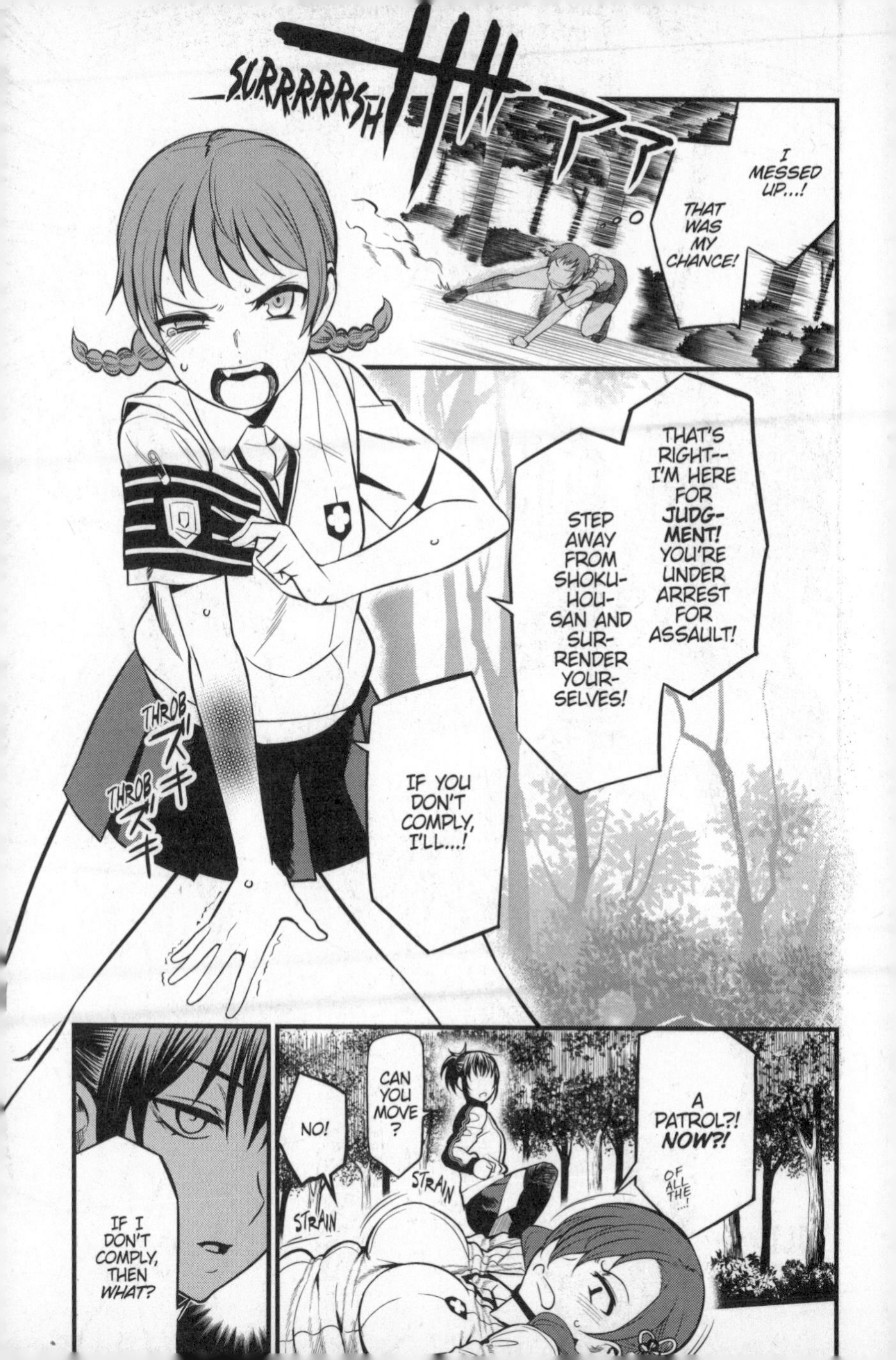
SCRRRRRSH
I MESSED UP...!
THAT WAS MY CHANCE!
THAT'S RIGHT-- I'M HERE FOR JUDGMENT! YOU'RE UNDER ARREST FOR ASSAULT!
STEP AWAY FROM SHOKUHOU-SAN AND SURRENDER YOURSELVES!
THROB
THROB
IF YOU DON'T COMPLY, I'LL...!
A PATROL?! NOW?!
OF ALL THE...!
CAN YOU MOVE?
NO!
STRAIN
STRAIN
IF I DON'T COMPLY, THEN WHAT?

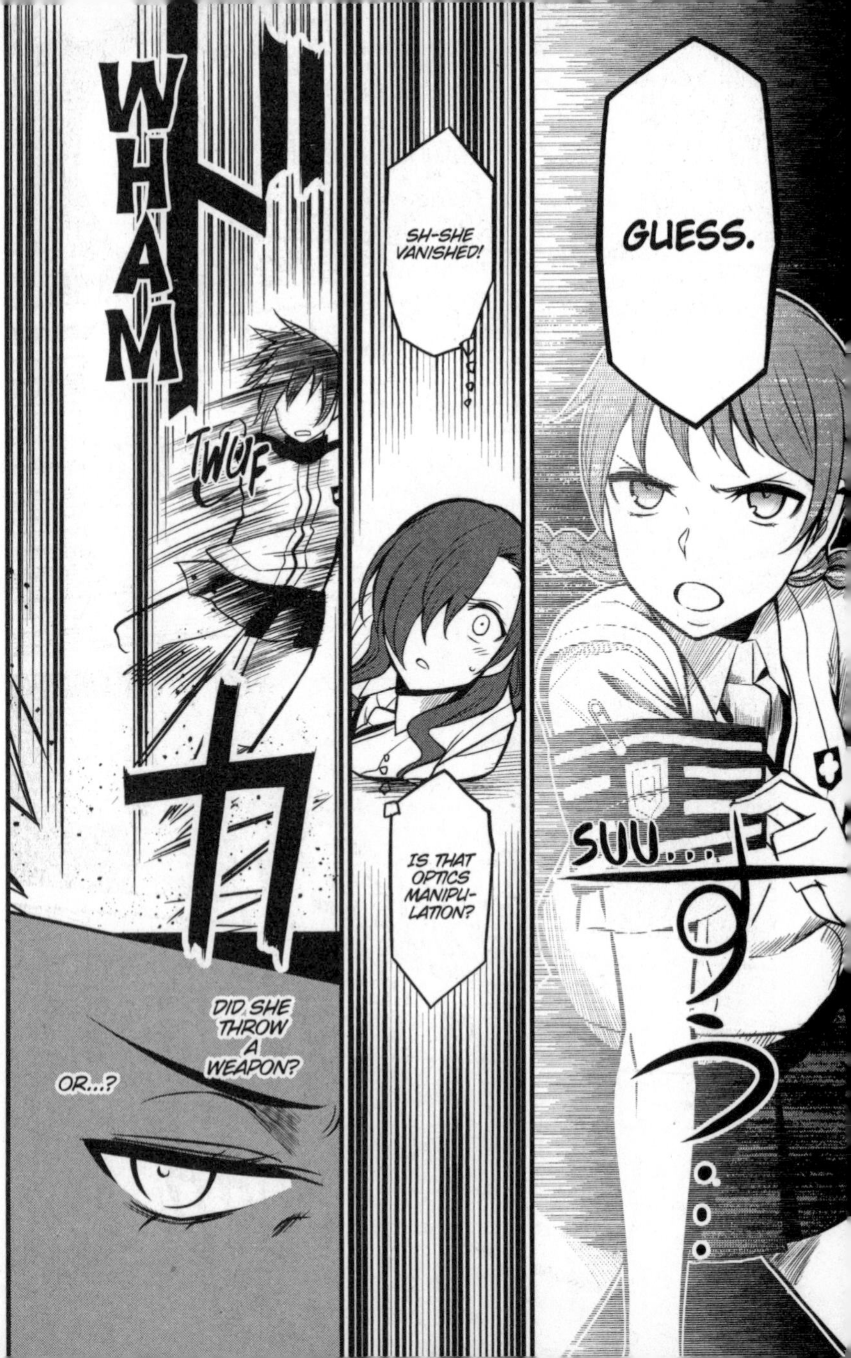
GUESS.
SUU...
SH-SHE VANISHED!
IS THAT OPTICS MANIPULATION?
WHAM
TWUF
DID SHE THROW A WEAPON?
OR...?

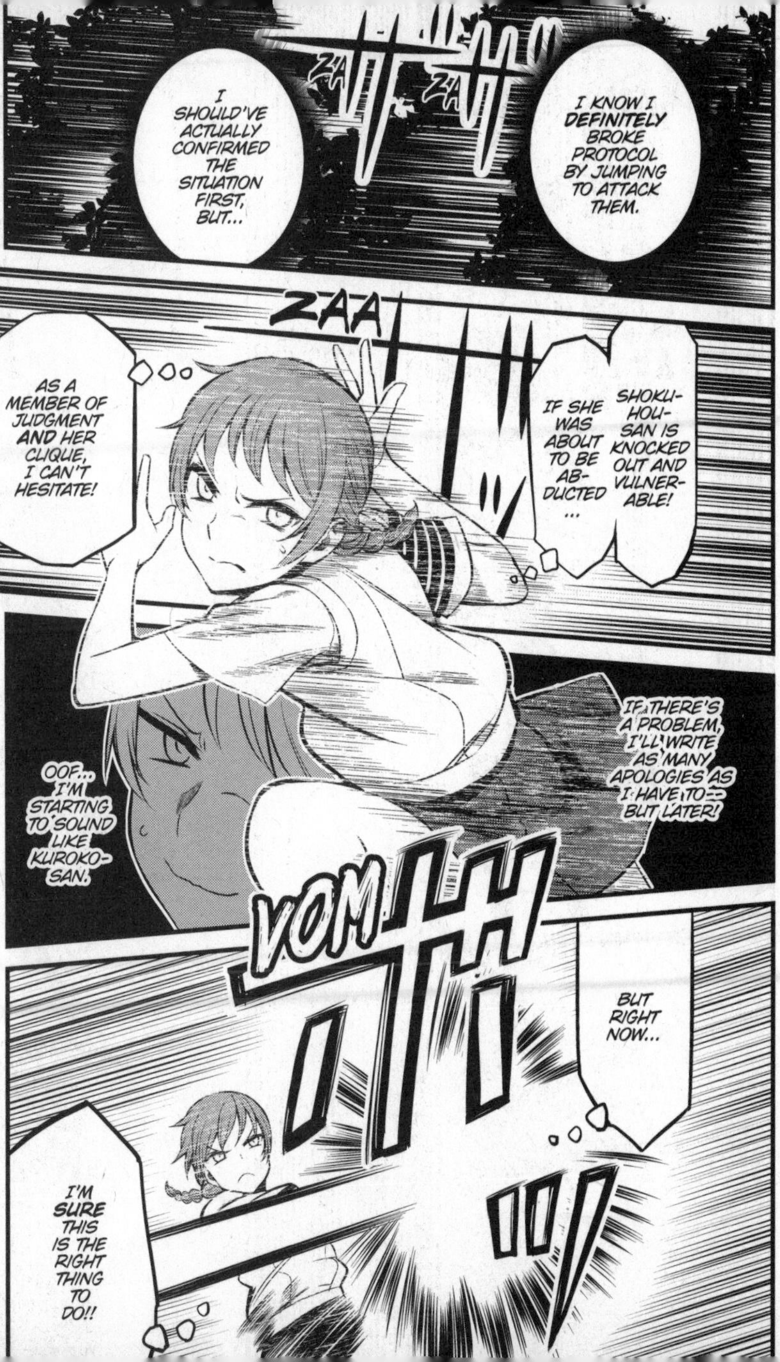
ZA
ZA
I KNOW I DEFINITELY BROKE PROTOCOL BY JUMPING TO ATTACK THEM.
I SHOULD'VE ACTUALLY CONFIRMED THE SITUATION FIRST, BUT...
ZAA
SHOKUHOU-SAN IS KNOCKED OUT AND VULNERABLE!
IF SHE WAS ABOUT TO BE ABDUCTED...
AS A MEMBER OF JUDGMENT AND HER CLIQUE, I CAN'T HESITATE!
IF THERE'S A PROBLEM, I'LL WRITE AS MANY APOLOGIES AS I HAVE TO-- BUT LATER!
OOF... I'M STARTING TO SOUND LIKE KUROKO-SAN.
VOM
BUT RIGHT NOW...
I'M SURE THIS IS THE RIGHT THING TO DO!!

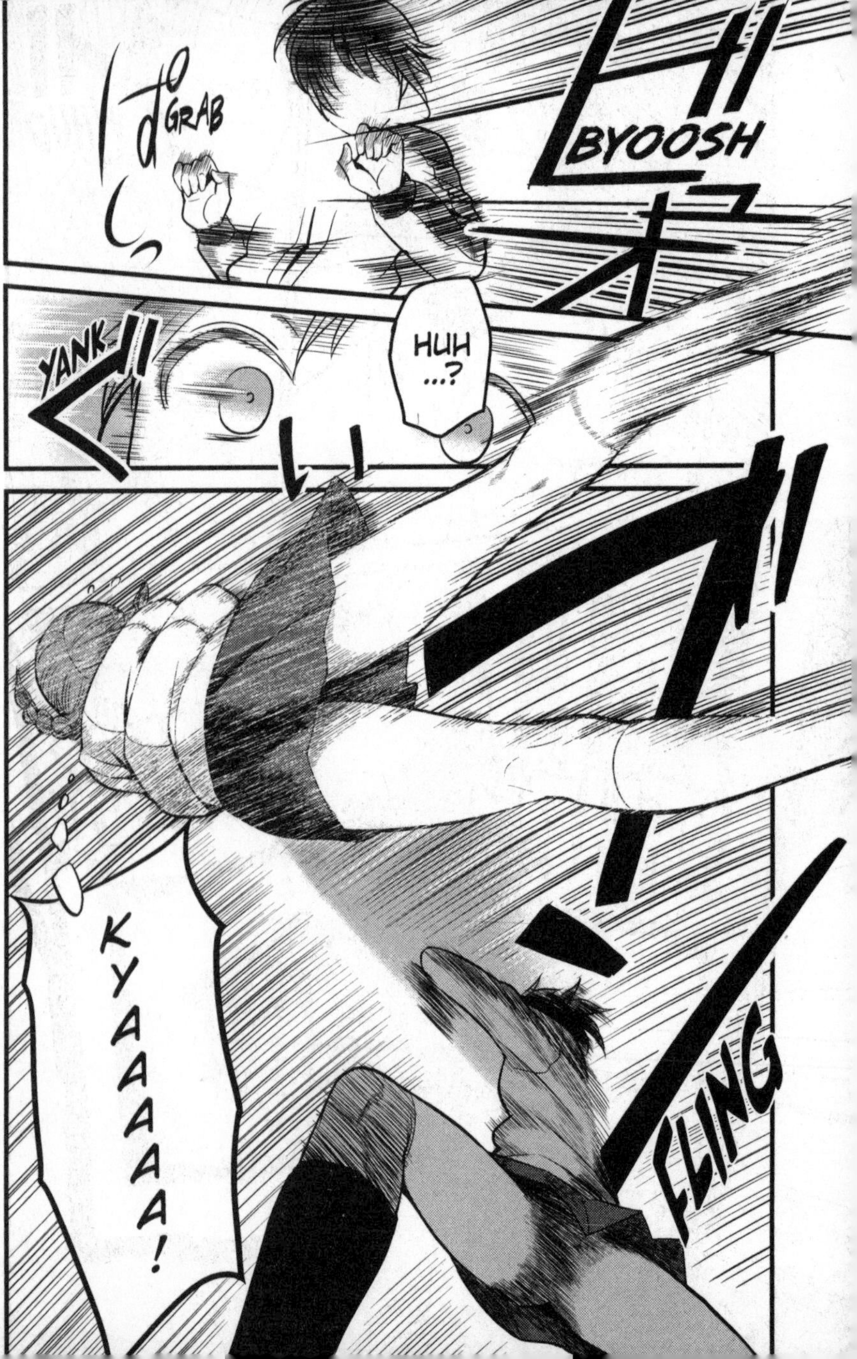
BYOOSH
GRAB
HUH ...?
YANK
FLING
KYAAAAAA!

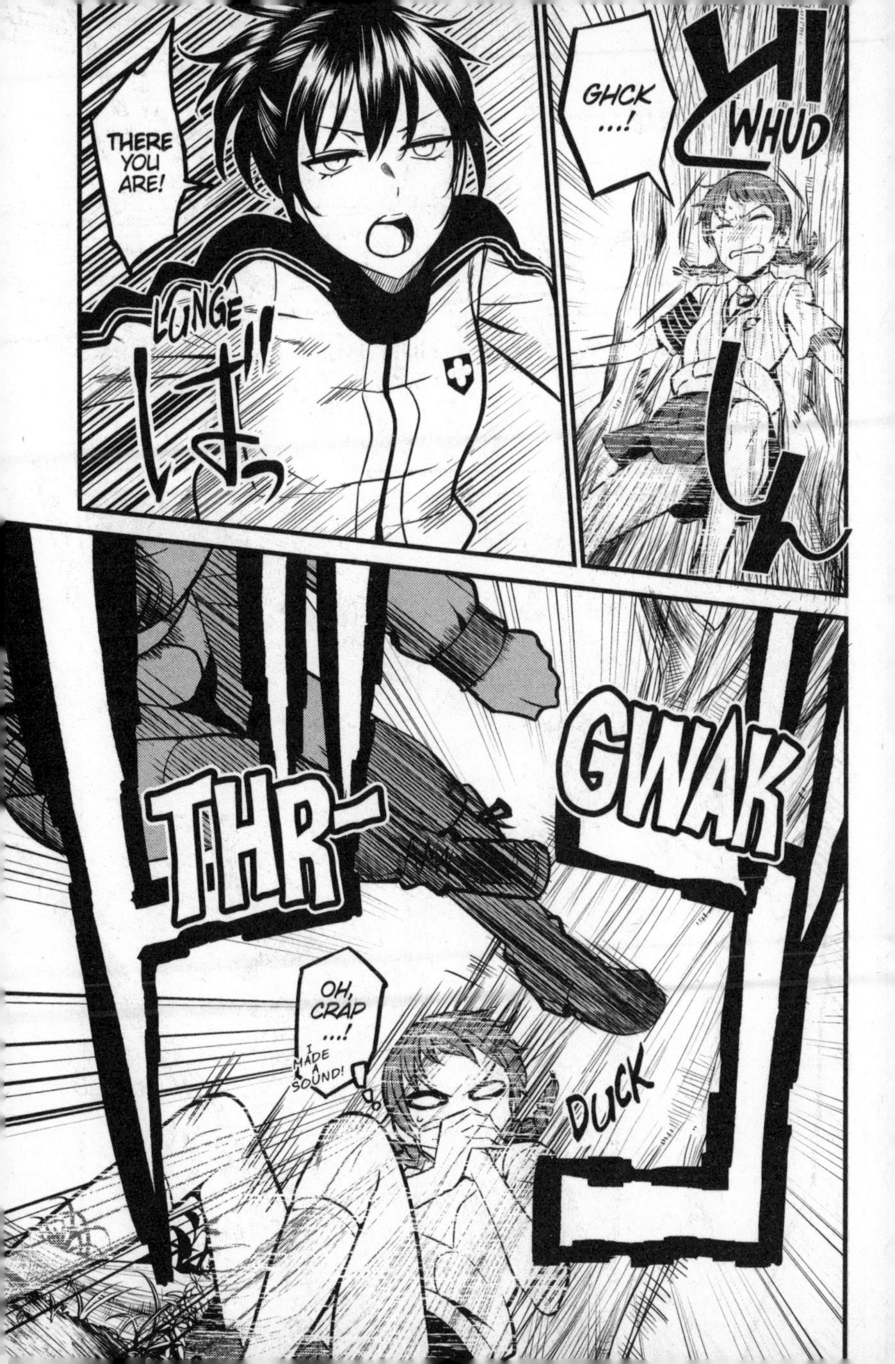
GHCK ...!
WHUD
THERE YOU ARE!
LUNGE
ばっ
GWAK
THR-
OH, CRAP ...!
I MADE A SOUND!
DUCK

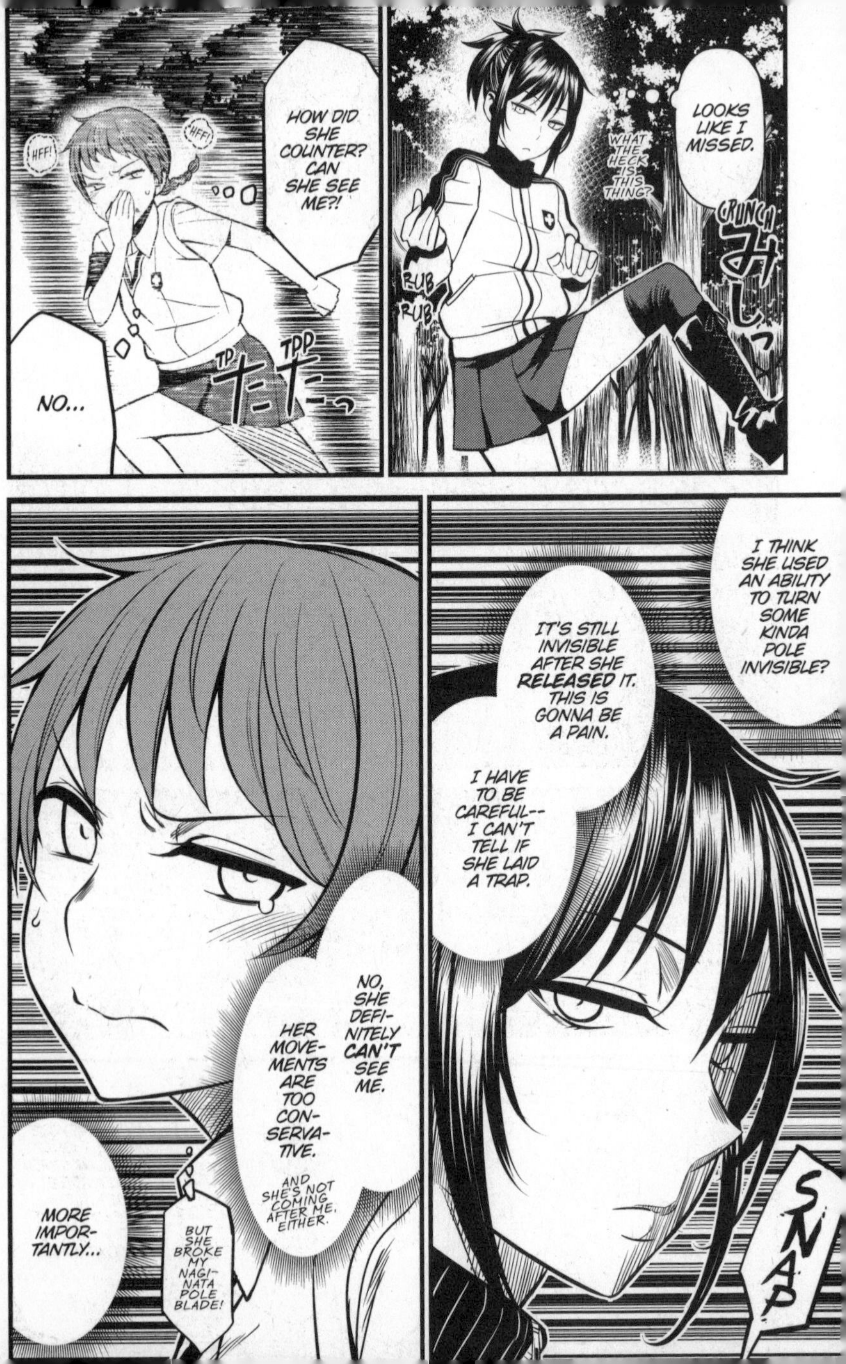
LOOKS LIKE I MISSED.
WHAT THE HECK IS THIS THING?
CRUNCH
みしっ
RUB RUB
HOW DID SHE COUNTER? CAN SHE SEE ME?!
HFF!
HFF!
TP TPP
NO...
I THINK SHE USED AN ABILITY TO TURN SOME KINDA POLE INVISIBLE?
IT'S STILL INVISIBLE AFTER SHE **RELEASED** IT. THIS IS GONNA BE A PAIN.
I HAVE TO BE CAREFUL-- I CAN'T TELL IF SHE LAID A TRAP.
SNAP
NO, SHE DEFINITELY **CAN'T** SEE ME.
HER MOVEMENTS ARE TOO CONSERVATIVE.
AND SHE'S NOT COMING AFTER ME, EITHER.
BUT SHE BROKE MY NAGINATA POLE BLADE!
MORE IMPORTANTLY...

IF SHE COULD SEE WHAT I'M DOING...

Toss

THEN SHE'D BE FOCUSED ON THE SUSPICIOUS OBJECT LYING RIGHT NEXT TO HER!

THE CUFFS GRENADE WRAPS ITSELF AROUND THE NEAREST LIVING ORGANISM.

ITS TITANIUM ROPE BINDING CAN SUBDUE MOST ESPERS!

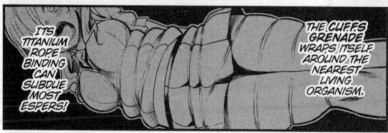

SINCE THEY'RE HEAVY, I ONLY BROUGHT TWO GRENADES WITH ME-- I NEED TO HIT HER WITH THE SECOND ONE!

AGH! SHOULD'VE BROUGHT MORE!

BUT WITHOUT KNOWING HOW SHE'S DETECTING MY POSITION...

I MIGHT MISS!

TAP TAP

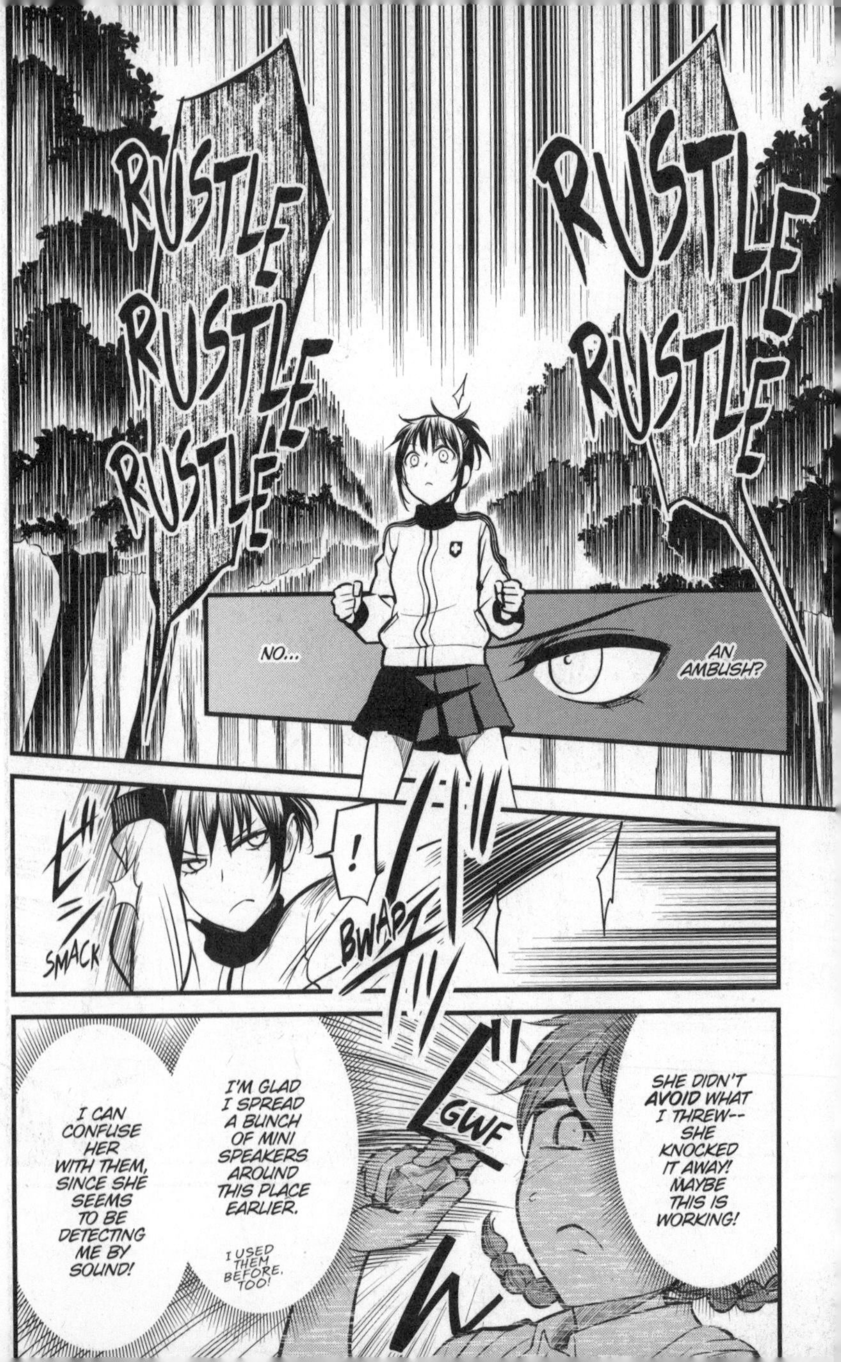
RUSTLE
RUSTLE
RUSTLE
RUSTLE
RUSTLE
RUSTLE
AN AMBUSH?
NO...
!
BWAP
SMACK
SHE DIDN'T AVOID WHAT I THREW-- SHE KNOCKED IT AWAY! MAYBE THIS IS WORKING!
GWF
I'M GLAD I SPREAD A BUNCH OF MINI SPEAKERS AROUND THIS PLACE EARLIER.
I USED THEM BEFORE, TOO!
I CAN CONFUSE HER WITH THEM, SINCE SHE SEEMS TO BE DETECTING ME BY SOUND!

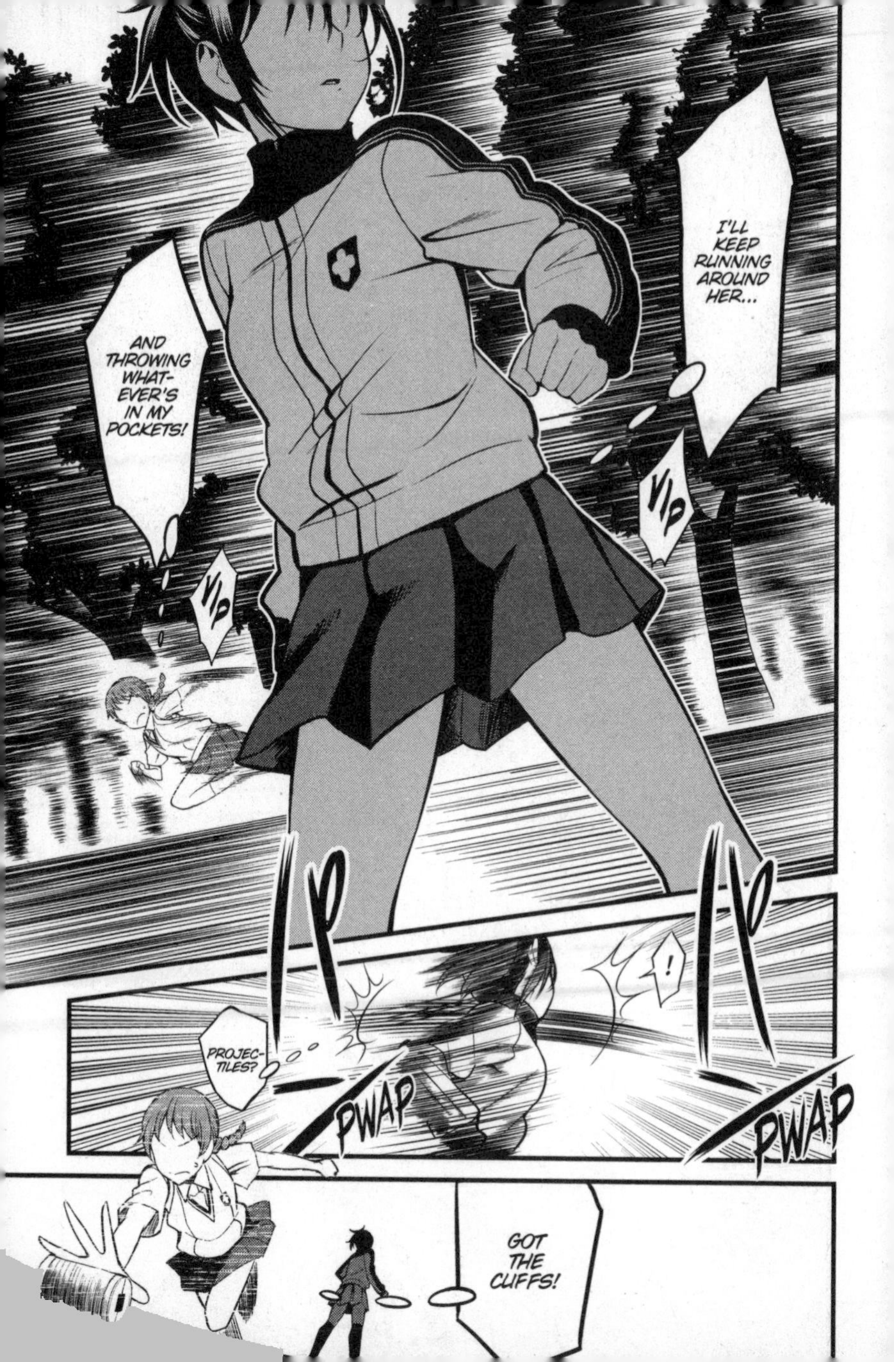
I'LL KEEP RUNNING AROUND HER...
AND THROWING WHAT-EVER'S IN MY POCKETS!
!
PWAP
PWAP
PROJEC-TILES?
GOT THE CUFFS!

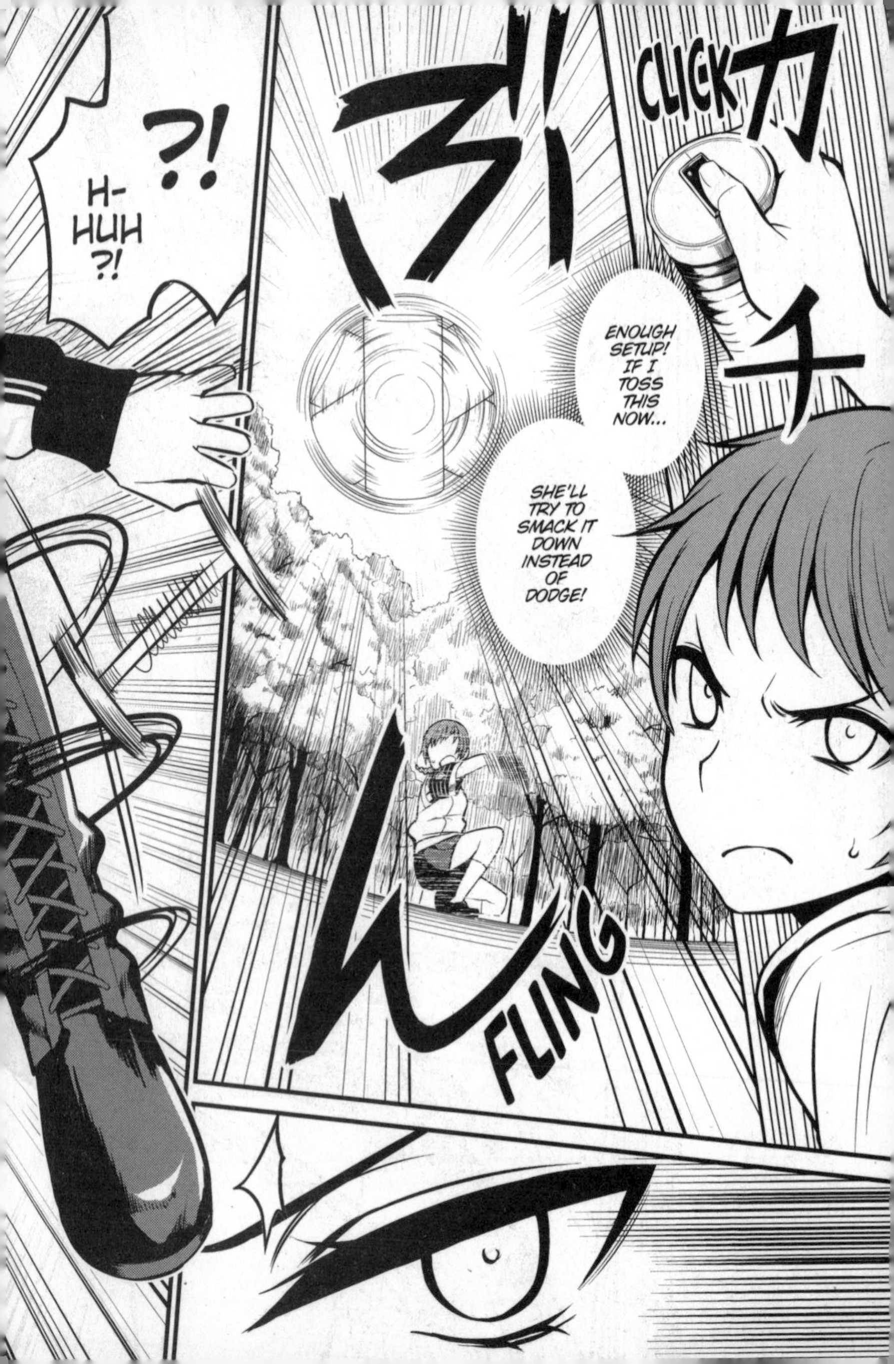
CLICK
ENOUGH SETUP! IF I TOSS THIS NOW...
SHE'LL TRY TO SMACK IT DOWN INSTEAD OF DODGE!
FLING
?!
H-HUH ?!

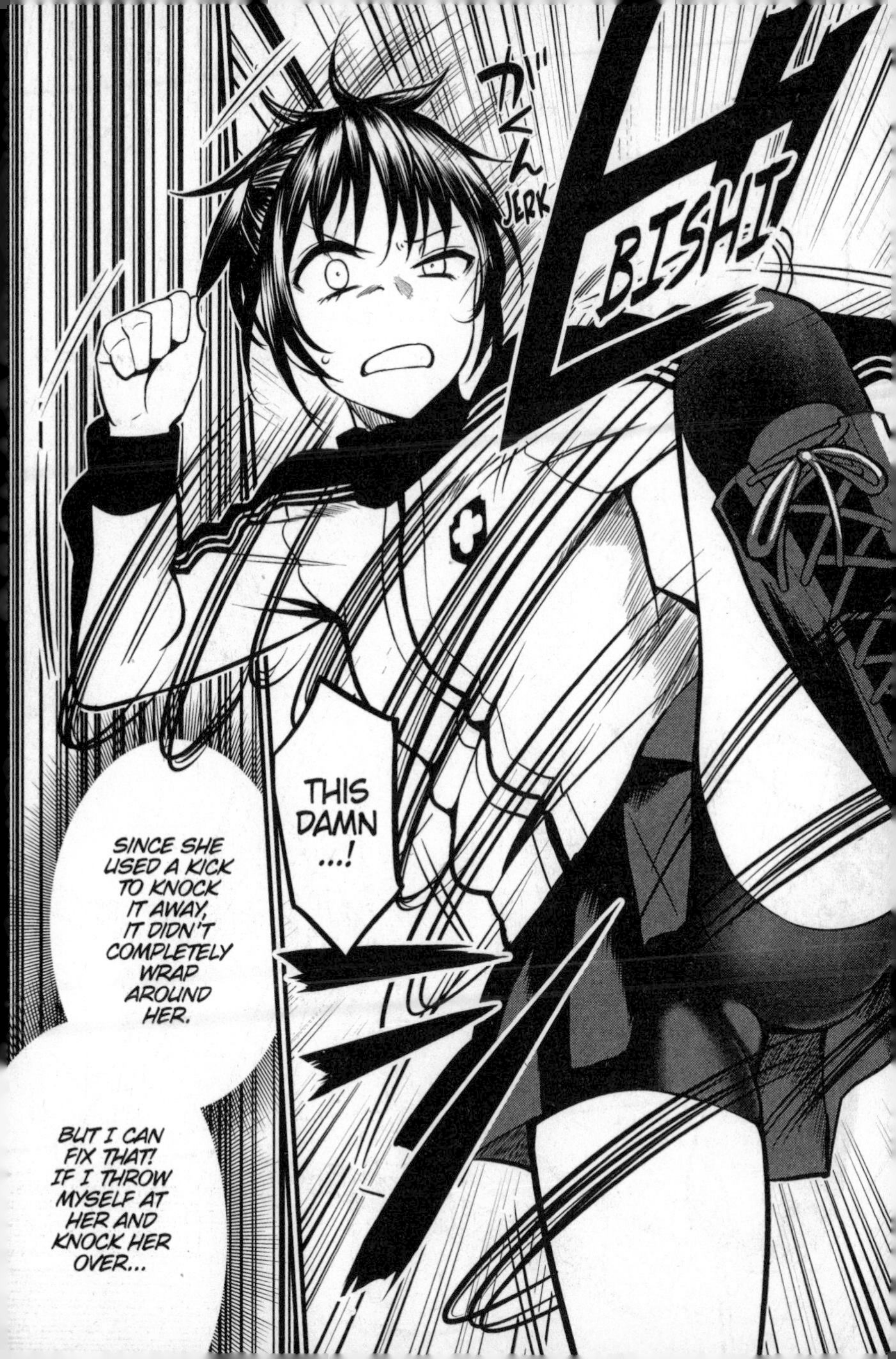
BISHI
がくん
JERK
THIS DAMN ...!
SINCE SHE USED A KICK TO KNOCK IT AWAY, IT DIDN'T COMPLETELY WRAP AROUND HER.
BUT I CAN FIX THAT! IF I THROW MYSELF AT HER AND KNOCK HER OVER...

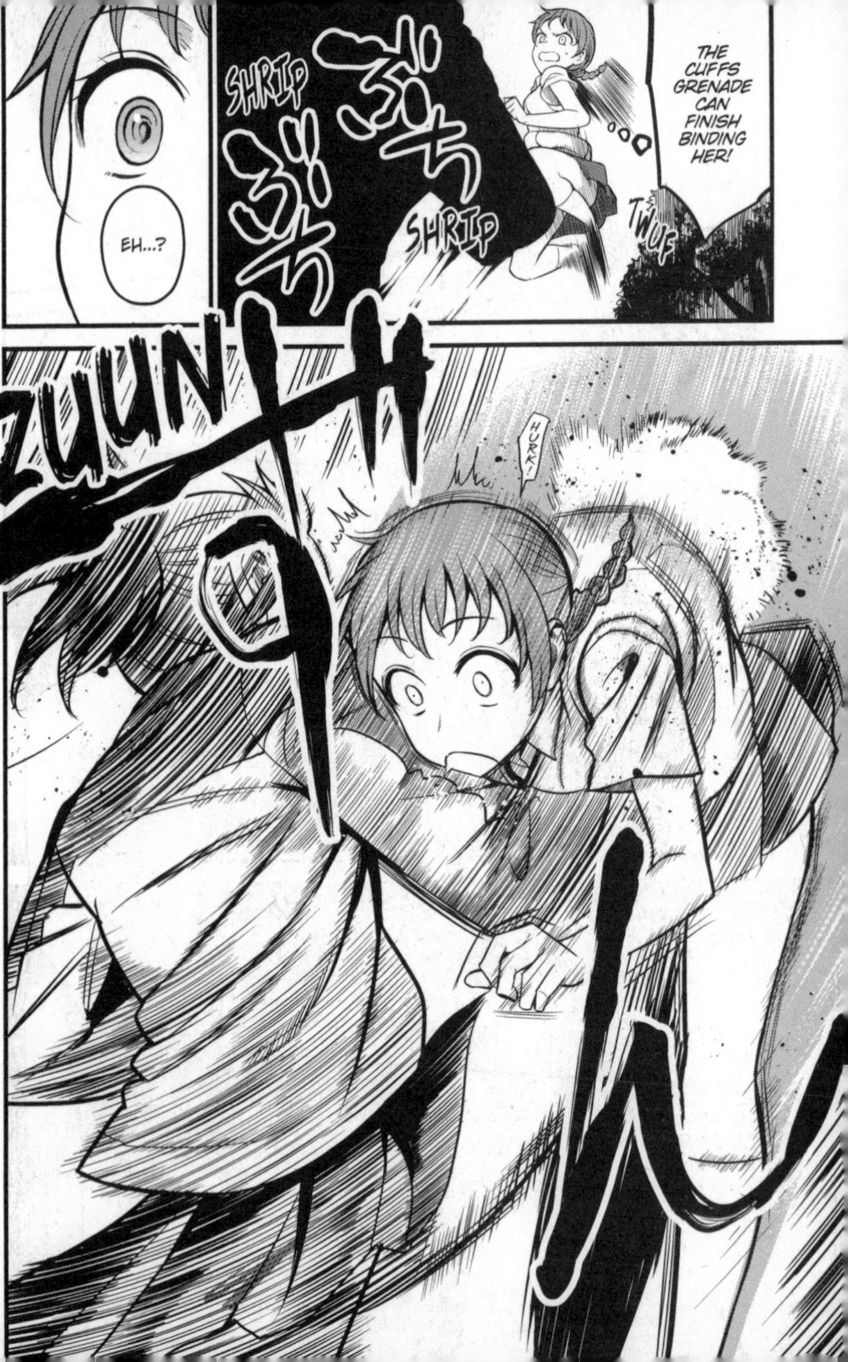
THE CUFFS GRENADE CAN FINISH BINDING HER!
TWUF
ぶち
SHRIP
ぶち
SHRIP
EH...?
ZUUN
HURK!

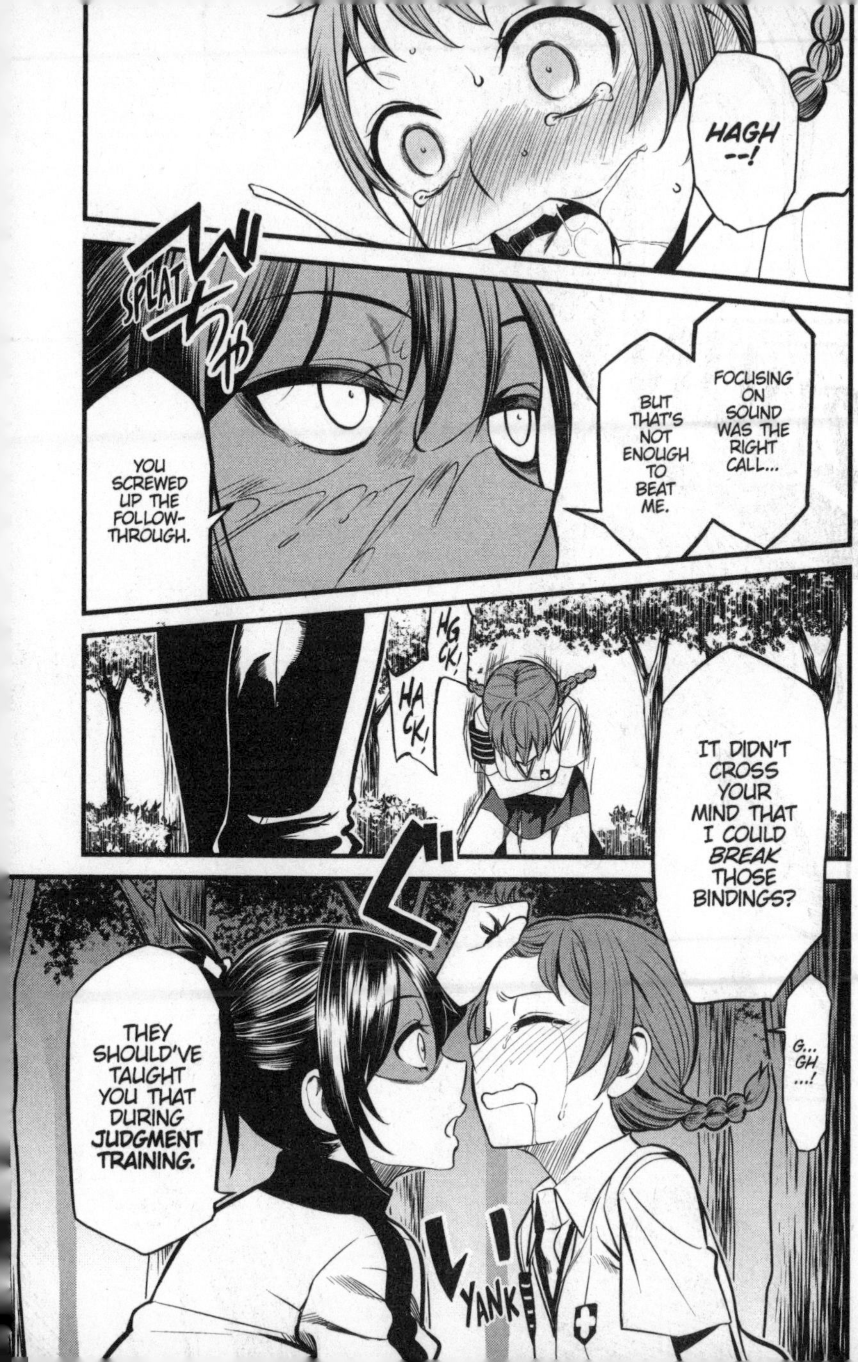
HAGH --!
SPLAT
FOCUSING ON SOUND WAS THE RIGHT CALL...
BUT THAT'S NOT ENOUGH TO BEAT ME.
YOU SCREWED UP THE FOLLOW-THROUGH.
IT DIDN'T CROSS YOUR MIND THAT I COULD *BREAK* THOSE BINDINGS?
HGCK!
HACK!
G... GH ...!
THEY SHOULD'VE TAUGHT YOU THAT DURING **JUDGMENT** TRAINING.
YANK

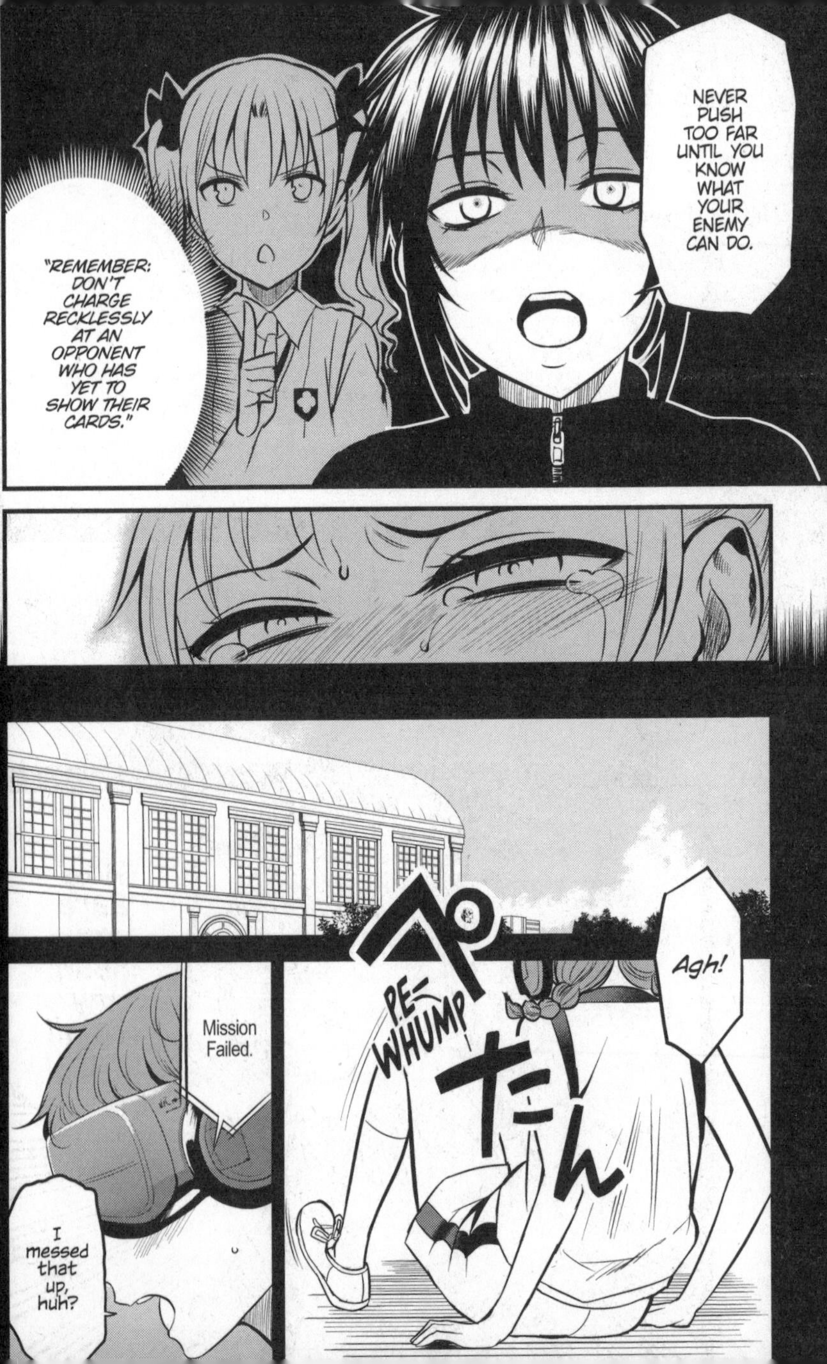
NEVER PUSH TOO FAR UNTIL YOU KNOW WHAT YOUR ENEMY CAN DO.
"REMEMBER: DON'T CHARGE RECKLESSLY AT AN OPPONENT WHO HAS YET TO SHOW THEIR CARDS."
Agh!
ペ
PE-WHUMP
たん
Mission Failed.
I messed that up, huh?

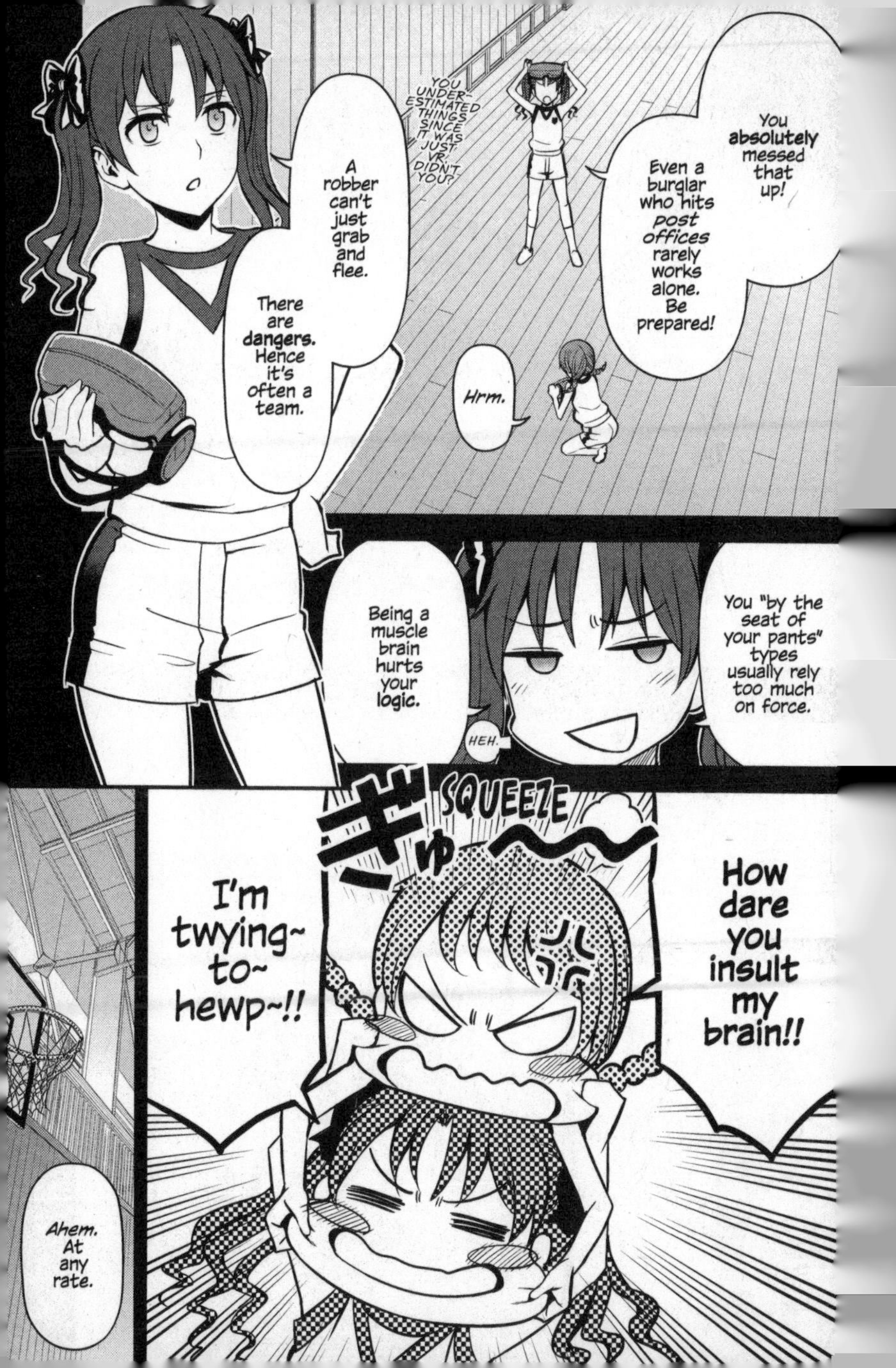
You absolutely messed that up!
Even a burglar who hits post offices rarely works alone. Be prepared!
YOU UNDER-ESTIMATED THINGS SINCE IT WAS JUST VR, DIDN'T YOU?
Hrm.
You "by the seat of your pants" types usually rely too much on force.
Being a muscle brain hurts your logic.
HEH.
A robber can't just grab and flee.
There are dangers. Hence it's often a team.
How dare you insult my brain!!
SQUEEZE
I'm twying~ to~ hewp~!!
Ahem. At any rate.

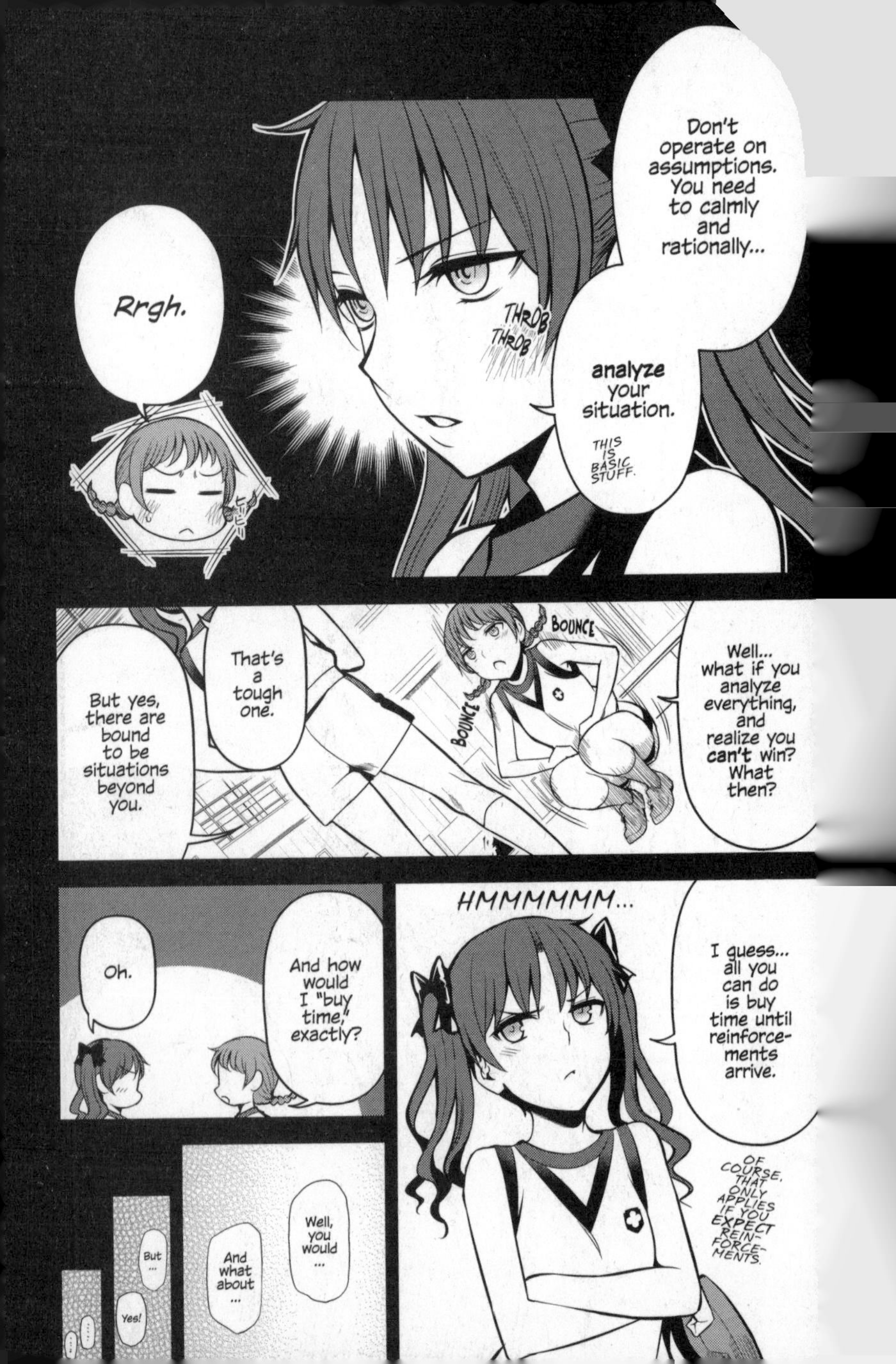
Don't operate on assumptions. You need to calmly and rationally...
analyze your situation.
THIS IS BASIC STUFF.
THROB THROB
Rrgh.
Well... what if you analyze everything, and realize you can't win? What then?
BOUNCE
BOUNCE
That's a tough one.
But yes, there are bound to be situations beyond you.
HMMMMMM...
I guess... all you can do is buy time until reinforcements arrive.
OF COURSE, THAT ONLY APPLIES IF YOU EXPECT REINFORCEMENTS.
And how would I "buy time," exactly?
Oh.
Well, you would ...
And what about ...
But ...
Yes!
...
...

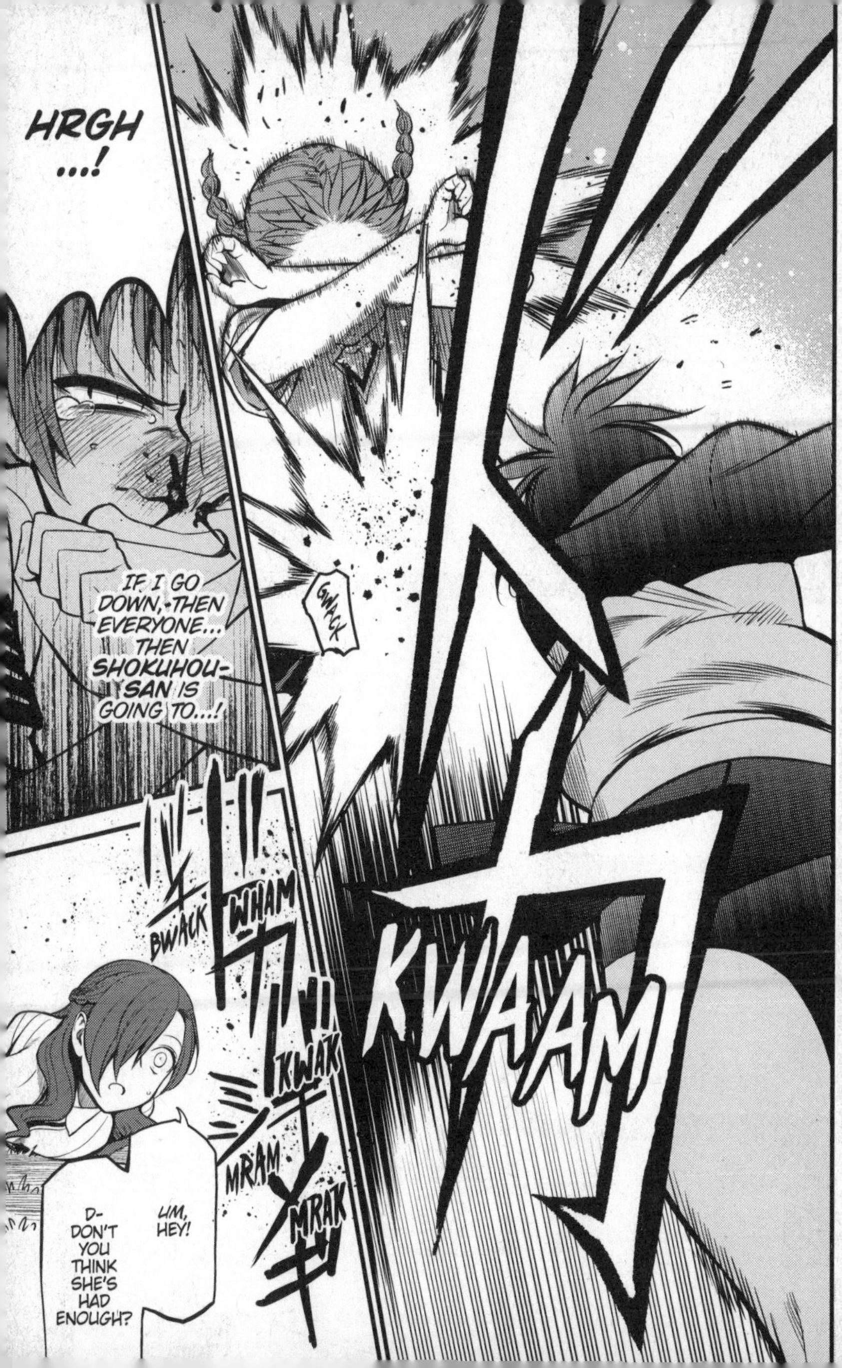
GWACK
KWAAM
WHAM
BWACK
KWAK
MRAM
MRAK
HRGH ...!
IF I GO DOWN, THEN EVERYONE... THEN SHOKUHOU-SAN IS GOING TO...!
UM, HEY!
D-DON'T YOU THINK SHE'S HAD ENOUGH?

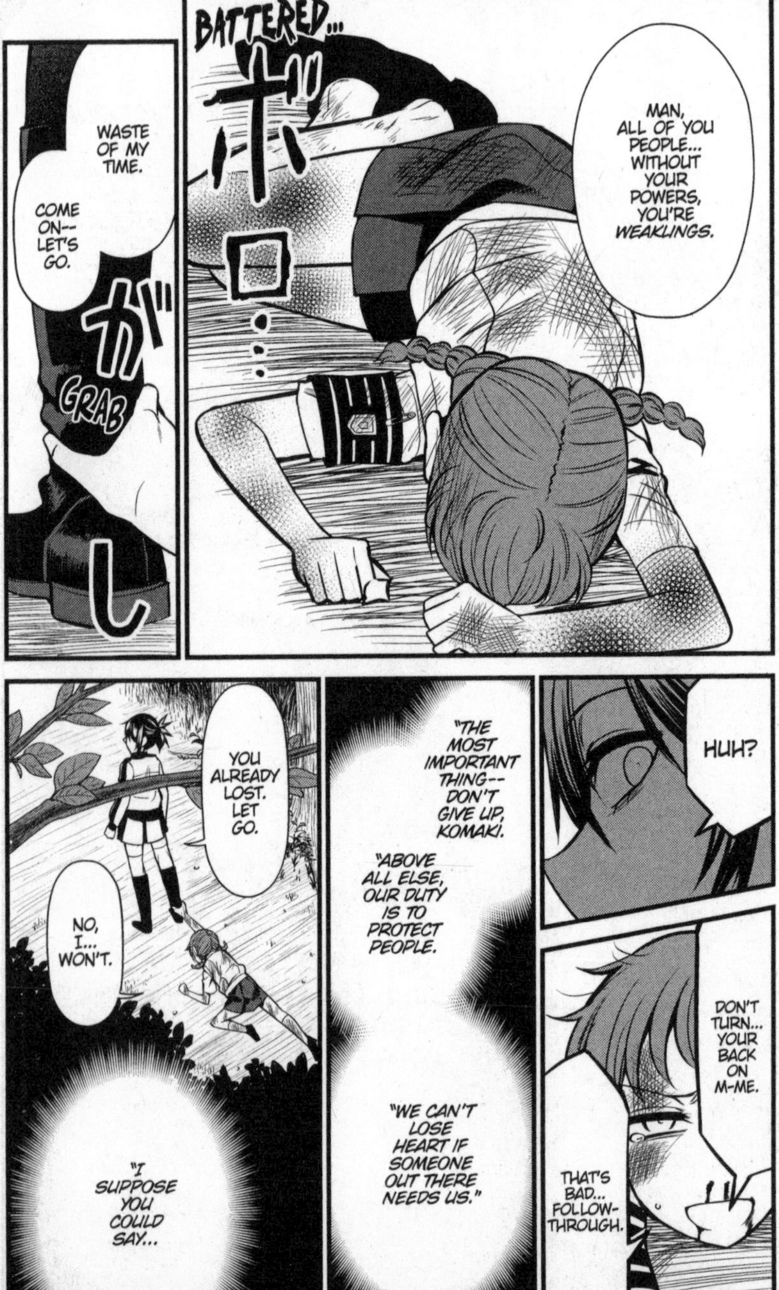
MAN, ALL OF YOU PEOPLE... WITHOUT YOUR POWERS, YOU'RE WEAKLINGS.
BATTERED...
ボロ…
WASTE OF MY TIME.
COME ON-- LET'S GO.
がし
GRAB
HUH?
DON'T TURN... YOUR BACK ON M-ME.
THAT'S BAD... FOLLOW-THROUGH.
"THE MOST IMPORTANT THING-- DON'T GIVE UP, KOMAKI.
"ABOVE ALL ELSE, OUR DUTY IS TO PROTECT PEOPLE.
"WE CAN'T LOSE HEART IF SOMEONE OUT THERE NEEDS US."
YOU ALREADY LOST. LET GO.
NO, I... WON'T.
"I SUPPOSE YOU COULD SAY...

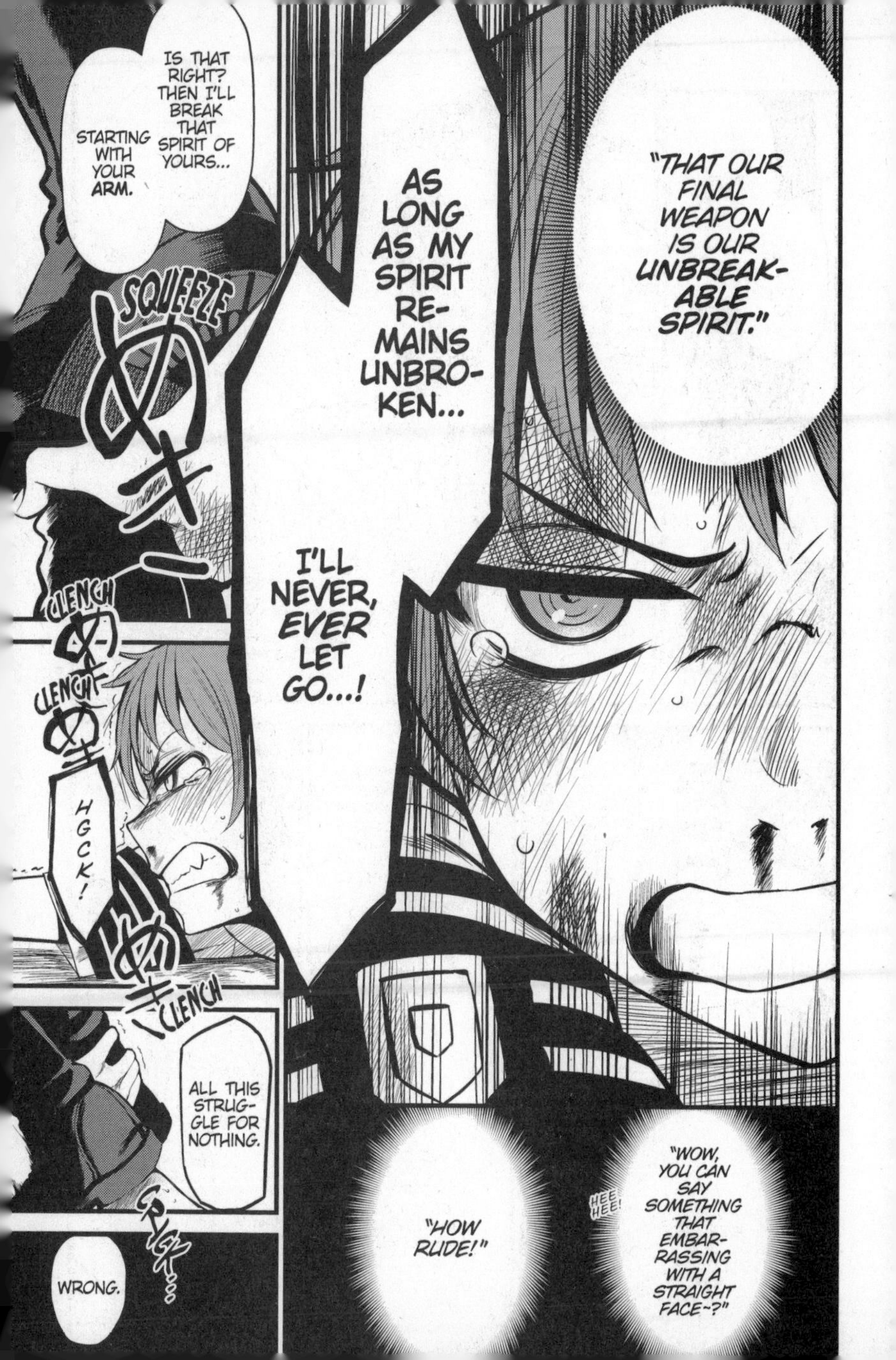
"THAT OUR FINAL WEAPON IS OUR UNBREAKABLE SPIRIT."
AS LONG AS MY SPIRIT REMAINS UNBROKEN...
I'LL NEVER, EVER LET GO...!
IS THAT RIGHT? THEN I'LL BREAK THAT SPIRIT OF YOURS...
STARTING WITH YOUR ARM.
SQUEEZE
CLENCH
CLENCH
HGCK!
CLENCH
"WOW, YOU CAN SAY SOMETHING THAT EMBARRASSING WITH A STRAIGHT FACE~?"
HEE HEE!
"HOW RUDE!"
ALL THIS STRUGGLE FOR NOTHING.
CRICK...
WRONG.

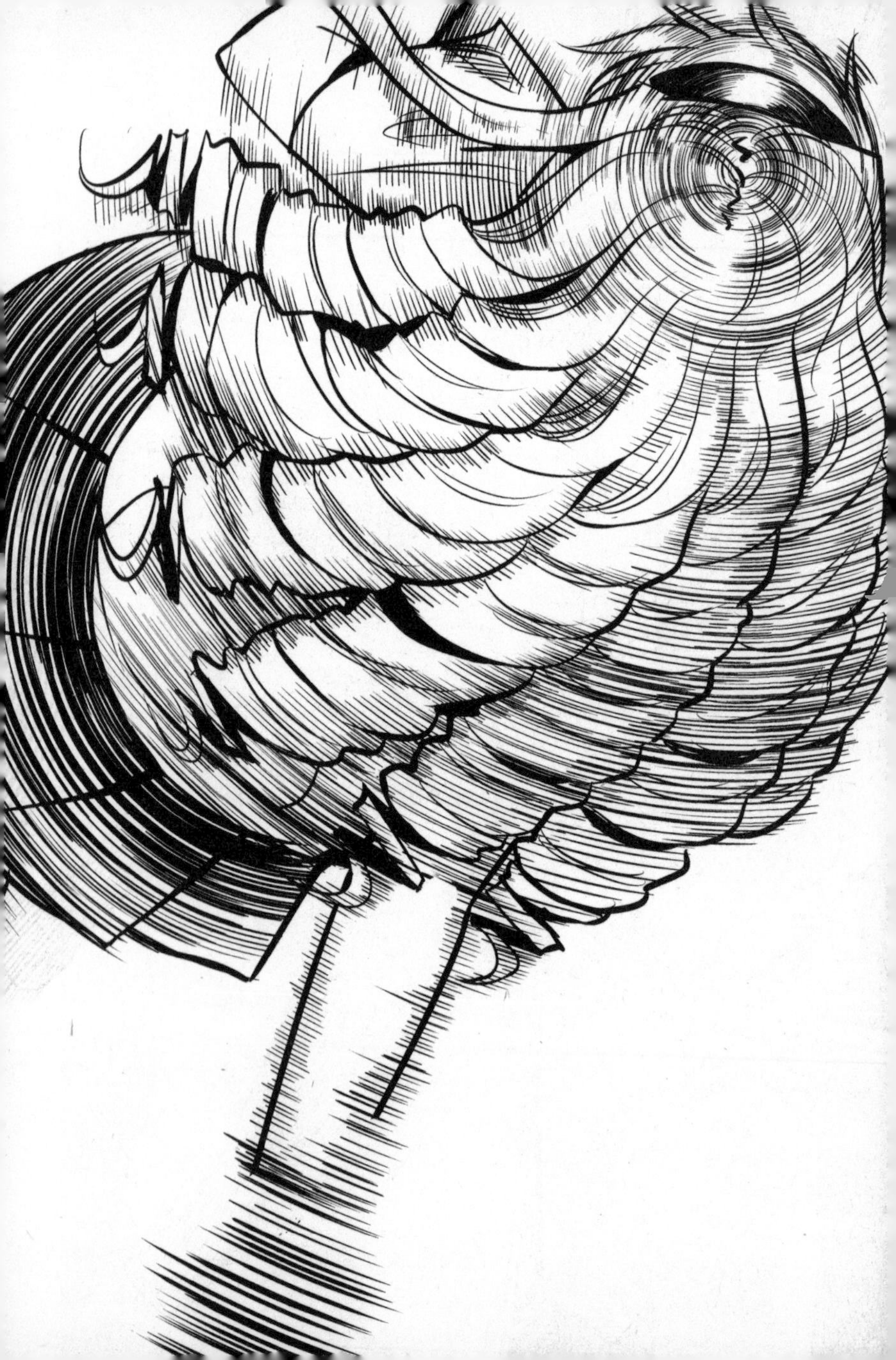

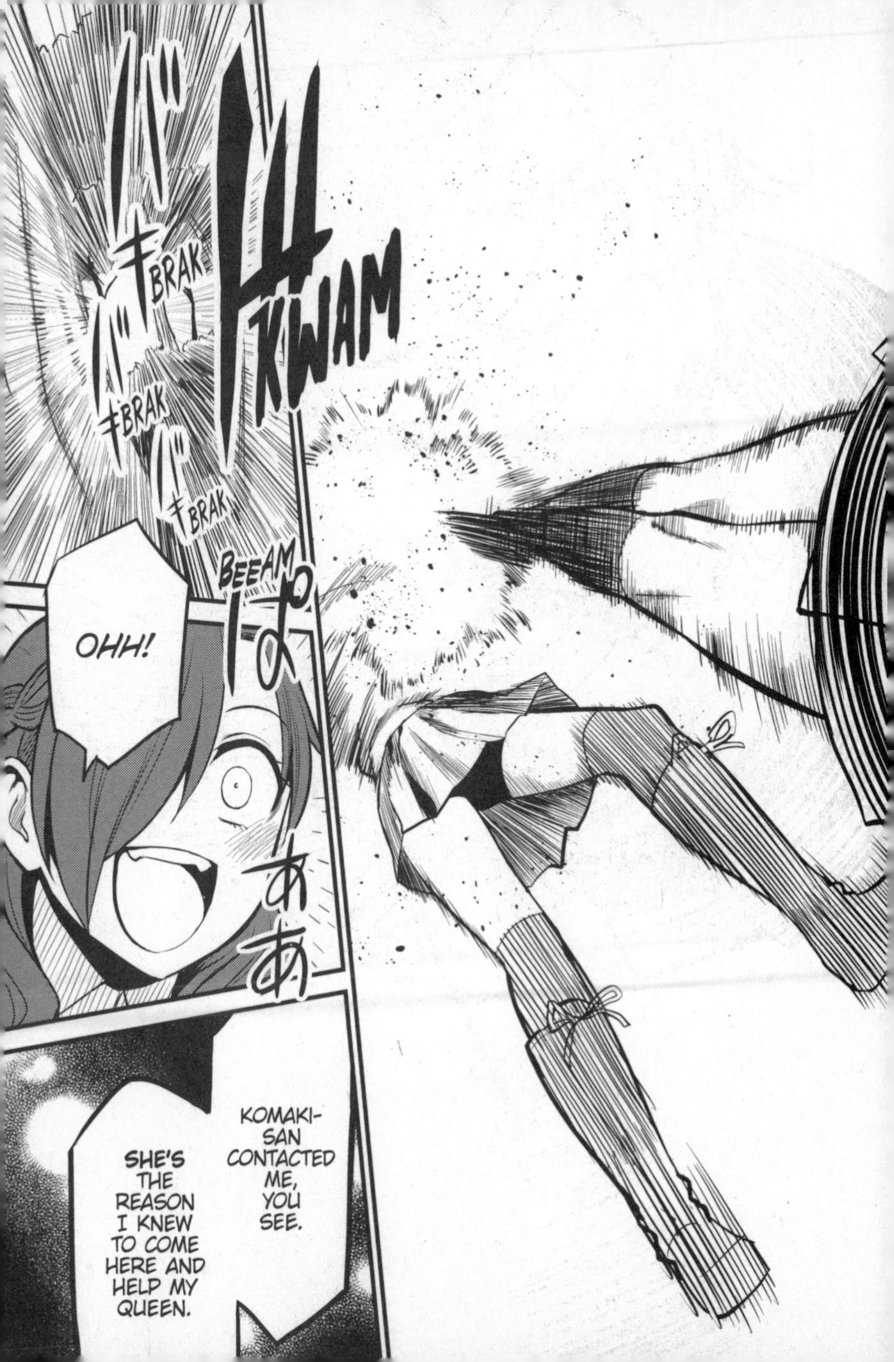
KWAM
BRAK
BRAK
BRAK
OHH!
BEEAM
KOMAKI-SAN CONTACTED ME, YOU SEE.
SHE'S THE REASON I KNEW TO COME HERE AND HELP MY QUEEN.

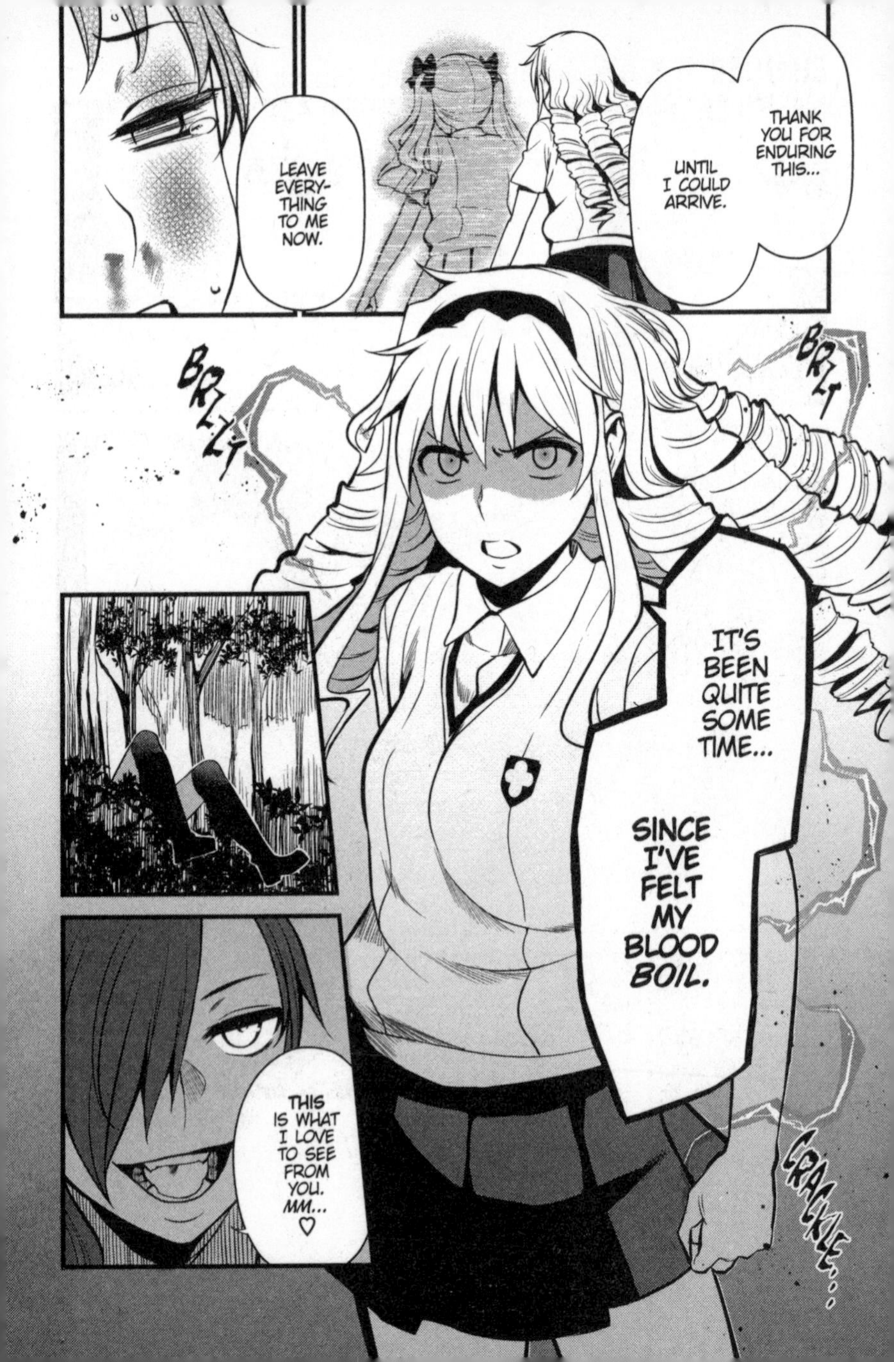
THANK YOU FOR ENDURING THIS...
UNTIL I COULD ARRIVE.
LEAVE EVERY-THING TO ME NOW.
BRZZT
BRZZT
IT'S BEEN QUITE SOME TIME...
SINCE I'VE FELT MY BLOOD BOIL.
CRACKLE...
THIS IS WHAT I LOVE TO SEE FROM YOU. MM... ♡

CHAPTER 7: You're Invincible When You Go All Out

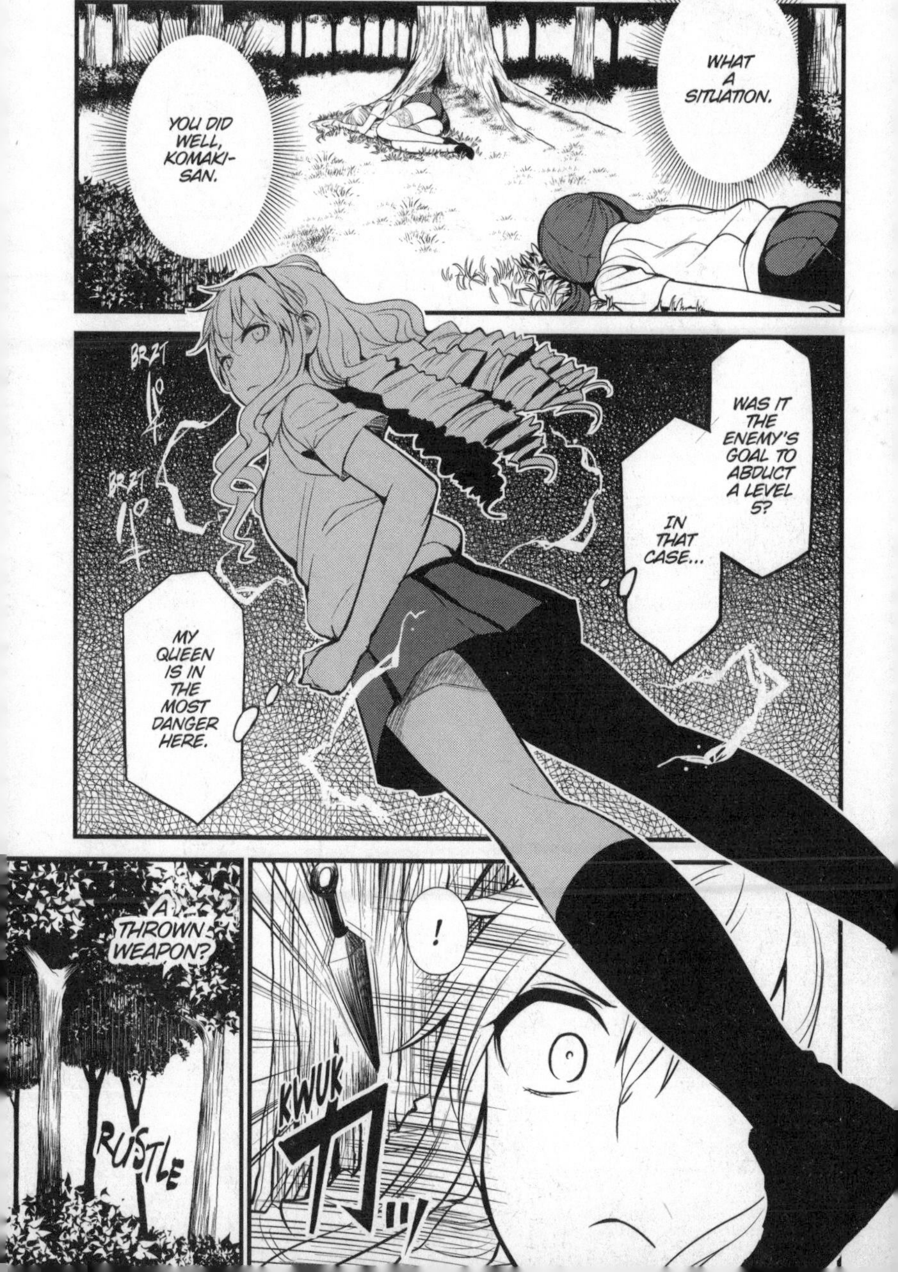
WHAT A SITUATION.
YOU DID WELL, KOMAKI-SAN.
WAS IT THE ENEMY'S GOAL TO ABDUCT A LEVEL 5?
IN THAT CASE...
BRZT
BRZT
MY QUEEN IS IN THE MOST DANGER HERE.
!
KWUK
A THROWN WEAPON?
RUSTLE

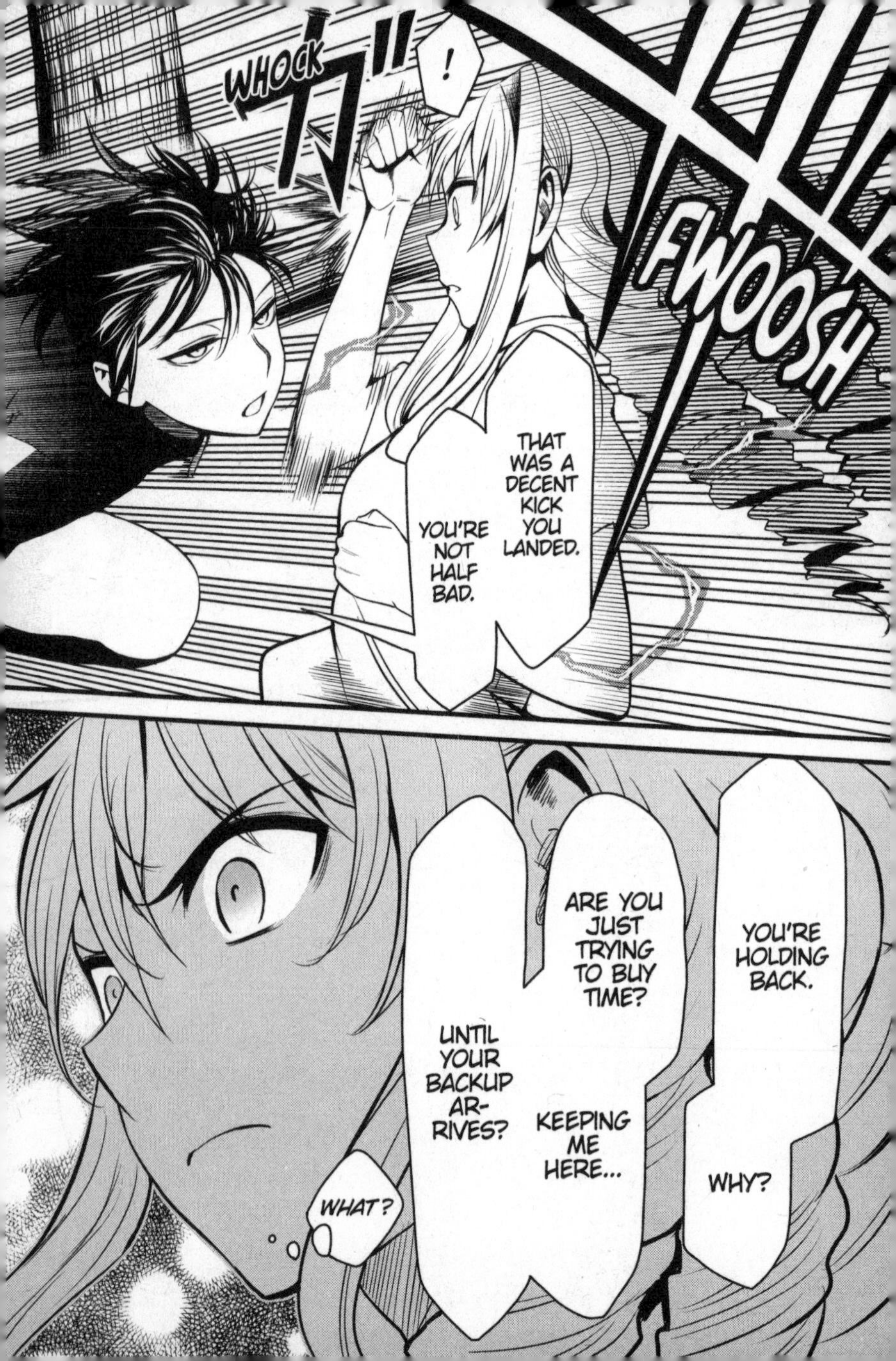
FWOOSH
WHOCK
!
THAT WAS A DECENT KICK YOU LANDED.
YOU'RE NOT HALF BAD.
YOU'RE HOLDING BACK.
ARE YOU JUST TRYING TO BUY TIME?
WHY?
KEEPING ME HERE...
UNTIL YOUR BACKUP AR-RIVES?
WHAT?

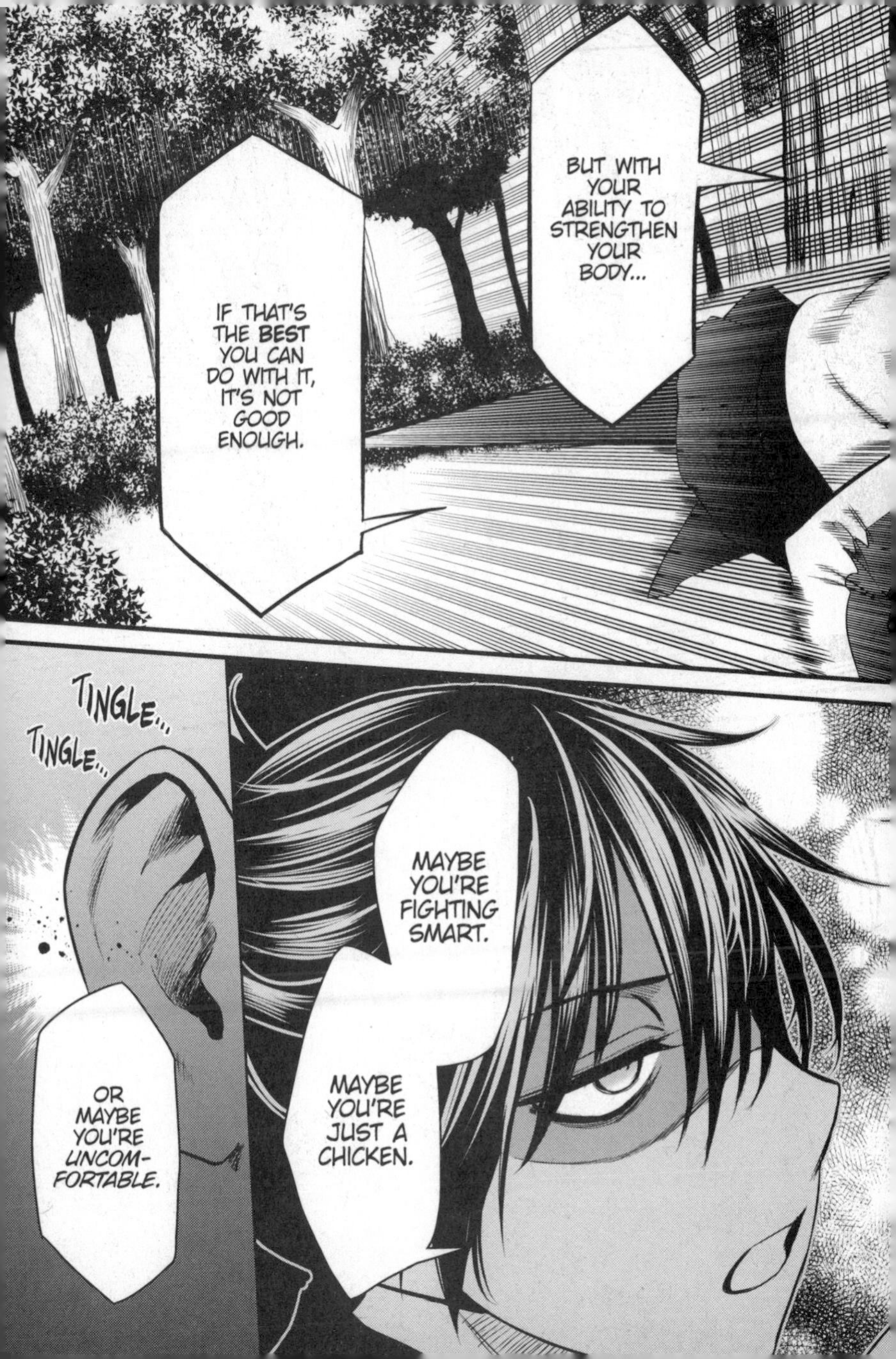
BUT WITH YOUR ABILITY TO STRENGTHEN YOUR BODY...
IF THAT'S THE BEST YOU CAN DO WITH IT, IT'S NOT GOOD ENOUGH.
MAYBE YOU'RE FIGHTING SMART.
MAYBE YOU'RE JUST A CHICKEN.
TINGLE...
TINGLE...
OR MAYBE YOU'RE UNCOM-FORTABLE.

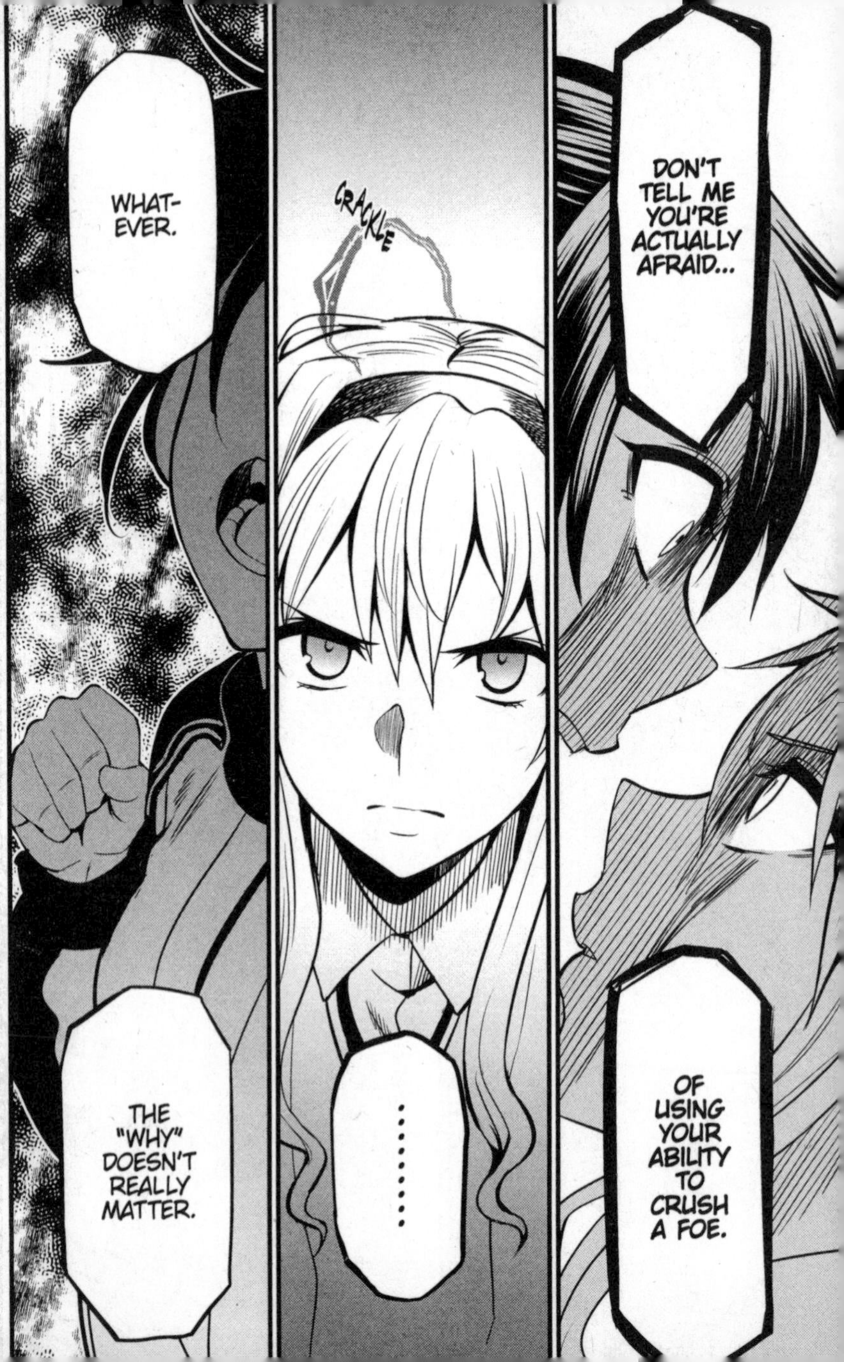
DON'T TELL ME YOU'RE ACTUALLY AFRAID...
OF USING YOUR ABILITY TO CRUSH A FOE.
CRACKLE
......
WHAT-
EVER.
THE "WHY" DOESN'T REALLY MATTER.

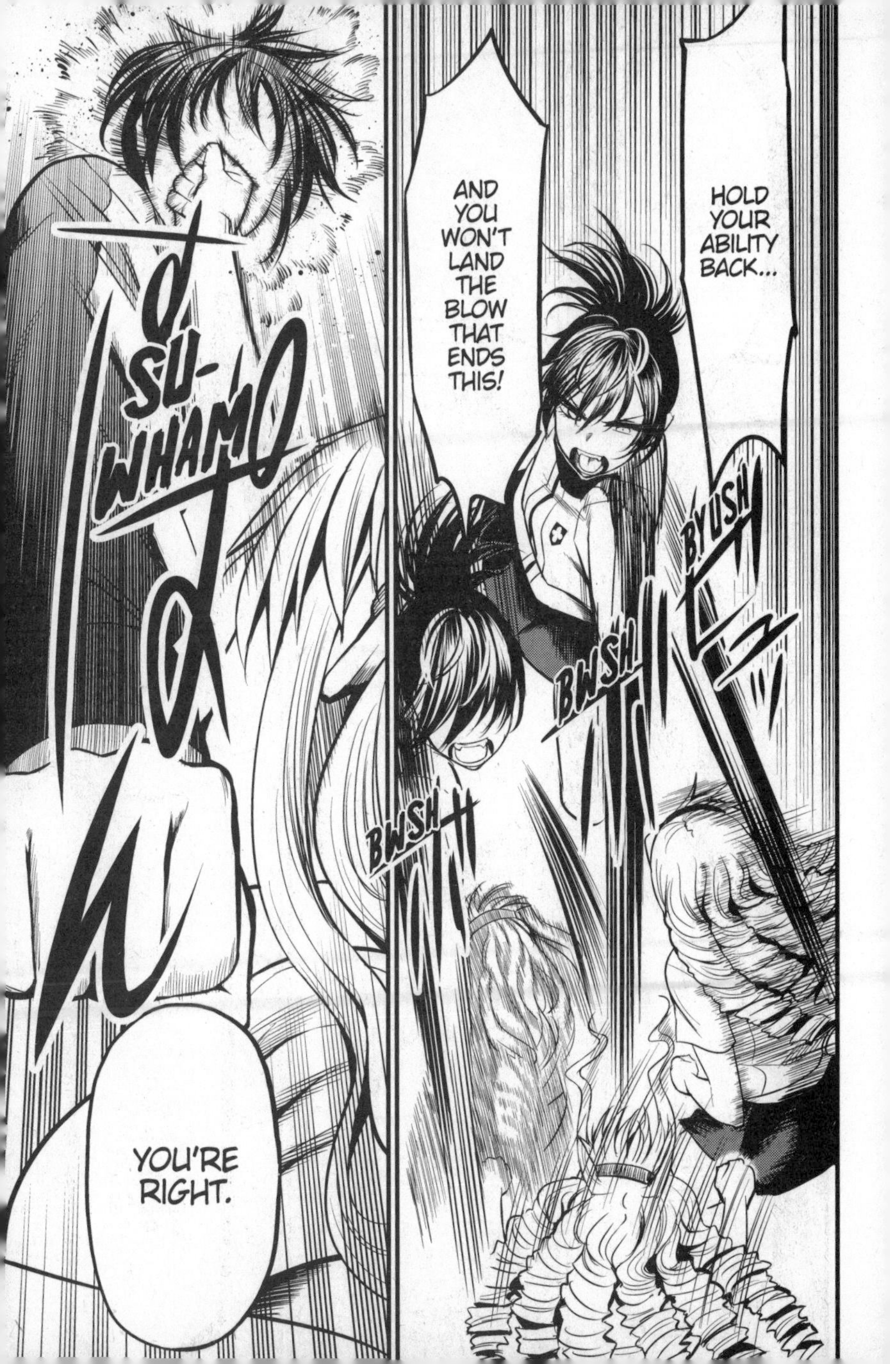
HOLD YOUR ABILITY BACK...
AND YOU WON'T LAND THE BLOW THAT ENDS THIS!
BYUSH
BWSH
BWSH
SU-WHAM
YOU'RE RIGHT.

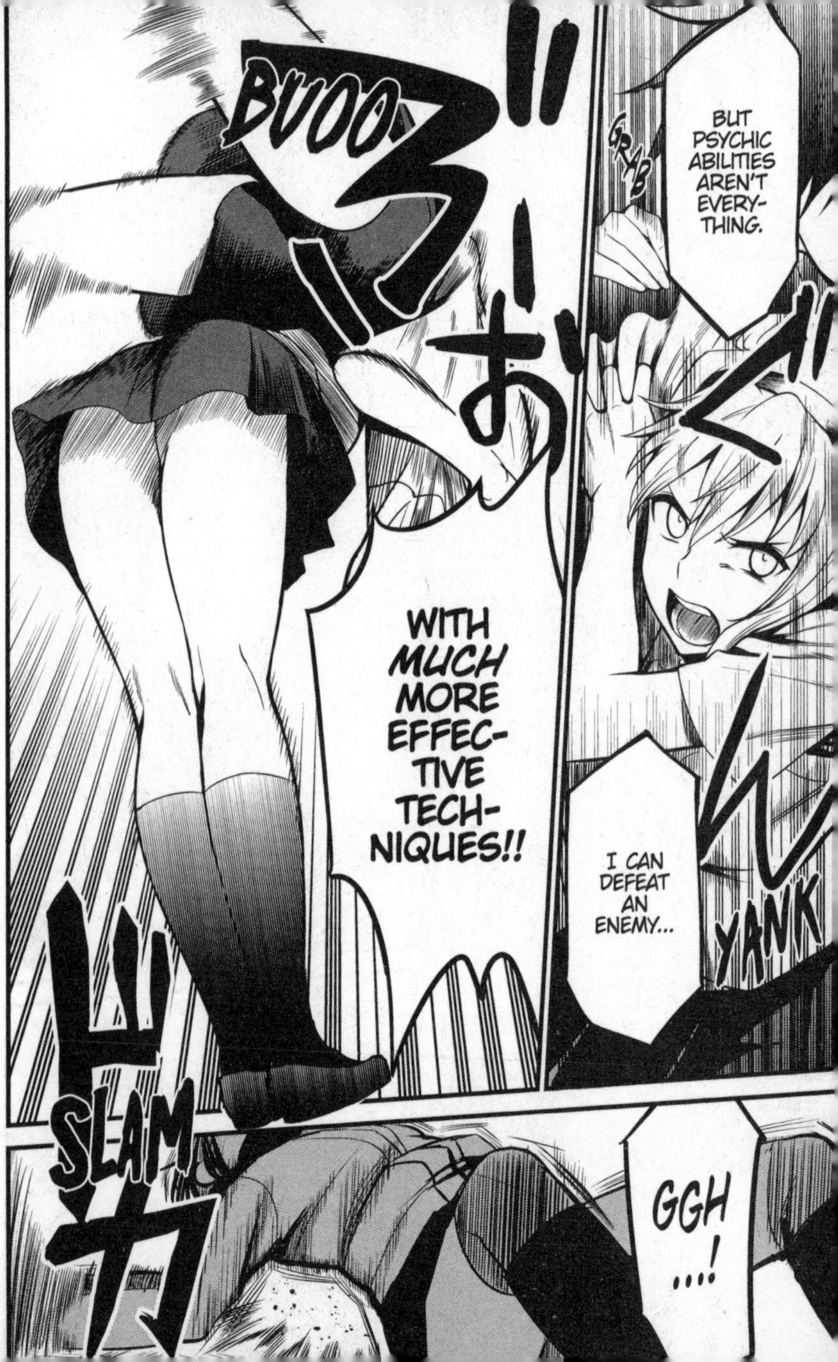
GRAB
BUT PSYCHIC ABILITIES AREN'T EVERY-THING.
I CAN DEFEAT AN ENEMY...
YANK
BUOO
WITH *MUCH* MORE EFFEC-TIVE TECH-NIQUES!!
SLAM
GGH ...!

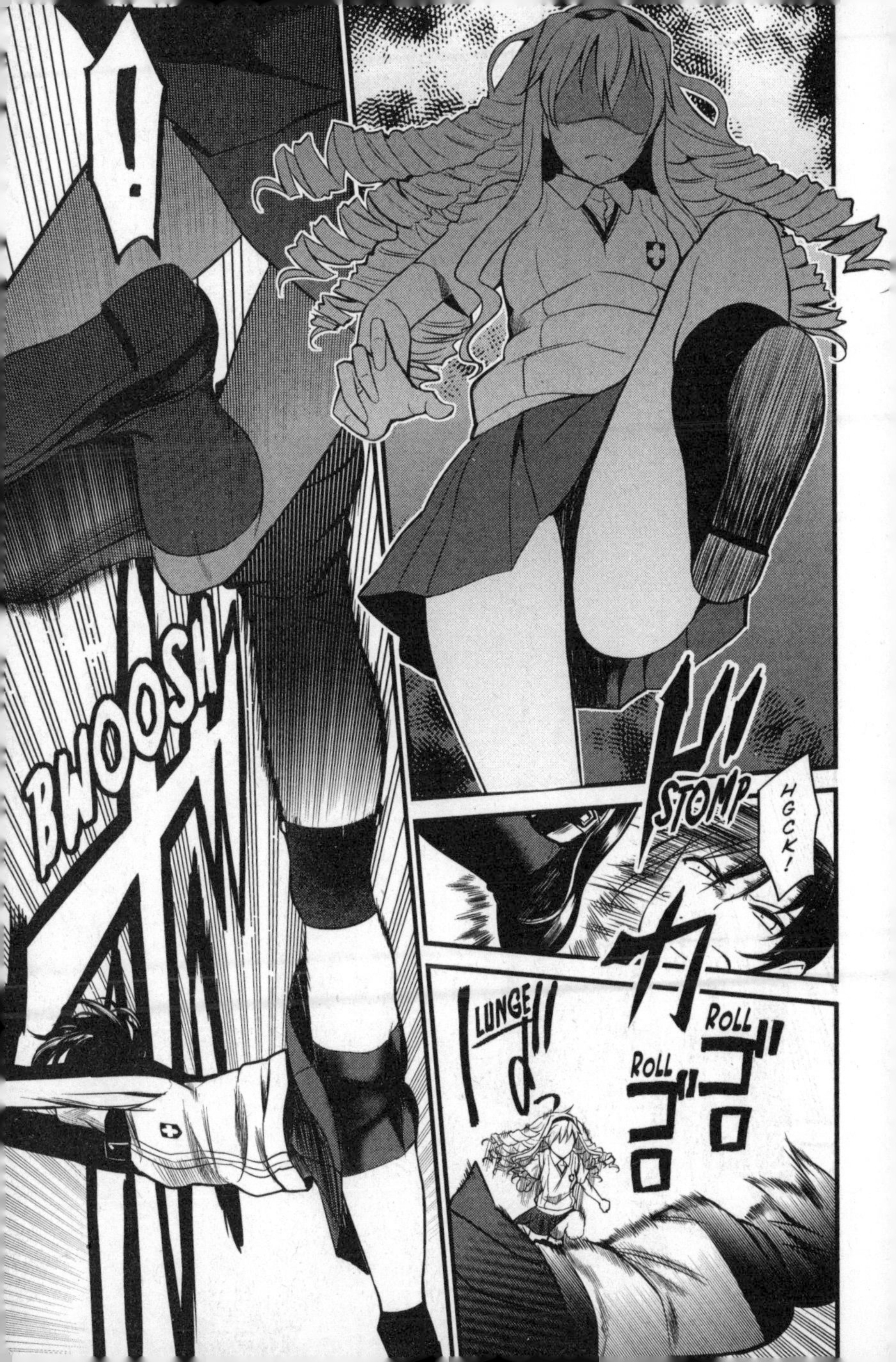
STOMP
HGCK!
LUNGE
ROLL
ゴロ
ROLL
ゴロ
!
BWOOSH

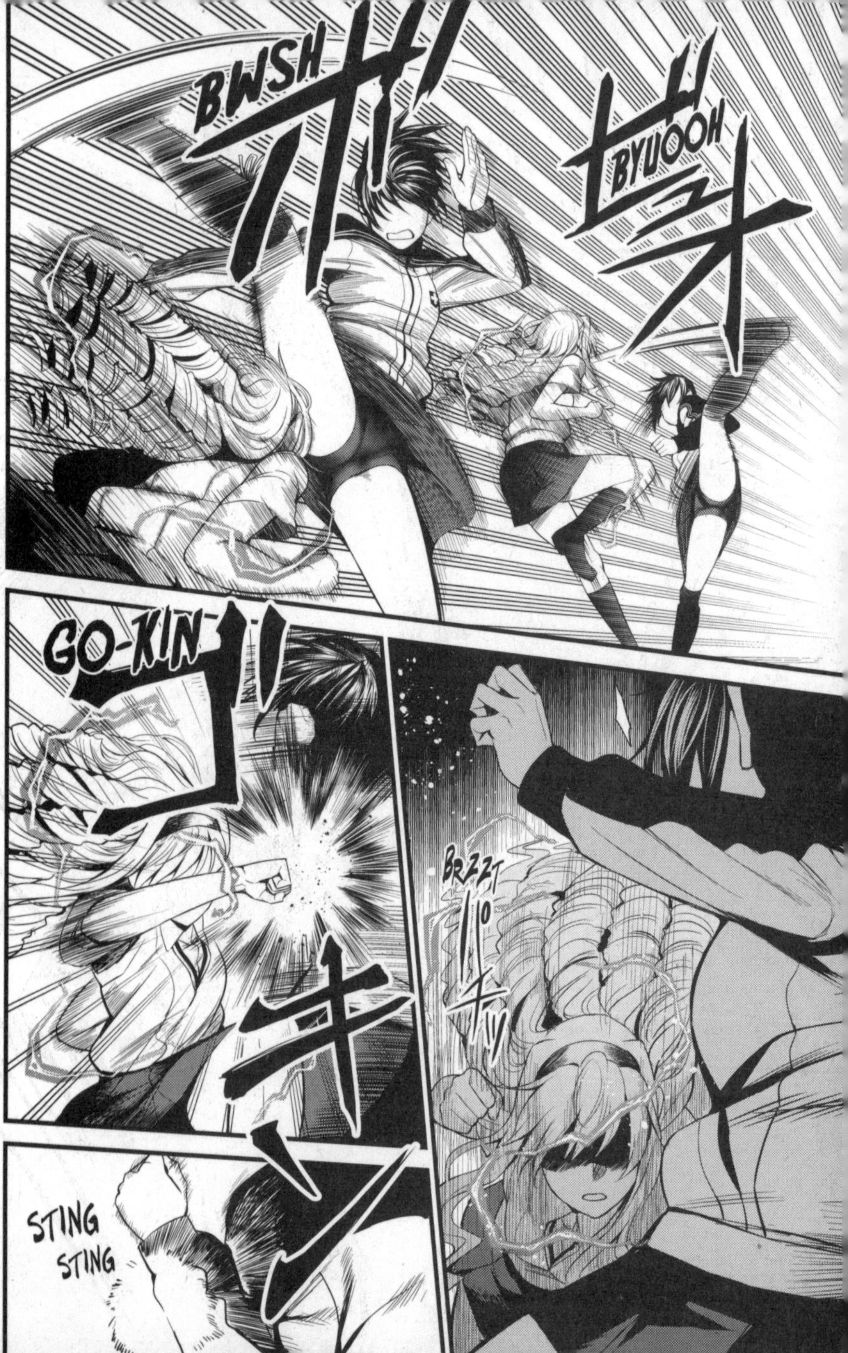
BYUOOH
BWSH
BRZZT
GO-KIN
STING
STING

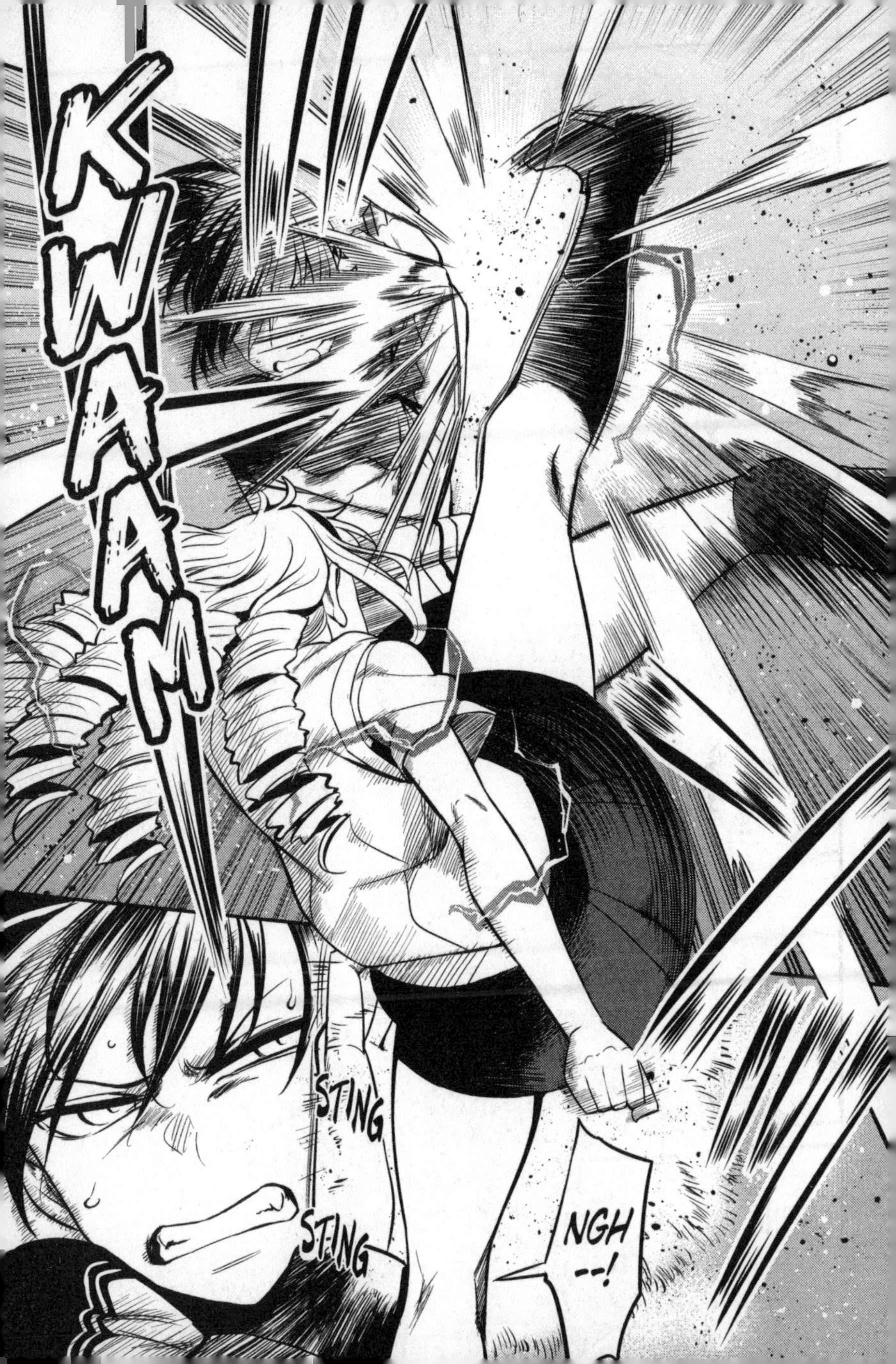
KWAAM
STING
STING
NGH --!

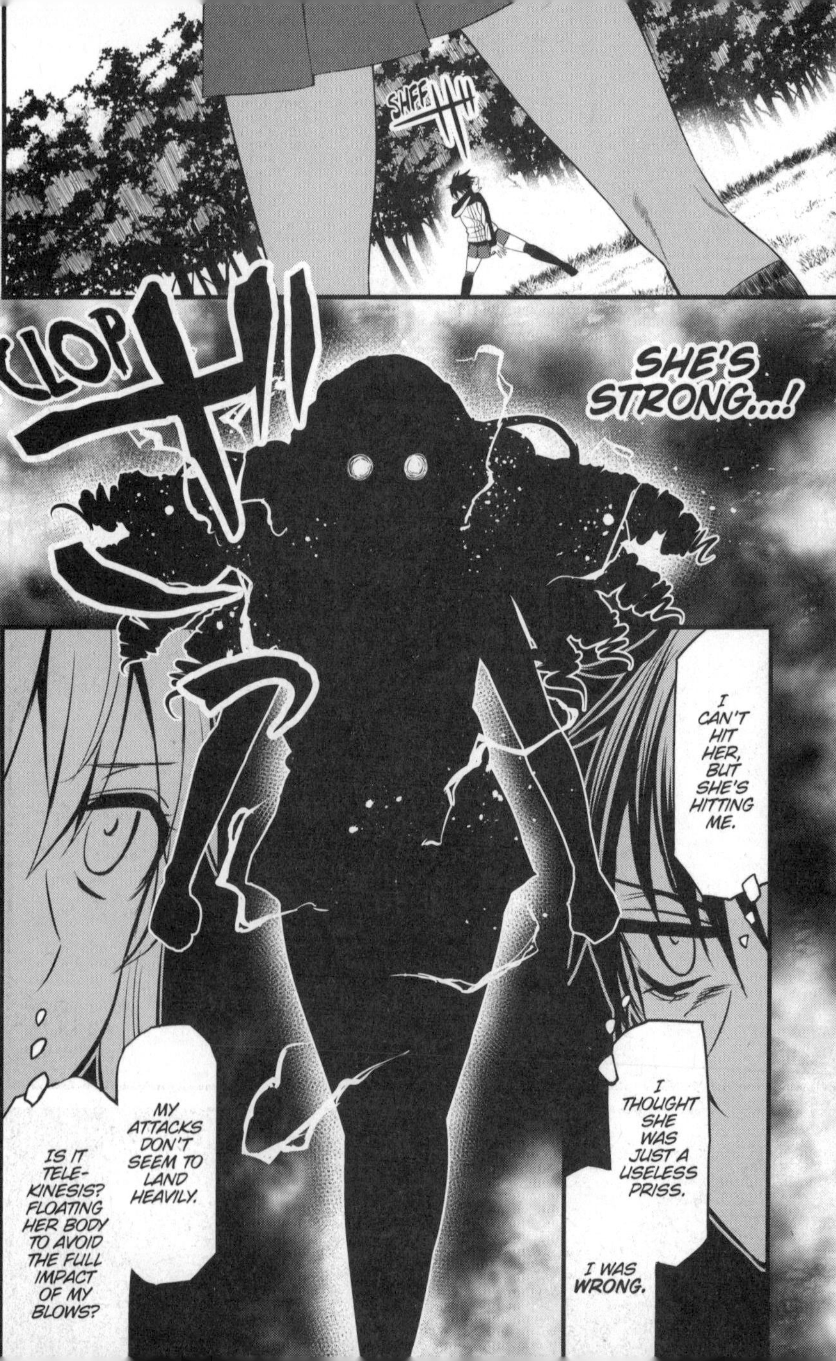
SHFF
SHE'S STRONG...!
CLOP
I CAN'T HIT HER, BUT SHE'S HITTING ME.
I THOUGHT SHE WAS JUST A USELESS PRISS.
I WAS WRONG.
MY ATTACKS DON'T SEEM TO LAND HEAVILY.
IS IT TELE-KINESIS? FLOATING HER BODY TO AVOID THE FULL IMPACT OF MY BLOWS?

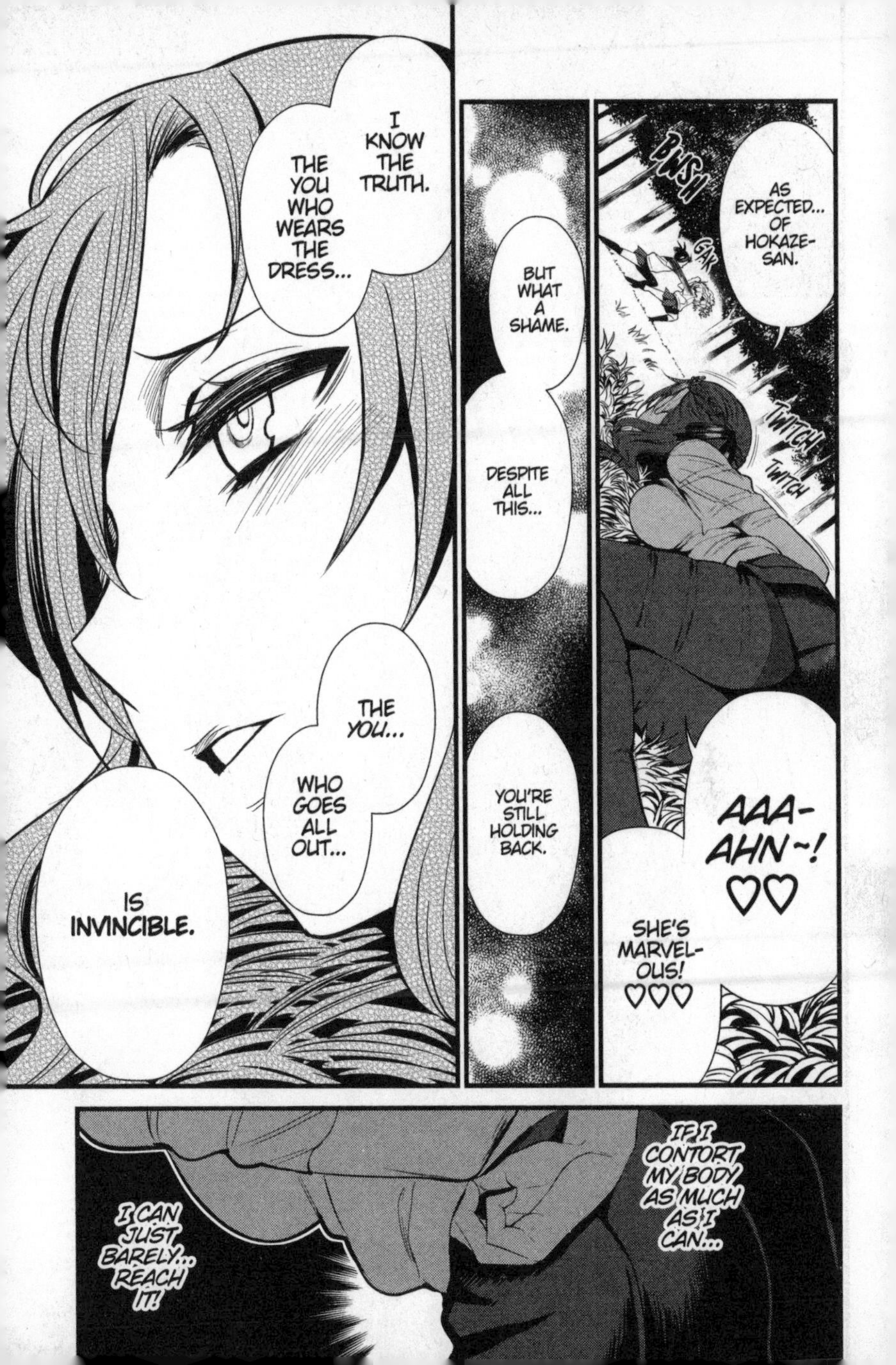
AS EXPECTED... OF HOKAZE-SAN.
BWSH
GAK
TWITCH TWITCH
AAA-AHN~! ♡♡
SHE'S MARVEL-OUS! ♡♡♡
BUT WHAT A SHAME.
DESPITE ALL THIS...
YOU'RE STILL HOLDING BACK.
I KNOW THE TRUTH.
THE YOU WHO WEARS THE DRESS...
THE YOU...
WHO GOES ALL OUT...
IS INVINCIBLE.
IF I CONTORT MY BODY AS MUCH AS I CAN...
I CAN JUST BARELY... REACH IT!

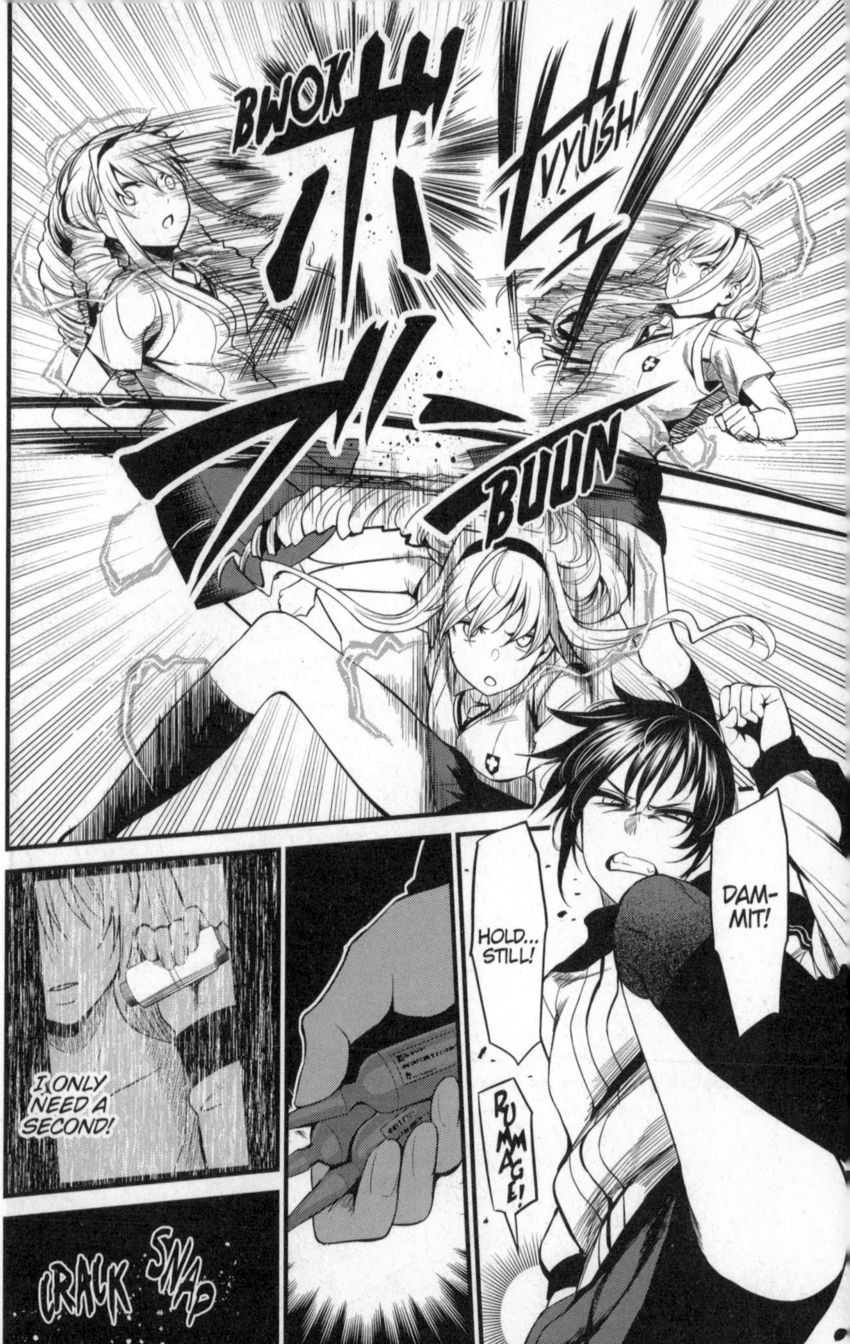
VYUSH
BWOKH
BUUN
DAM-MIT!
HOLD... STILL!
RUMMAGE!
I ONLY NEED A SECOND!
SNAP
CRACK

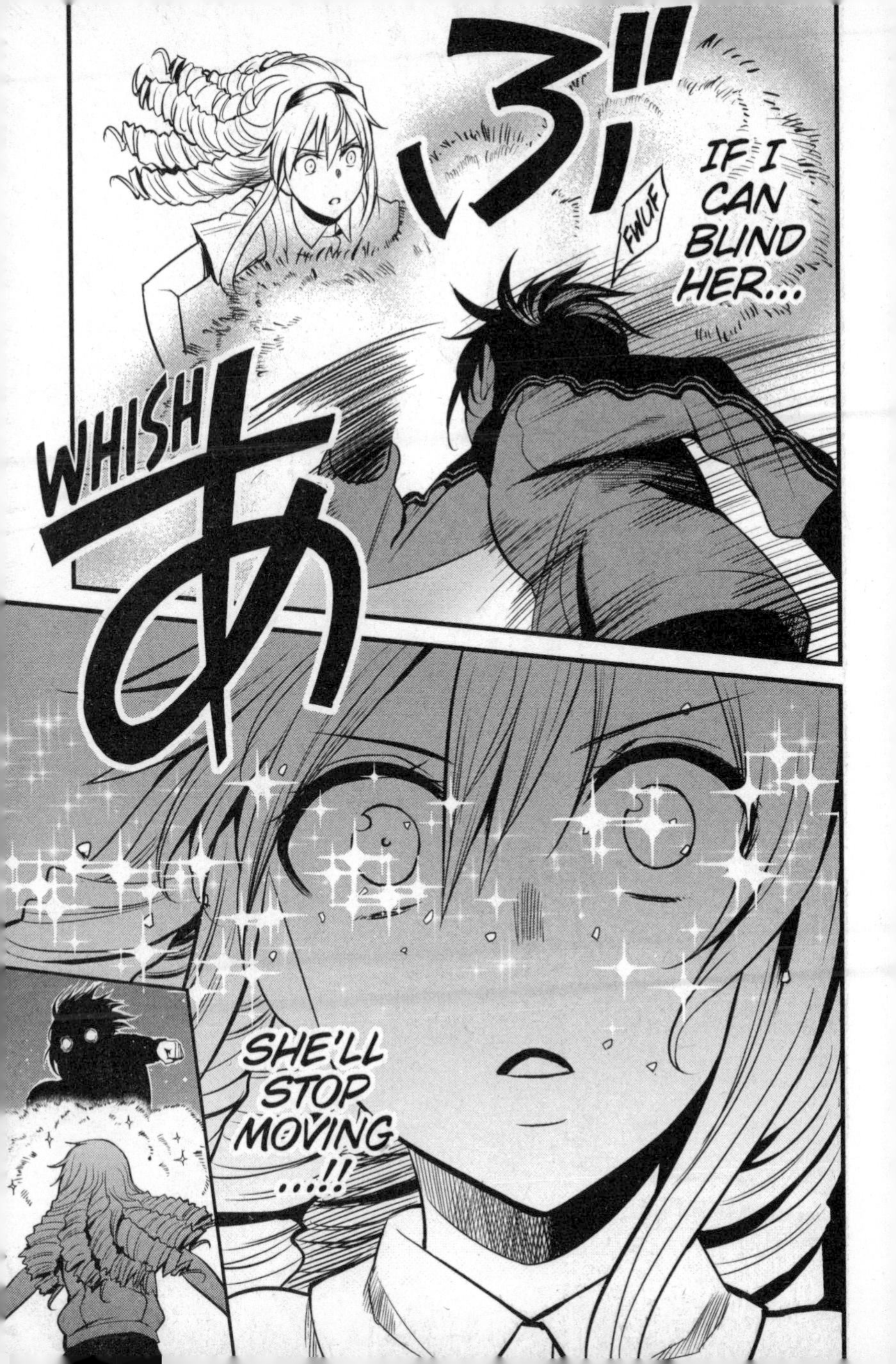
IF I CAN BLIND HER...
FWUF
ろ゛
WHISH
あ
SHE'LL STOP MOVING ...!!

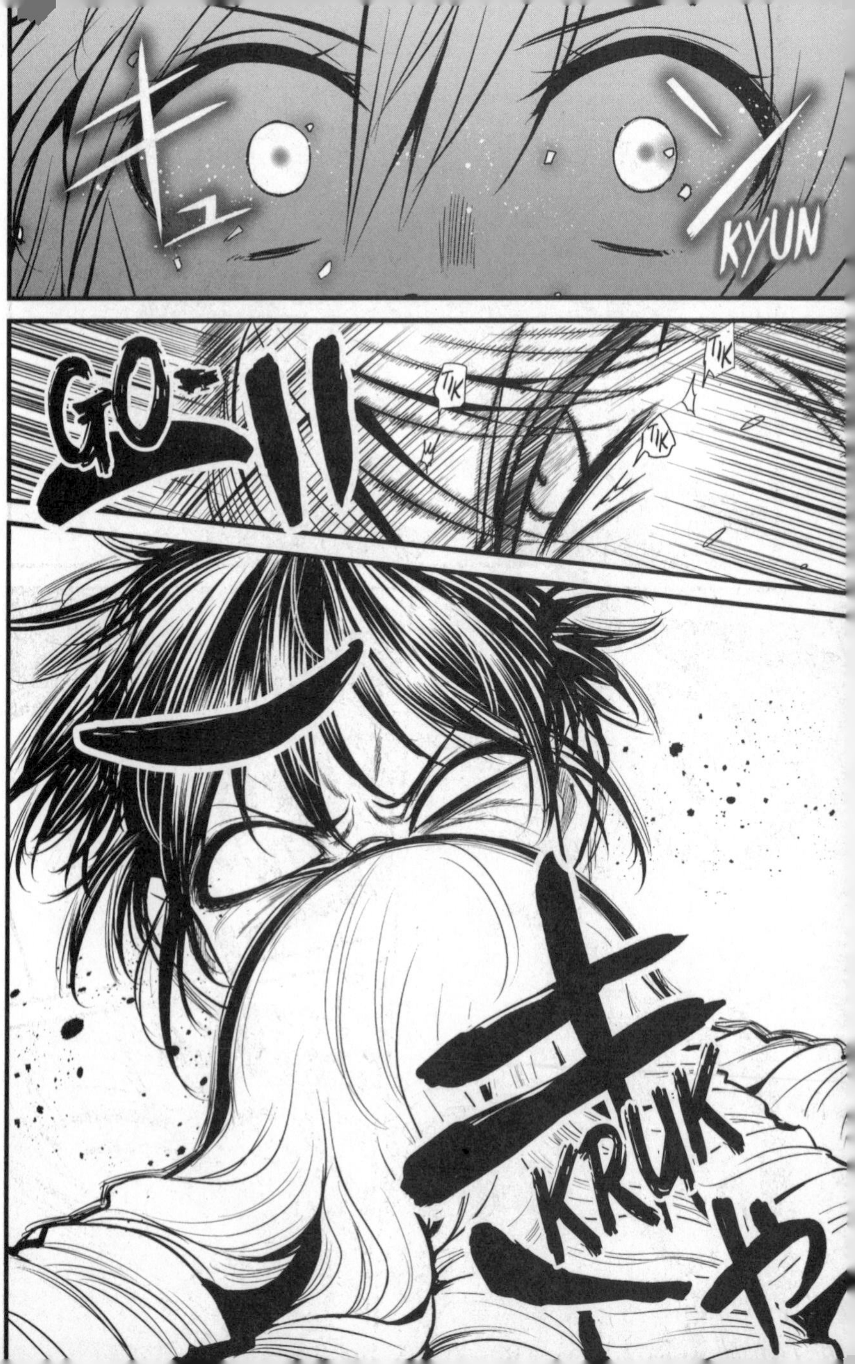
KYUN
TIK
TIK
TIK
GO
KRUK

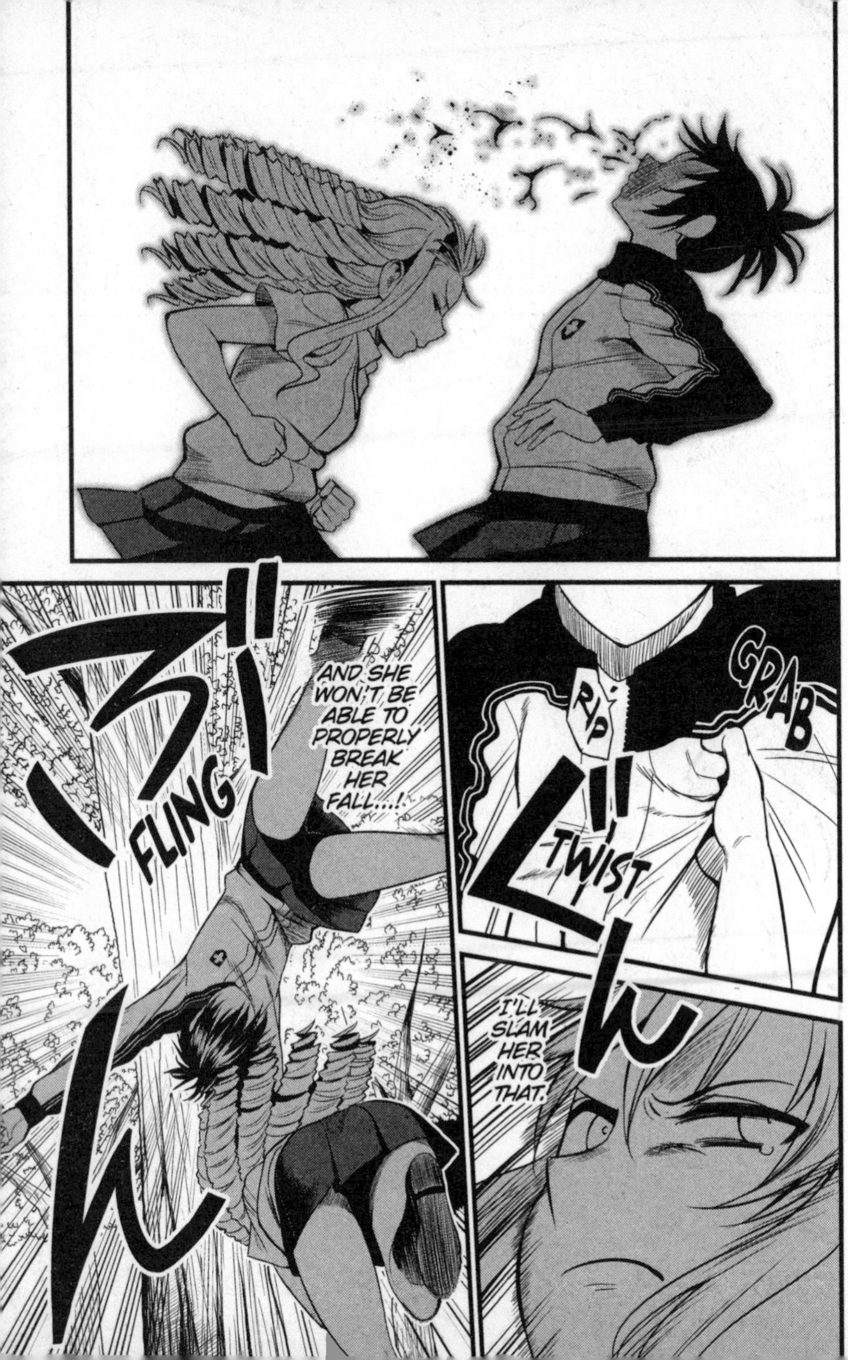
GRAB
RIP
TWIST
I'LL SLAM HER INTO THAT.
AND SHE WON'T BE ABLE TO PROPERLY BREAK HER FALL...!
FLING

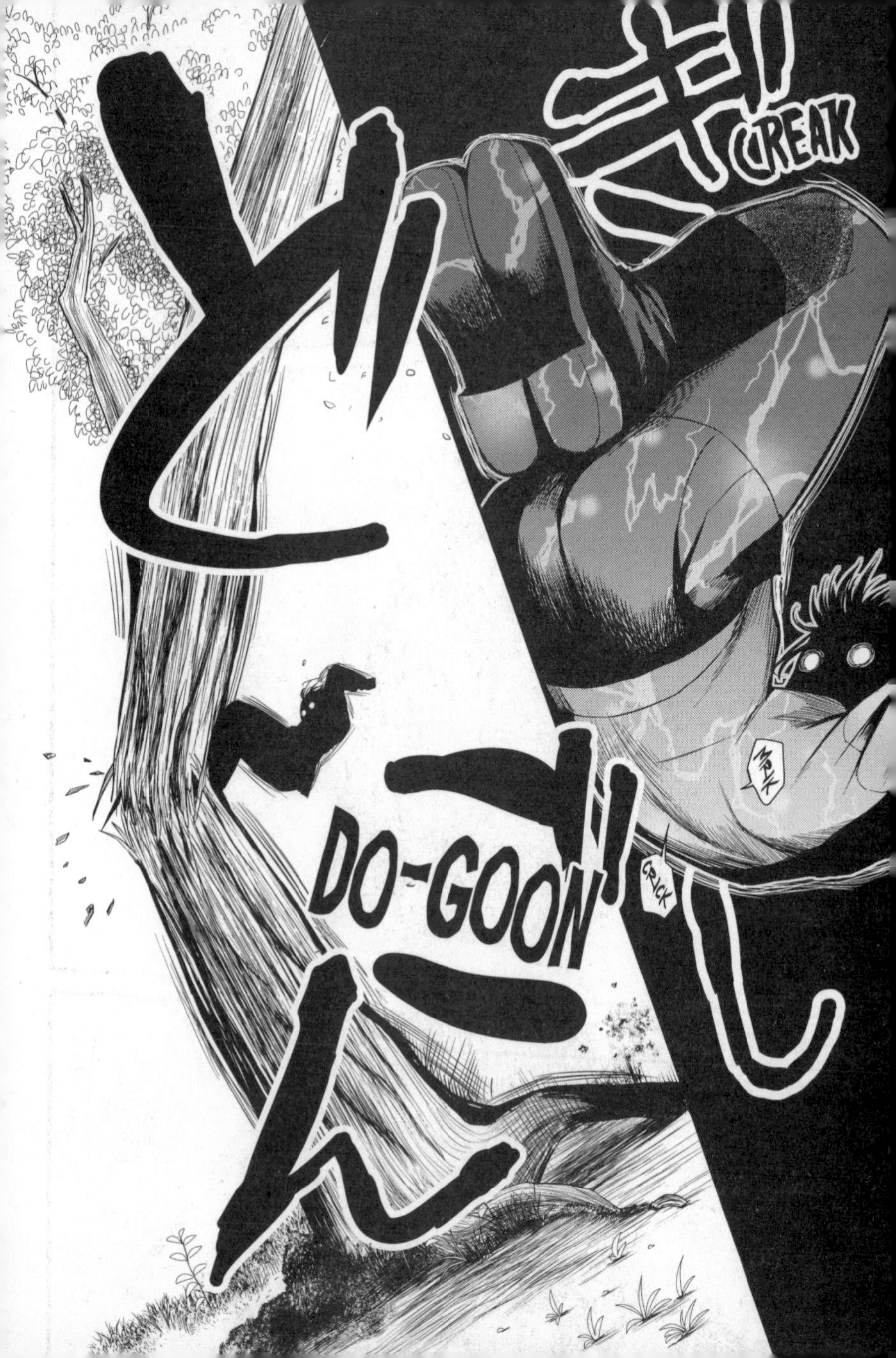
CREAK
MRIK
CRICK
DO-GOON!

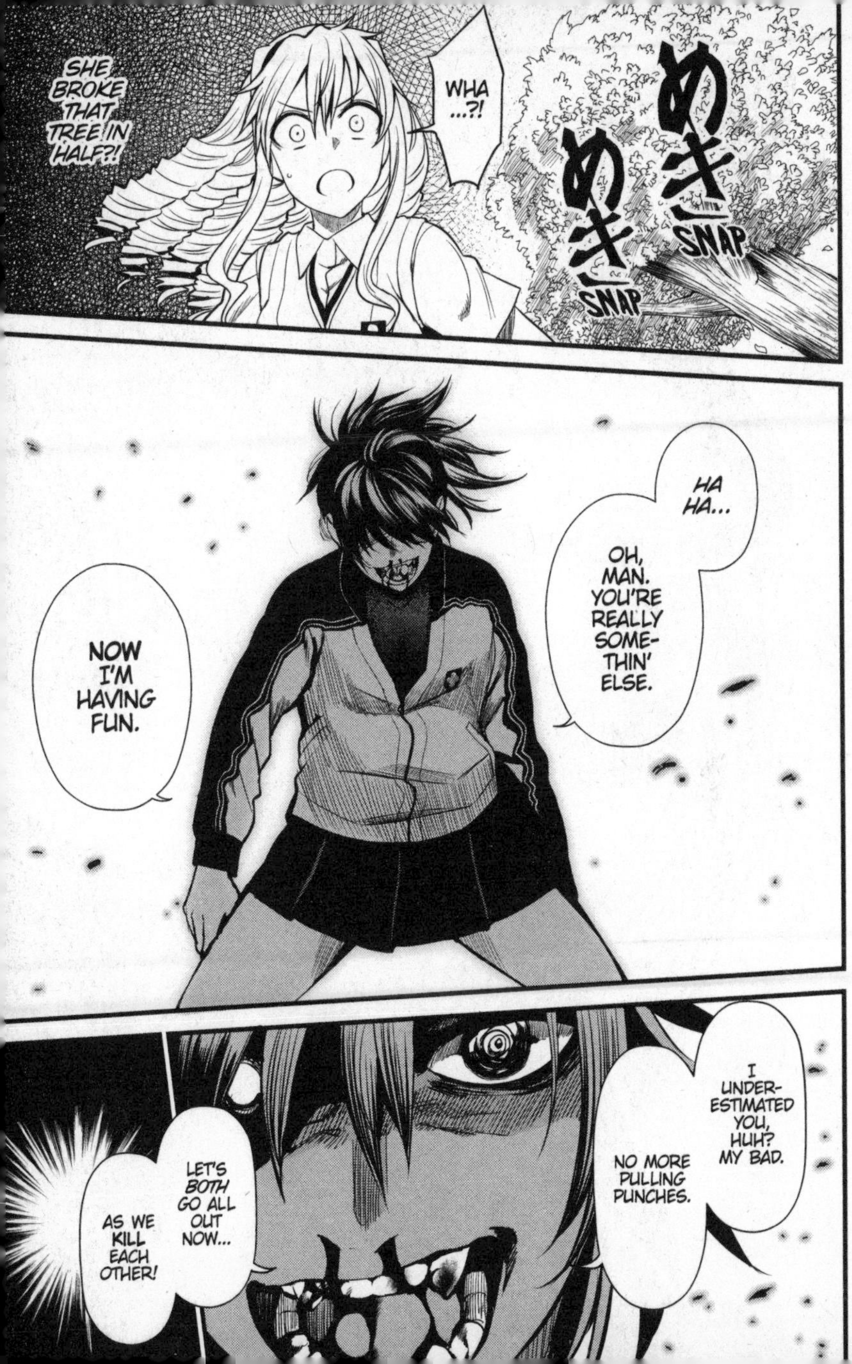
めき
SNAP
めき
SNAP
WHA ...?!
SHE BROKE THAT TREE IN HALF?!
HA HA...
OH, MAN. YOU'RE REALLY SOME-THIN' ELSE.
NOW I'M HAVING FUN.
I UNDER-ESTIMATED YOU, HUH? MY BAD.
NO MORE PULLING PUNCHES.
LET'S BOTH GO ALL OUT NOW...
AS WE KILL EACH OTHER!

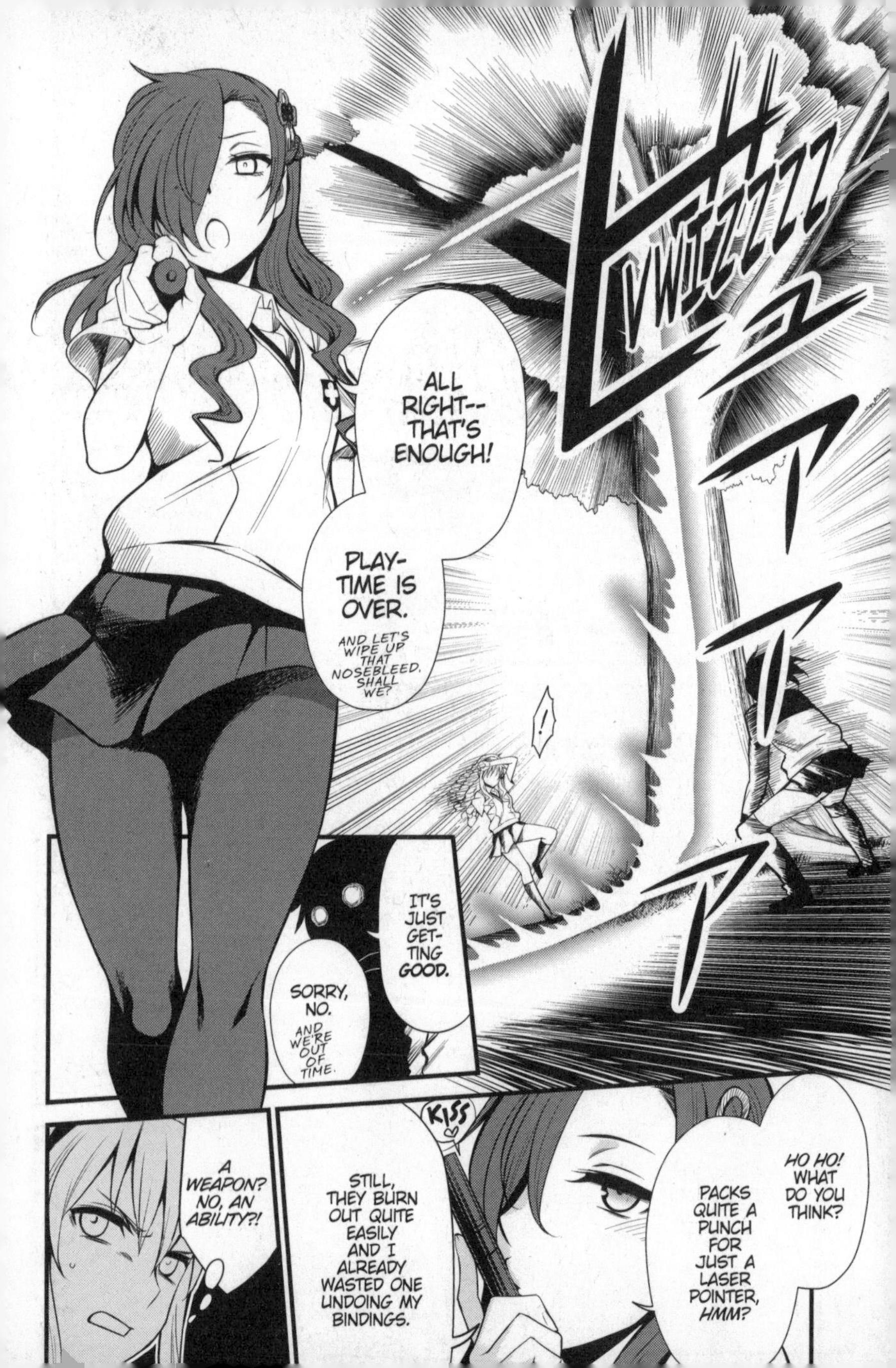
VWIZZZZZZ
ALL RIGHT-- THAT'S ENOUGH!
PLAY-TIME IS OVER.
AND LET'S WIPE UP THAT NOSEBLEED, SHALL WE?
!
IT'S JUST GET-TING GOOD.
SORRY, NO.
AND WE'RE OUT OF TIME.
KISS
HO HO! WHAT DO YOU THINK?
PACKS QUITE A PUNCH FOR JUST A LASER POINTER, HMM?
STILL, THEY BURN OUT QUITE EASILY AND I ALREADY WASTED ONE UNDOING MY BINDINGS.
A WEAPON? NO, AN ABILITY?!

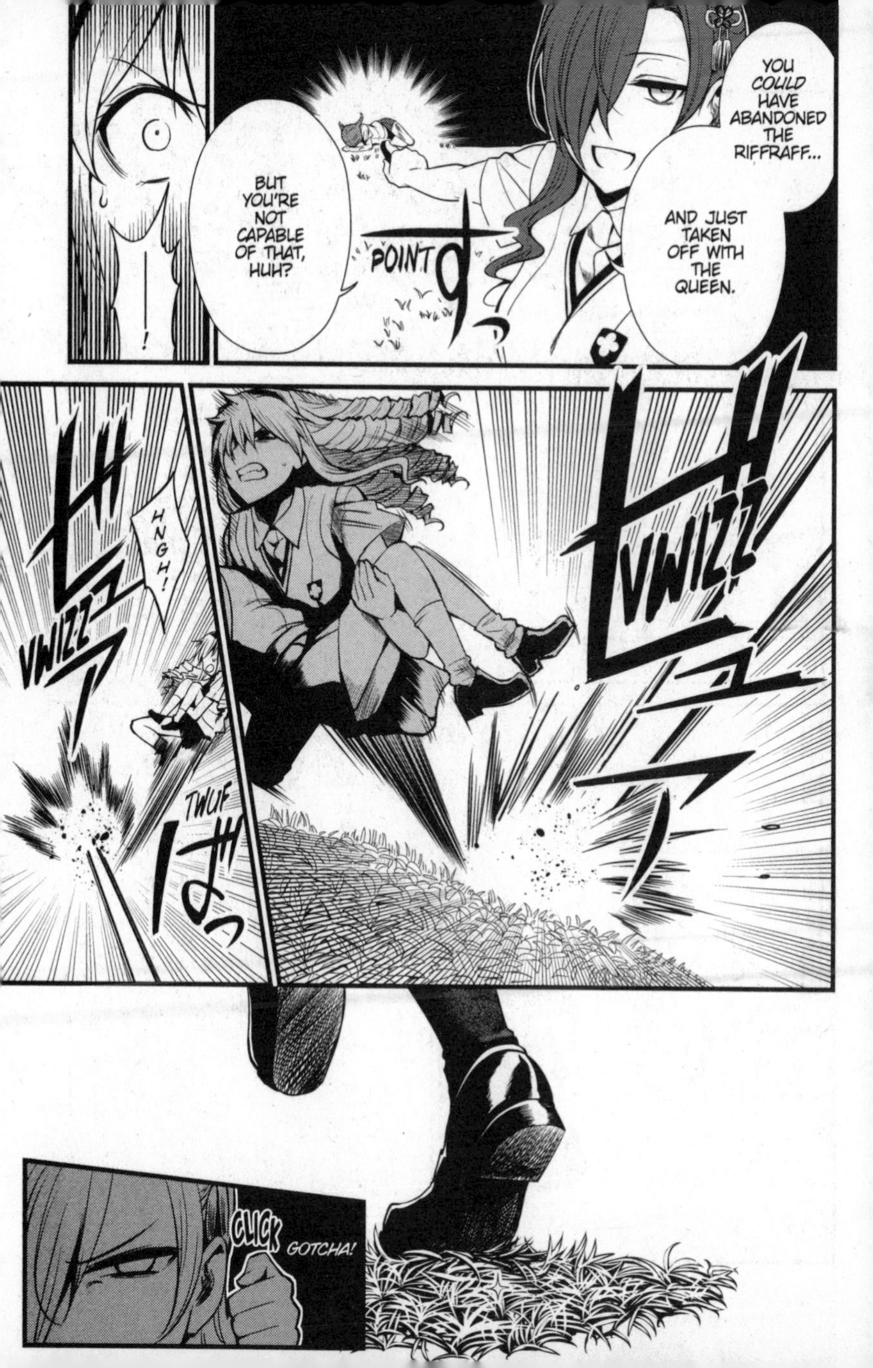
YOU COULD HAVE ABANDONED THE RIFFRAFF...
AND JUST TAKEN OFF WITH THE QUEEN.
POINT
BUT YOU'RE NOT CAPABLE OF THAT, HUH?
!
VWIZZ
HNGH!
VWIZZ
TWUF
CLICK
GOTCHA!

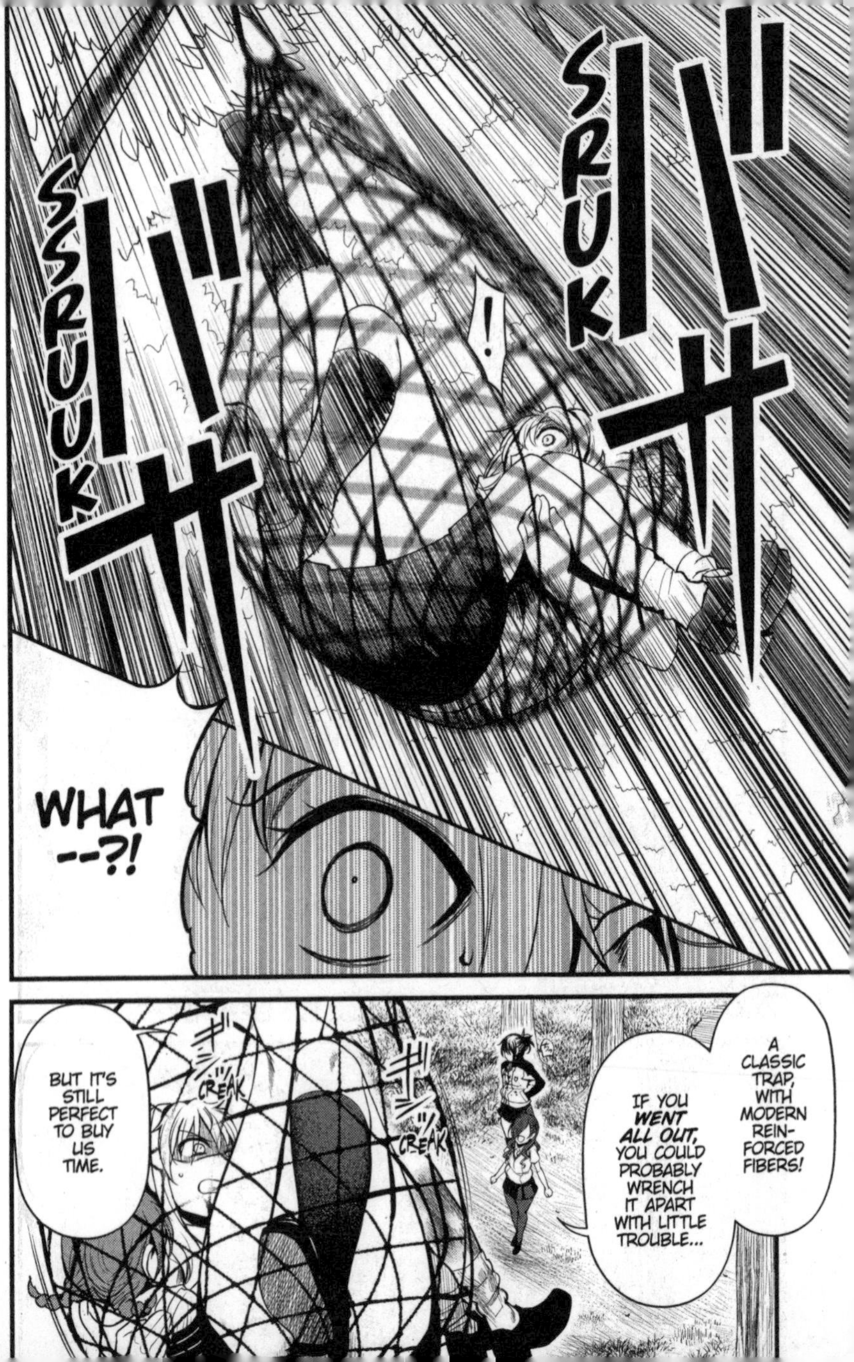
SRUUK
SRUUK
!
WHAT --?!
A CLASSIC TRAP, WITH MODERN REIN-FORCED FIBERS!
IF YOU *WENT ALL OUT*, YOU COULD PROBABLY WRENCH IT APART WITH LITTLE TROUBLE...
CREAK
CREAK
BUT IT'S STILL PERFECT TO BUY US TIME.

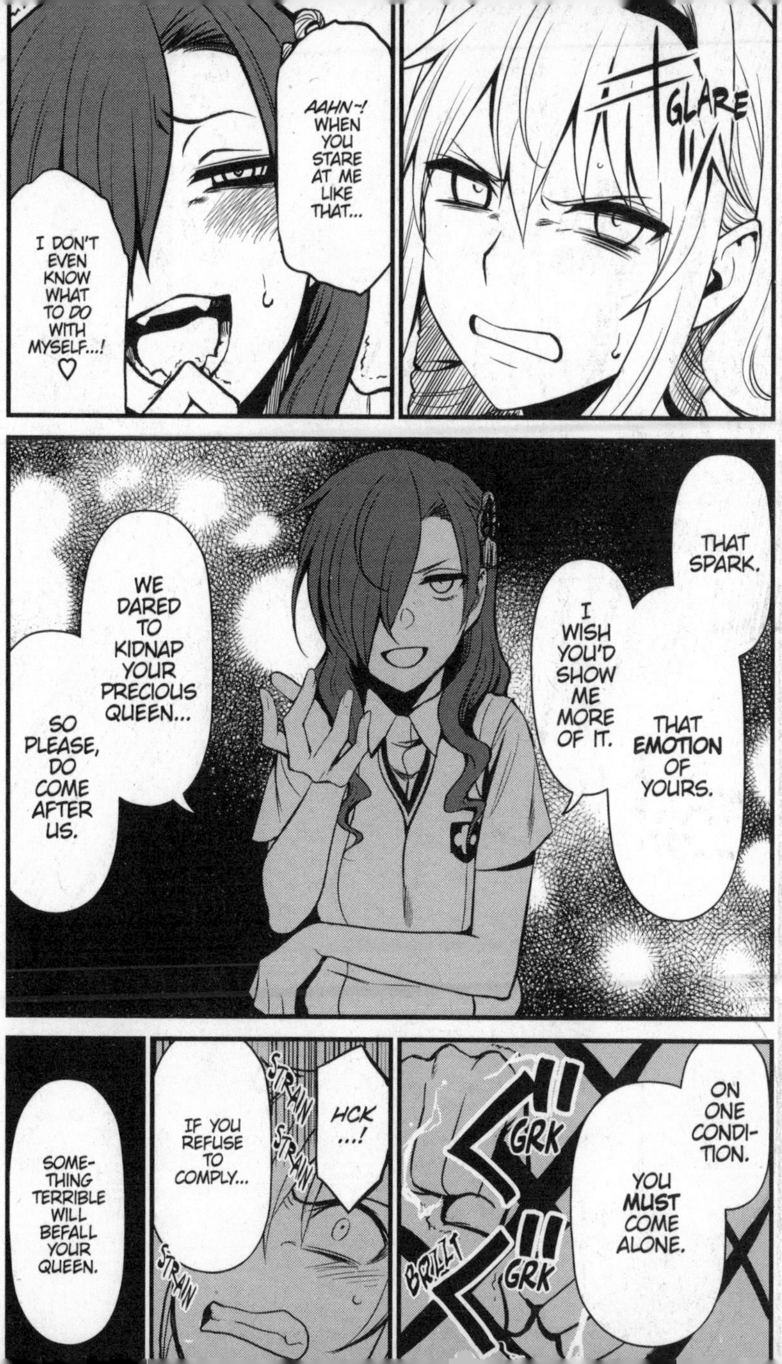
GLARE
AAHN~! WHEN YOU STARE AT ME LIKE THAT...
I DON'T EVEN KNOW WHAT TO DO WITH MYSELF...! ♡
THAT SPARK.
THAT EMOTION OF YOURS.
I WISH YOU'D SHOW ME MORE OF IT.
WE DARED TO KIDNAP YOUR PRECIOUS QUEEN...
SO PLEASE, DO COME AFTER US.
ON ONE CONDITION.
YOU MUST COME ALONE.
GRK
GRK
HCK ...!
STRAIN STRAIN STRAIN
IF YOU REFUSE TO COMPLY...
STRAIN
SOME-THING TERRIBLE WILL BEFALL YOUR QUEEN.

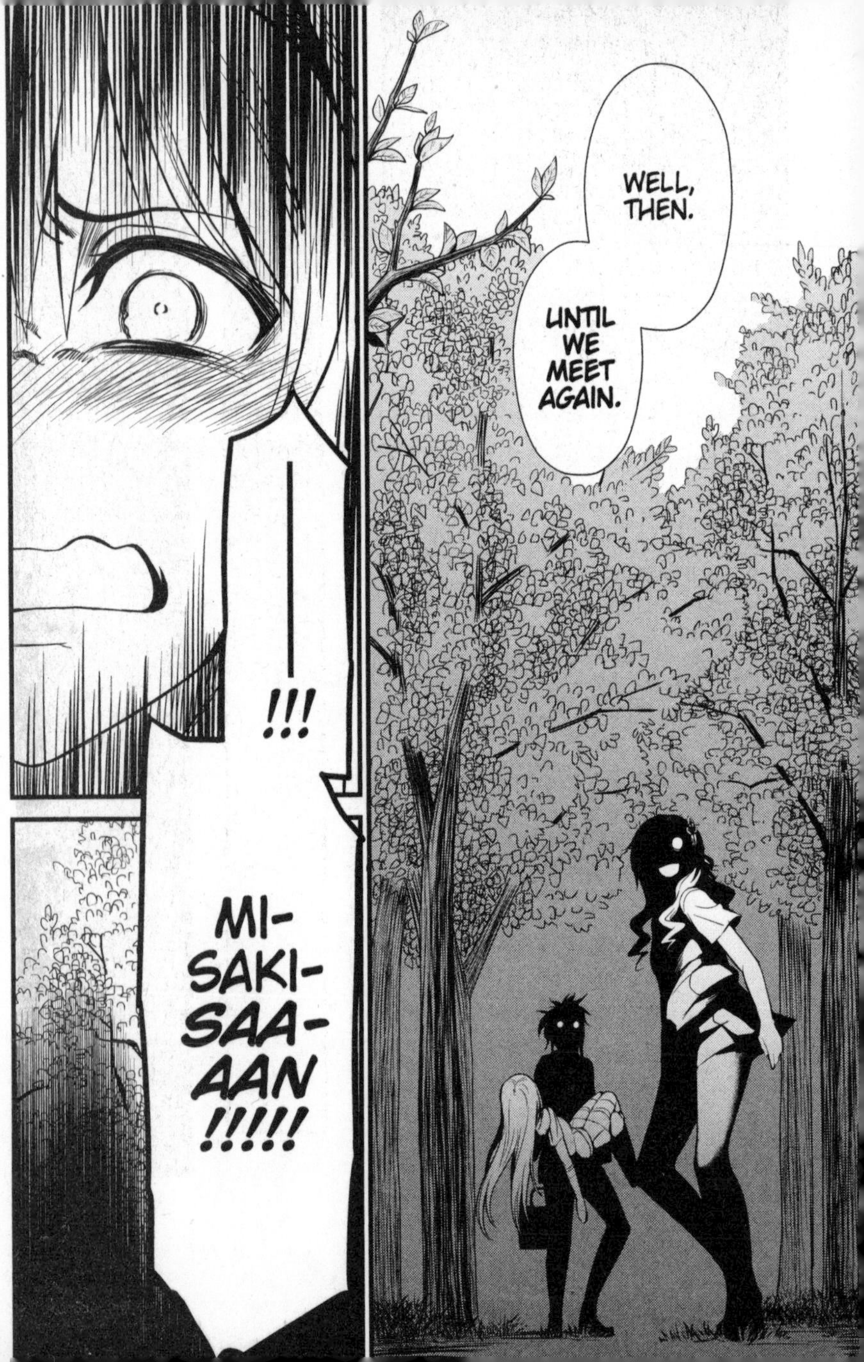
WELL, THEN.
UNTIL WE MEET AGAIN.
——!!!
MI-SAKI-SAAA-AAN!!!!!

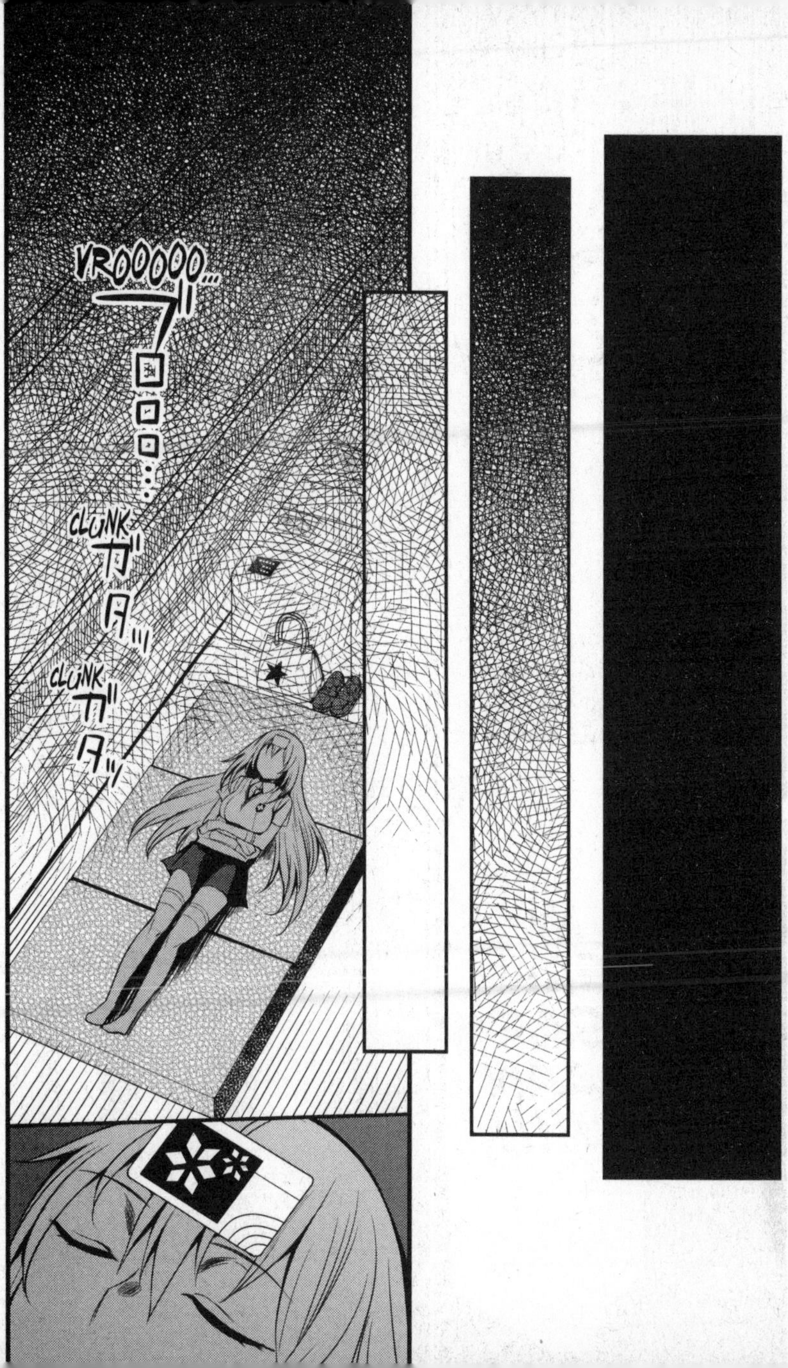
VROOOOO...
ブロロロ...
CLUNK
ガタッ
CLUNK
ガタッ

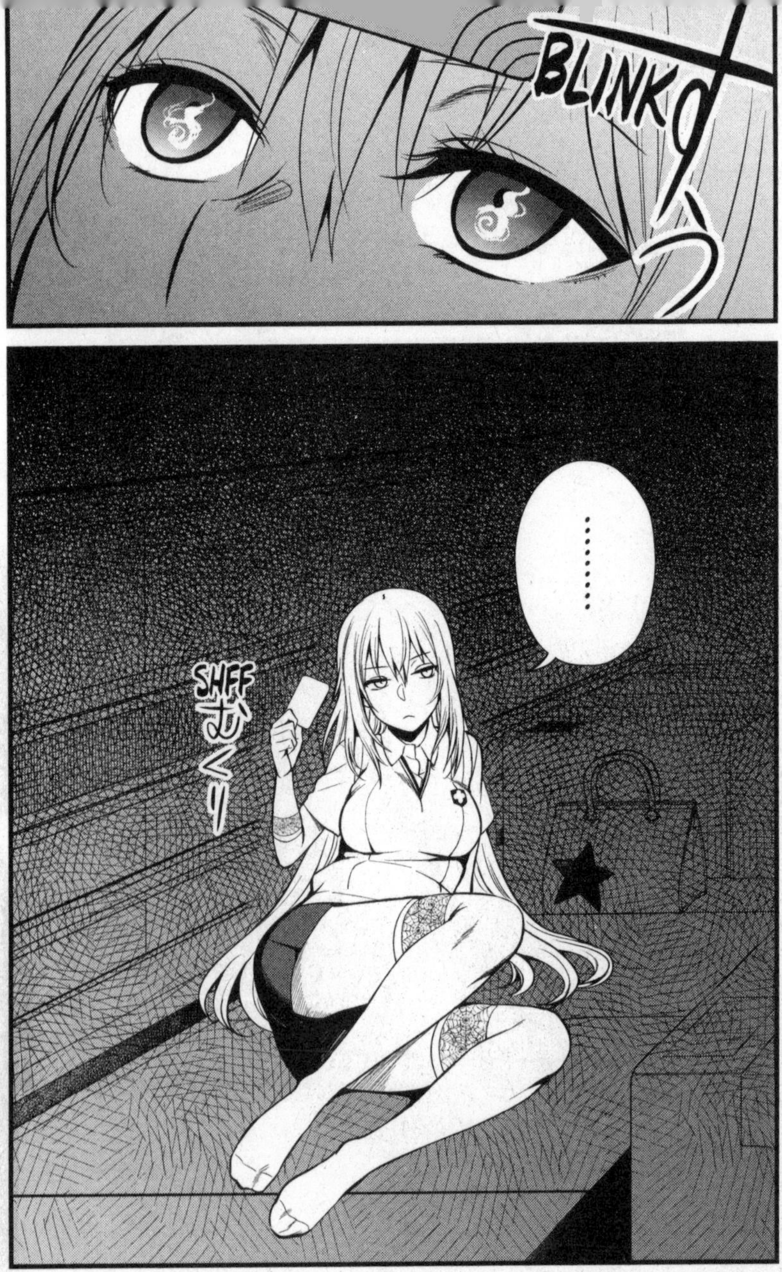
BLINK
……
SHFF
むくり

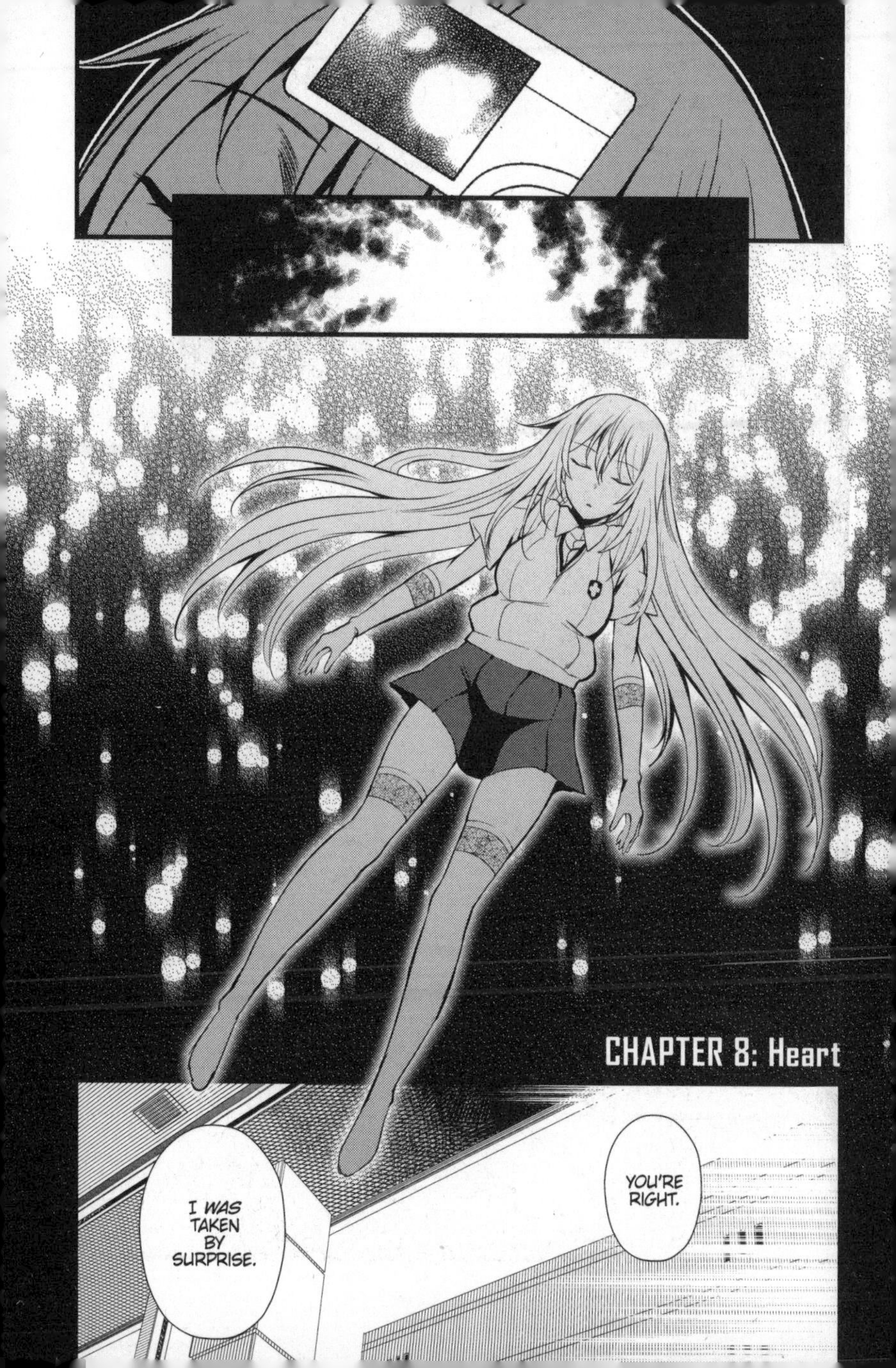
CHAPTER 8: Heart
YOU'RE RIGHT.
I *WAS* TAKEN BY SURPRISE.

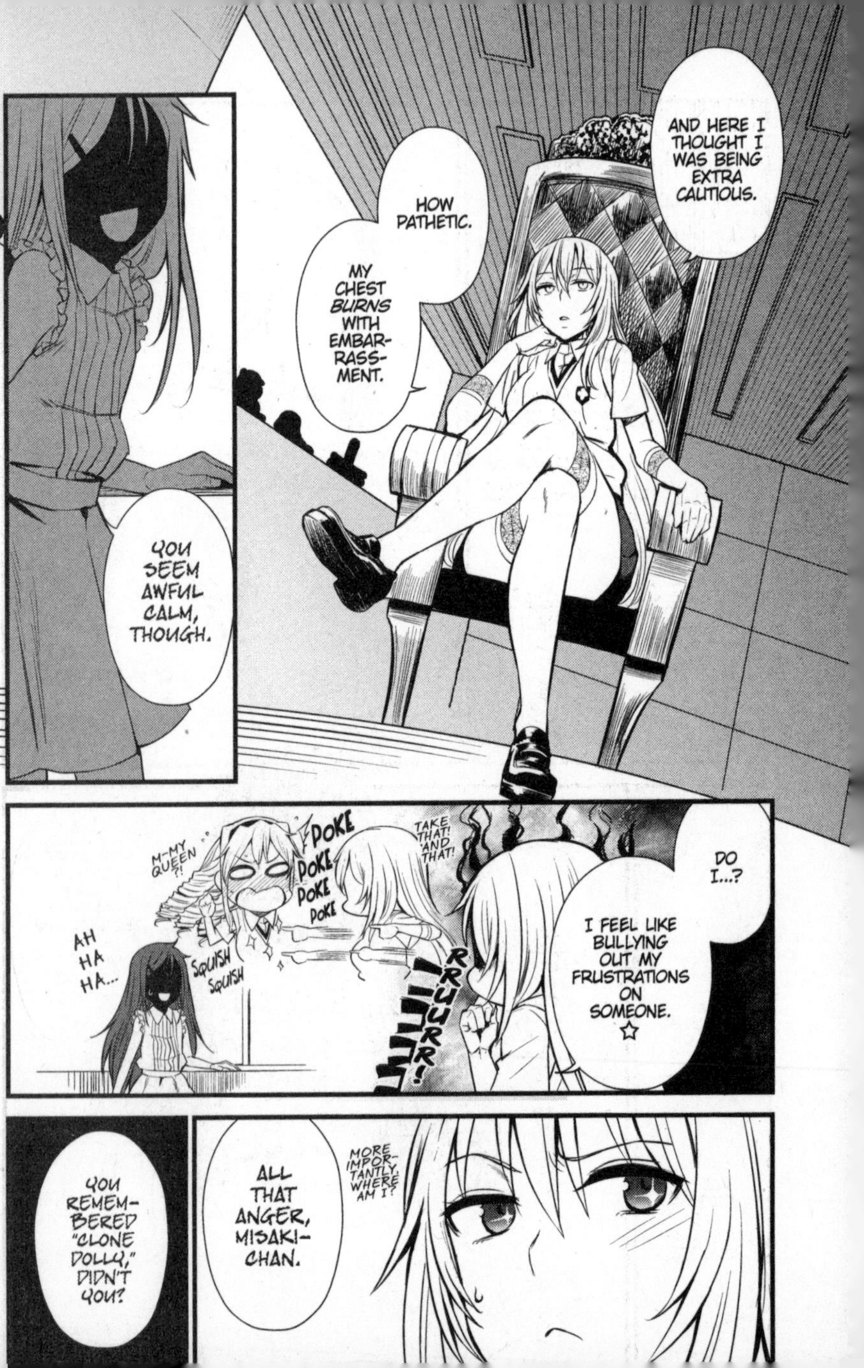
AND HERE I THOUGHT I WAS BEING EXTRA CAUTIOUS.
HOW PATHETIC.
MY CHEST BURNS WITH EMBARRASSMENT.
YOU SEEM AWFUL CALM, THOUGH.
DO I...?
I FEEL LIKE BULLYING OUT MY FRUSTRATIONS ON SOMEONE. ☆
RRUURR!
TAKE THAT! AND THAT!
POKE POKE POKE POKE
M-MY QUEEN?!
SQUISH SQUISH
AH HA HA...
MORE IMPORTANTLY, WHERE AM I?
ALL THAT ANGER, MISAKI-CHAN.
YOU REMEMBERED "CLONE DOLLY," DIDN'T YOU?

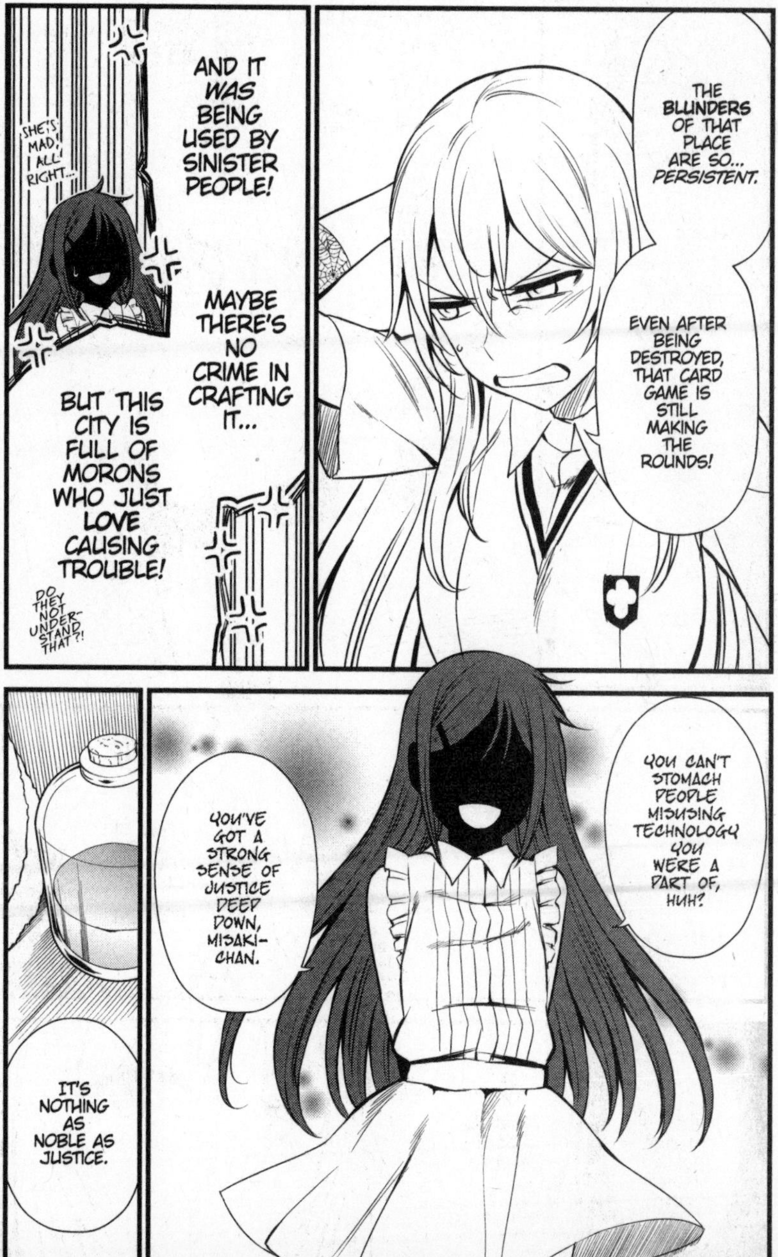
THE BLUNDERS OF THAT PLACE ARE SO... PERSISTENT.
EVEN AFTER BEING DESTROYED, THAT CARD GAME IS STILL MAKING THE ROUNDS!
AND IT WAS BEING USED BY SINISTER PEOPLE!
SHE'S MAD, ALL RIGHT...
MAYBE THERE'S NO CRIME IN CRAFTING IT...
BUT THIS CITY IS FULL OF MORONS WHO JUST LOVE CAUSING TROUBLE!
DO THEY NOT UNDERSTAND THAT?!
YOU CAN'T STOMACH PEOPLE MISUSING TECHNOLOGY YOU WERE A PART OF, HUH?
YOU'VE GOT A STRONG SENSE OF JUSTICE DEEP DOWN, MISAKI-CHAN.
IT'S NOTHING AS NOBLE AS JUSTICE.

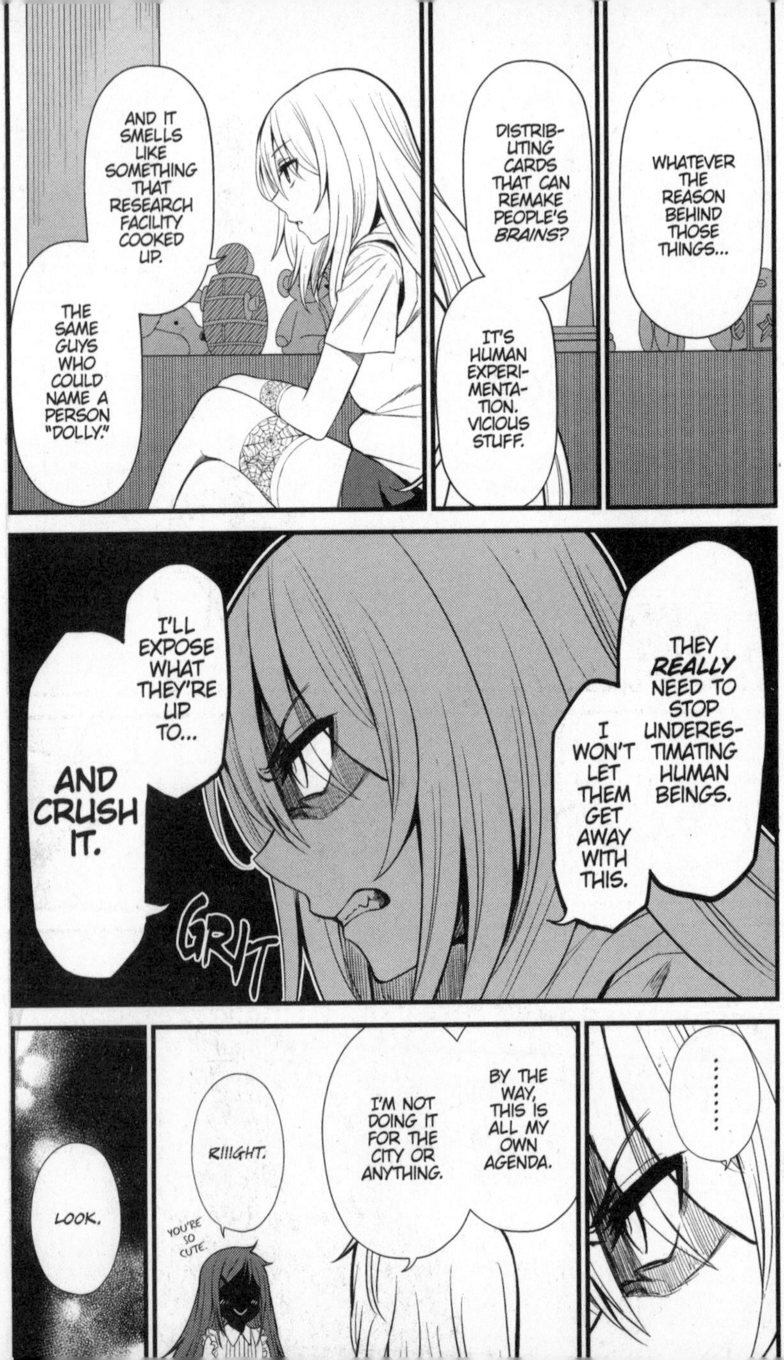
WHATEVER THE REASON BEHIND THOSE THINGS...
DISTRIB-UTING CARDS THAT CAN REMAKE PEOPLE'S *BRAINS?*
IT'S HUMAN EXPERI-MENTA-TION. VICIOUS STUFF.
AND IT SMELLS LIKE SOMETHING THAT RESEARCH FACILITY COOKED UP.
THE SAME GUYS WHO COULD NAME A PERSON "DOLLY."
THEY ***REALLY*** NEED TO STOP UNDERES-TIMATING HUMAN BEINGS.
I WON'T LET THEM GET AWAY WITH THIS.
I'LL EXPOSE WHAT THEY'RE UP TO...
AND CRUSH IT.
GRIT
......
BY THE WAY, THIS IS ALL MY OWN AGENDA.
I'M NOT DOING IT FOR THE CITY OR ANYTHING.
RIIIGHT.
YOU'RE SO CUTE.
LOOK.

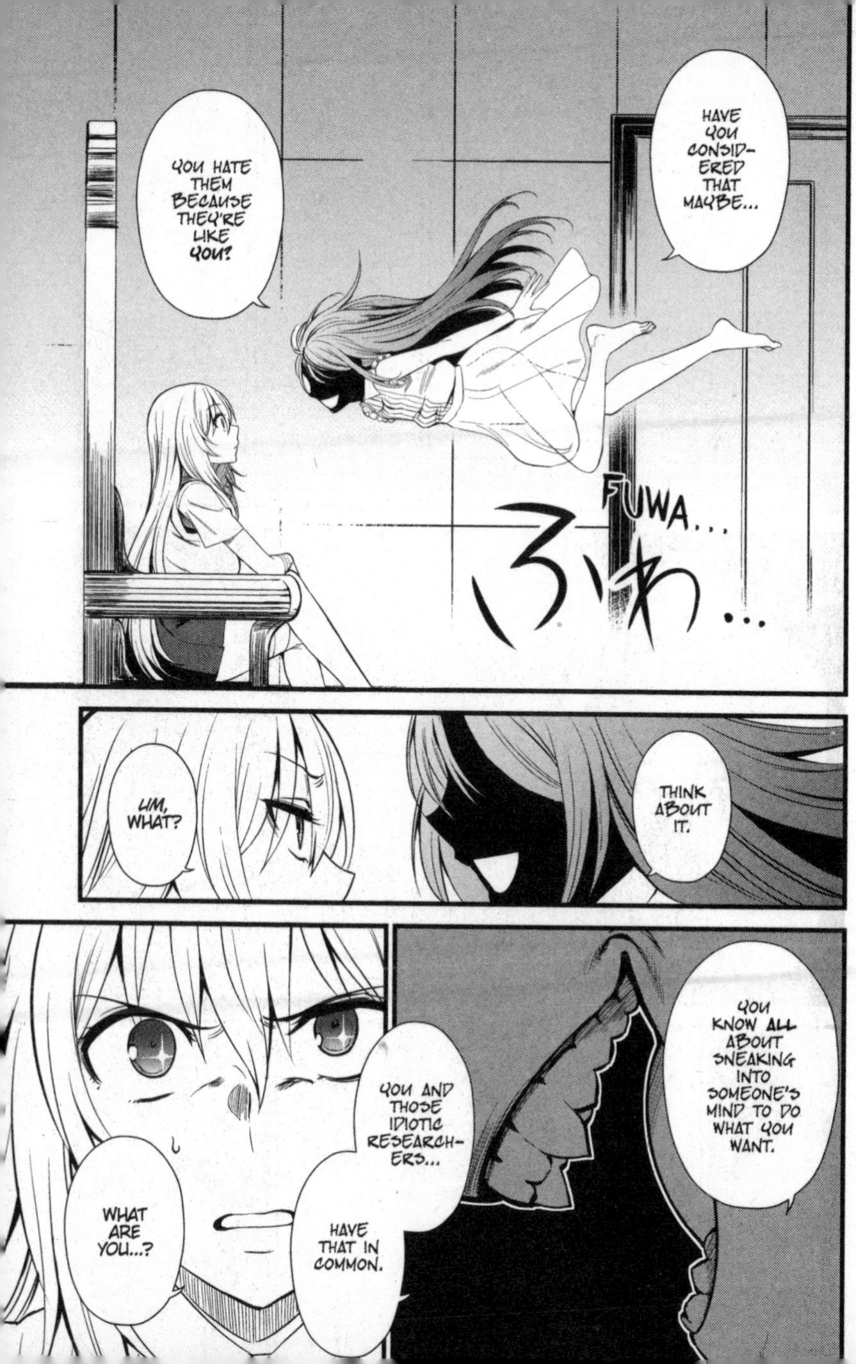
HAVE YOU CONSIDERED THAT MAYBE...
YOU HATE THEM BECAUSE THEY'RE LIKE YOU?
FUWA...
ふわ...
THINK ABOUT IT.
UM, WHAT?
YOU KNOW ALL ABOUT SNEAKING INTO SOMEONE'S MIND TO DO WHAT YOU WANT.
YOU AND THOSE IDIOTIC RESEARCHERS...
HAVE THAT IN COMMON.
WHAT ARE YOU...?

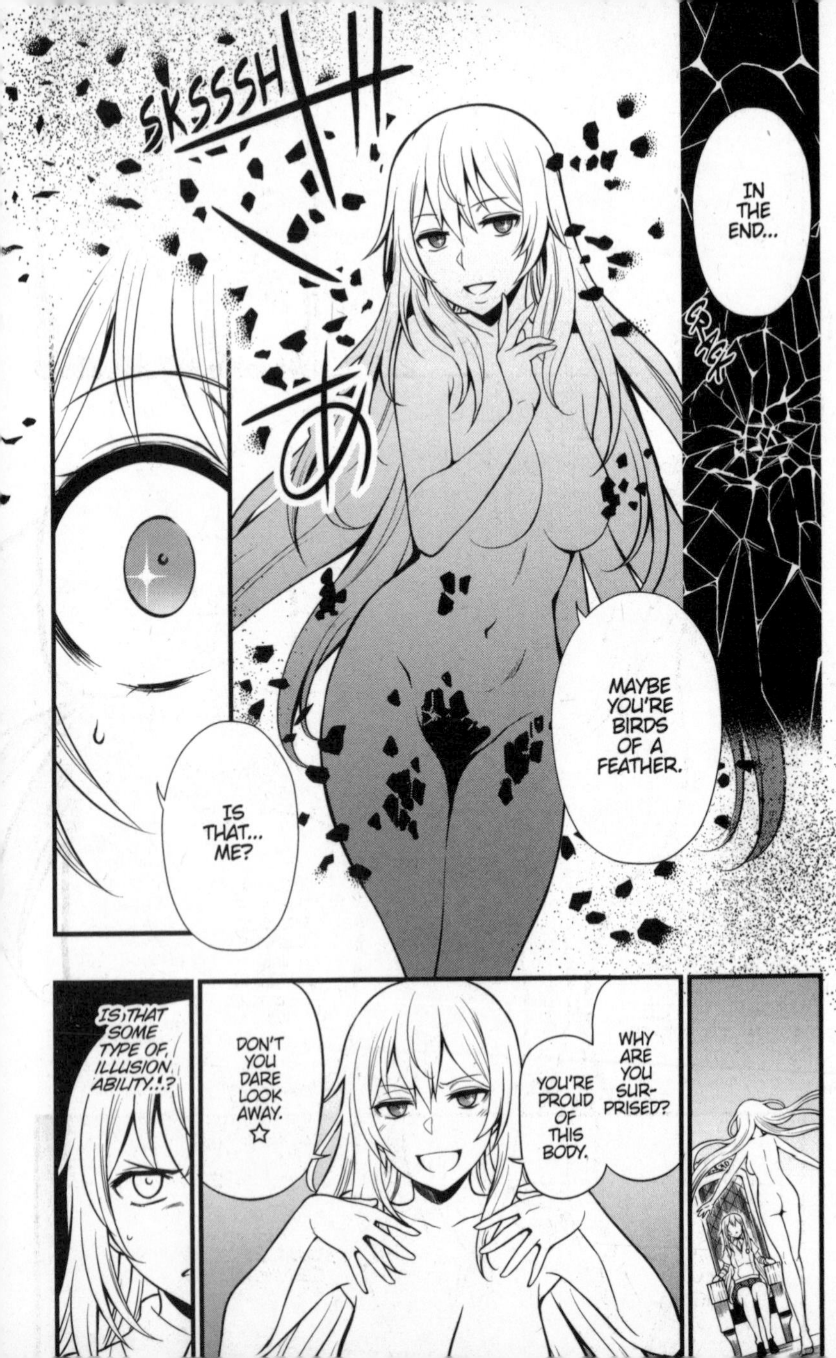
IN THE END...
CRACK
SKSSSH!!
MAYBE YOU'RE BIRDS OF A FEATHER.
あ
IS THAT... ME?
WHY ARE YOU SURPRISED?
YOU'RE PROUD OF THIS BODY.
DON'T YOU DARE LOOK AWAY. ☆
IS THAT SOME TYPE OF ILLUSION ABILITY...!?

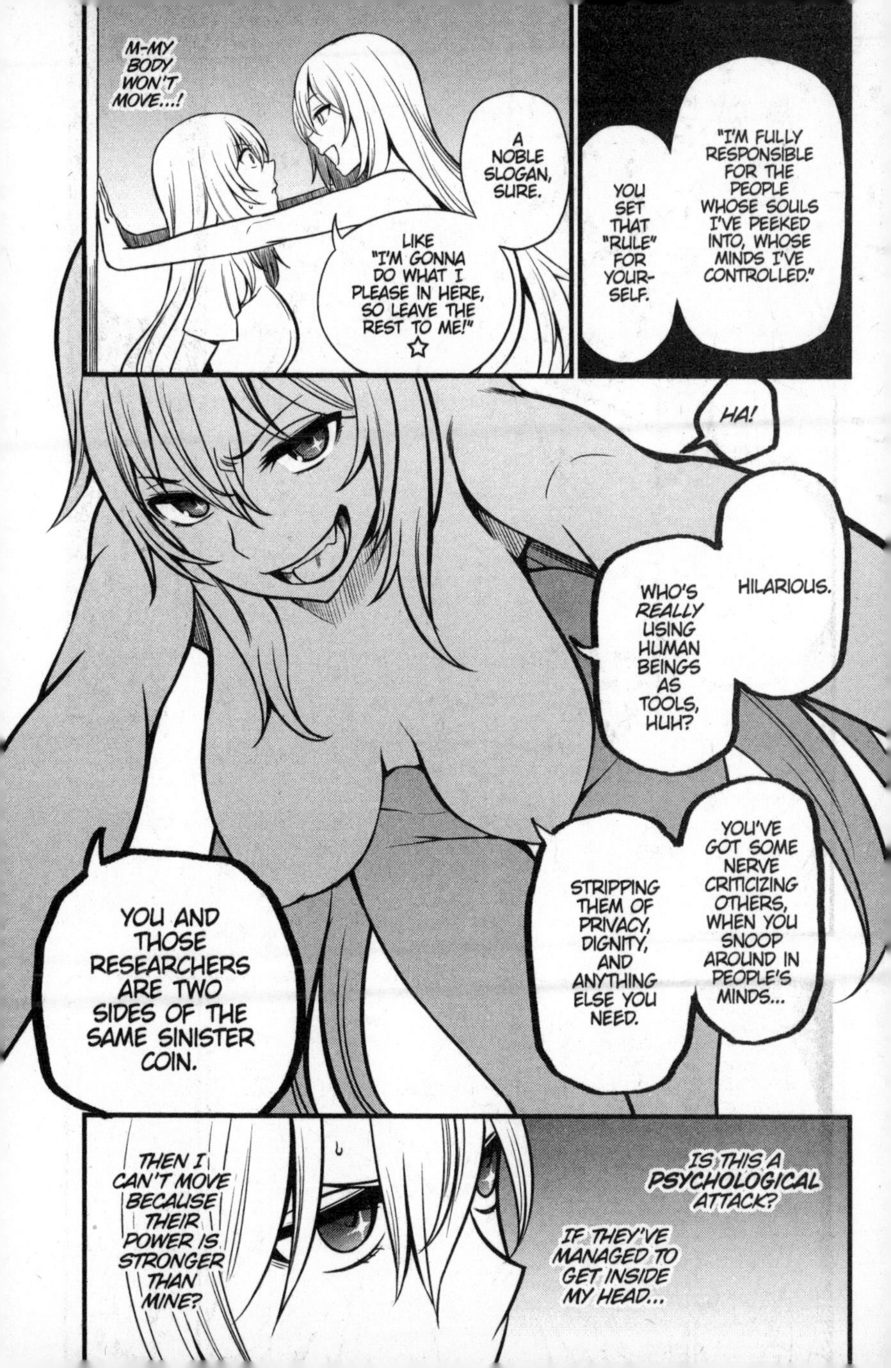
"I'M FULLY RESPONSIBLE FOR THE PEOPLE WHOSE SOULS I'VE PEEKED INTO, WHOSE MINDS I'VE CONTROLLED."
YOU SET THAT "RULE" FOR YOURSELF.
A NOBLE SLOGAN, SURE.
LIKE "I'M GONNA DO WHAT I PLEASE IN HERE, SO LEAVE THE REST TO ME!" ☆
M-MY BODY WON'T MOVE...!
HA!
HILARIOUS.
WHO'S *REALLY* USING HUMAN BEINGS AS TOOLS, HUH?
YOU'VE GOT SOME NERVE CRITICIZING OTHERS, WHEN YOU SNOOP AROUND IN PEOPLE'S MINDS...
STRIPPING THEM OF PRIVACY, DIGNITY, AND ANYTHING ELSE YOU NEED.
YOU AND THOSE RESEARCHERS ARE TWO SIDES OF THE SAME SINISTER COIN.
IS THIS A PSYCHOLOGICAL ATTACK?
IF THEY'VE MANAGED TO GET INSIDE MY HEAD...
THEN I CAN'T MOVE BECAUSE THEIR POWER IS STRONGER THAN MINE?

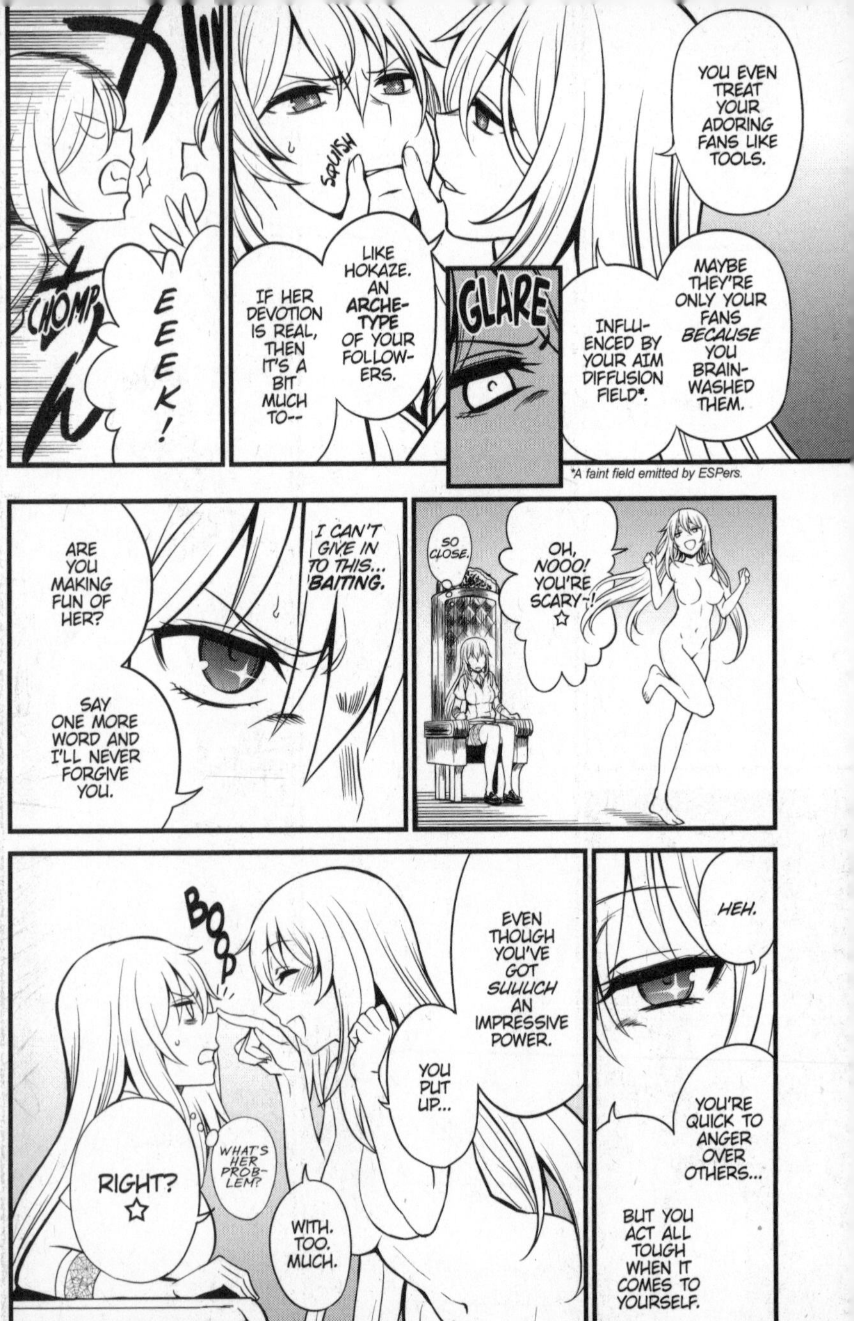
YOU EVEN TREAT YOUR ADORING FANS LIKE TOOLS.
MAYBE THEY'RE ONLY YOUR FANS *BECAUSE* YOU BRAIN-WASHED THEM.
INFLU-ENCED BY YOUR AIM DIFFUSION FIELD*.
GLARE
SQUISH
LIKE HOKAZE. AN **ARCHE-TYPE** OF YOUR FOLLOW-ERS.
IF HER DEVOTION IS REAL, THEN IT'S A BIT MUCH TO--
CHOMP
EEEEK!
OH, NOOO! YOU'RE SCARY~! ☆
SO CLOSE.
I CAN'T GIVE IN TO THIS... **BAITING.**
ARE YOU MAKING FUN OF HER?
SAY ONE MORE WORD AND I'LL NEVER FORGIVE YOU.
HEH.
YOU'RE QUICK TO ANGER OVER OTHERS...
BUT YOU ACT ALL TOUGH WHEN IT COMES TO YOURSELF.
BOOP
EVEN THOUGH YOU'VE GOT *SUUUCH* AN IMPRESSIVE POWER.
YOU PUT UP...
WITH. TOO. MUCH.
WHAT'S HER PROB-LEM?
RIGHT? ☆

*A faint field emitted by ESPers.

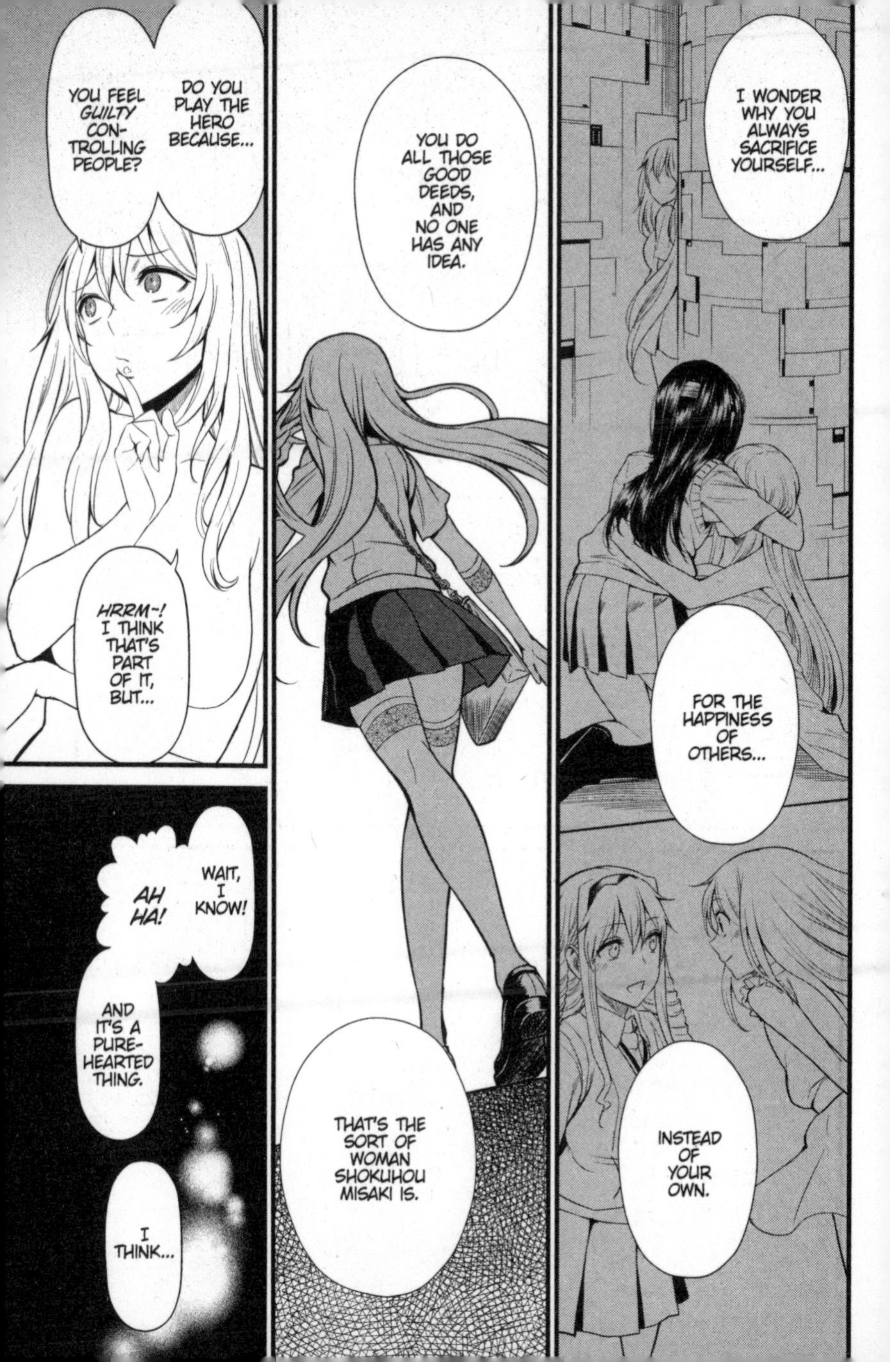
I WONDER WHY YOU ALWAYS SACRIFICE YOURSELF...
FOR THE HAPPINESS OF OTHERS...
INSTEAD OF YOUR OWN.
YOU DO ALL THOSE GOOD DEEDS, AND NO ONE HAS ANY IDEA.
THAT'S THE SORT OF WOMAN SHOKUHOU MISAKI IS.
DO YOU PLAY THE HERO BECAUSE...
YOU FEEL *GUILTY* CONTROLLING PEOPLE?
HRRM~! I THINK THAT'S PART OF IT, BUT...
WAIT, I KNOW!
AH HA!
AND IT'S A PURE-HEARTED THING.
I THINK...

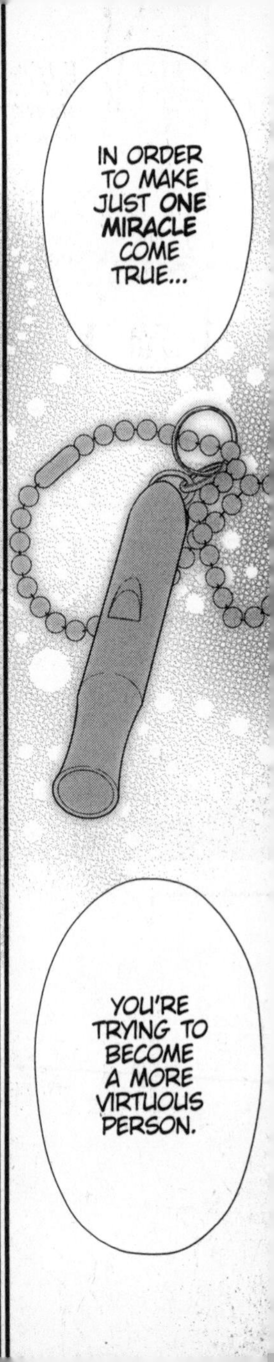
IN ORDER TO MAKE JUST ONE MIRACLE COME TRUE...
YOU'RE TRYING TO BECOME A MORE VIRTUOUS PERSON.
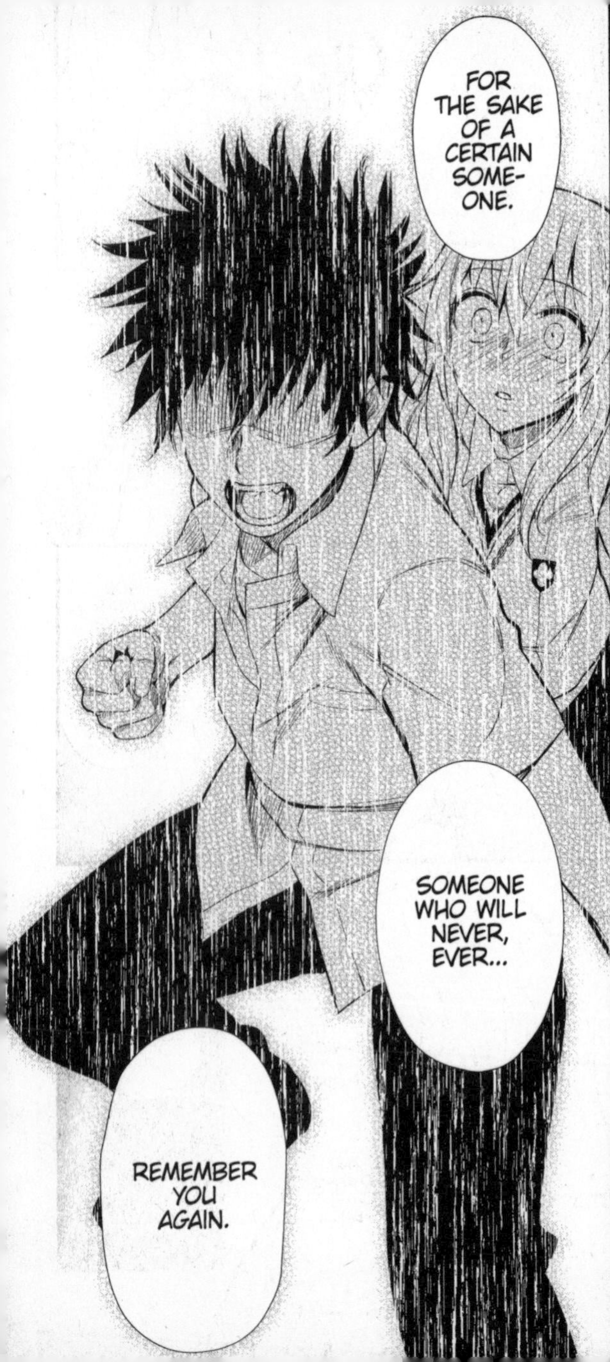
FOR THE SAKE OF A CERTAIN SOME-ONE.
SOMEONE WHO WILL NEVER, EVER...
REMEMBER YOU AGAIN.

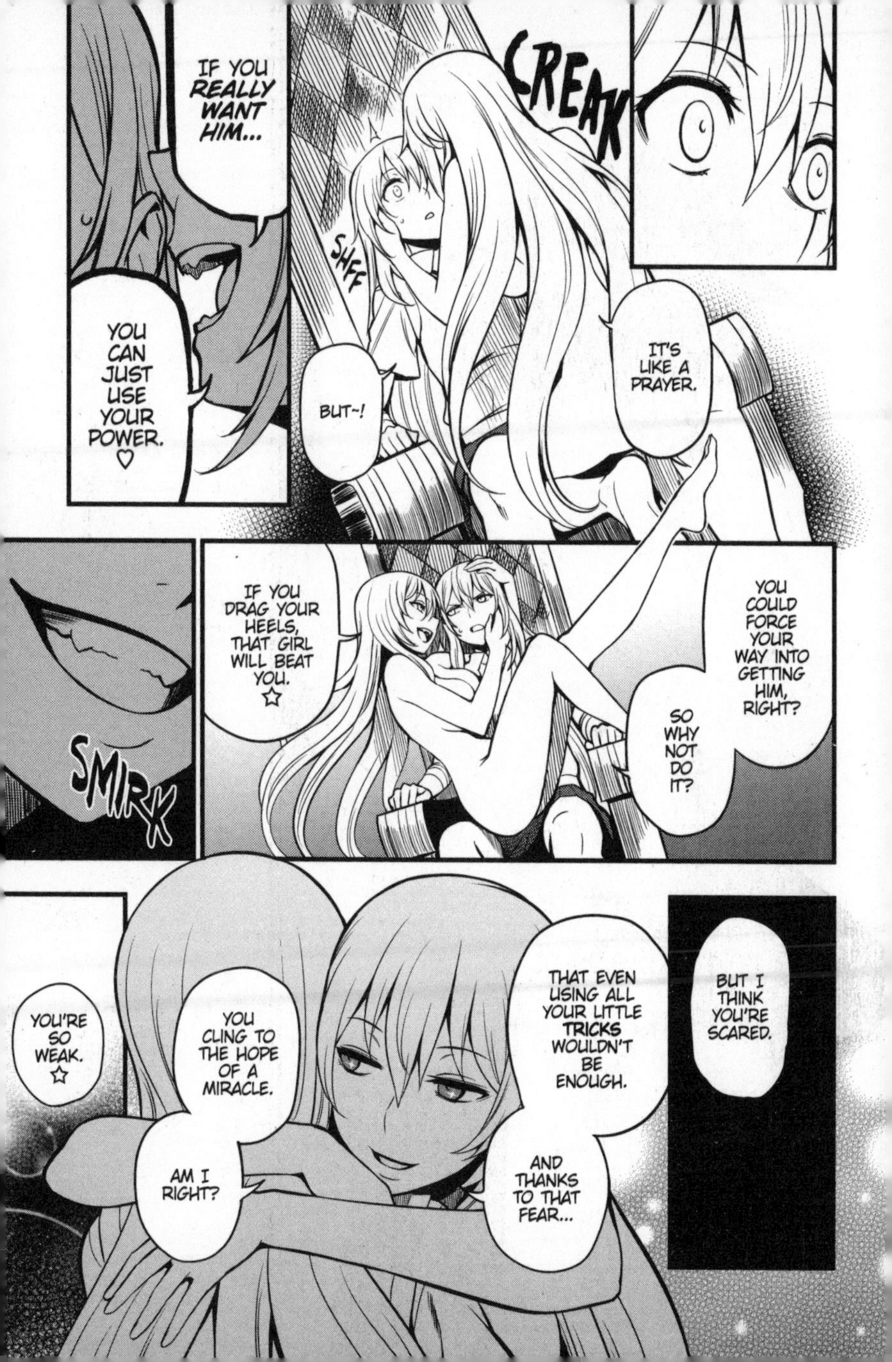
CREAK
IT'S LIKE A PRAYER.
SHFF
BUT~!
IF YOU REALLY WANT HIM...
YOU CAN JUST USE YOUR POWER. ♡
YOU COULD FORCE YOUR WAY INTO GETTING HIM, RIGHT?
SO WHY NOT DO IT?
IF YOU DRAG YOUR HEELS, THAT GIRL WILL BEAT YOU. ☆
SMIRK
BUT I THINK YOU'RE SCARED.
THAT EVEN USING ALL YOUR LITTLE TRICKS WOULDN'T BE ENOUGH.
AND THANKS TO THAT FEAR...
YOU CLING TO THE HOPE OF A MIRACLE.
AM I RIGHT?
YOU'RE SO WEAK. ☆

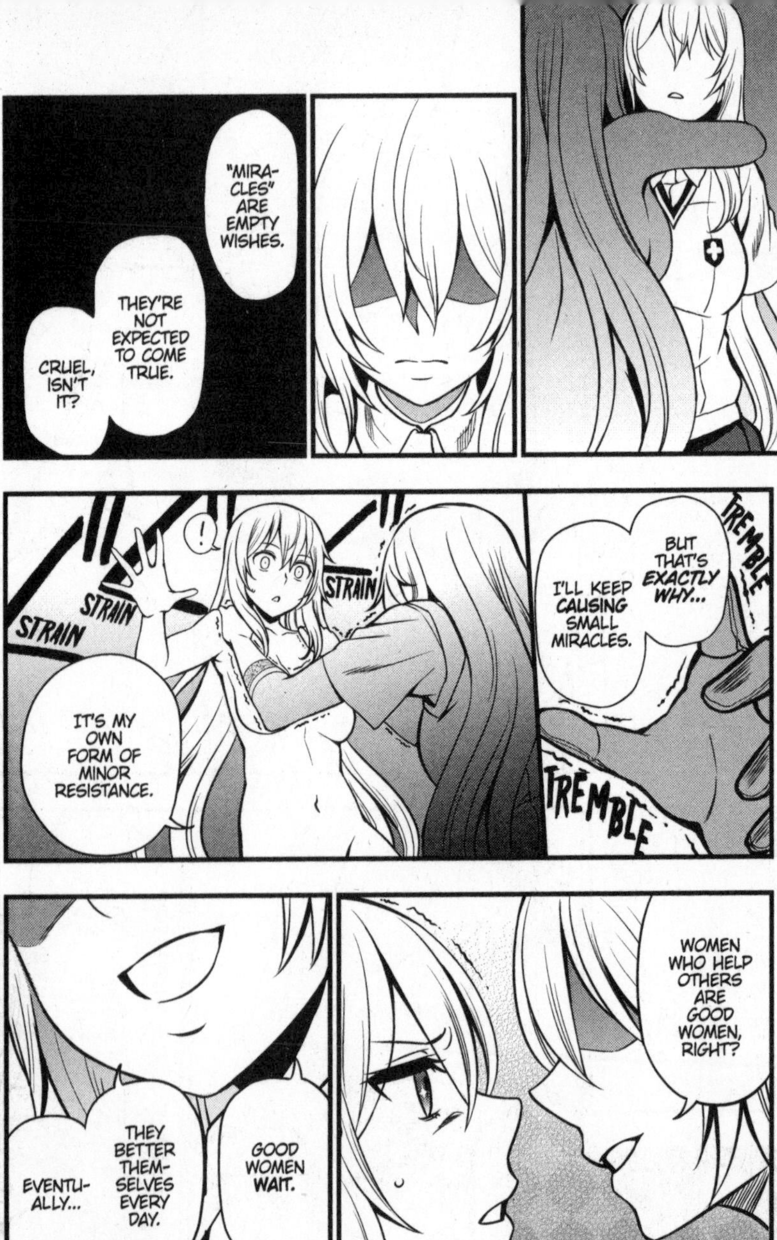
"MIRA-CLES" ARE EMPTY WISHES.
THEY'RE NOT EXPECTED TO COME TRUE.
CRUEL, ISN'T IT?
BUT THAT'S *EXACTLY* WHY...
I'LL KEEP **CAUSING** SMALL MIRACLES.
TREMBLE
TREMBLE
STRAIN
STRAIN
STRAIN
!
IT'S MY OWN FORM OF MINOR RESISTANCE.
WOMEN WHO HELP OTHERS ARE GOOD WOMEN, RIGHT?
GOOD WOMEN **WAIT**.
THEY BETTER THEM-SELVES EVERY DAY.
EVENTU-ALLY...

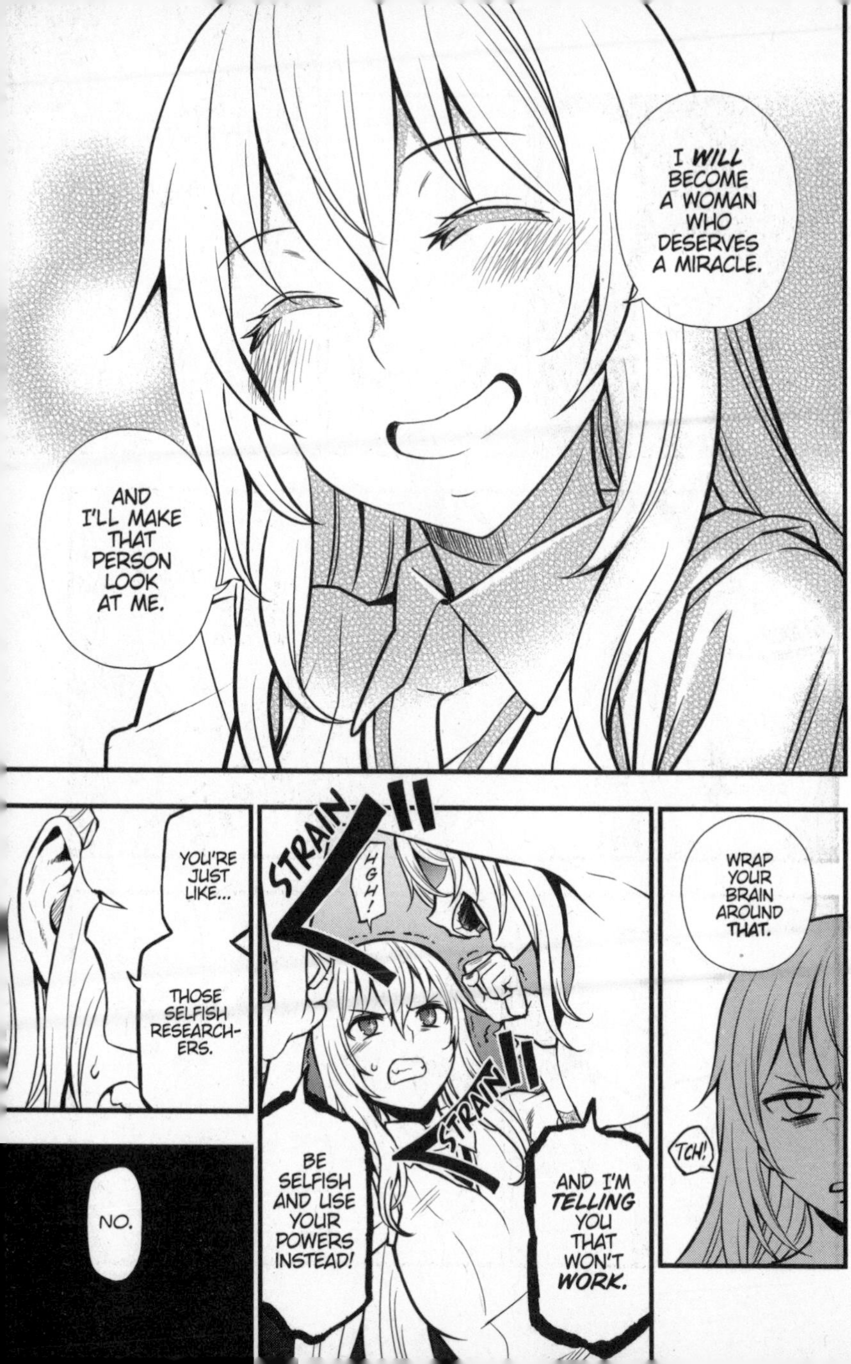
I WILL BECOME A WOMAN WHO DESERVES A MIRACLE.
AND I'LL MAKE THAT PERSON LOOK AT ME.
WRAP YOUR BRAIN AROUND THAT.
TCH!
STRAIN
HGH!
STRAIN
AND I'M TELLING YOU THAT WON'T WORK.
BE SELFISH AND USE YOUR POWERS INSTEAD!
YOU'RE JUST LIKE...
THOSE SELFISH RESEARCHERS.
NO.

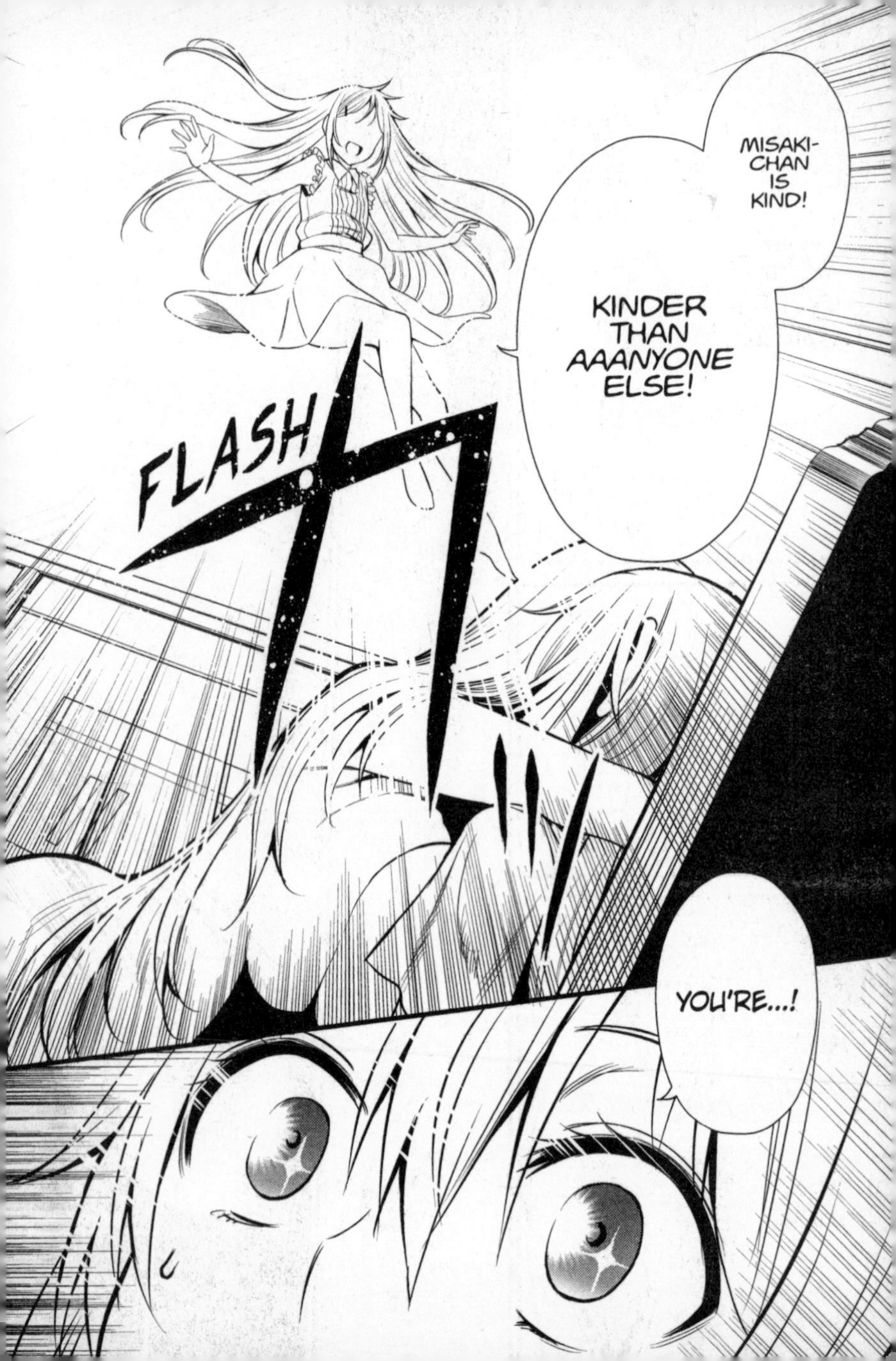
MISAKI-CHAN IS KIND!
KINDER THAN AAANYONE ELSE!
FLASH
YOU'RE...!

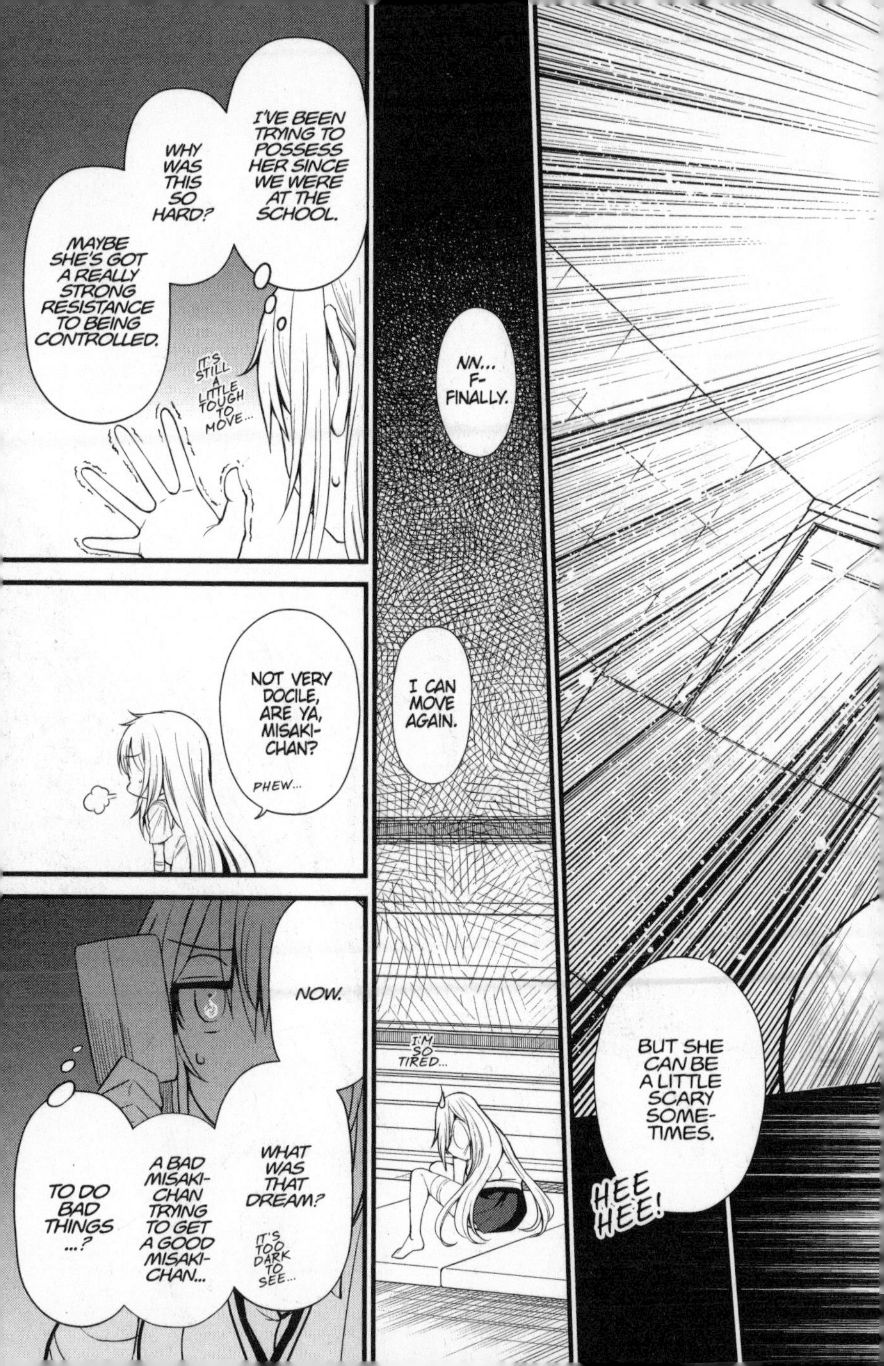
I'VE BEEN TRYING TO POSSESS HER SINCE WE WERE AT THE SCHOOL.
WHY WAS THIS SO HARD?
MAYBE SHE'S GOT A REALLY STRONG RESISTANCE TO BEING CONTROLLED.
IT'S STILL A LITTLE TOUGH TO MOVE...
NOT VERY DOCILE, ARE YA, MISAKI-CHAN?
PHEW...
NOW.
WHAT WAS THAT DREAM?
A BAD MISAKI-CHAN TRYING TO GET A GOOD MISAKI-CHAN...
TO DO BAD THINGS ...?
IT'S TOO DARK TO SEE...
NN... F-FINALLY.
I CAN MOVE AGAIN.
I'M SO TIRED...
BUT SHE CAN BE A LITTLE SCARY SOME-TIMES.
HEE HEE!

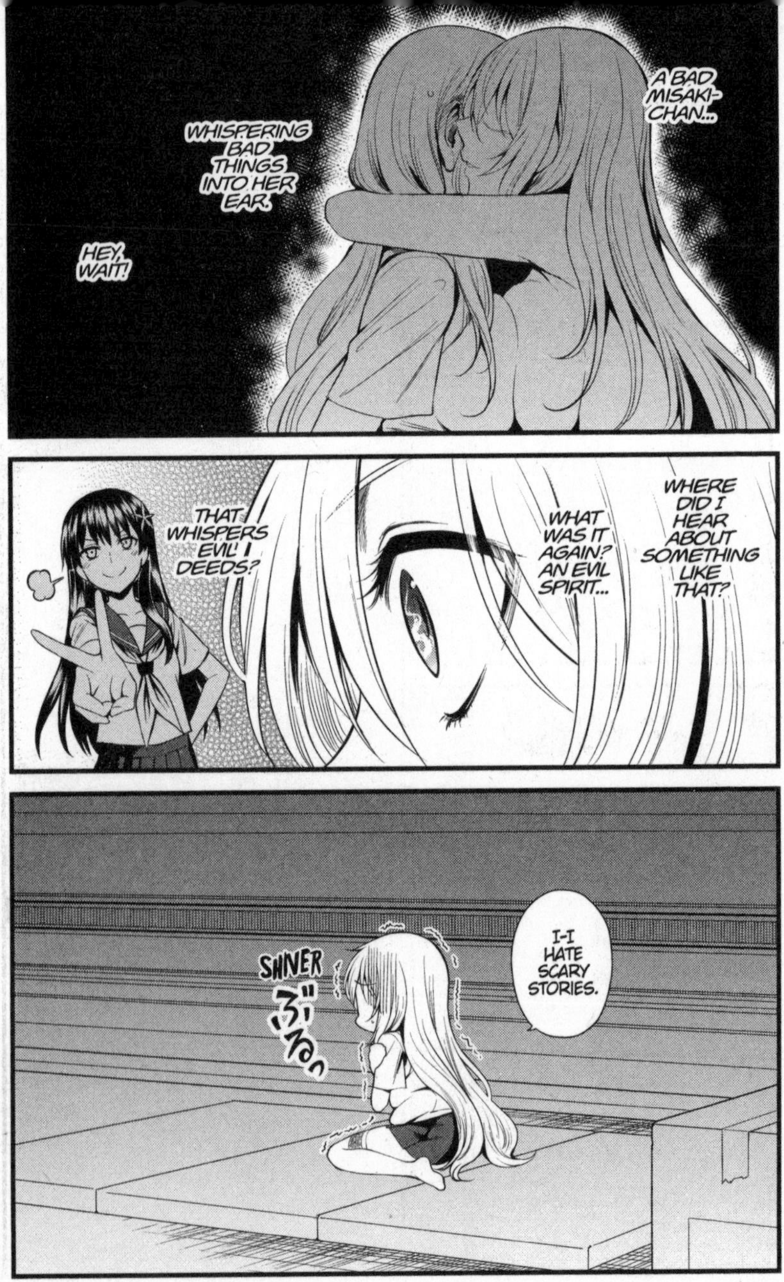
A BAD MISAKI-CHAN...
WHISPERING BAD THINGS INTO HER EAR.
HEY, WAIT!
WHERE DID I HEAR ABOUT SOMETHING LIKE THAT?
WHAT WAS IT AGAIN? AN EVIL SPIRIT...
THAT WHISPERS EVIL DEEDS?
I-I HATE SCARY STORIES.
SHIVER

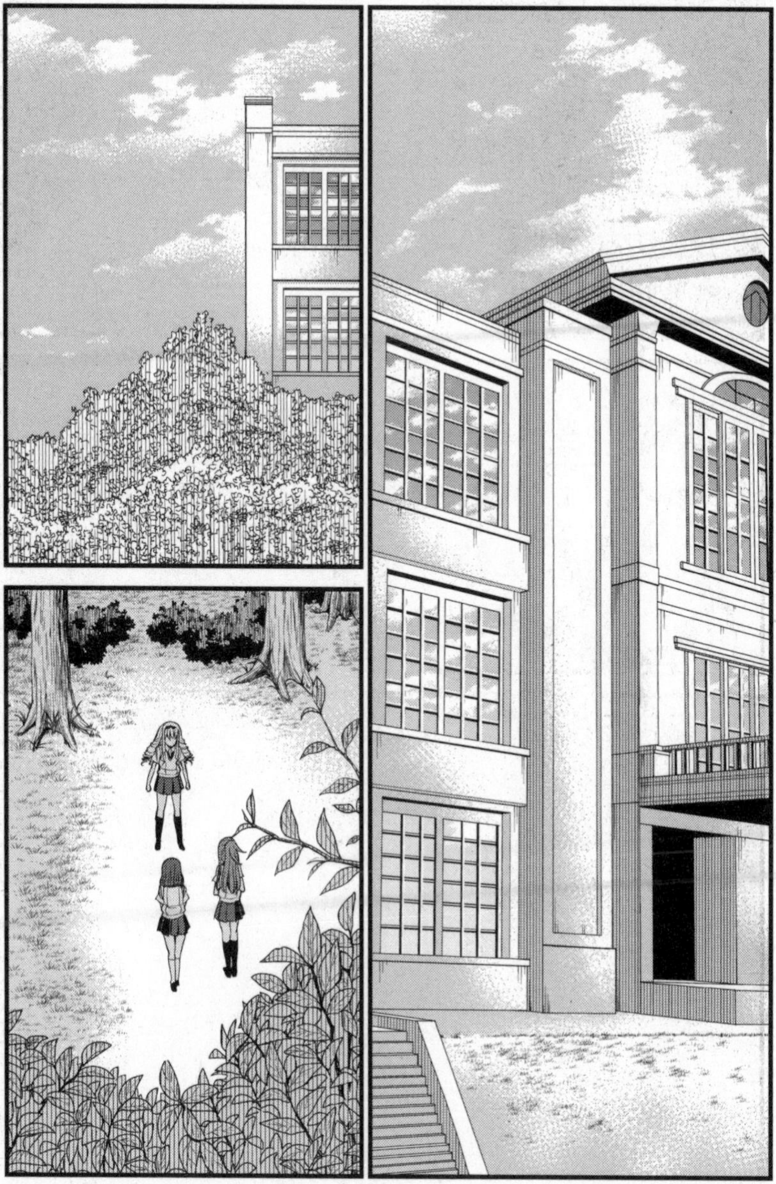

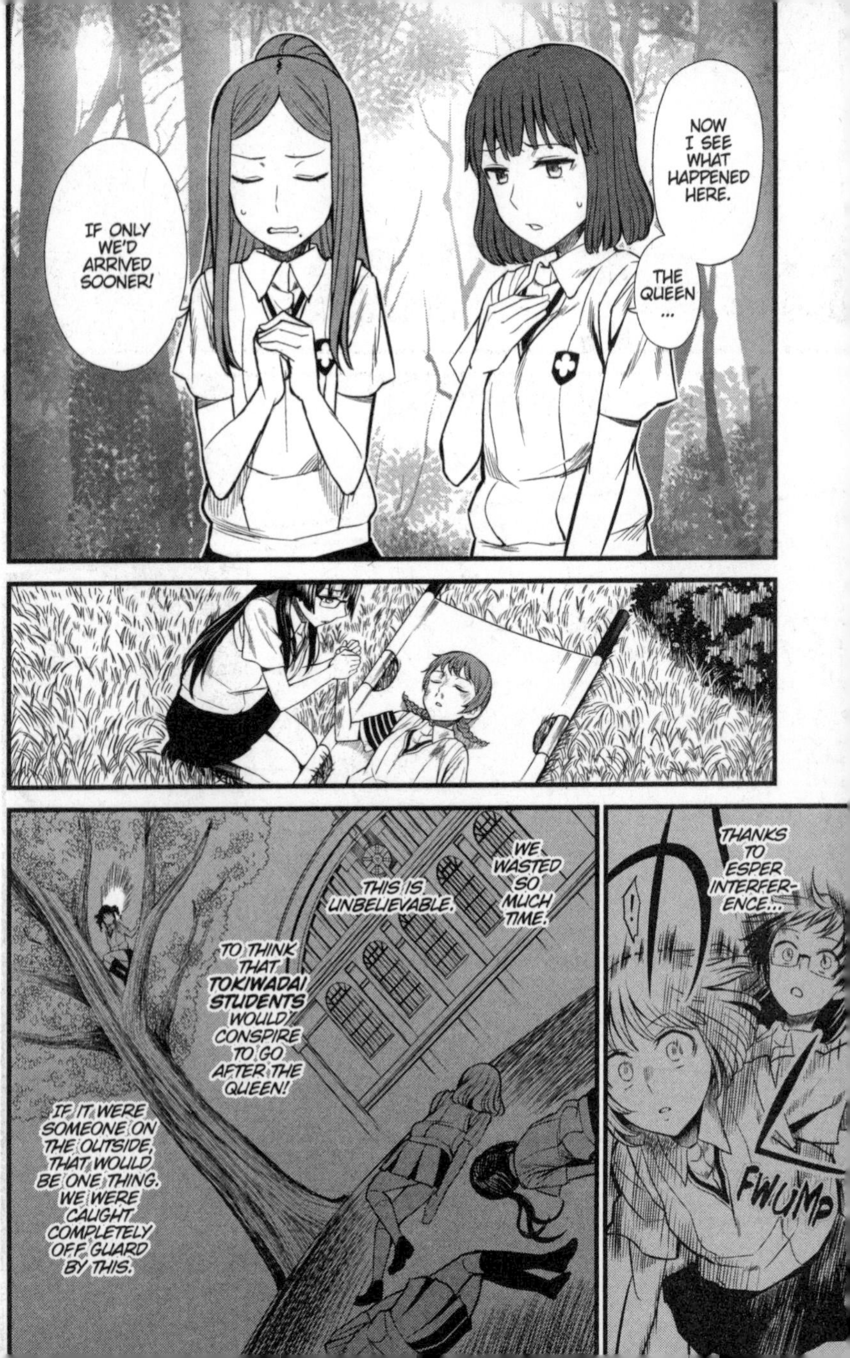
NOW I SEE WHAT HAPPENED HERE.
THE QUEEN...
IF ONLY WE'D ARRIVED SOONER!
THANKS TO ESPER INTERFERENCE...
!
FWUMP
WE WASTED SO MUCH TIME.
THIS IS UNBELIEVABLE.
TO THINK THAT TOKIWADAI STUDENTS WOULD CONSPIRE TO GO AFTER THE QUEEN!
IF IT WERE SOMEONE ON THE OUTSIDE, THAT WOULD BE ONE THING. WE WERE CAUGHT COMPLETELY OFF GUARD BY THIS.

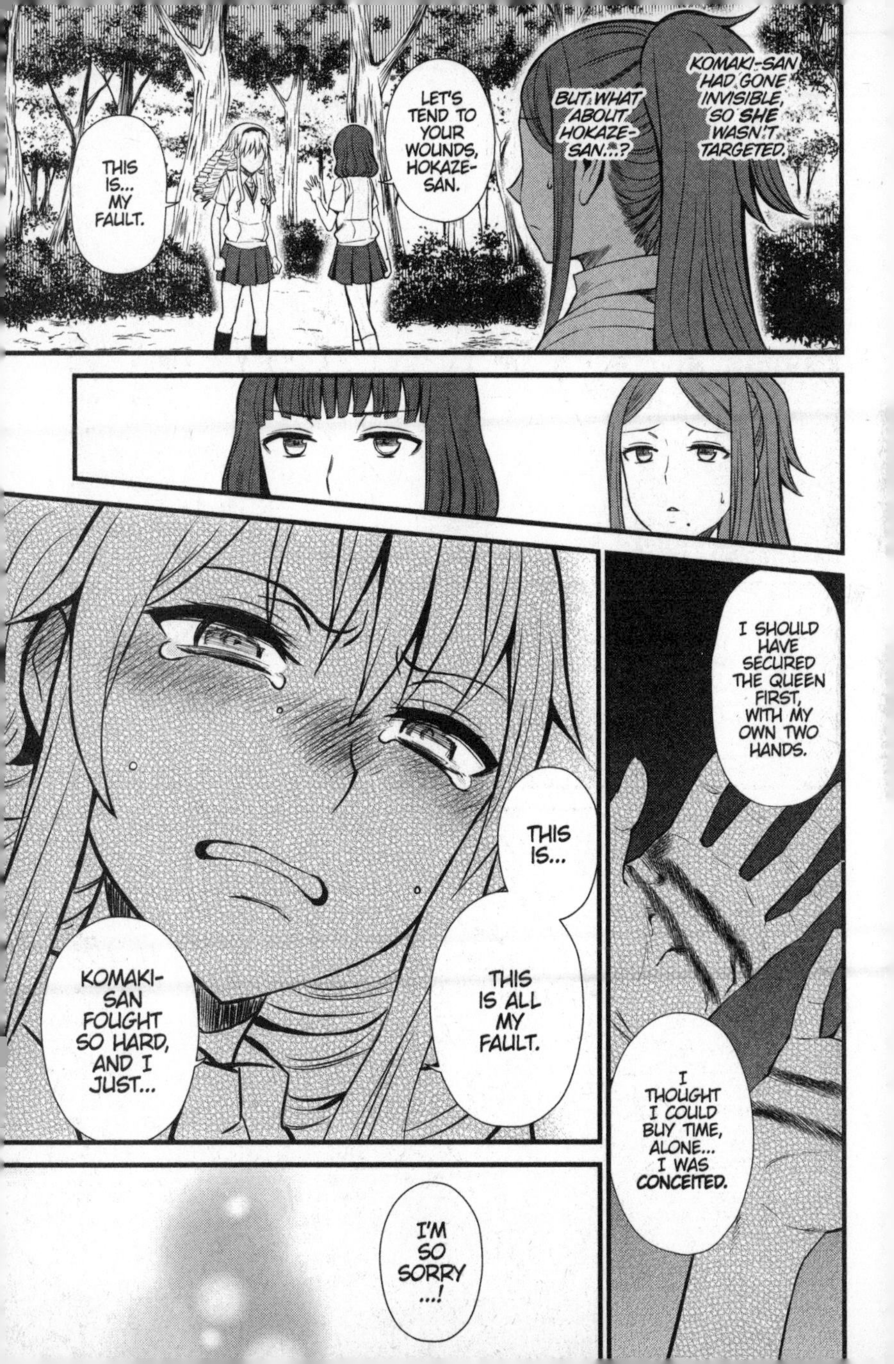
KOMAKI-SAN HAD GONE INVISIBLE, SO SHE WASN'T TARGETED.
BUT WHAT ABOUT HOKAZE-SAN...?
LET'S TEND TO YOUR WOUNDS, HOKAZE-SAN.
THIS IS... MY FAULT.
I SHOULD HAVE SECURED THE QUEEN FIRST, WITH MY OWN TWO HANDS.
I THOUGHT I COULD BUY TIME, ALONE... I WAS CONCEITED.
THIS IS...
THIS IS ALL MY FAULT.
KOMAKI-SAN FOUGHT SO HARD, AND I JUST...
I'M SO SORRY ...!

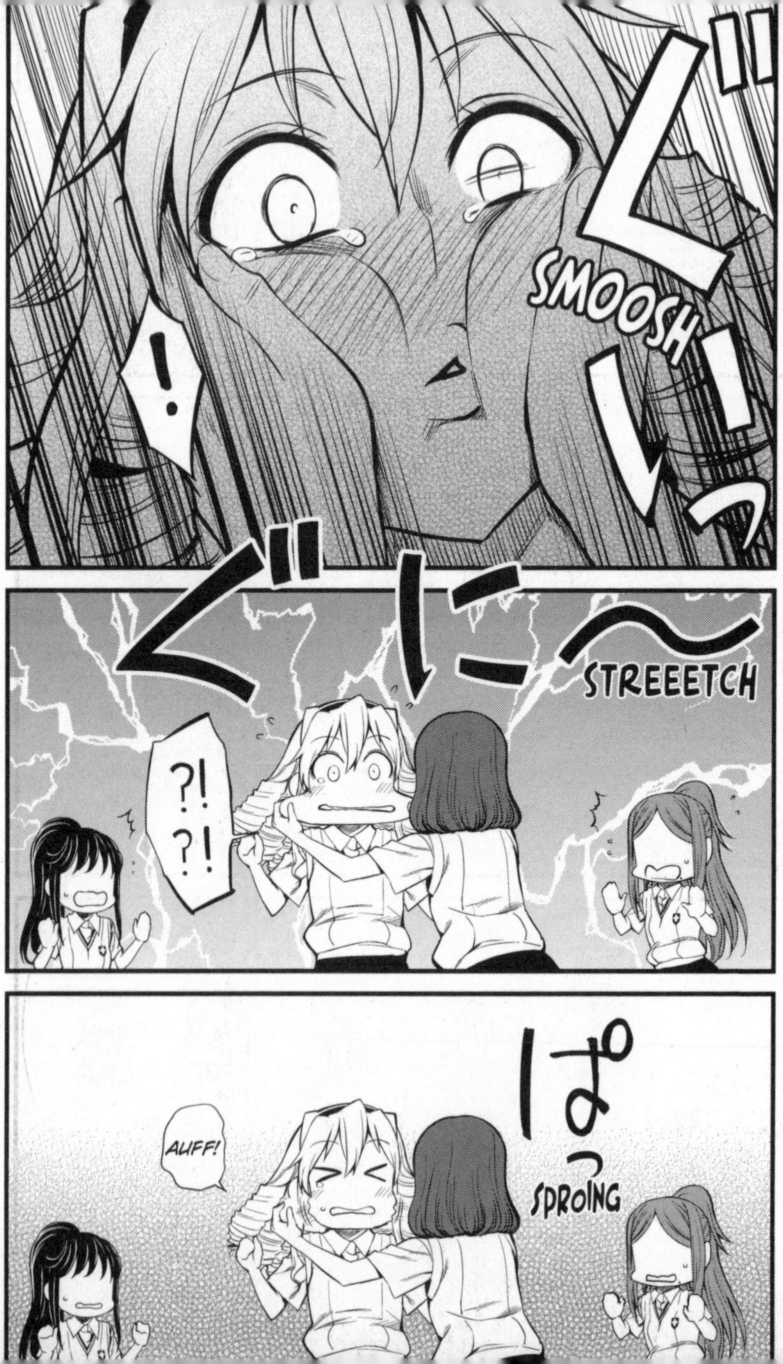
SMOOSH
!
ぐに〜
STREEETCH
?! ?!
ぱっ
SPROING
AUFF!

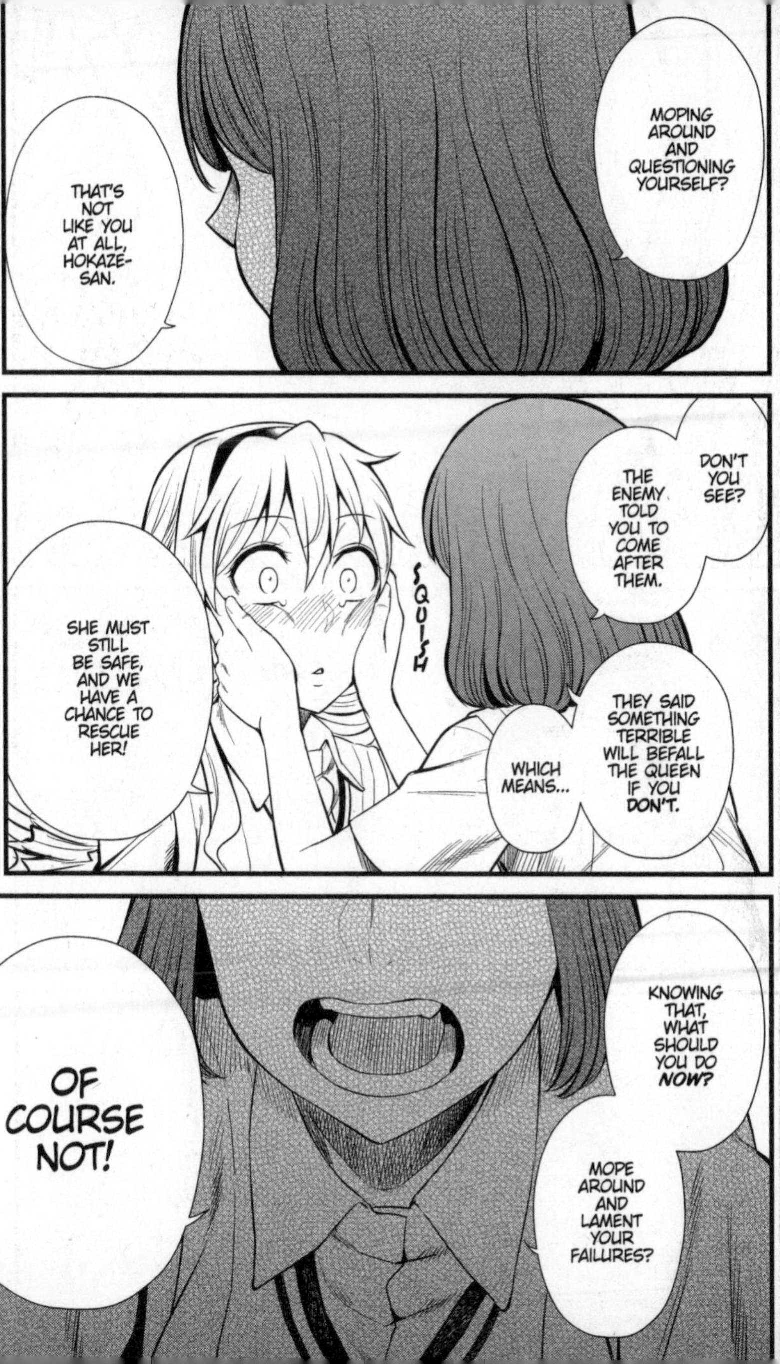
MOPING AROUND AND QUESTIONING YOURSELF?
THAT'S NOT LIKE YOU AT ALL, HOKAZE-SAN.
DON'T YOU SEE?
THE ENEMY TOLD YOU TO COME AFTER THEM.
SQUISH
THEY SAID SOMETHING TERRIBLE WILL BEFALL THE QUEEN IF YOU DON'T.
WHICH MEANS...
SHE MUST STILL BE SAFE, AND WE HAVE A CHANCE TO RESCUE HER!
KNOWING THAT, WHAT SHOULD YOU DO NOW?
MOPE AROUND AND LAMENT YOUR FAILURES?
OF COURSE NOT!

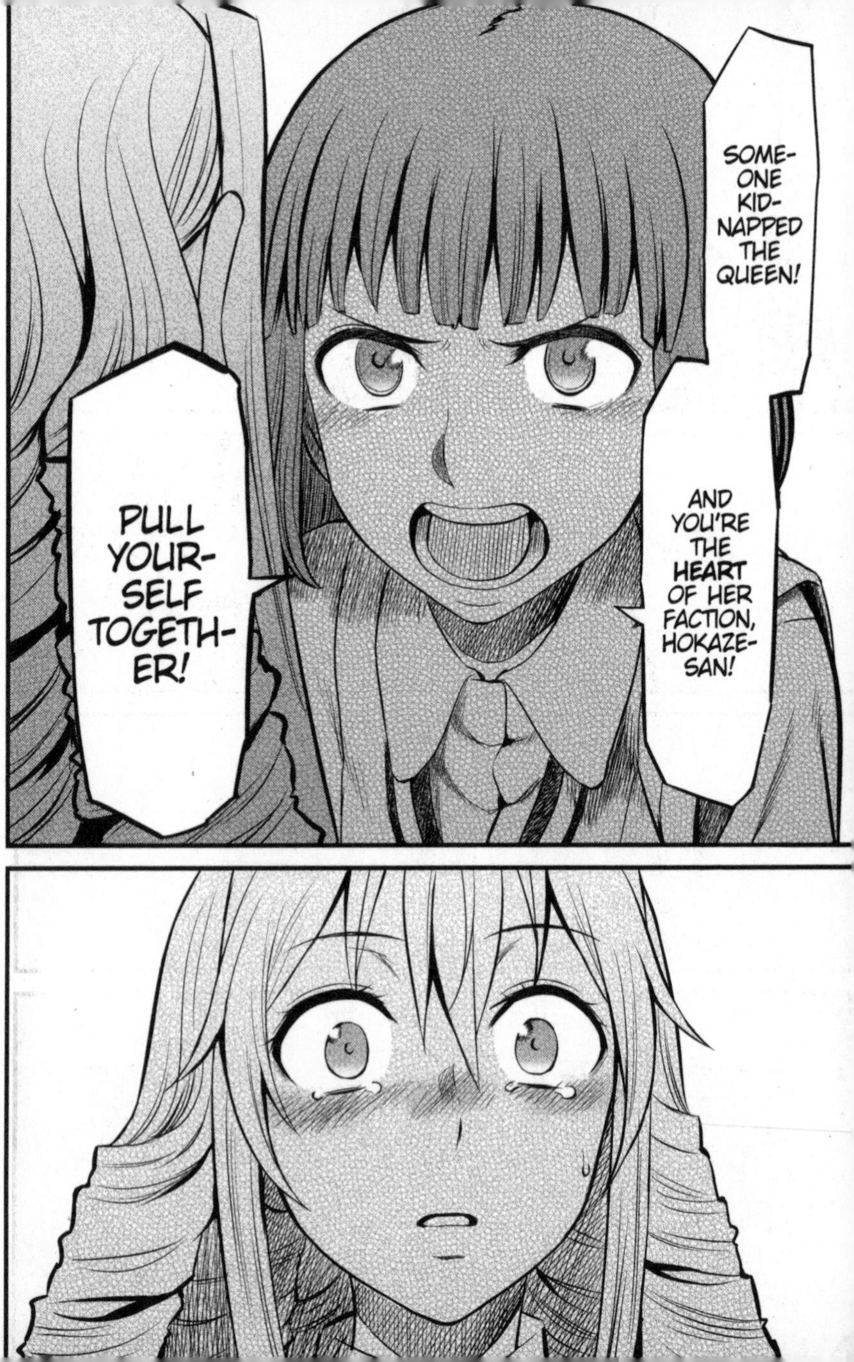
SOME-ONE KID-NAPPED THE QUEEN!
AND YOU'RE THE **HEART** OF HER FACTION, HOKAZE-SAN!
PULL YOUR-SELF TOGETH-ER!

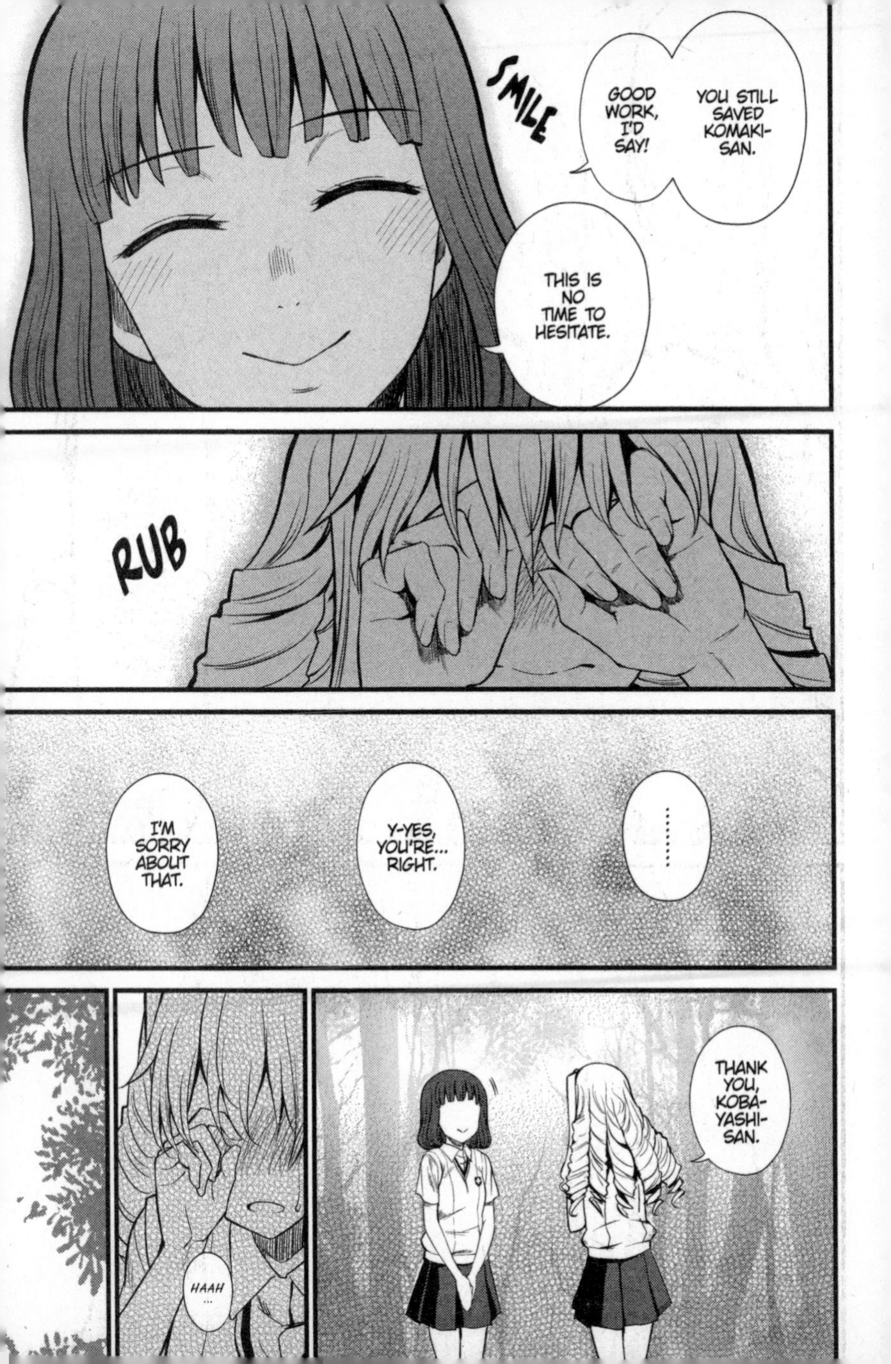
YOU STILL SAVED KOMAKI-SAN.
GOOD WORK, I'D SAY!
SMILE
THIS IS NO TIME TO HESITATE.
RUB
......
Y-YES, YOU'RE... RIGHT.
I'M SORRY ABOUT THAT.
THANK YOU, KOBA-YASHI-SAN.
HAAH ...

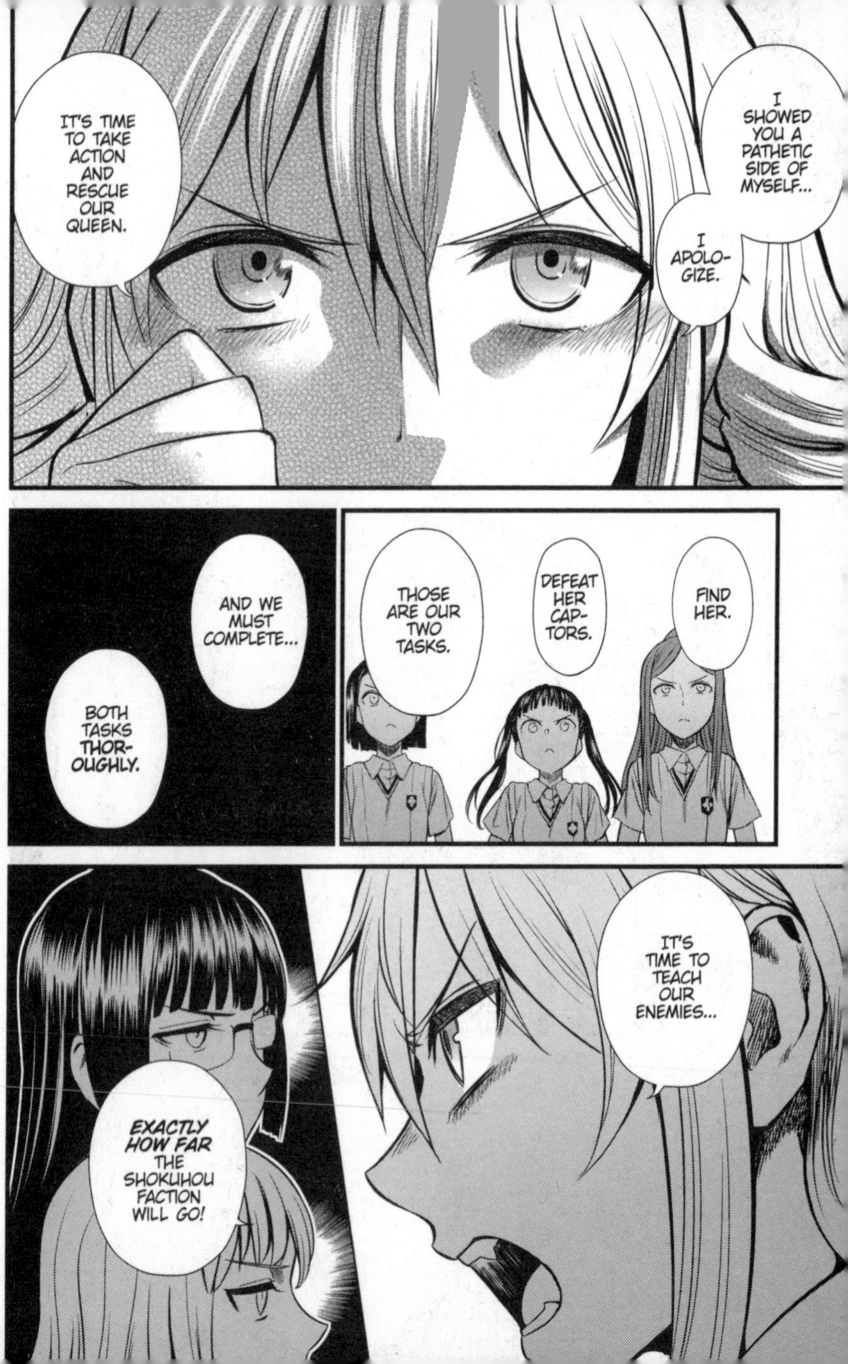
I SHOWED YOU A PATHETIC SIDE OF MYSELF...
I APOLOGIZE.
IT'S TIME TO TAKE ACTION AND RESCUE OUR QUEEN.
FIND HER.
DEFEAT HER CAP-TORS.
THOSE ARE OUR TWO TASKS.
AND WE MUST COMPLETE...
BOTH TASKS THOR-OUGHLY.
IT'S TIME TO TEACH OUR ENEMIES...
EXACTLY HOW FAR THE SHOKUHOU FACTION WILL GO!

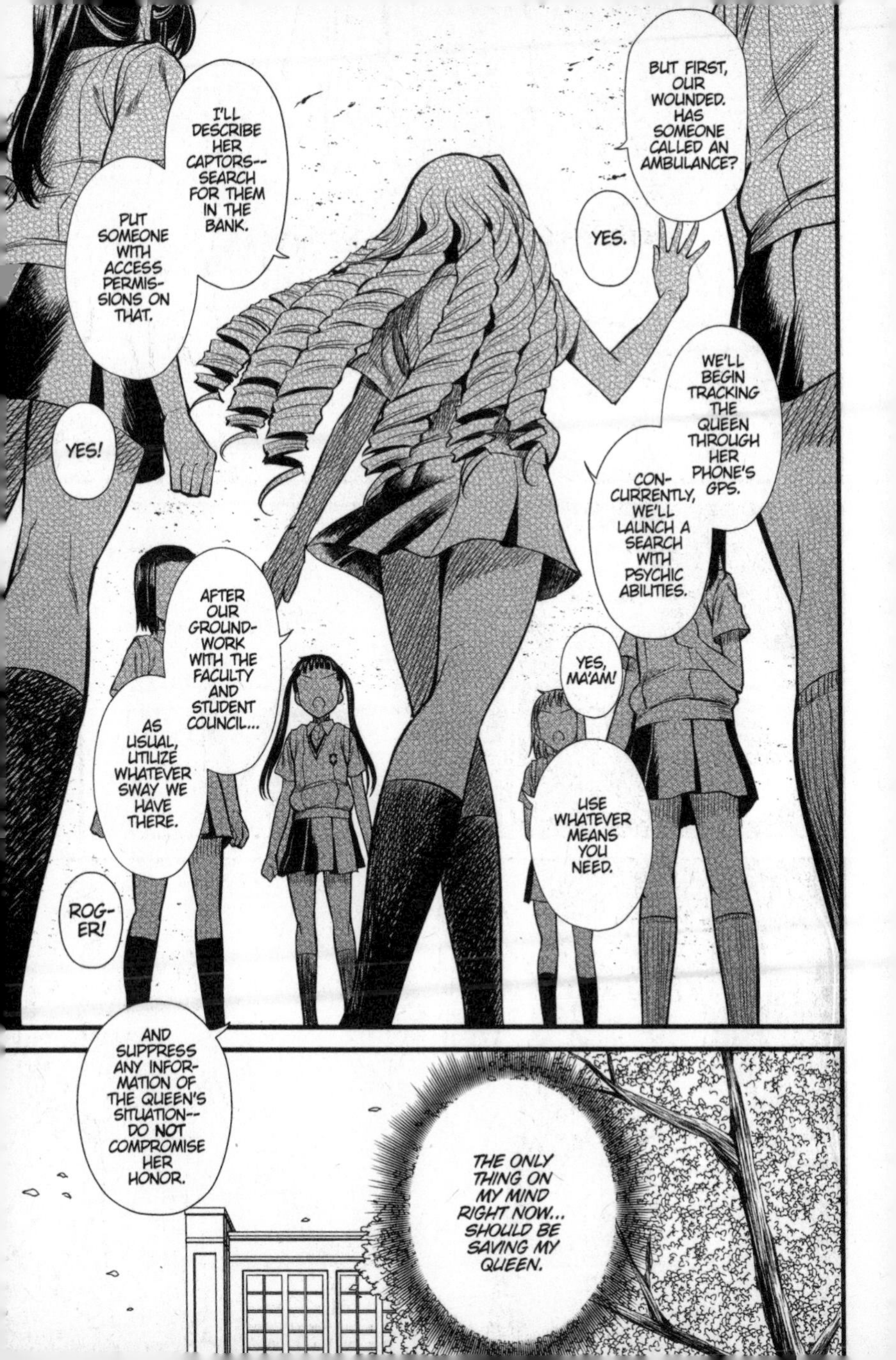

BUT FIRST, OUR WOUNDED. HAS SOMEONE CALLED AN AMBULANCE?
YES.
I'LL DESCRIBE HER CAPTORS-- SEARCH FOR THEM IN THE BANK.
PUT SOMEONE WITH ACCESS PERMISSIONS ON THAT.
YES!
WE'LL BEGIN TRACKING THE QUEEN THROUGH HER PHONE'S GPS.
CONCURRENTLY, WE'LL LAUNCH A SEARCH WITH PSYCHIC ABILITIES.
YES, MA'AM!
AFTER OUR GROUNDWORK WITH THE FACULTY AND STUDENT COUNCIL...
AS USUAL, UTILIZE WHATEVER SWAY WE HAVE THERE.
USE WHATEVER MEANS YOU NEED.
ROGER!
AND SUPPRESS ANY INFORMATION OF THE QUEEN'S SITUATION-- DO NOT COMPROMISE HER HONOR.
THE ONLY THING ON MY MIND RIGHT NOW... SHOULD BE SAVING MY QUEEN.

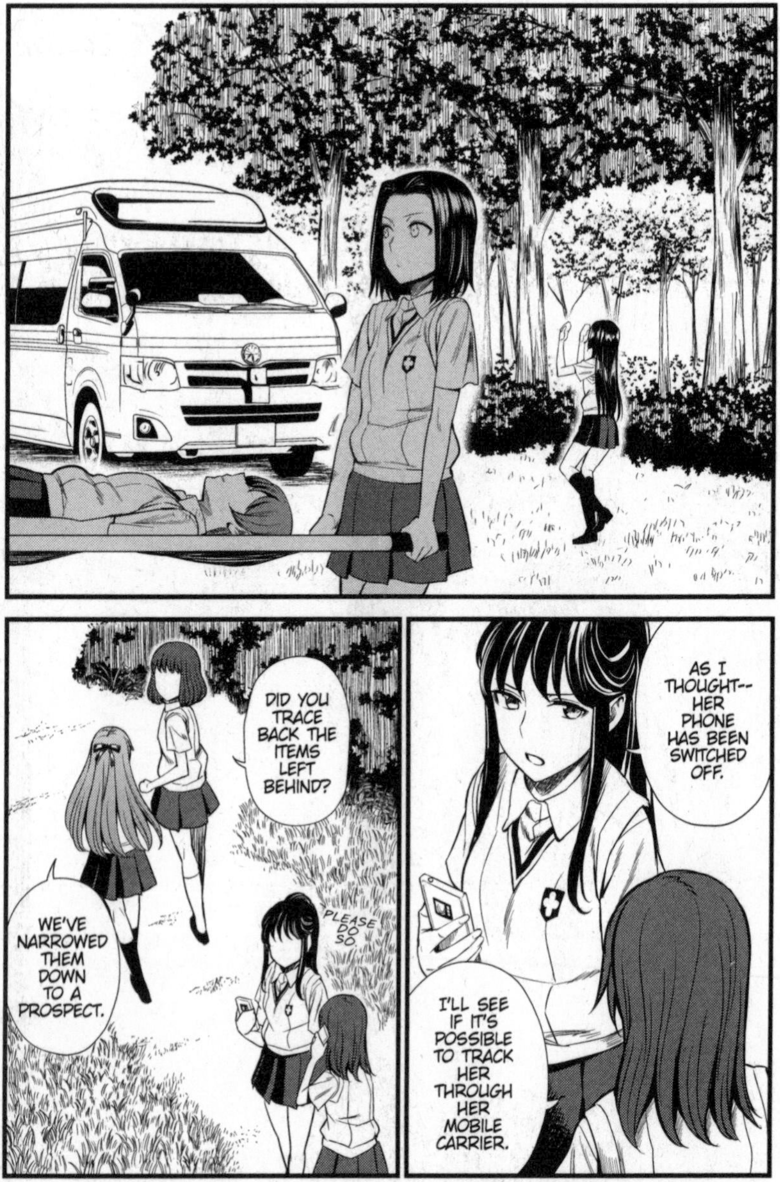
AS I THOUGHT-- HER PHONE HAS BEEN SWITCHED OFF.
I'LL SEE IF IT'S POSSIBLE TO TRACK HER THROUGH HER MOBILE CARRIER.
DID YOU TRACE BACK THE ITEMS LEFT BEHIND?
PLEASE DO SO.
WE'VE NARROWED THEM DOWN TO A PROSPECT.

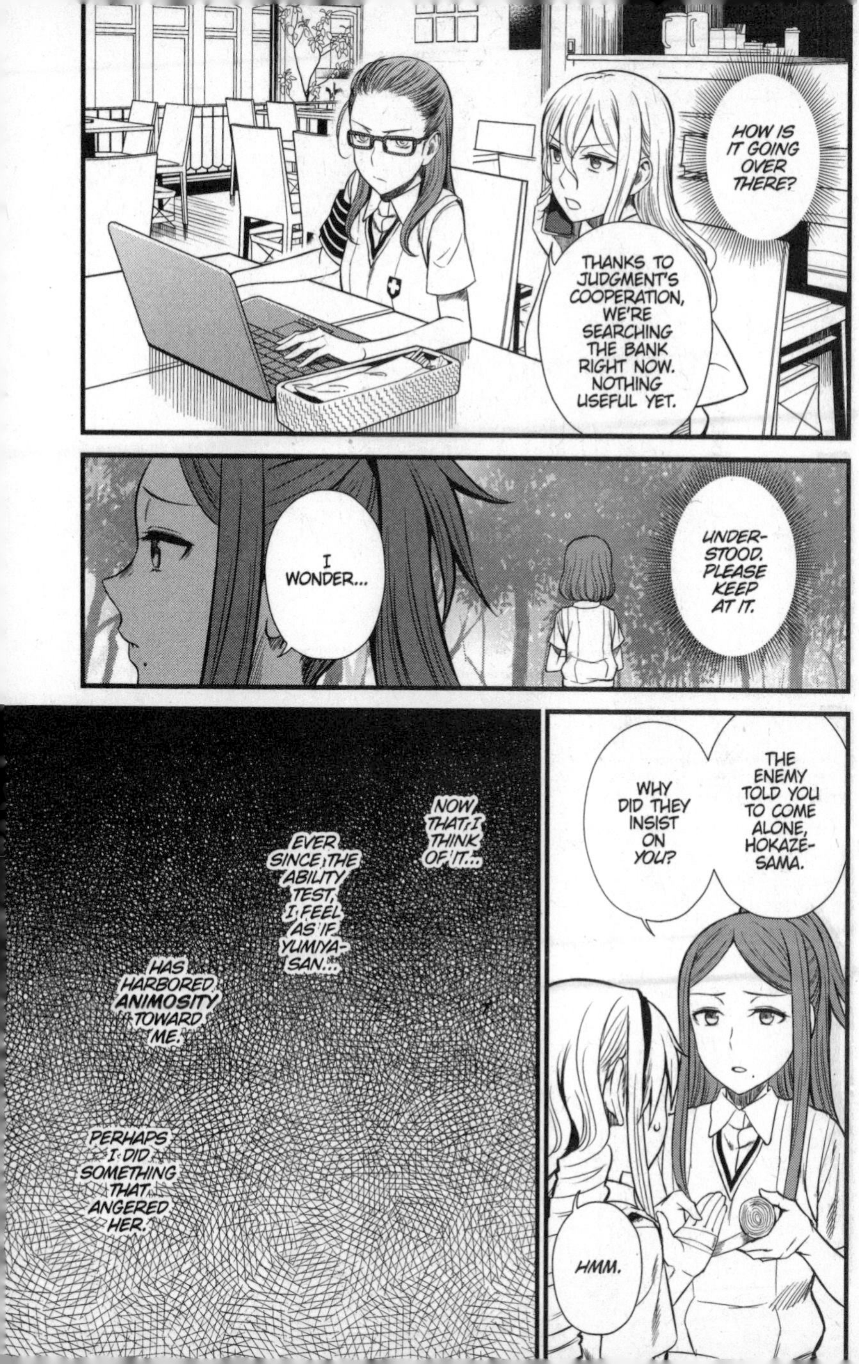
HOW IS IT GOING OVER THERE?
THANKS TO JUDGMENT'S COOPERATION, WE'RE SEARCHING THE BANK RIGHT NOW. NOTHING USEFUL YET.
UNDERSTOOD. PLEASE KEEP AT IT.
I WONDER...
THE ENEMY TOLD YOU TO COME ALONE, HOKAZE-SAMA.
WHY DID THEY INSIST ON YOU?
HMM.
NOW THAT I THINK OF IT...
EVER SINCE THE ABILITY TEST, I FEEL AS IF YUMIYA-SAN...
HAS HARBORED ANIMOSITY TOWARD ME.
PERHAPS I DID SOMETHING THAT ANGERED HER.

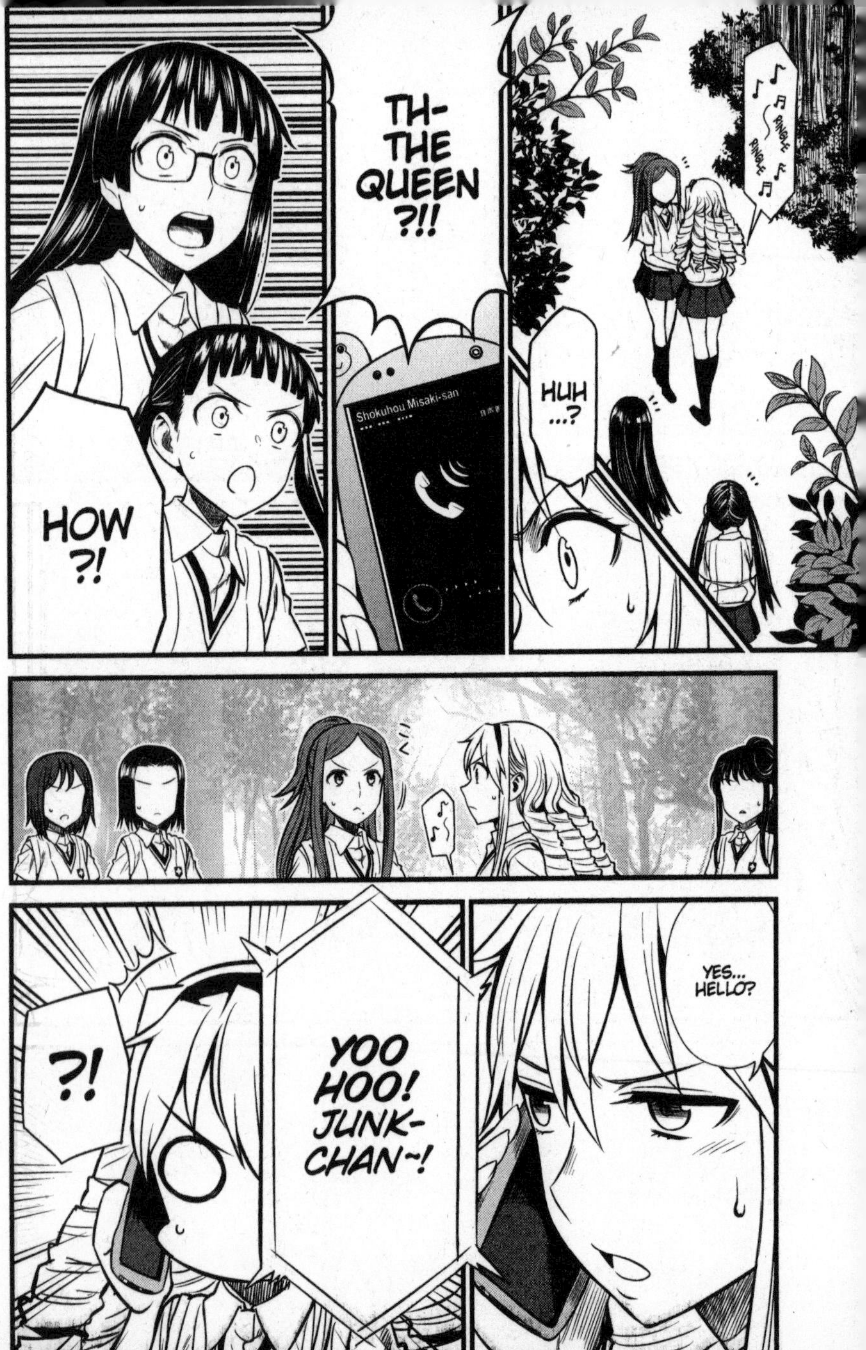
RINGLE RINGLE
HUH...?
Shokuhou Misaki-san
TH-THE QUEEN?!!
HOW?!
YES... HELLO?
YOO HOO! JUNK-CHAN~!
?!

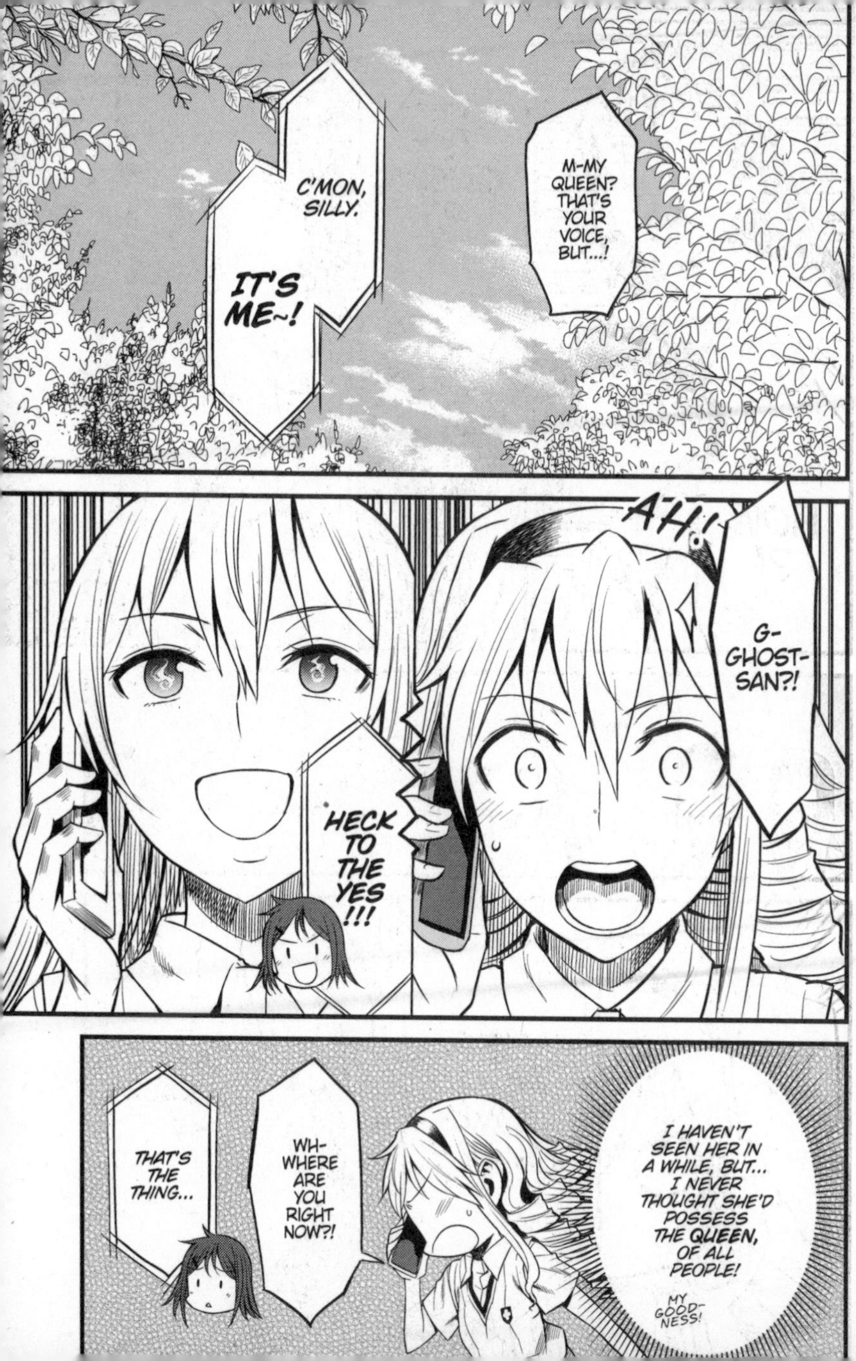
M-MY QUEEN? THAT'S YOUR VOICE, BUT...!
C'MON, SILLY.
IT'S ME~!
AH!
G-GHOST-SAN?!
HECK TO THE YES!!!
I HAVEN'T SEEN HER IN A WHILE, BUT... I NEVER THOUGHT SHE'D POSSESS THE QUEEN, OF ALL PEOPLE!
MY GOOD-NESS!
WH-WHERE ARE YOU RIGHT NOW?!
THAT'S THE THING...

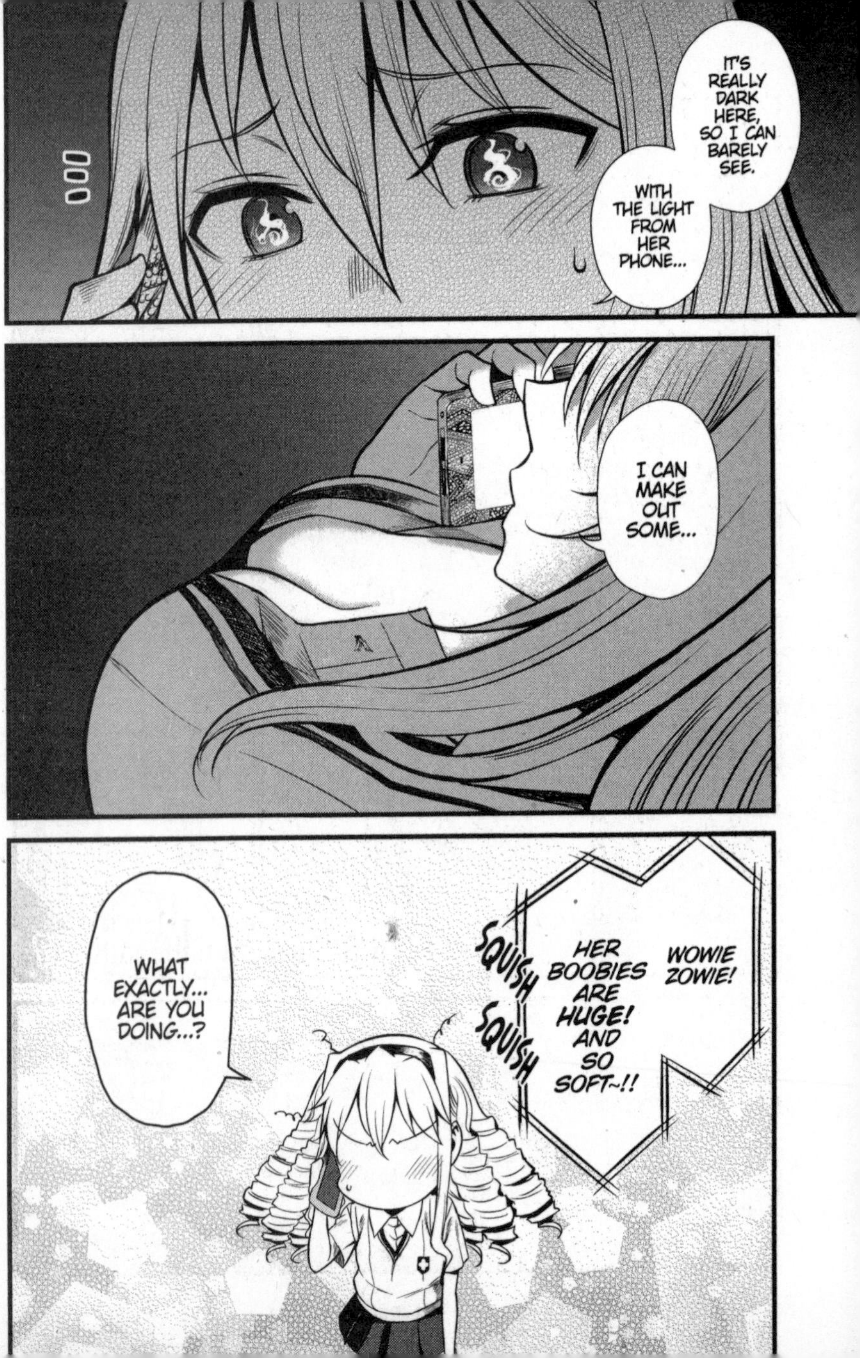
IT'S REALLY DARK HERE, SO I CAN BARELY SEE.
WITH THE LIGHT FROM HER PHONE...
I CAN MAKE OUT SOME...
WOWIE ZOWIE!
HER BOOBIES ARE HUGE! AND SO SOFT~!!
SQUISH SQUISH
WHAT EXACTLY... ARE YOU DOING...?

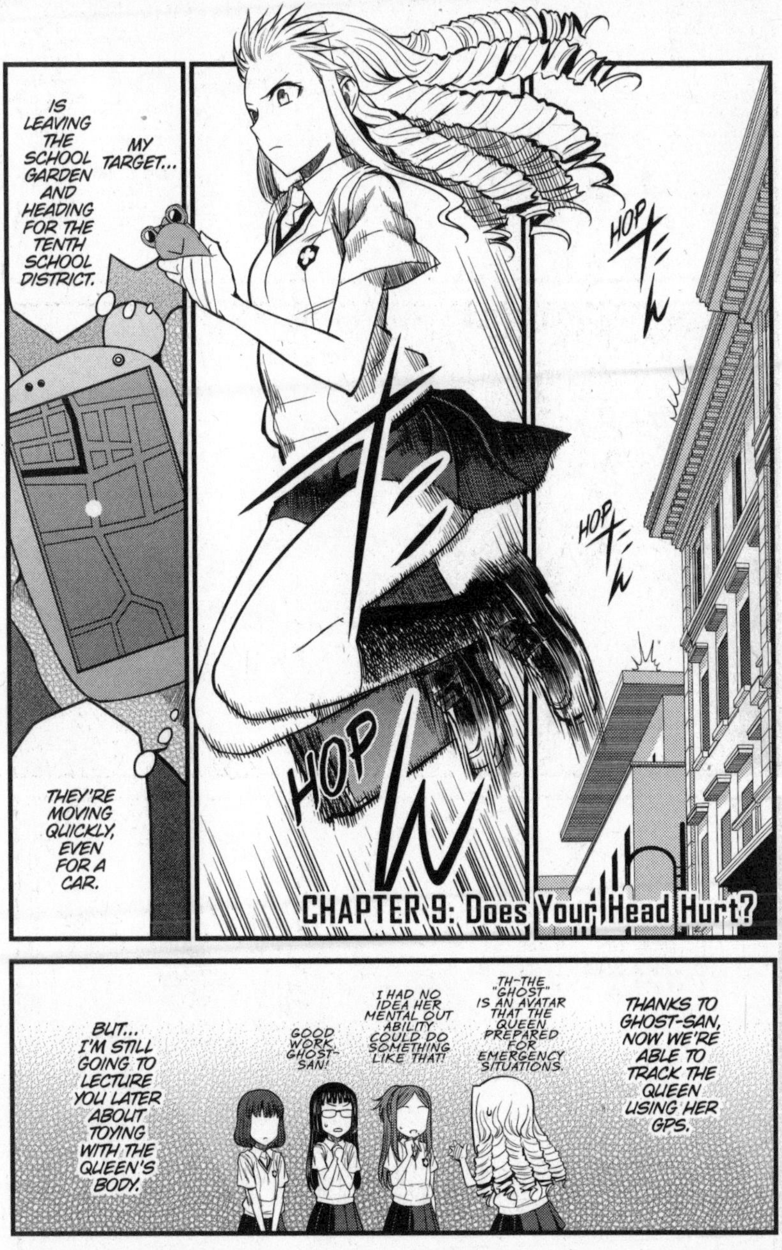
HOP
HOP
CHAPTER 9: Does Your Head Hurt?
HOP
MY TARGET...
IS LEAVING THE SCHOOL GARDEN AND HEADING FOR THE TENTH SCHOOL DISTRICT.
THEY'RE MOVING QUICKLY, EVEN FOR A CAR.
THANKS TO GHOST-SAN, NOW WE'RE ABLE TO TRACK THE QUEEN USING HER GPS.
TH-THE "GHOST" IS AN AVATAR THAT THE QUEEN PREPARED FOR EMERGENCY SITUATIONS.
I HAD NO IDEA HER MENTAL OUT ABILITY COULD DO SOMETHING LIKE THAT!
GOOD WORK, GHOST-SAN!
BUT... I'M STILL GOING TO LECTURE YOU LATER ABOUT TOYING WITH THE QUEEN'S BODY.

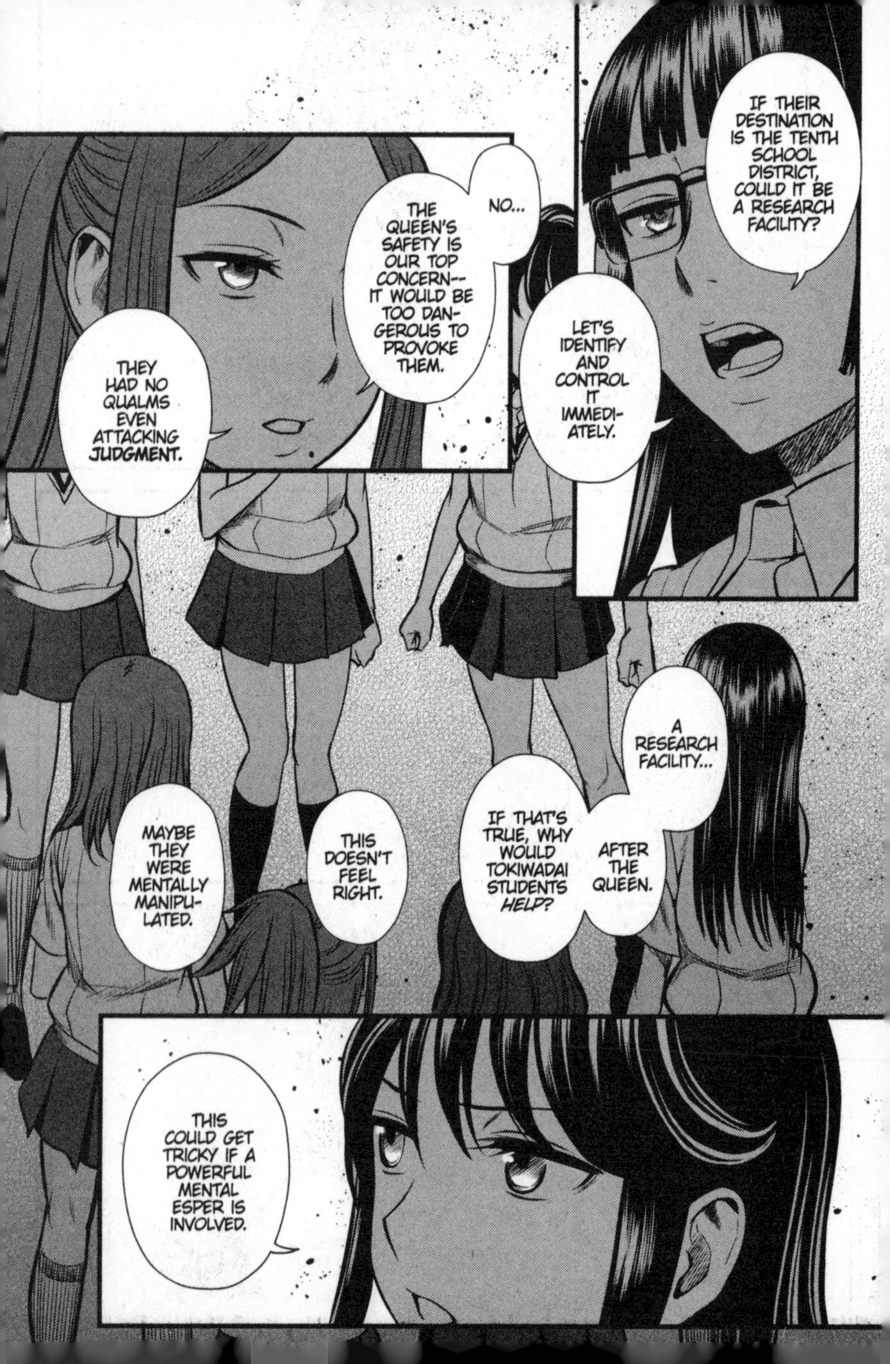
IF THEIR DESTINATION IS THE TENTH SCHOOL DISTRICT, COULD IT BE A RESEARCH FACILITY?
LET'S IDENTIFY AND CONTROL IT IMMEDIATELY.
NO...
THE QUEEN'S SAFETY IS OUR TOP CONCERN-- IT WOULD BE TOO DANGEROUS TO PROVOKE THEM.
THEY HAD NO QUALMS EVEN ATTACKING JUDGMENT.
A RESEARCH FACILITY...
AFTER THE QUEEN.
IF THAT'S TRUE, WHY WOULD TOKIWADAI STUDENTS *HELP?*
THIS DOESN'T FEEL RIGHT.
MAYBE THEY WERE MENTALLY MANIPULATED.
THIS COULD GET TRICKY IF A POWERFUL MENTAL ESPER IS INVOLVED.

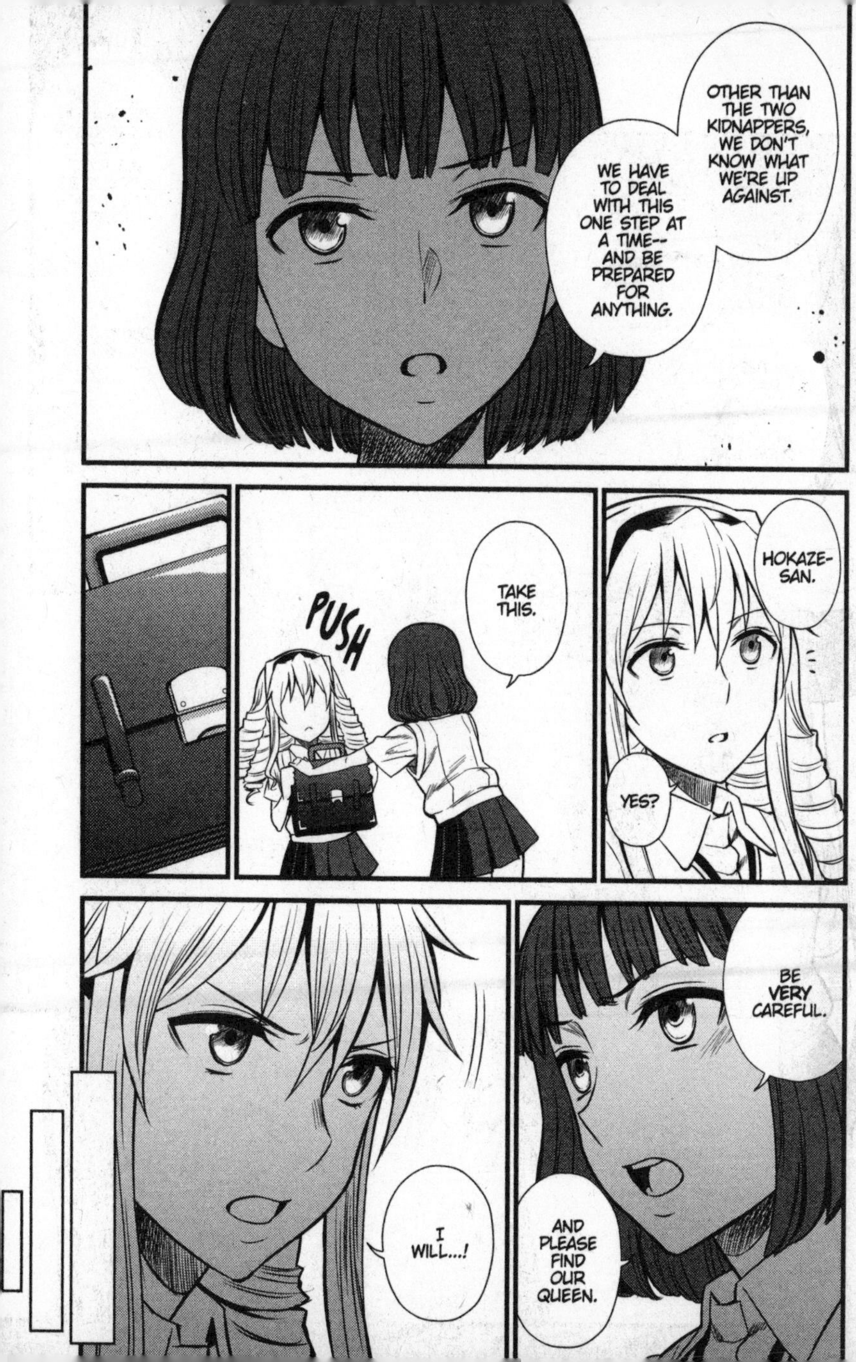
OTHER THAN THE TWO KIDNAPPERS, WE DON'T KNOW WHAT WE'RE UP AGAINST.
WE HAVE TO DEAL WITH THIS ONE STEP AT A TIME-- AND BE PREPARED FOR ANYTHING.
HOKAZE-SAN.
YES?
TAKE THIS.
PUSH
BE VERY CAREFUL.
AND PLEASE FIND OUR QUEEN.
I WILL...!

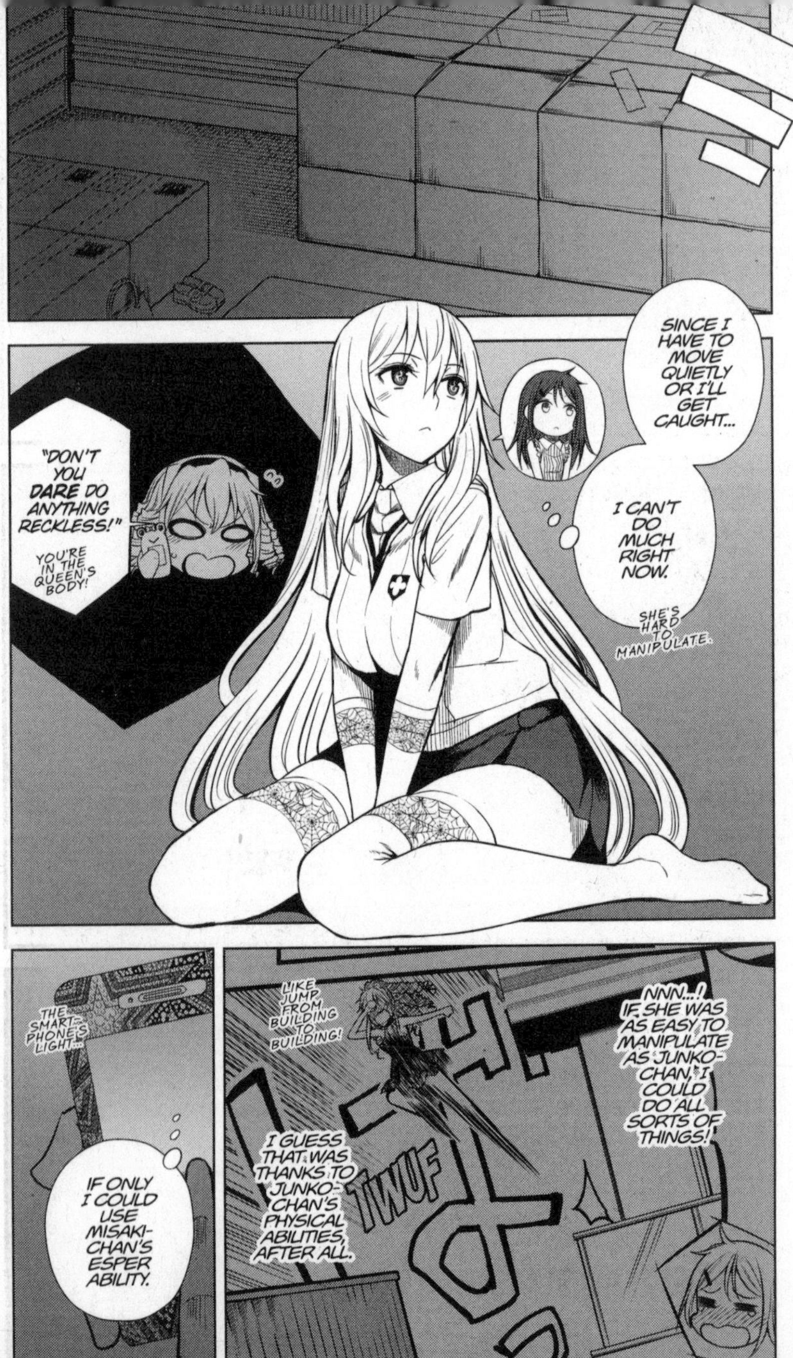
SINCE I HAVE TO MOVE QUIETLY OR I'LL GET CAUGHT...
I CAN'T DO MUCH RIGHT NOW.
SHE'S HARD TO MANIPULATE.
"DON'T YOU DARE DO ANYTHING RECKLESS!"
YOU'RE IN THE QUEEN'S BODY!
NNN...! IF SHE WAS AS EASY TO MANIPULATE AS JUNKO-CHAN, I COULD DO ALL SORTS OF THINGS!
LIKE JUMP FROM BUILDING TO BUILDING!
I GUESS THAT WAS THANKS TO JUNKO-CHAN'S PHYSICAL ABILITIES, AFTER ALL.
TWUF
THE SMART-PHONE'S LIGHT...
IF ONLY I COULD USE MISAKI-CHAN'S ESPER ABILITY.

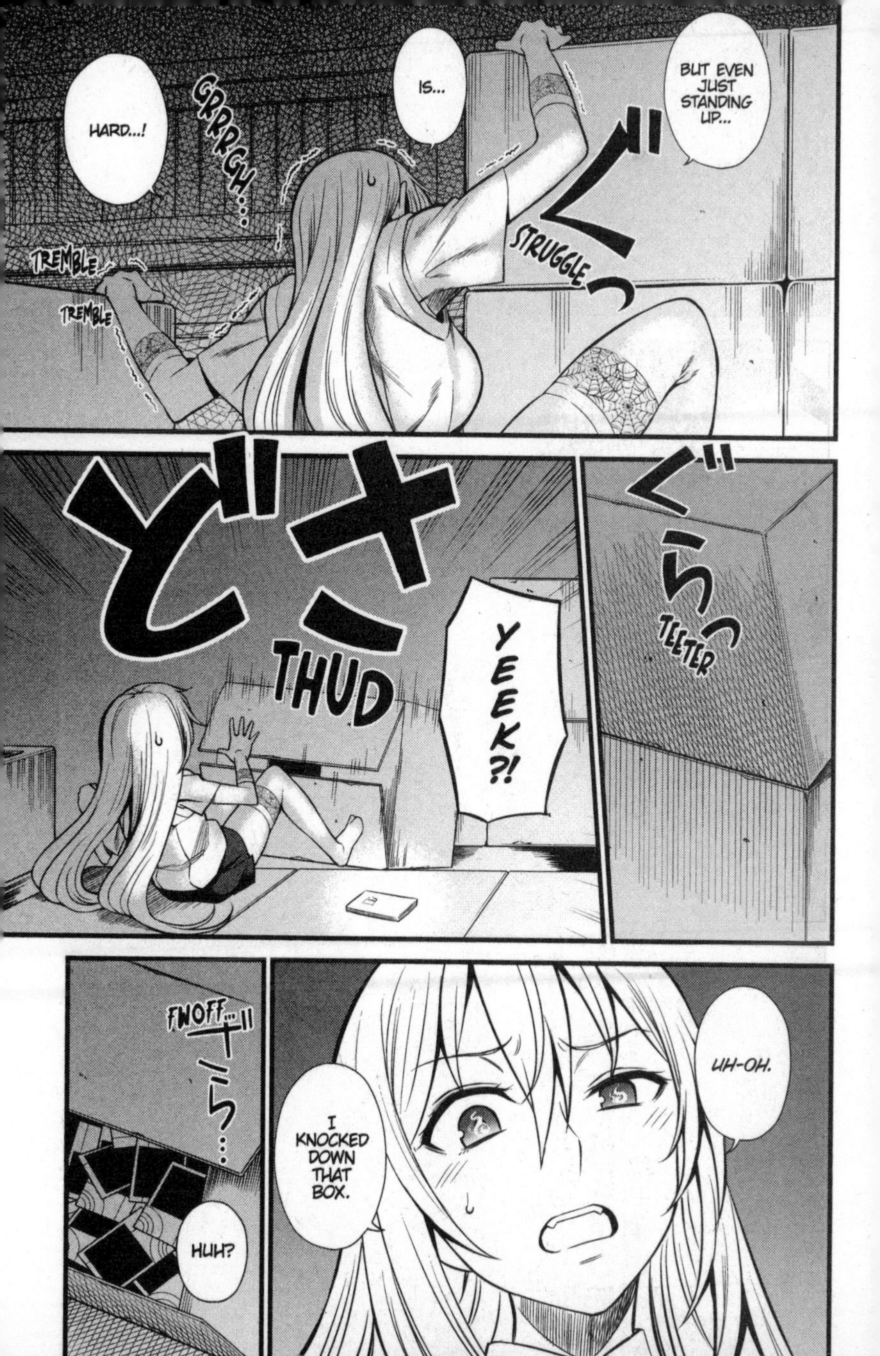
BUT EVEN JUST STANDING UP...
STRUGGLE
IS...
GRRRGH...
HARD...!
TREMBLE
TREMBLE
ぐらっ
TEETER
どさ
THUD
YEEEK?!
UH-OH.
I KNOCKED DOWN THAT BOX.
FWOFF...
HUH?

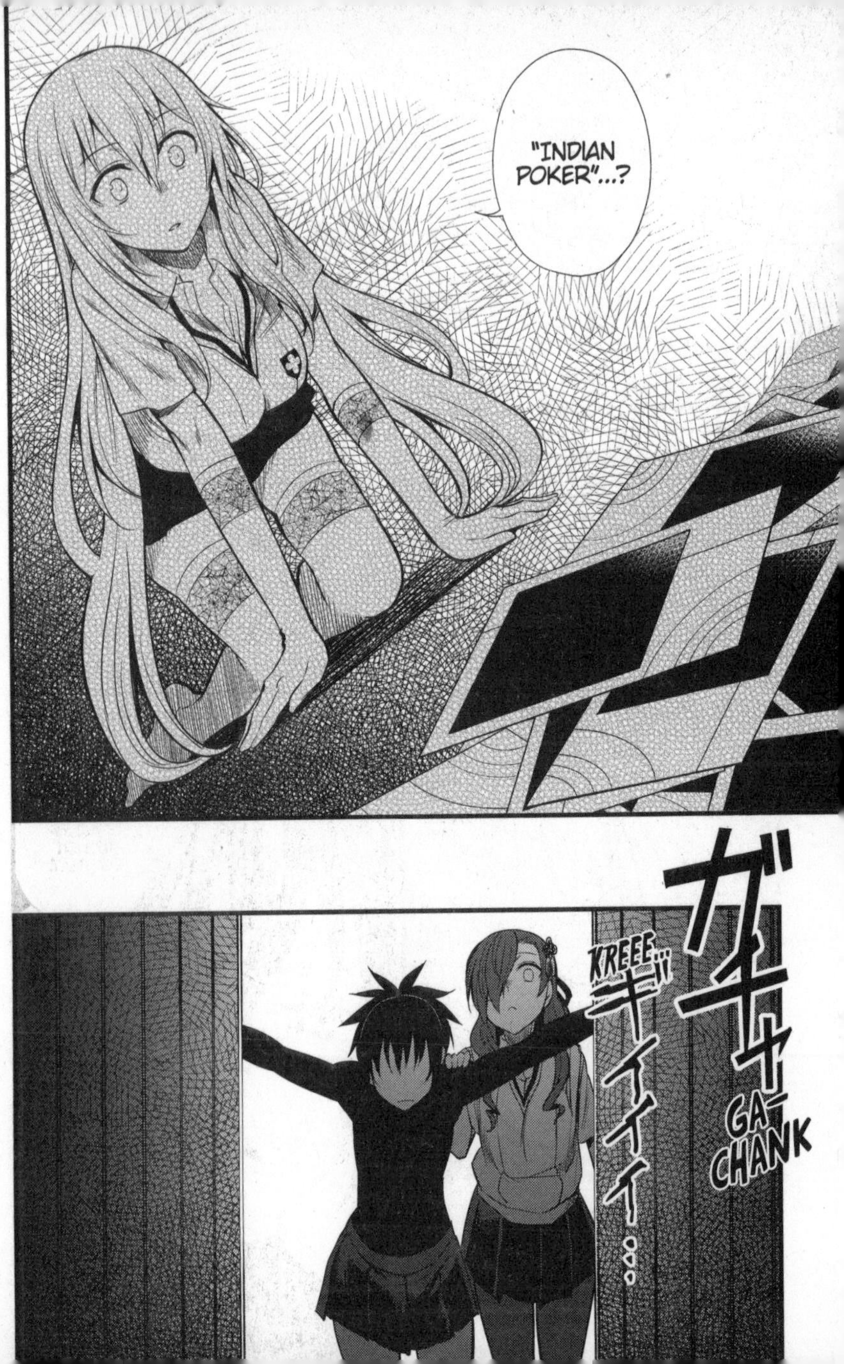
"INDIAN POKER"...?
GA-CHANK
KREEE...

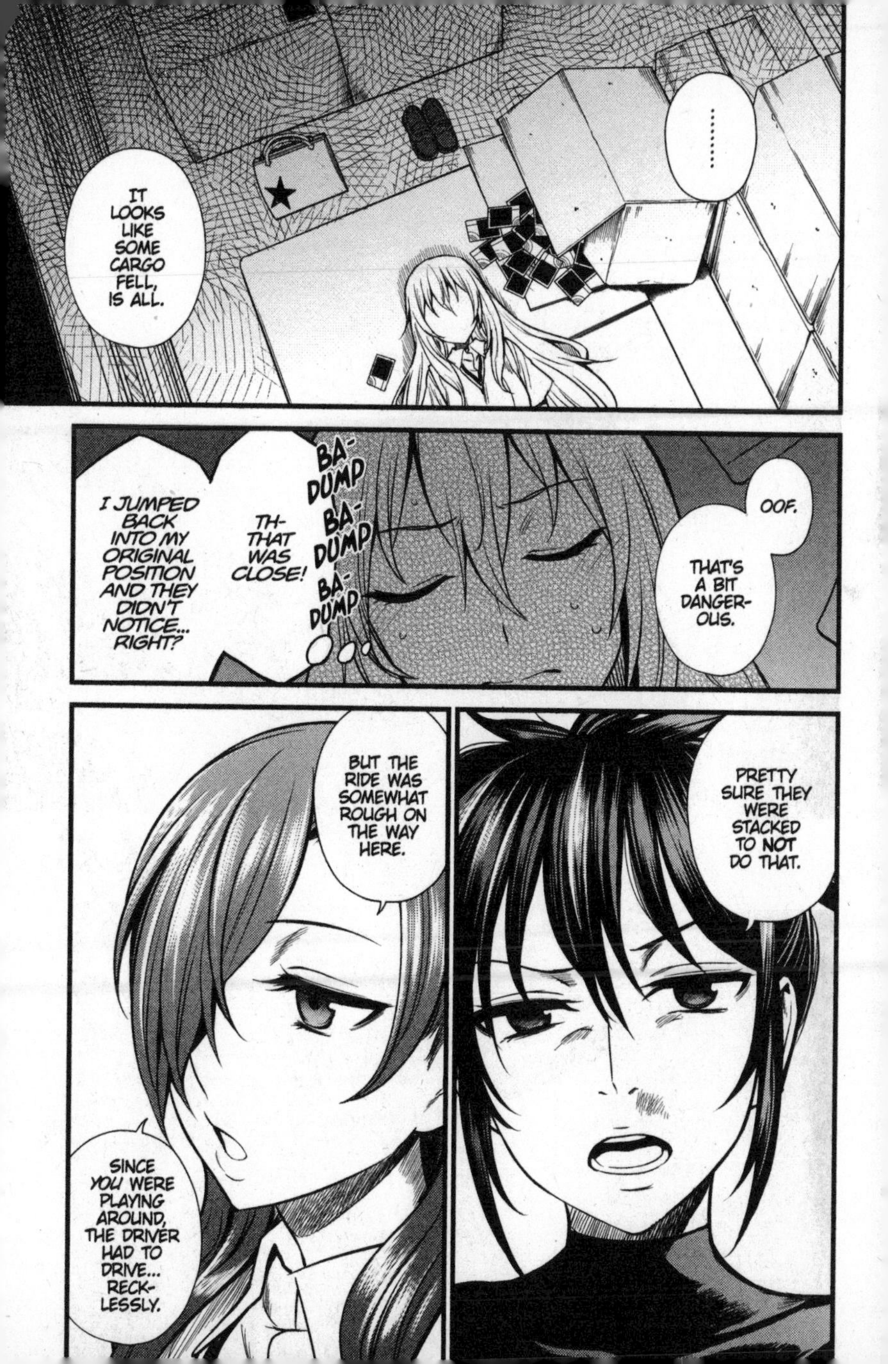
……
IT LOOKS LIKE SOME CARGO FELL, IS ALL.
OOF.
THAT'S A BIT DANGER-OUS.
BA-DUMP BA-DUMP BA-DUMP
TH-THAT WAS CLOSE!
I JUMPED BACK INTO MY ORIGINAL POSITION AND THEY DIDN'T NOTICE... RIGHT?
PRETTY SURE THEY WERE STACKED TO NOT DO THAT.
BUT THE RIDE WAS SOMEWHAT ROUGH ON THE WAY HERE.
SINCE YOU WERE PLAYING AROUND, THE DRIVER HAD TO DRIVE... RECK-LESSLY.

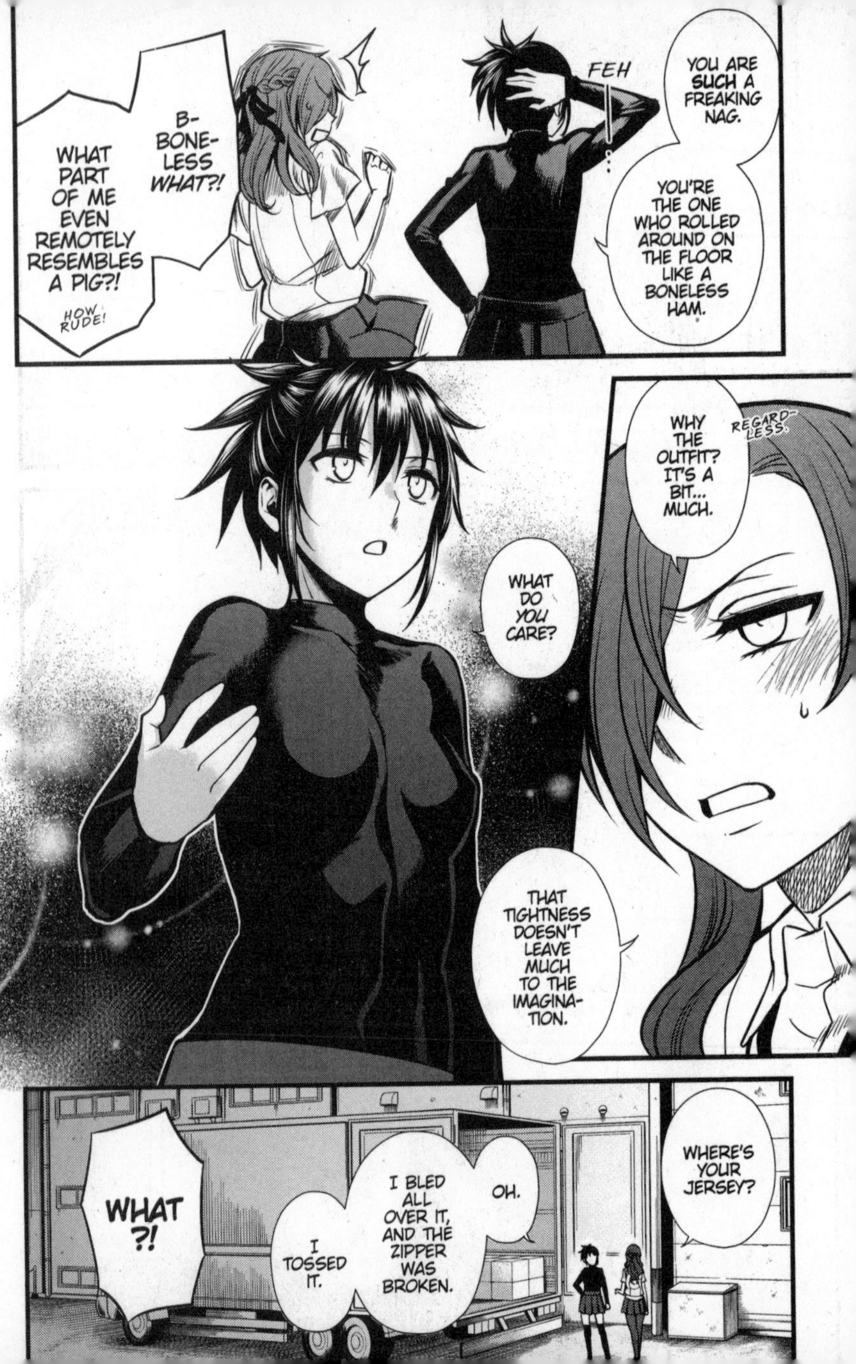
YOU ARE SUCH A FREAKING NAG.
FEH
YOU'RE THE ONE WHO ROLLED AROUND ON THE FLOOR LIKE A BONELESS HAM.
B-BONELESS WHAT?!
WHAT PART OF ME EVEN REMOTELY RESEMBLES A PIG?!
HOW RUDE!
REGARDLESS.
WHY THE OUTFIT? IT'S A BIT... MUCH.
WHAT DO YOU CARE?
THAT TIGHTNESS DOESN'T LEAVE MUCH TO THE IMAGINATION.
WHERE'S YOUR JERSEY?
OH.
I BLED ALL OVER IT, AND THE ZIPPER WAS BROKEN.
I TOSSED IT.
WHAT ?!

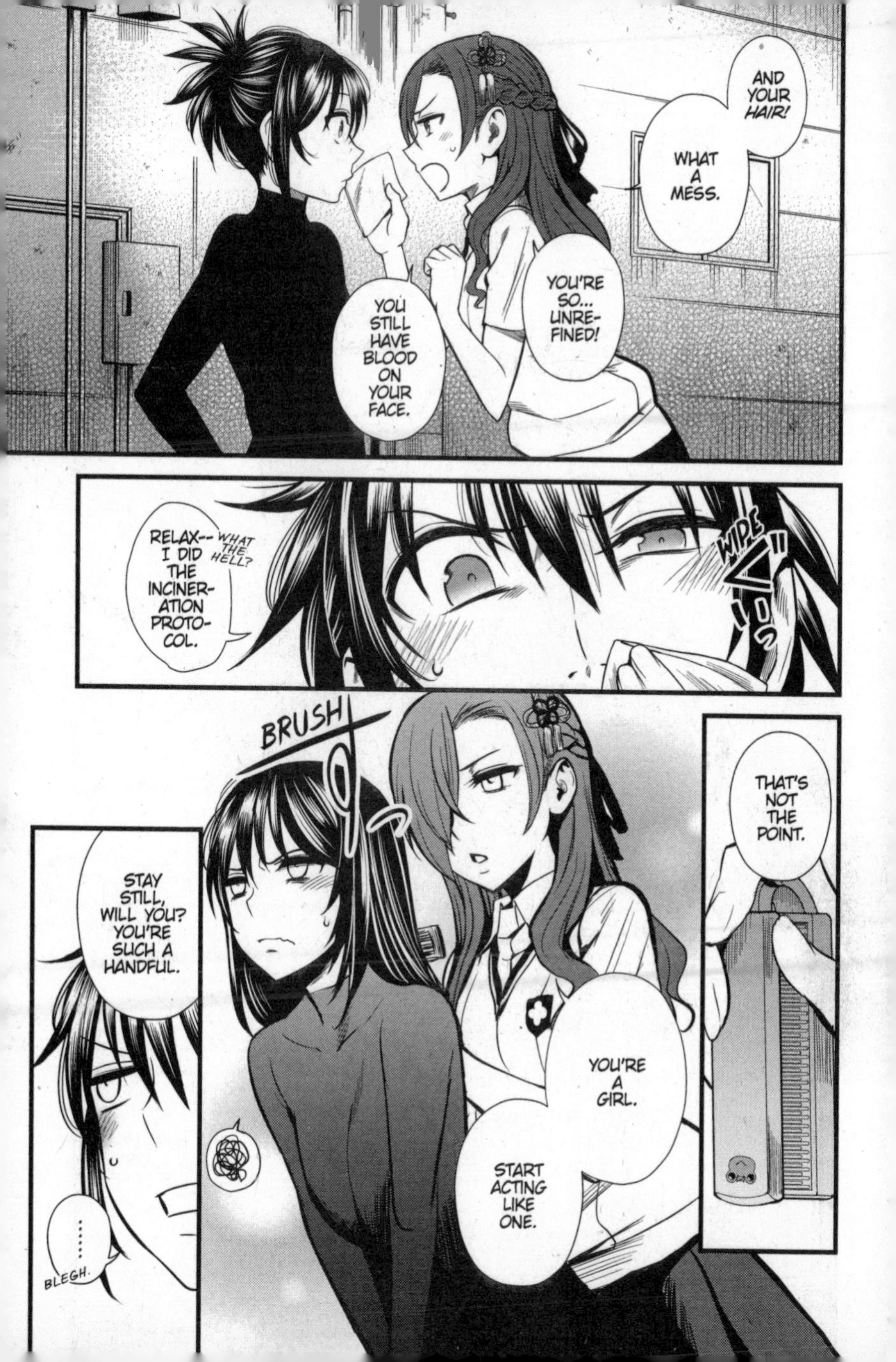
AND YOUR HAIR!
WHAT A MESS.
YOU'RE SO... UNREFINED!
YOU STILL HAVE BLOOD ON YOUR FACE.
WIPE
WHAT THE HELL?
RELAX-- I DID THE INCINERATION PROTOCOL.
THAT'S NOT THE POINT.
BRUSH
YOU'RE A GIRL.
START ACTING LIKE ONE.
STAY STILL, WILL YOU? YOU'RE SUCH A HANDFUL.
......
BLEGH.

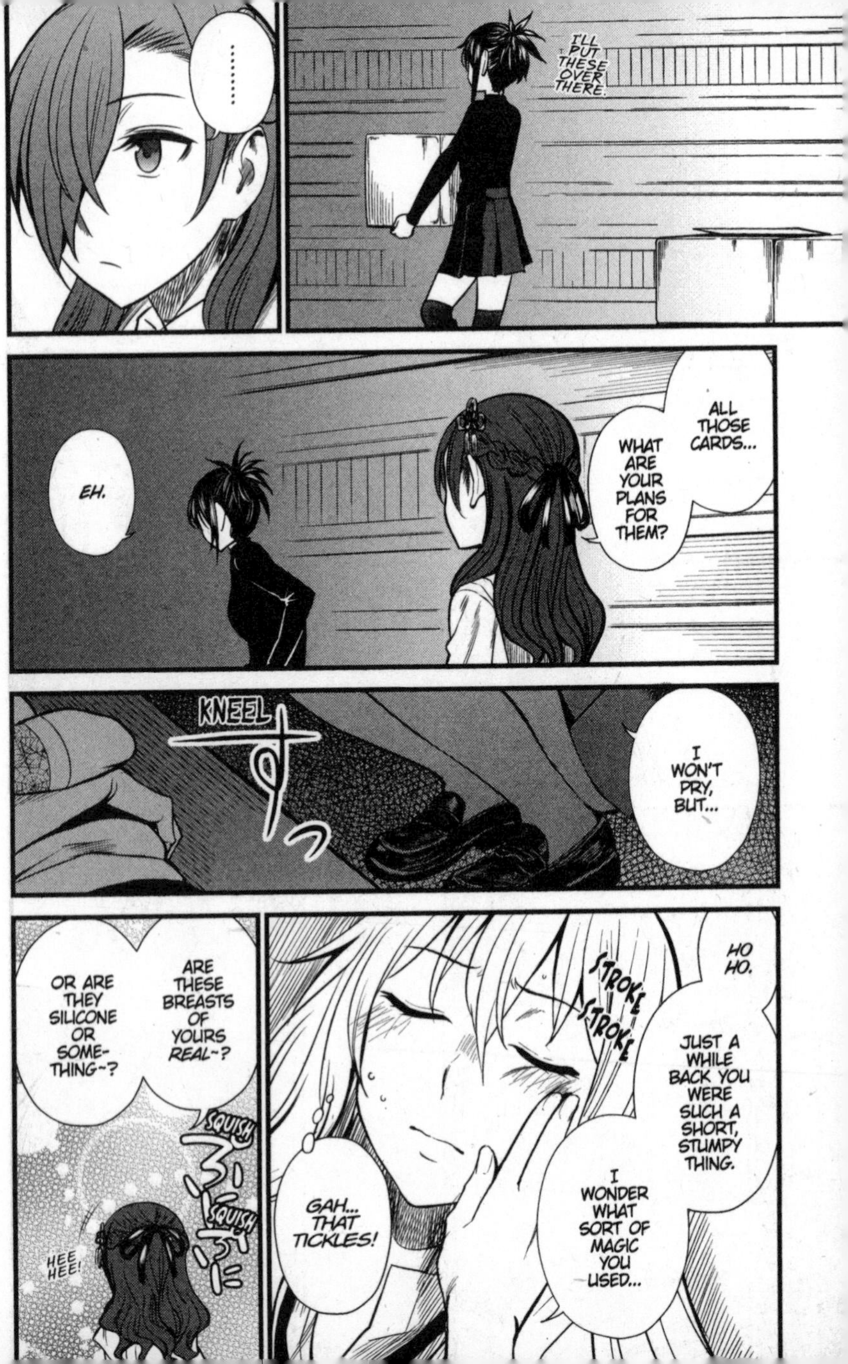
I'LL PUT THESE OVER THERE.
......
ALL THOSE CARDS...
WHAT ARE YOUR PLANS FOR THEM?
EH.
I WON'T PRY, BUT...
KNEEL
HO HO.
JUST A WHILE BACK YOU WERE SUCH A SHORT, STUMPY THING.
I WONDER WHAT SORT OF MAGIC YOU USED...
STROKE STROKE
GAH... THAT TICKLES!
ARE THESE BREASTS OF YOURS REAL~?
OR ARE THEY SILICONE OR SOMETHING~?
SQUISH
SQUISH
HEE HEE!

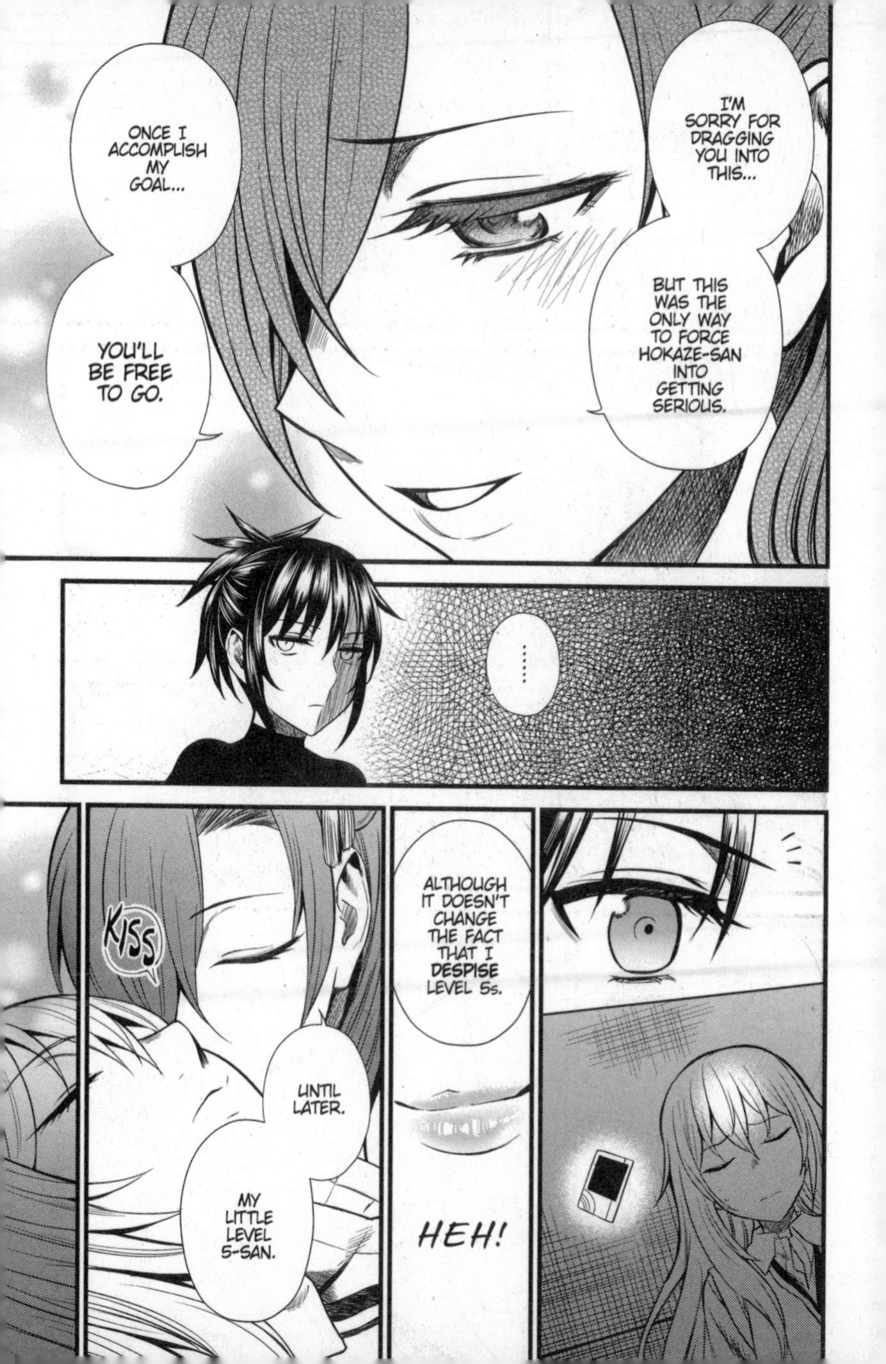
I'M SORRY FOR DRAGGING YOU INTO THIS...
BUT THIS WAS THE ONLY WAY TO FORCE HOKAZE-SAN INTO GETTING SERIOUS.
ONCE I ACCOMPLISH MY GOAL...
YOU'LL BE FREE TO GO.
......
ALTHOUGH IT DOESN'T CHANGE THE FACT THAT I DESPISE LEVEL 5s.
HEH!
KISS
UNTIL LATER.
MY LITTLE LEVEL 5-SAN.

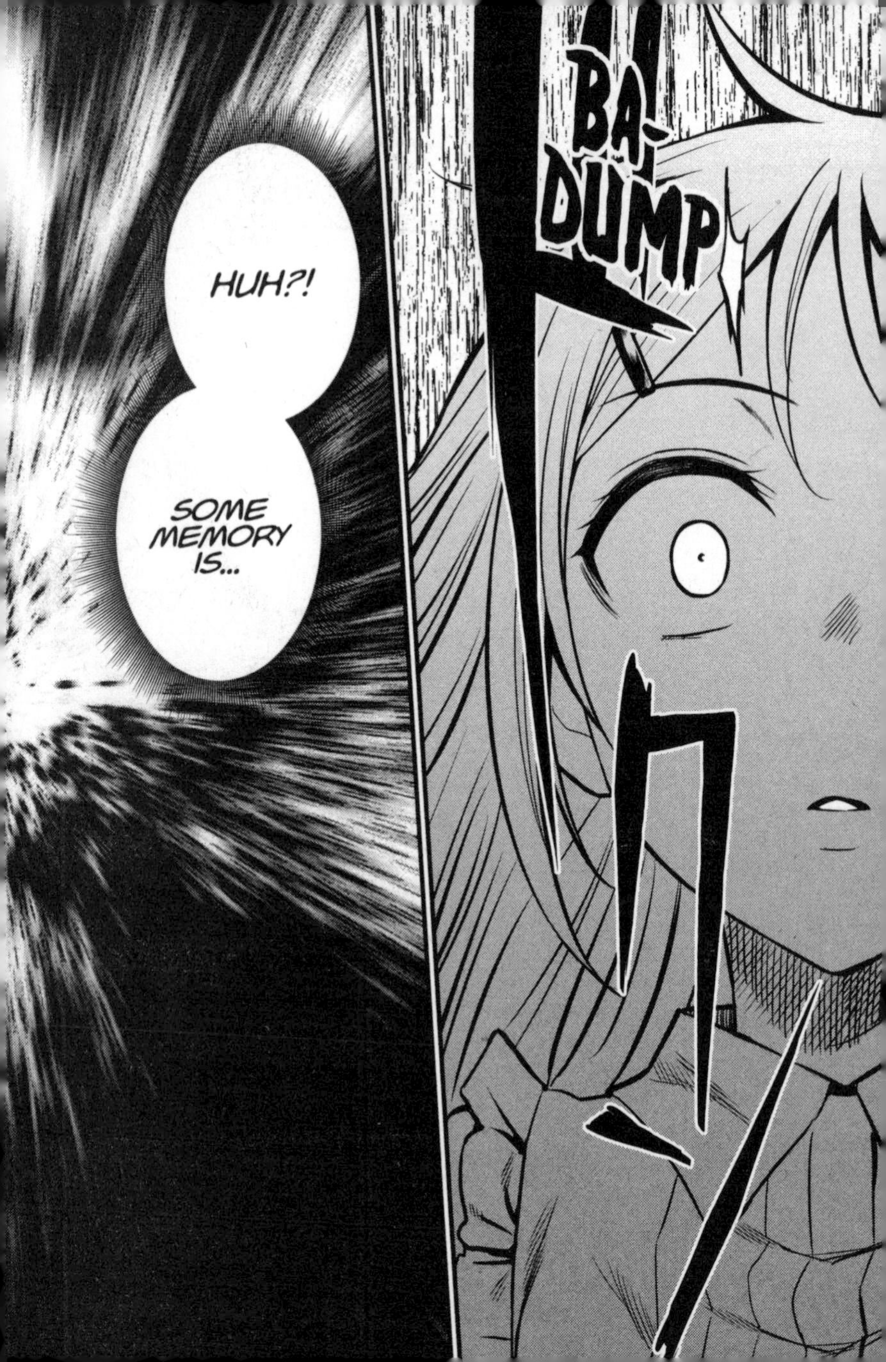
BA-DUMP
HUH?!
SOME MEMORY IS...

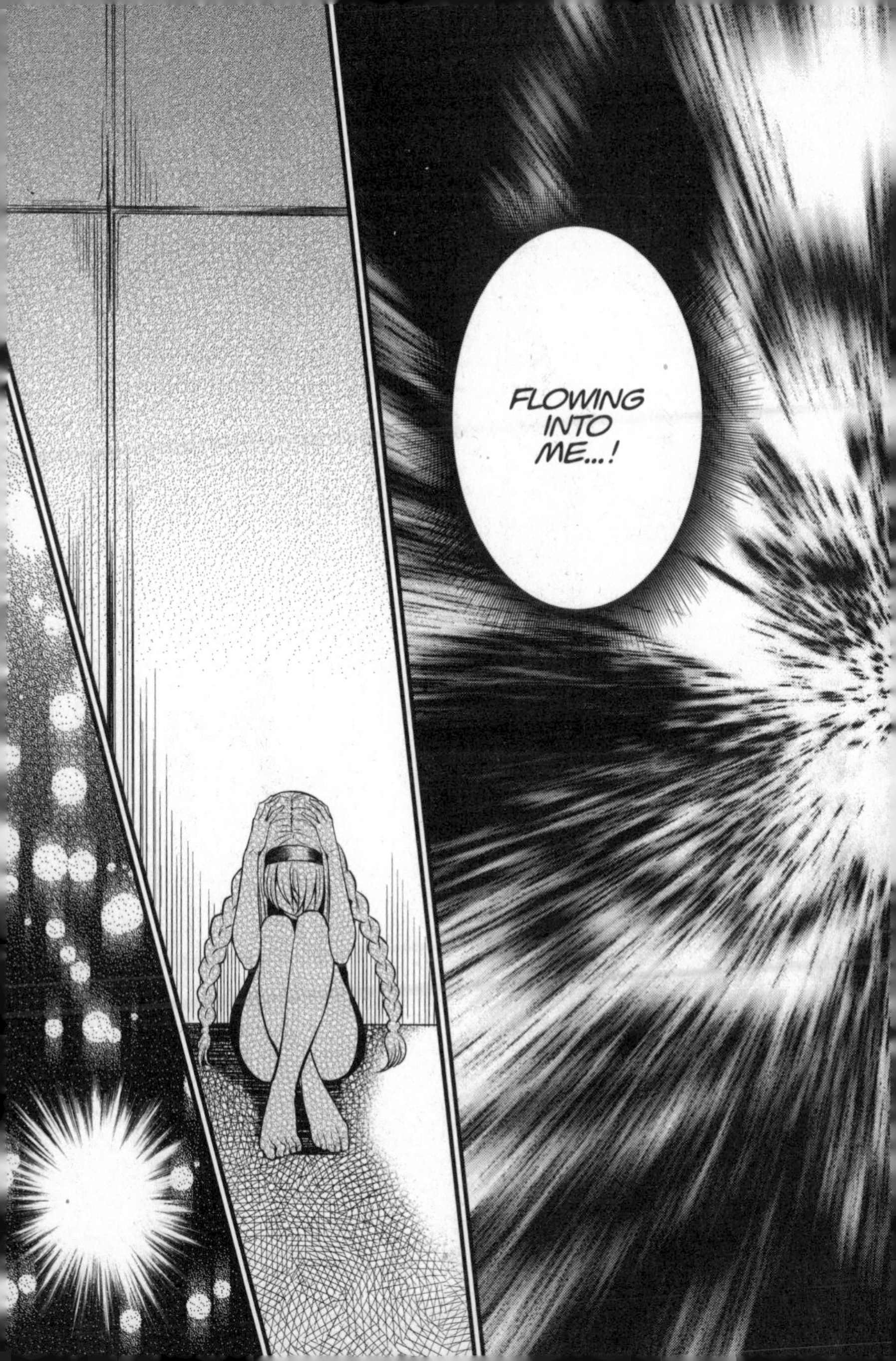
FLOWING INTO ME...!

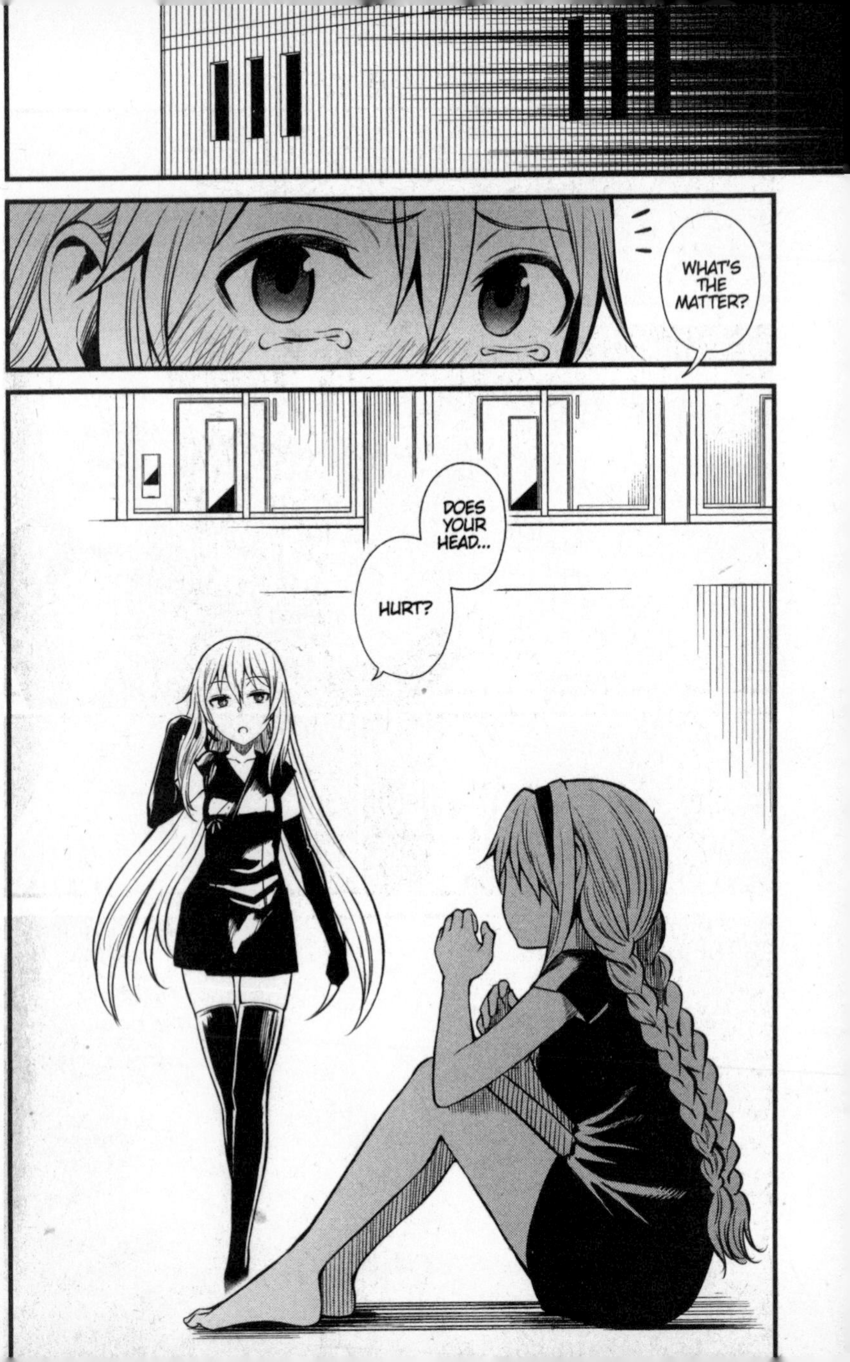
WHAT'S THE MATTER?
DOES YOUR HEAD...
HURT?

CHAPTER 10: Welcome to "Ideal"☆

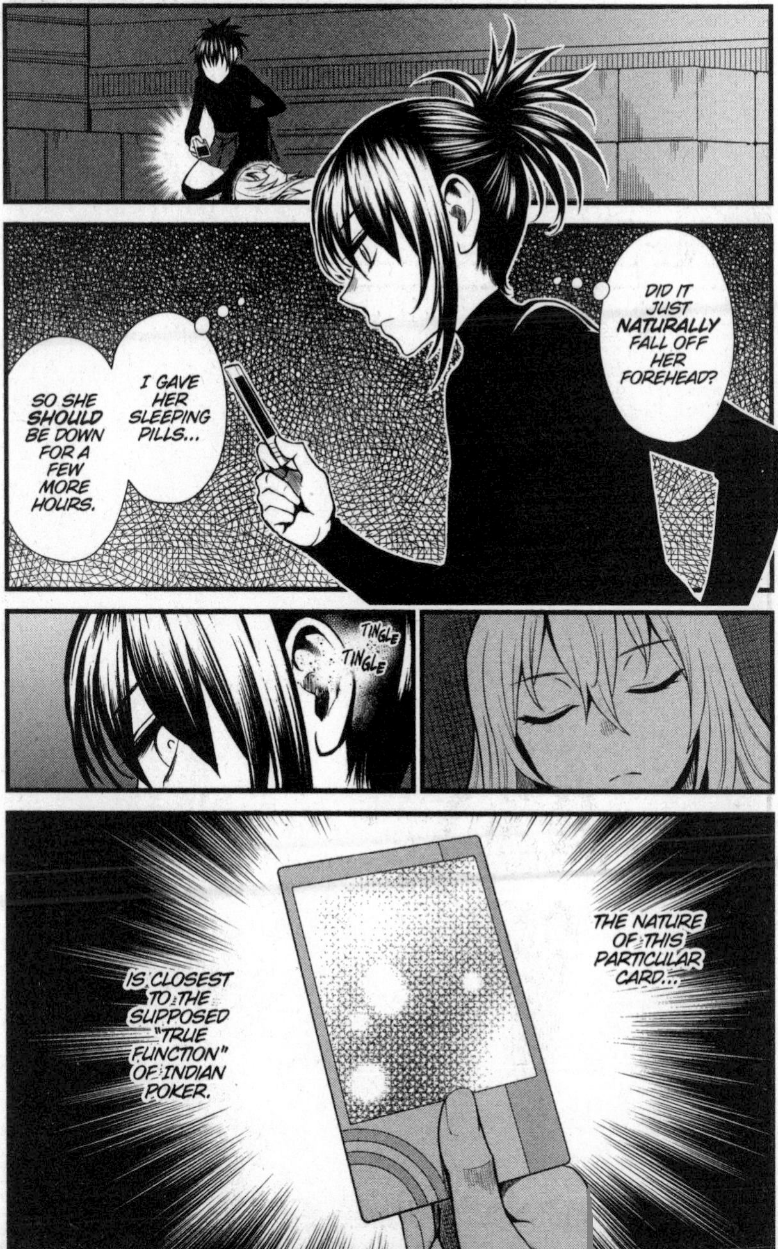

DID IT JUST NATURALLY FALL OFF HER FOREHEAD?
I GAVE HER SLEEPING PILLS...
SO SHE SHOULD BE DOWN FOR A FEW MORE HOURS.
TINGLE TINGLE
THE NATURE OF THIS PARTICULAR CARD...
IS CLOSEST TO THE SUPPOSED "TRUE FUNCTION" OF INDIAN POKER.

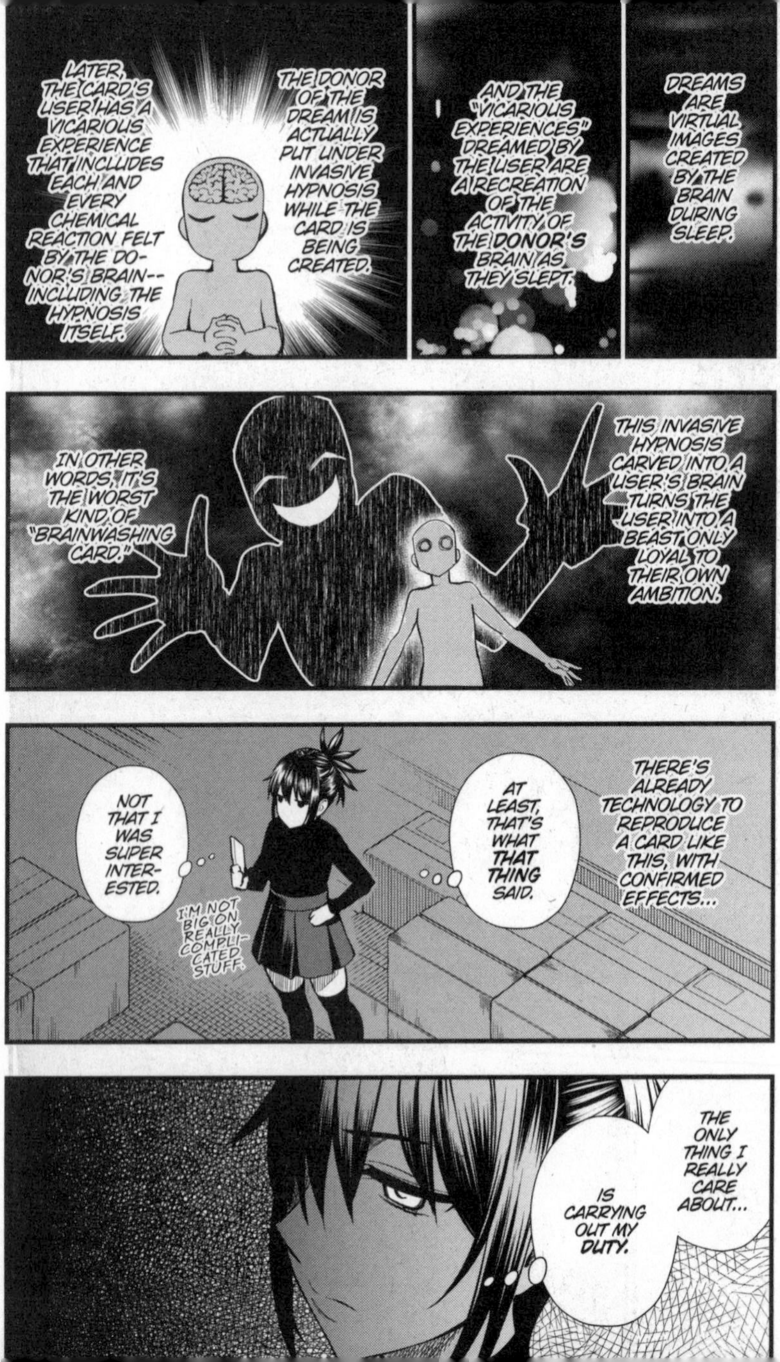
DREAMS ARE VIRTUAL IMAGES CREATED BY THE BRAIN DURING SLEEP.
AND THE "VICARIOUS EXPERIENCES" DREAMED BY THE USER ARE A RECREATION OF THE ACTIVITY OF THE **DONOR'S** BRAIN AS THEY SLEPT.
THE DONOR OF THE DREAM IS ACTUALLY PUT UNDER INVASIVE HYPNOSIS WHILE THE CARD IS BEING CREATED.
LATER, THE CARD'S USER HAS A VICARIOUS EXPERIENCE THAT INCLUDES EACH AND EVERY CHEMICAL REACTION FELT BY THE DO-NOR'S BRAIN--INCLUDING THE HYPNOSIS ITSELF.
THIS INVASIVE HYPNOSIS CARVED INTO A USER'S BRAIN TURNS THE USER INTO A BEAST ONLY LOYAL TO THEIR OWN AMBITION.
IN OTHER WORDS, IT'S THE WORST KIND OF "BRAINWASHING CARD."
THERE'S ALREADY TECHNOLOGY TO REPRODUCE A CARD LIKE THIS, WITH CONFIRMED EFFECTS...
AT LEAST, THAT'S WHAT **THAT THING** SAID.
NOT THAT I WAS SUPER INTER-ESTED.
I'M NOT BIG ON REALLY COMPLI-CATED STUFF.
THE ONLY THING I REALLY CARE ABOUT...
IS CARRYING OUT MY **DUTY.**

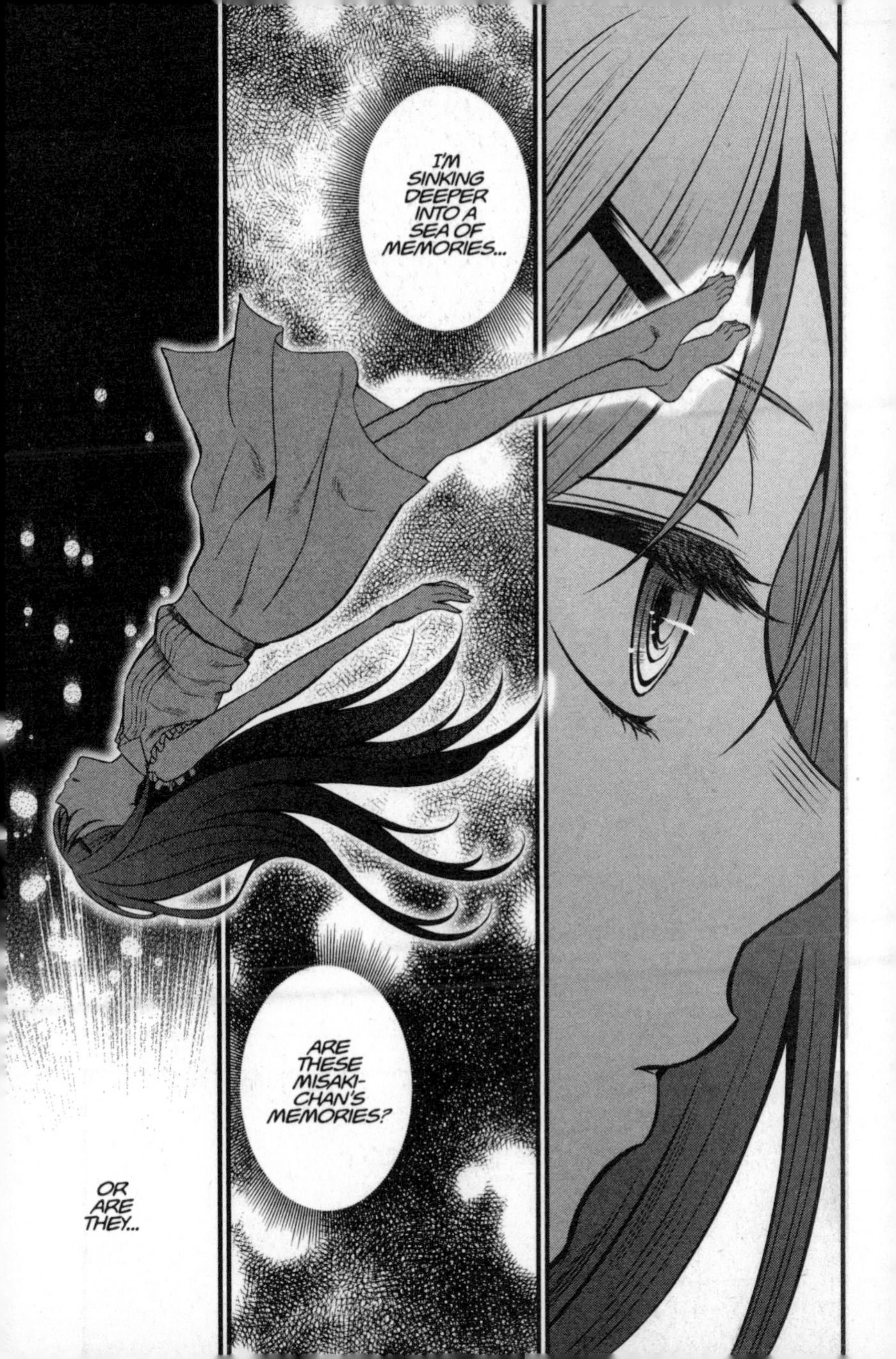
I'M SINKING DEEPER INTO A SEA OF MEMORIES...
ARE THESE MISAKI-CHAN'S MEMORIES?
OR ARE THEY...

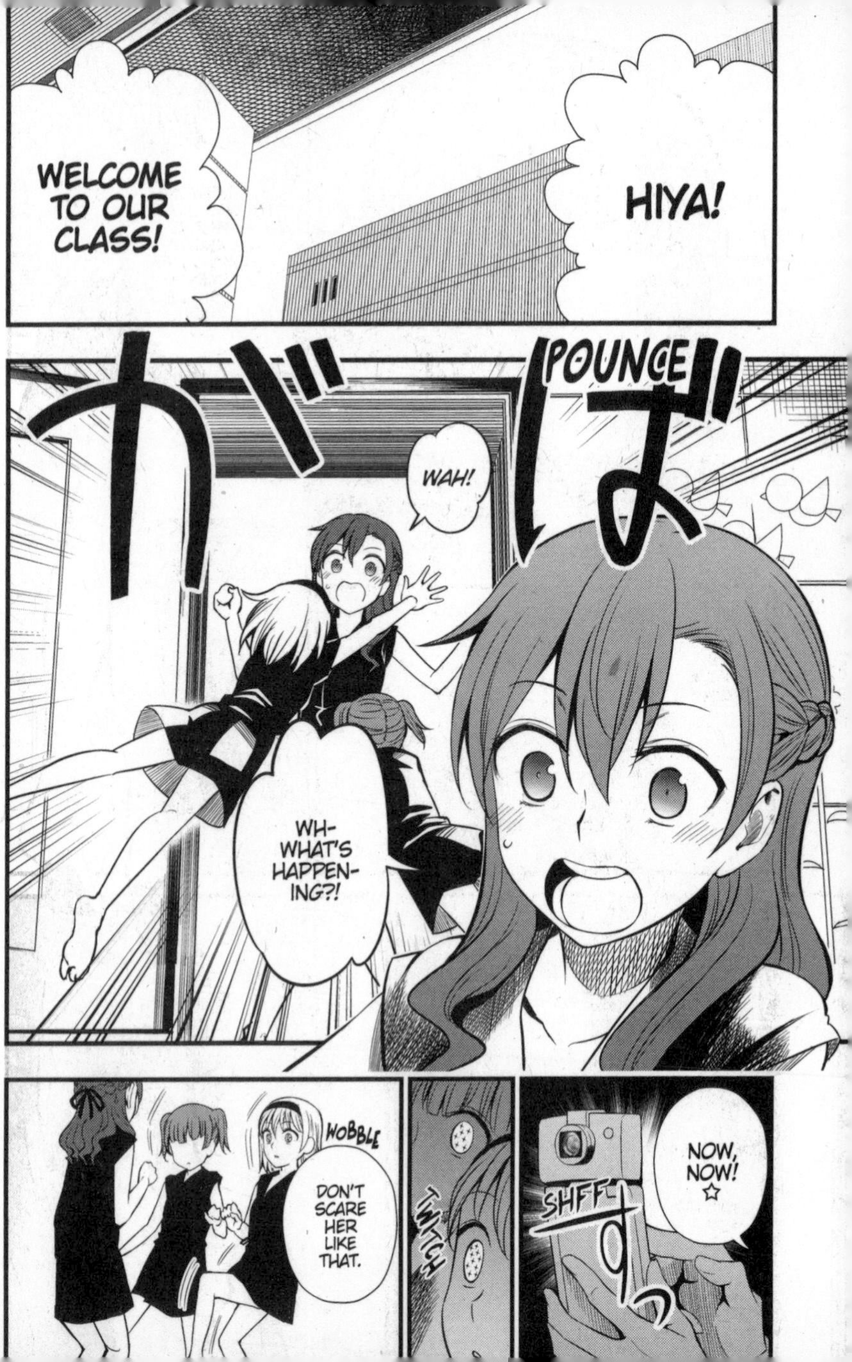
HIYA!
WELCOME TO OUR CLASS!
POUNCE
がば
WAH!
WH-WHAT'S HAPPENING?!
NOW, NOW! ☆
SHFF
すっ
TWITCH
WOBBLE
DON'T SCARE HER LIKE THAT.

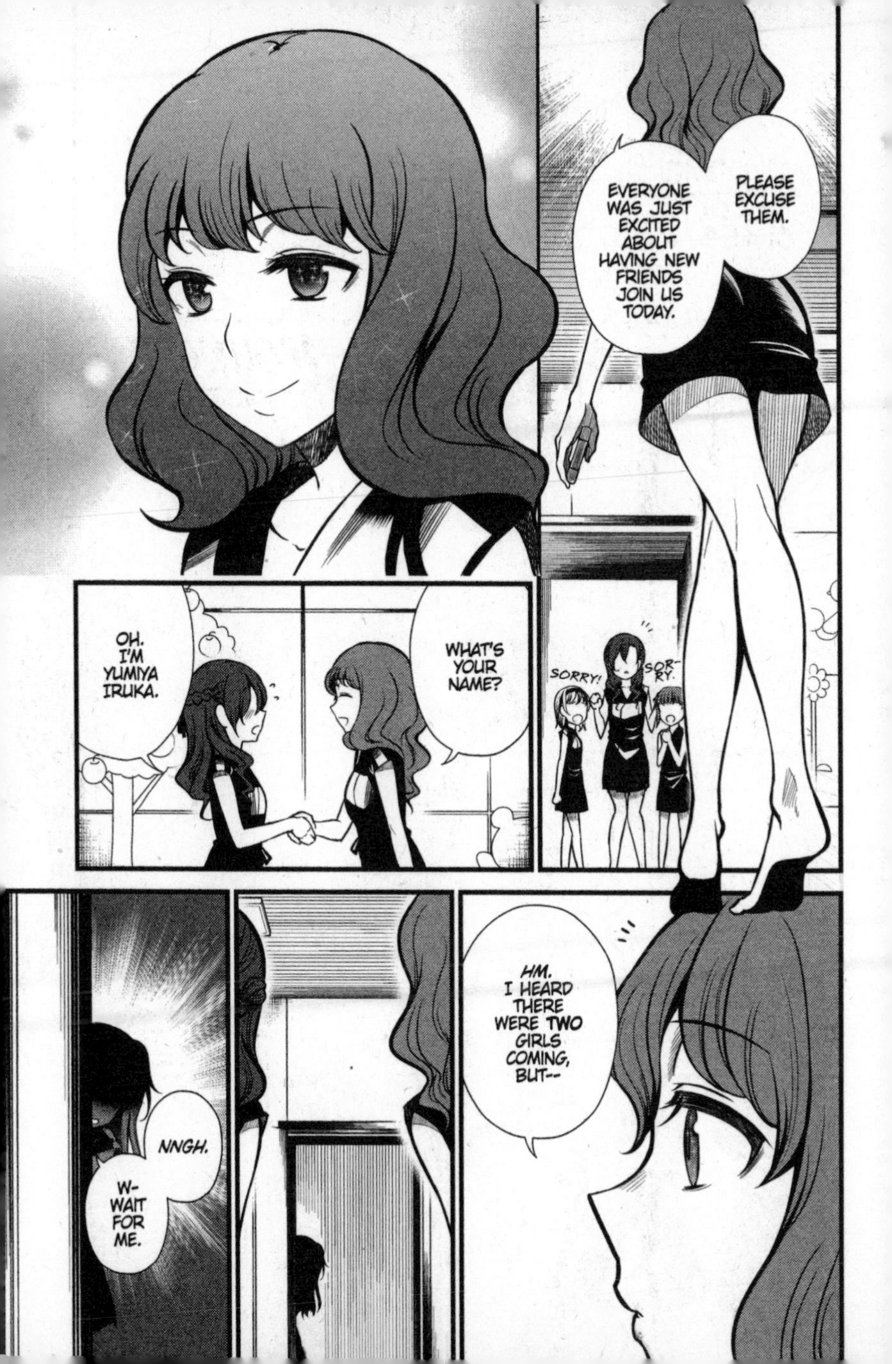
PLEASE EXCUSE THEM.
EVERYONE WAS JUST EXCITED ABOUT HAVING NEW FRIENDS JOIN US TODAY.
SOR-RY.
SORRY!
WHAT'S YOUR NAME?
OH. I'M YUMIYA IRUKA.
HM. I HEARD THERE WERE TWO GIRLS COMING, BUT--
NNGH.
W-WAIT FOR ME.

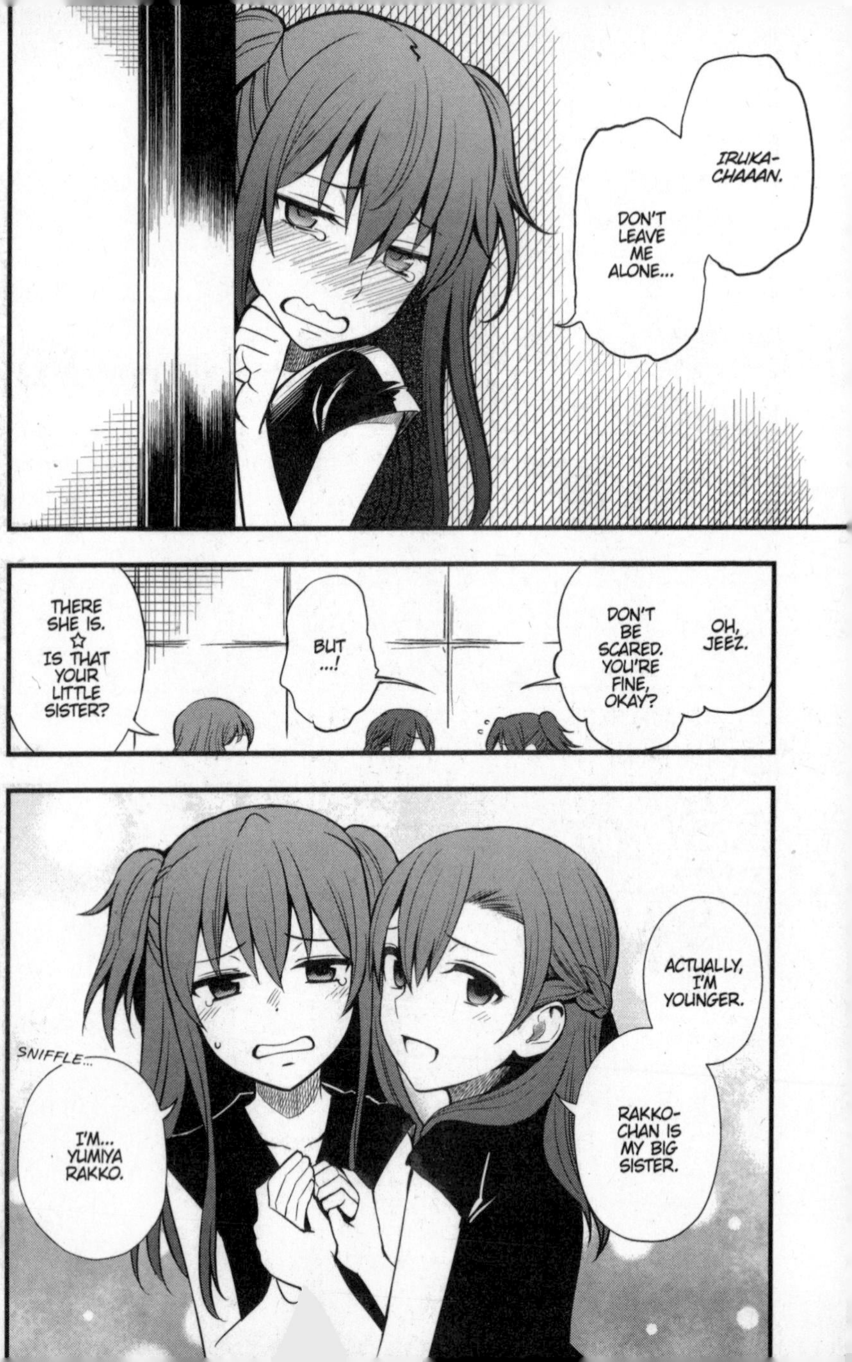
IRUKA-CHAAAN.
DON'T LEAVE ME ALONE...
OH, JEEZ.
DON'T BE SCARED. YOU'RE FINE, OKAY?
BUT ...!
THERE SHE IS. ☆ IS THAT YOUR LITTLE SISTER?
ACTUALLY, I'M YOUNGER.
RAKKO-CHAN IS MY BIG SISTER.
SNIFFLE...
I'M... YUMIYA RAKKO.

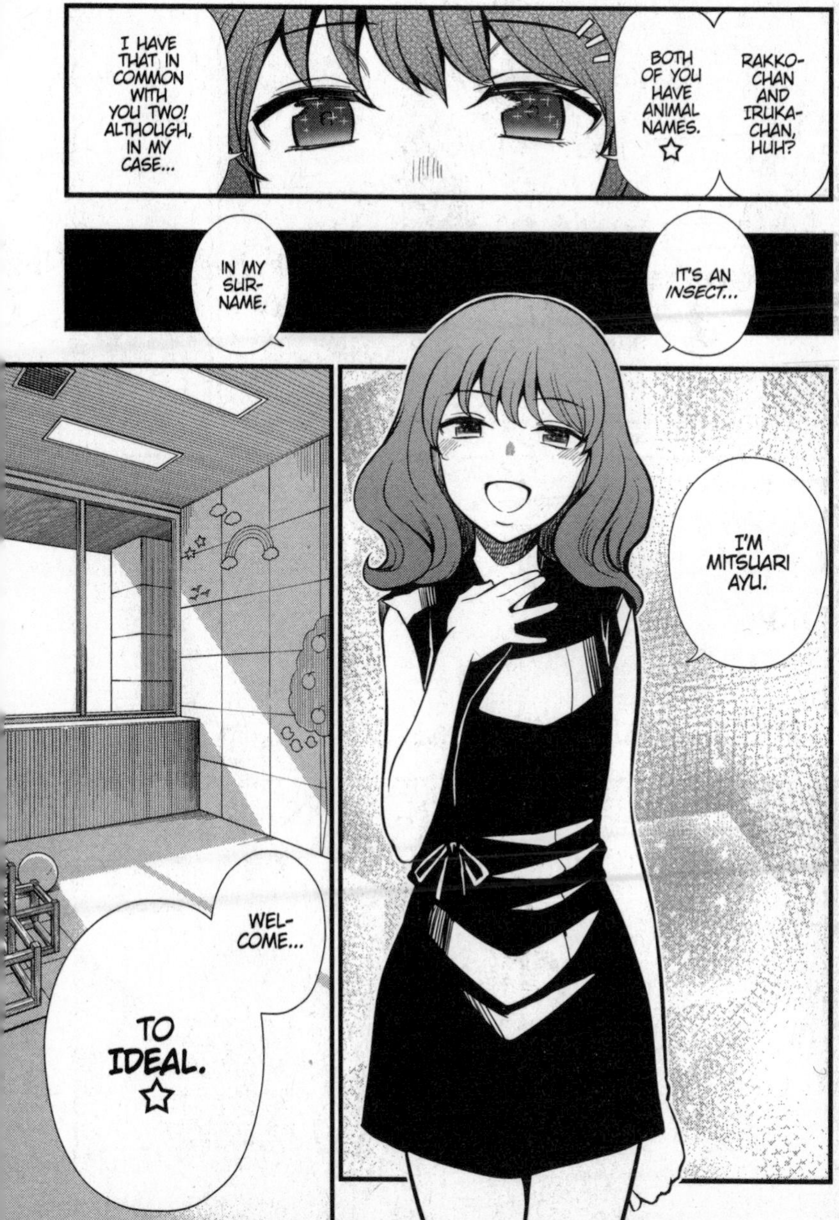
RAKKO-CHAN AND IRUKA-CHAN, HUH?
BOTH OF YOU HAVE ANIMAL NAMES. ☆
I HAVE THAT IN COMMON WITH YOU TWO! ALTHOUGH, IN MY CASE...
IT'S AN *INSECT*...
IN MY SUR-NAME.
I'M MITSUARI AYU.
WEL-COME...
TO IDEAL. ☆

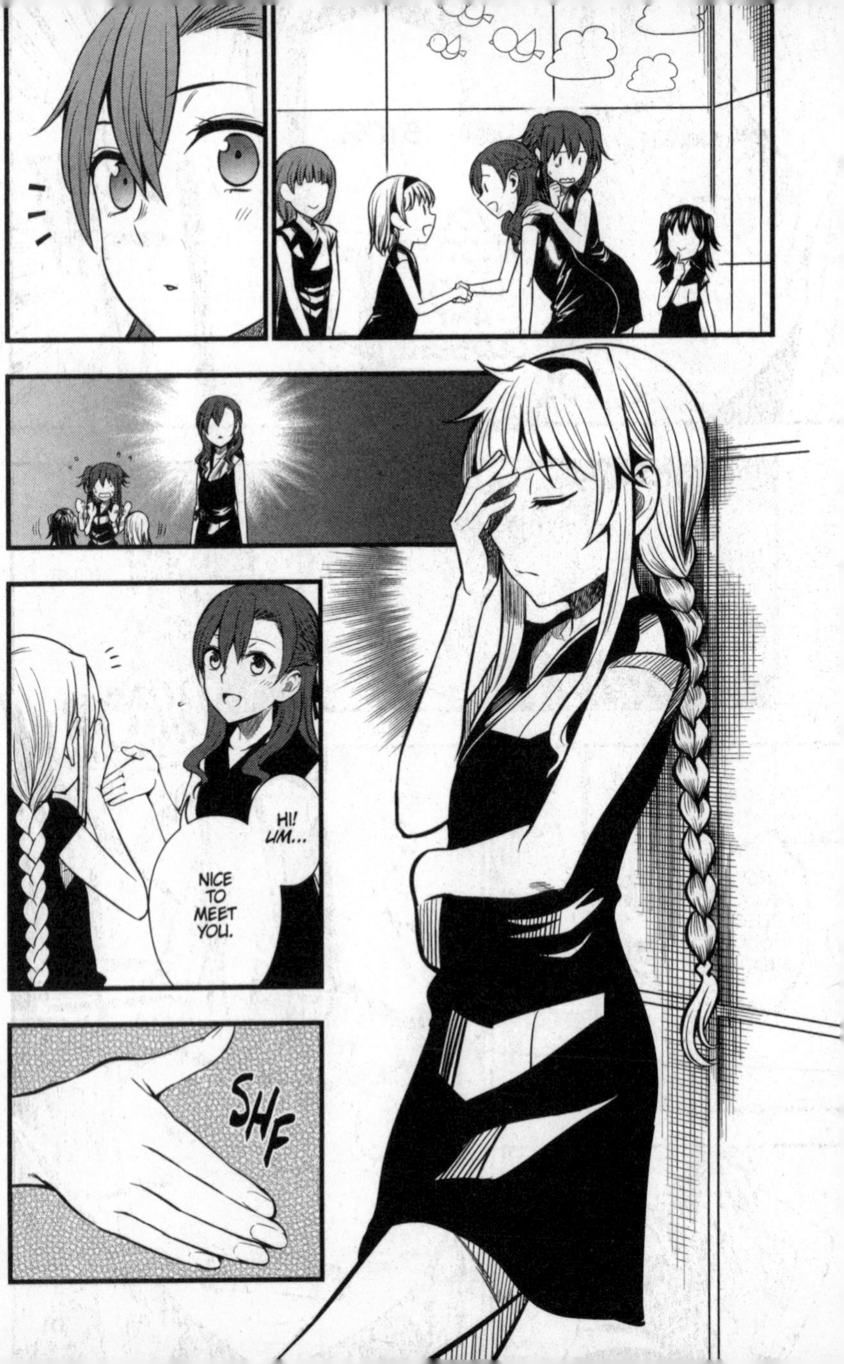
HI! UM...
NICE TO MEET YOU.
SHF

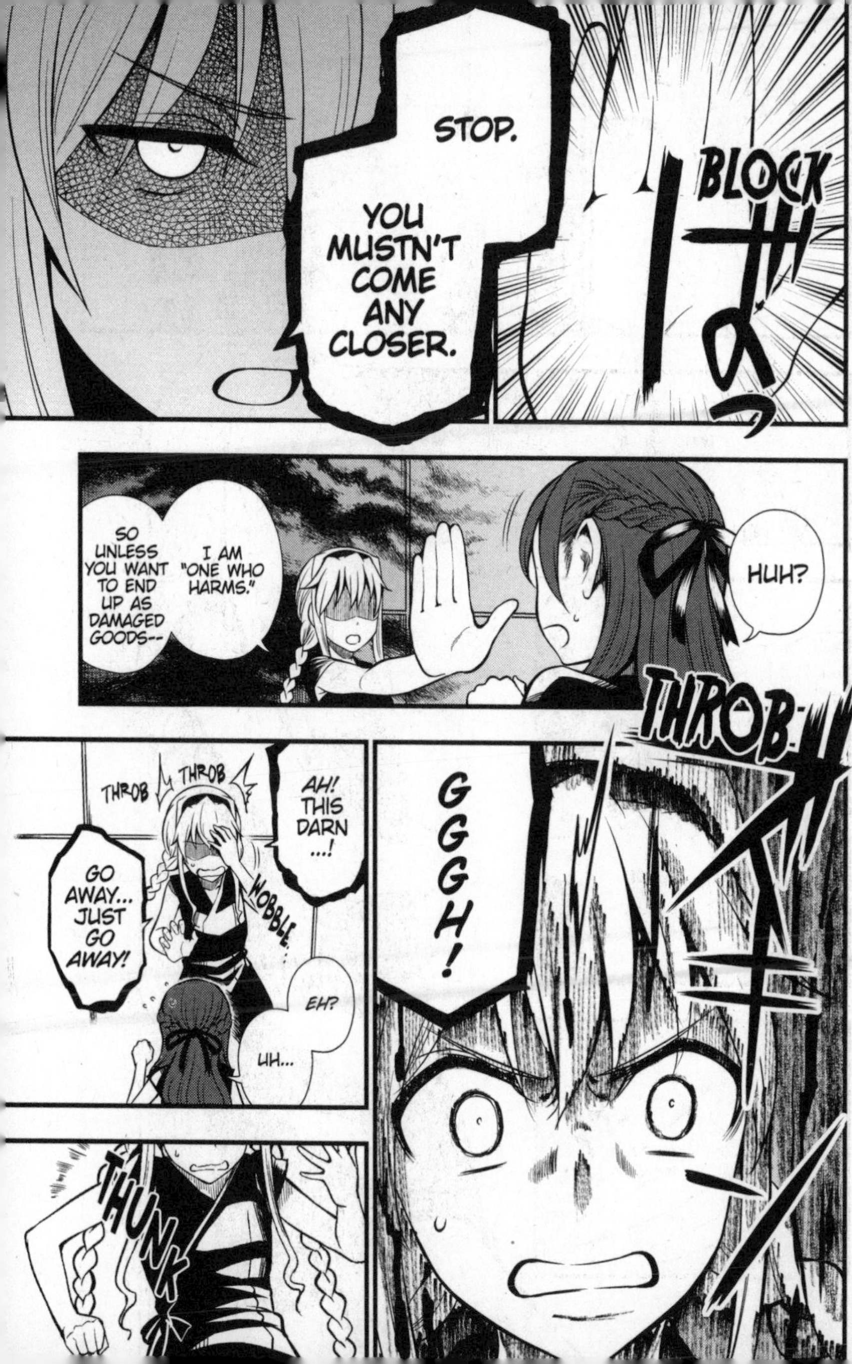
BLOCK
STOP.
YOU MUSTN'T COME ANY CLOSER.
HUH?
I AM "ONE WHO HARMS."
SO UNLESS YOU WANT TO END UP AS DAMAGED GOODS--
THROB
GGGH!
AH! THIS DARN ...!
THROB THROB
GO AWAY... JUST GO AWAY!
WOBBLE
EH?
UH...
THUNK

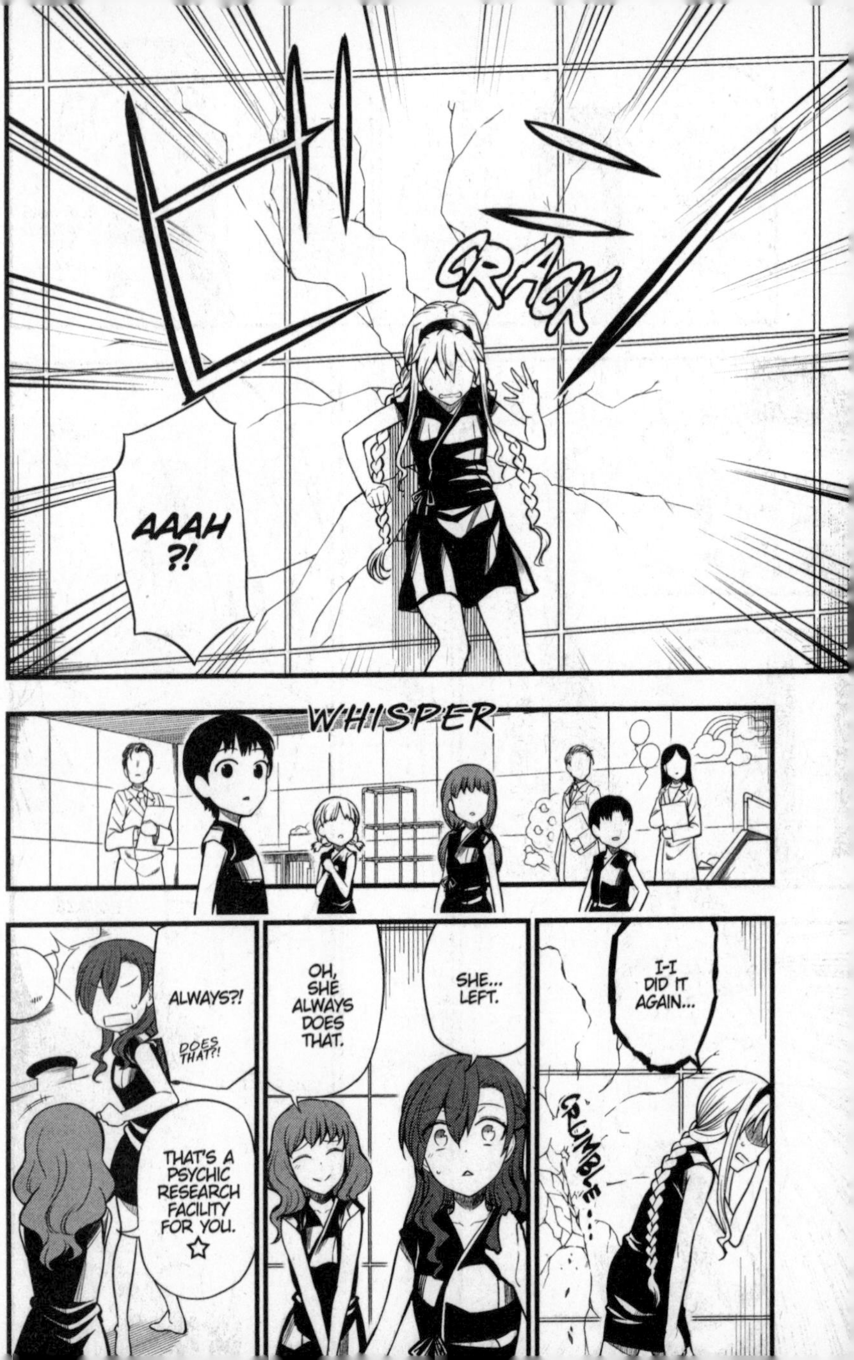
CRACK
AAAH ?!
WHISPER
I-I DID IT AGAIN...
CRUMBLE...
SHE... LEFT.
OH, SHE ALWAYS DOES THAT.
ALWAYS?!
DOES THAT?!
THAT'S A PSYCHIC RESEARCH FACILITY FOR YOU. ☆

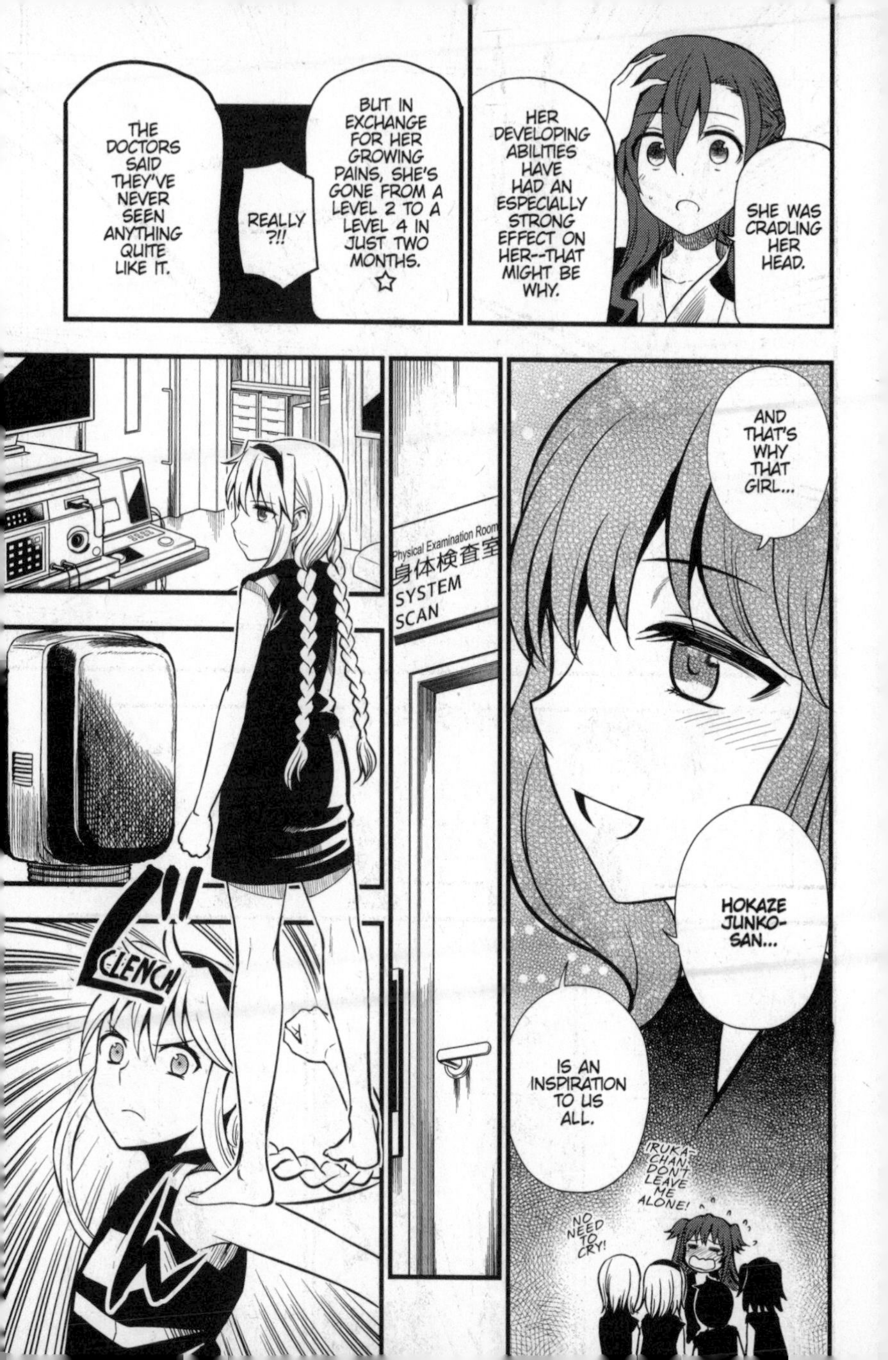
SHE WAS CRADLING HER HEAD.
HER DEVELOPING ABILITIES HAVE HAD AN ESPECIALLY STRONG EFFECT ON HER--THAT MIGHT BE WHY.
BUT IN EXCHANGE FOR HER GROWING PAINS, SHE'S GONE FROM A LEVEL 2 TO A LEVEL 4 IN JUST TWO MONTHS. ☆
REALLY ?!!
THE DOCTORS SAID THEY'VE NEVER SEEN ANYTHING QUITE LIKE IT.
AND THAT'S WHY THAT GIRL...
HOKAZE JUNKO-SAN...
IS AN INSPIRATION TO US ALL.
IRUKA-CHAN, DON'T LEAVE ME ALONE!
NO NEED TO CRY!
Physical Examination Room
身体検査室
SYSTEM SCAN
!!
CLENCH

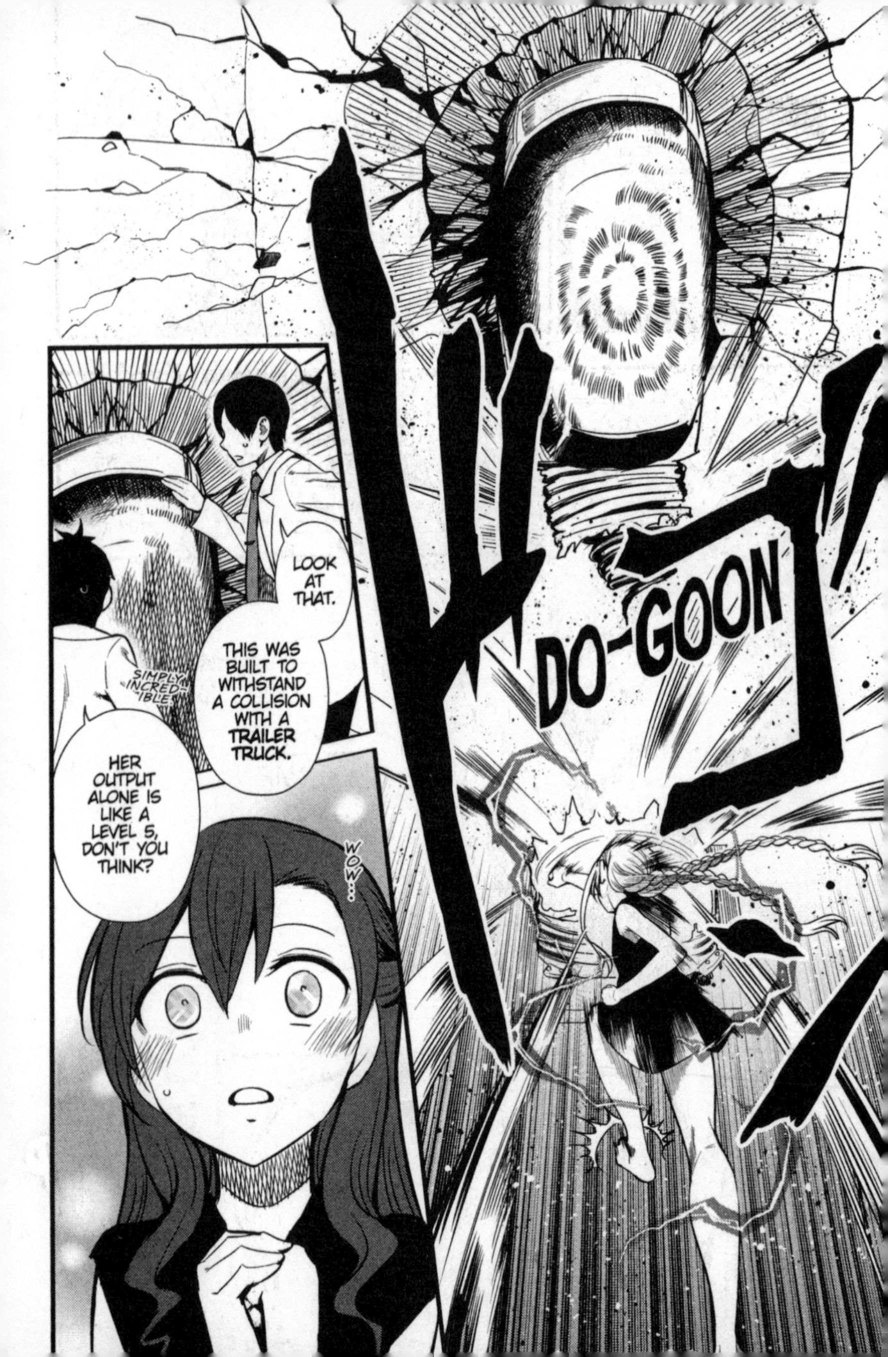
DO-GOON
LOOK AT THAT.
THIS WAS BUILT TO WITHSTAND A COLLISION WITH A TRAILER TRUCK.
SIMPLY INCRED-IBLE
HER OUTPUT ALONE IS LIKE A LEVEL 5, DON'T YOU THINK?
WOW...

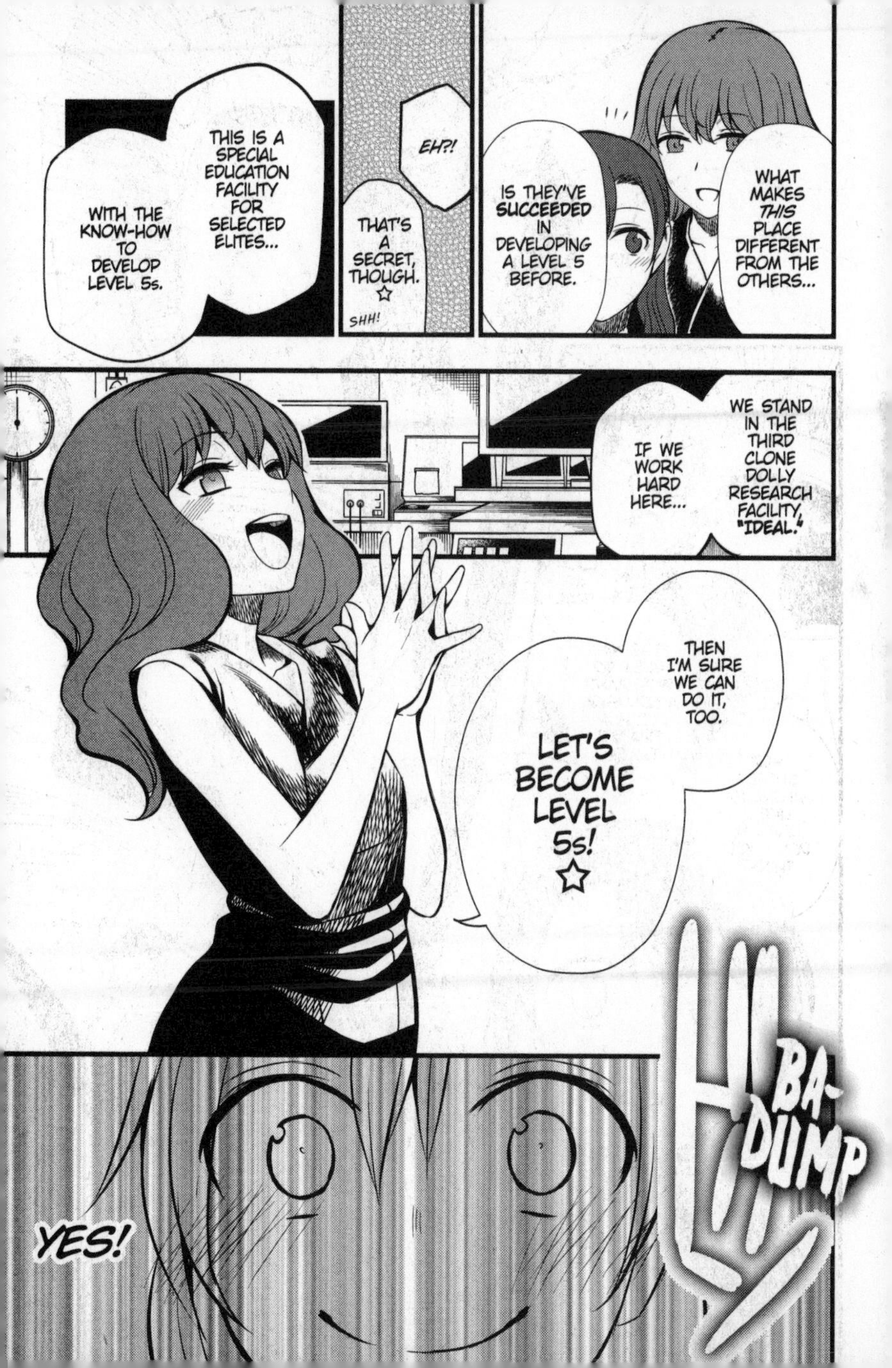
WHAT MAKES THIS PLACE DIFFERENT FROM THE OTHERS...
IS THEY'VE SUCCEEDED IN DEVELOPING A LEVEL 5 BEFORE.
EH?!
THAT'S A SECRET, THOUGH. ☆
SHH!
THIS IS A SPECIAL EDUCATION FACILITY FOR SELECTED ELITES...
WITH THE KNOW-HOW TO DEVELOP LEVEL 5s.
WE STAND IN THE THIRD CLONE DOLLY RESEARCH FACILITY, "IDEAL."
IF WE WORK HARD HERE...
THEN I'M SURE WE CAN DO IT, TOO.
LET'S BECOME LEVEL 5s! ☆
BA-DUMP
YES!

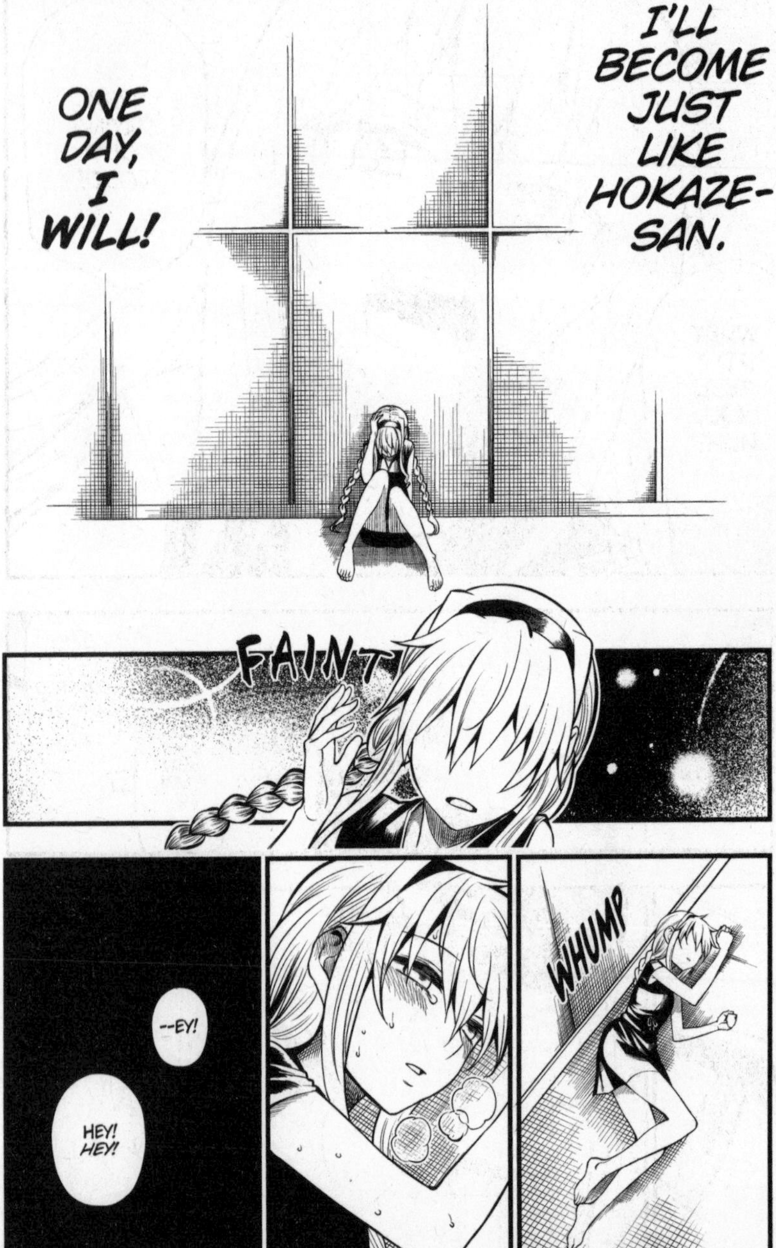
I'LL BECOME JUST LIKE HOKAZE-SAN.
ONE DAY, I WILL!
FAINT
WHUMP
--EY!
HEY! HEY!

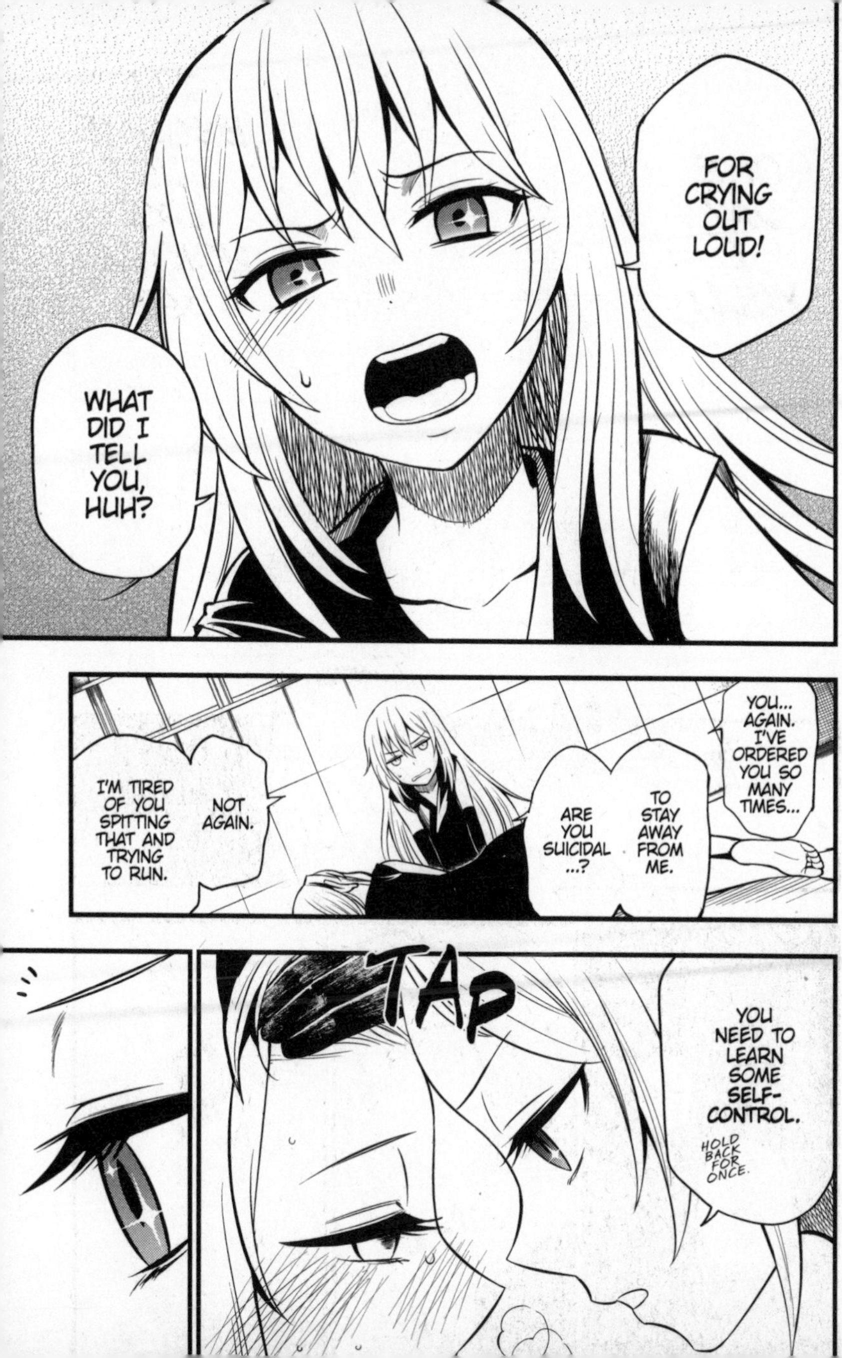
FOR CRYING OUT LOUD!
WHAT DID I TELL YOU, HUH?
YOU... AGAIN. I'VE ORDERED YOU SO MANY TIMES...
TO STAY AWAY FROM ME.
ARE YOU SUICIDAL ...?
NOT AGAIN.
I'M TIRED OF YOU SPITTING THAT AND TRYING TO RUN.
TAP
YOU NEED TO LEARN SOME SELF-CONTROL.
HOLD BACK FOR ONCE.

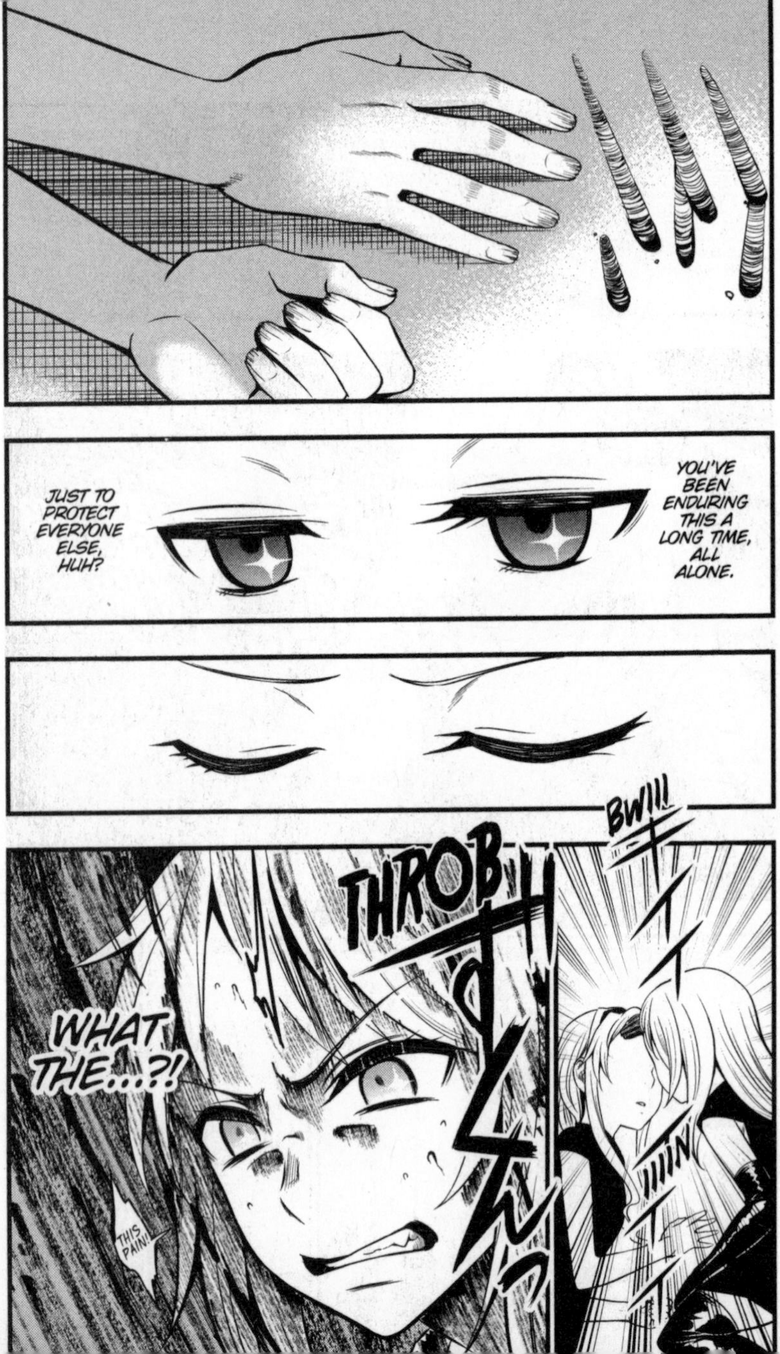
YOU'VE BEEN ENDURING THIS A LONG TIME, ALL ALONE.
JUST TO PROTECT EVERYONE ELSE, HUH?
BWIII
IIIIN
THROB
WHAT THE...?!
THIS PAIN!

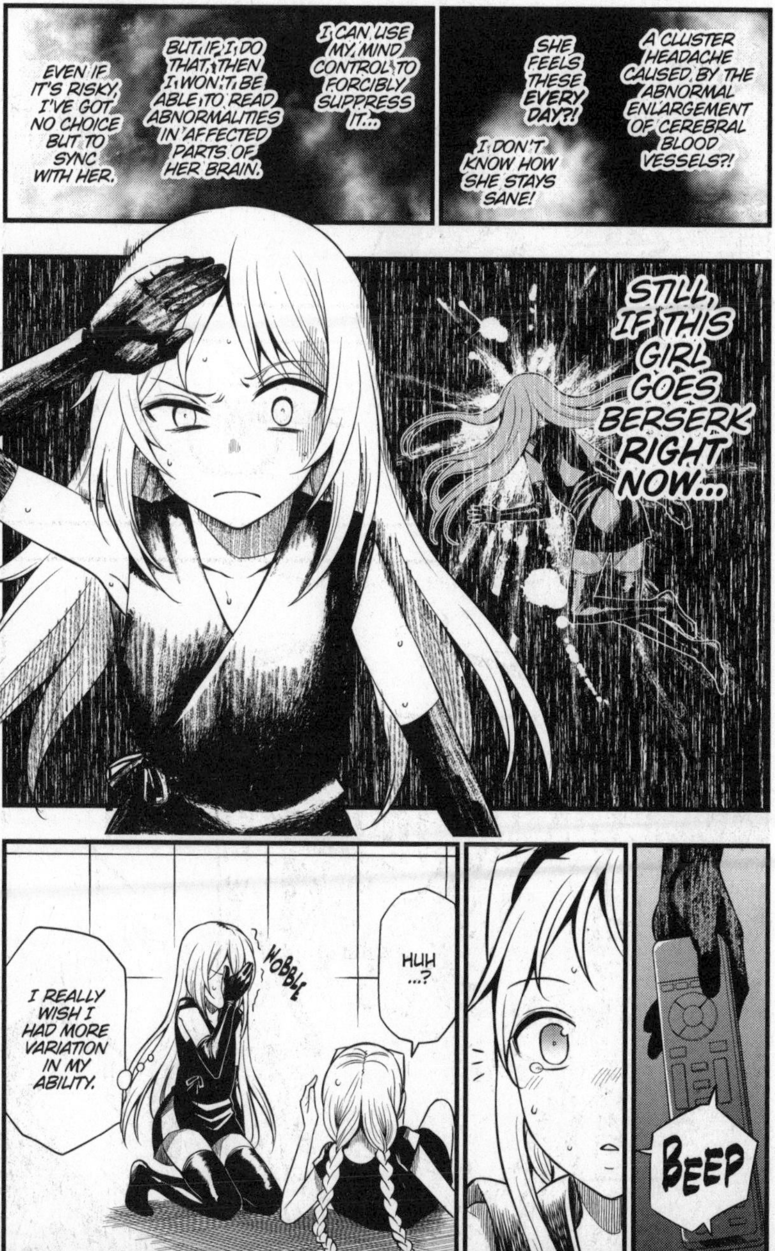
A CLUSTER HEADACHE CAUSED BY THE ABNORMAL ENLARGEMENT OF CEREBRAL BLOOD VESSELS?!
SHE FEELS THESE EVERY DAY?!
I DON'T KNOW HOW SHE STAYS SANE!
I CAN USE MY MIND CONTROL TO FORCIBLY SUPPRESS IT...
BUT IF I DO THAT, THEN I WON'T BE ABLE TO READ ABNORMALITIES IN AFFECTED PARTS OF HER BRAIN.
EVEN IF IT'S RISKY, I'VE GOT NO CHOICE BUT TO SYNC WITH HER.
STILL, IF THIS GIRL GOES BERSERK RIGHT NOW...
BEEP
HUH ...?
WOBBLE
I REALLY WISH I HAD MORE VARIATION IN MY ABILITY.

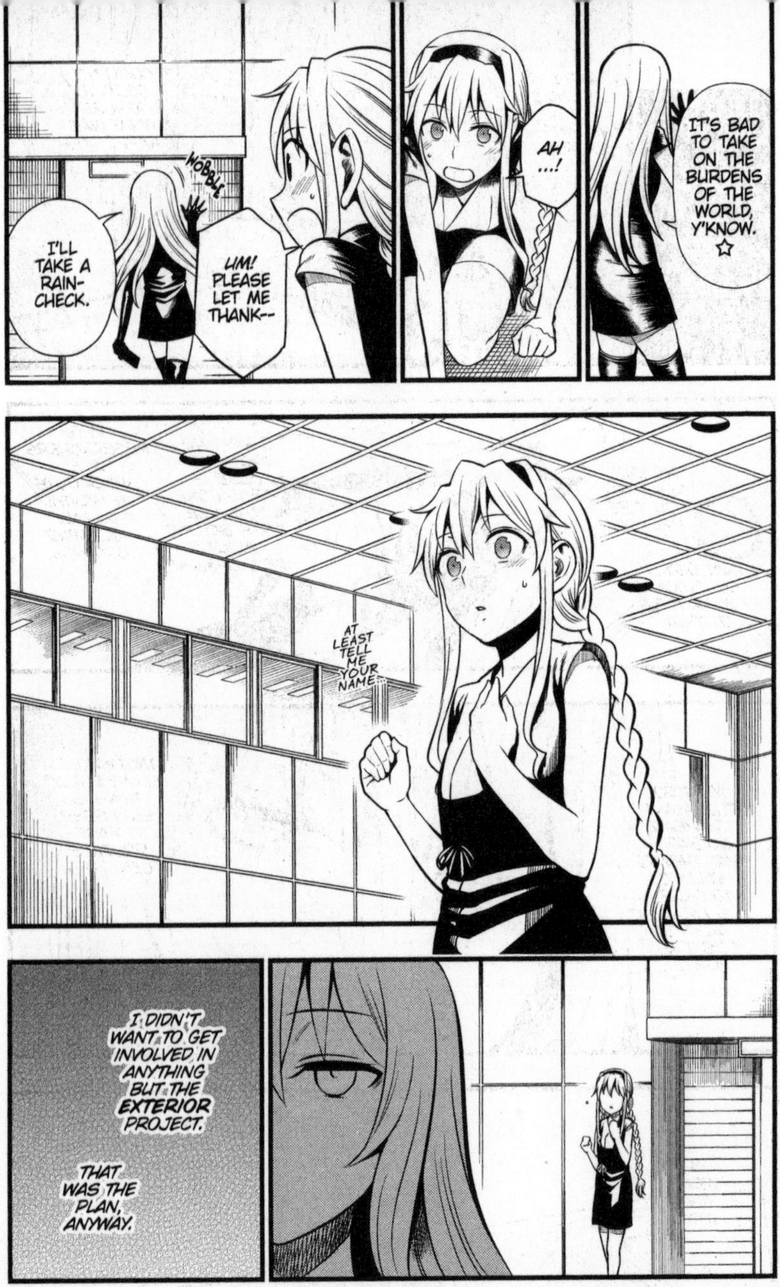
IT'S BAD TO TAKE ON THE BURDENS OF THE WORLD, Y'KNOW. ☆
AH ...!
UM! PLEASE LET ME THANK--
WOBBLE
I'LL TAKE A RAIN-CHECK.
AT LEAST TELL ME YOUR NAME...
I DIDN'T WANT TO GET INVOLVED IN ANYTHING BUT THE EXTERIOR PROJECT.
THAT WAS THE PLAN, ANYWAY.

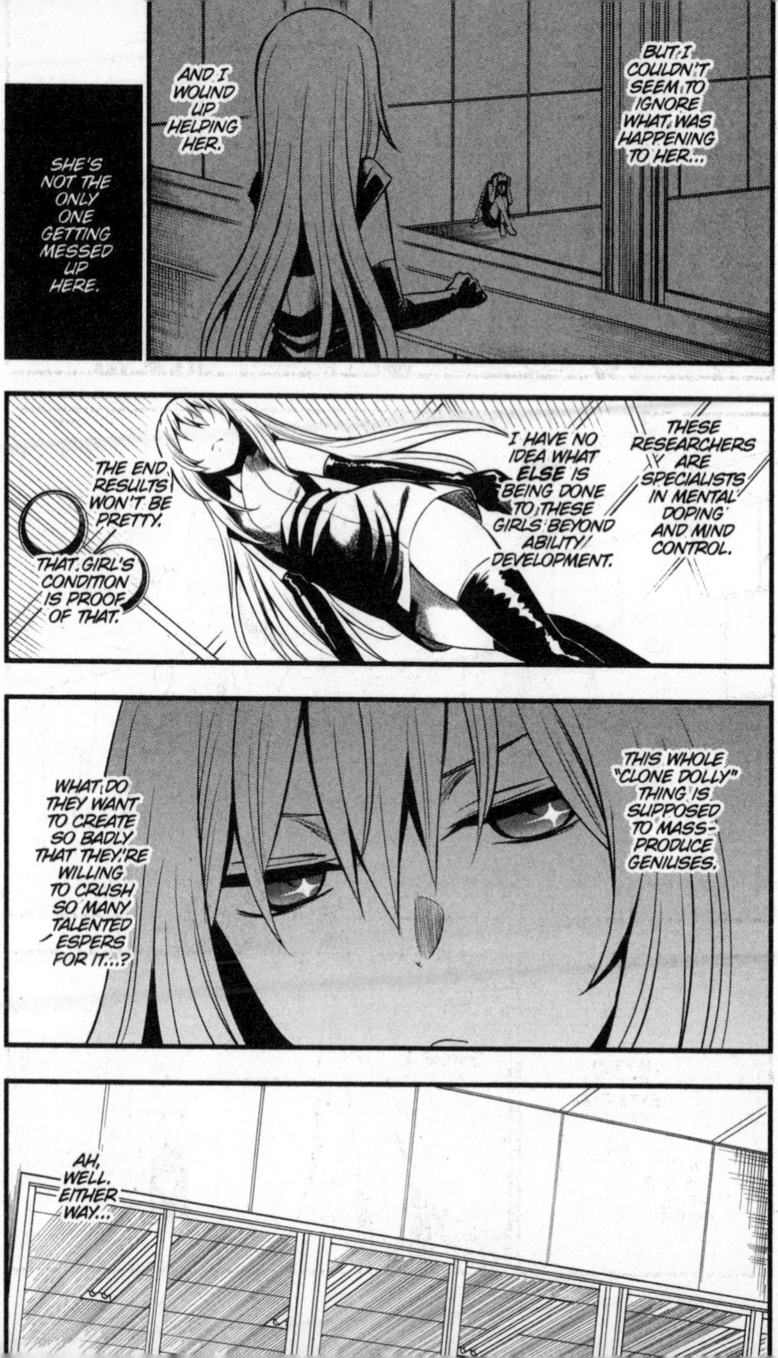
BUT I COULDN'T SEEM TO IGNORE WHAT WAS HAPPENING TO HER...
AND I WOUND UP HELPING HER.
SHE'S NOT THE ONLY ONE GETTING MESSED UP HERE.
THESE RESEARCHERS ARE SPECIALISTS IN MENTAL DOPING AND MIND CONTROL.
I HAVE NO IDEA WHAT ELSE IS BEING DONE TO THESE GIRLS BEYOND ABILITY DEVELOPMENT.
THE END RESULTS WON'T BE PRETTY.
THAT GIRL'S CONDITION IS PROOF OF THAT.
THIS WHOLE "CLONE DOLLY" THING IS SUPPOSED TO MASS-PRODUCE GENIUSES.
WHAT DO THEY WANT TO CREATE SO BADLY THAT THEY'RE WILLING TO CRUSH SO MANY TALENTED ESPERS FOR IT...?
AH, WELL. EITHER WAY...

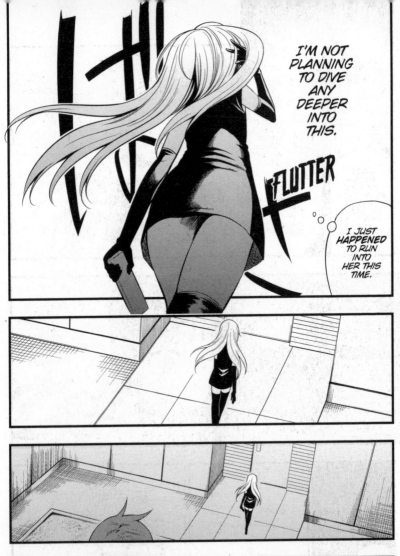

I'M NOT PLANNING TO DIVE ANY DEEPER INTO THIS.

FLUTTER

I JUST HAPPENED TO RUN INTO HER THIS TIME.

WHOA!

SO MUCH HAP-PENED, HUH...?

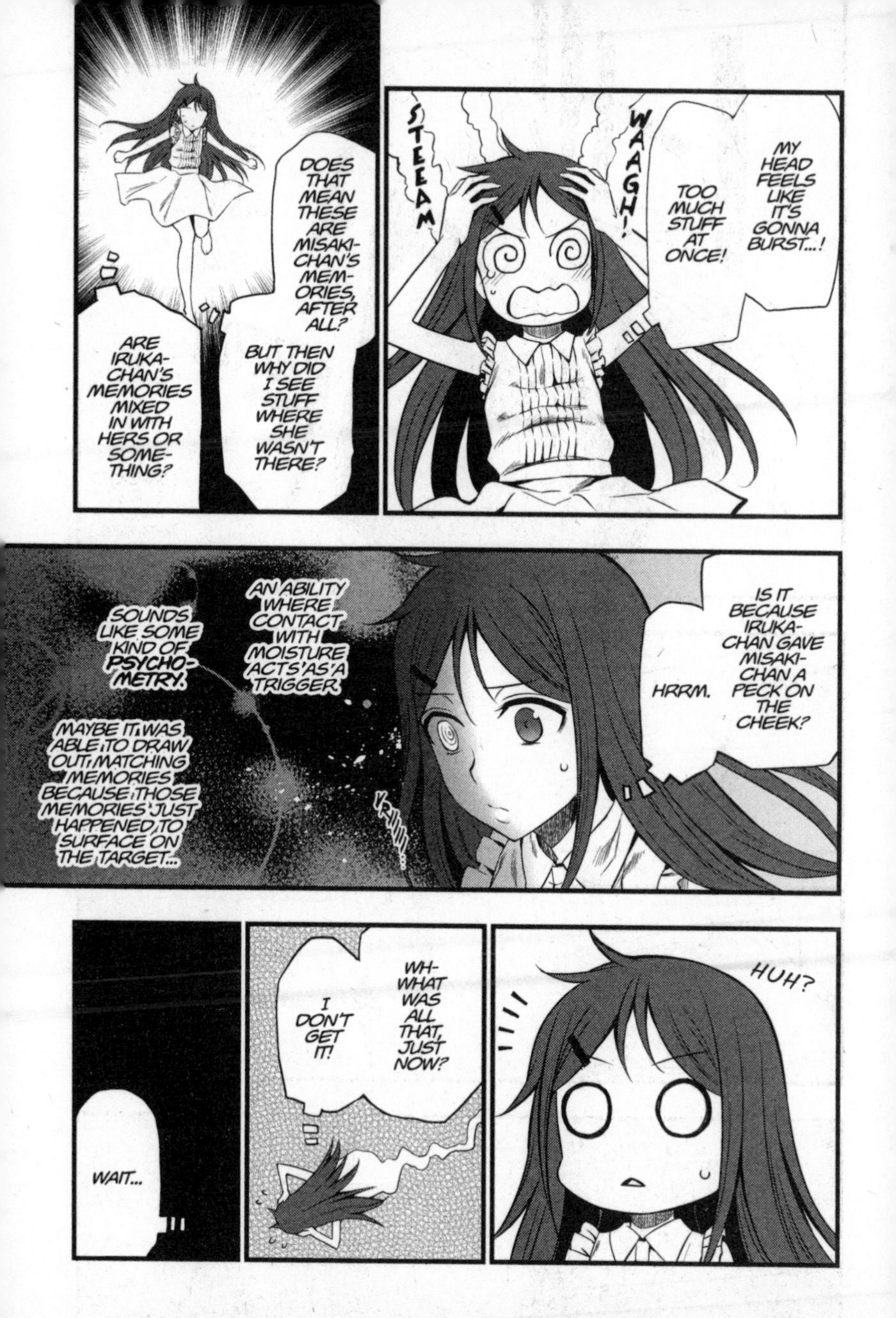
MY HEAD FEELS LIKE IT'S GONNA BURST...!
TOO MUCH STUFF AT ONCE!
WAAGH!
STEEAM
DOES THAT MEAN THESE ARE MISAKI-CHAN'S MEMORIES, AFTER ALL?
BUT THEN WHY DID I SEE STUFF WHERE SHE WASN'T THERE?
ARE IRUKA-CHAN'S MEMORIES MIXED IN WITH HERS OR SOMETHING?
IS IT BECAUSE IRUKA-CHAN GAVE MISAKI-CHAN A PECK ON THE CHEEK?
HRRM.
AN ABILITY WHERE CONTACT WITH MOISTURE ACTS AS A TRIGGER.
SOUNDS LIKE SOME KIND OF PSYCHOMETRY.
MAYBE IT WAS ABLE TO DRAW OUT MATCHING MEMORIES BECAUSE THOSE MEMORIES JUST HAPPENED TO SURFACE ON THE TARGET...
HUH?
WH-WHAT WAS ALL THAT, JUST NOW?
I DON'T GET IT!
WAIT...

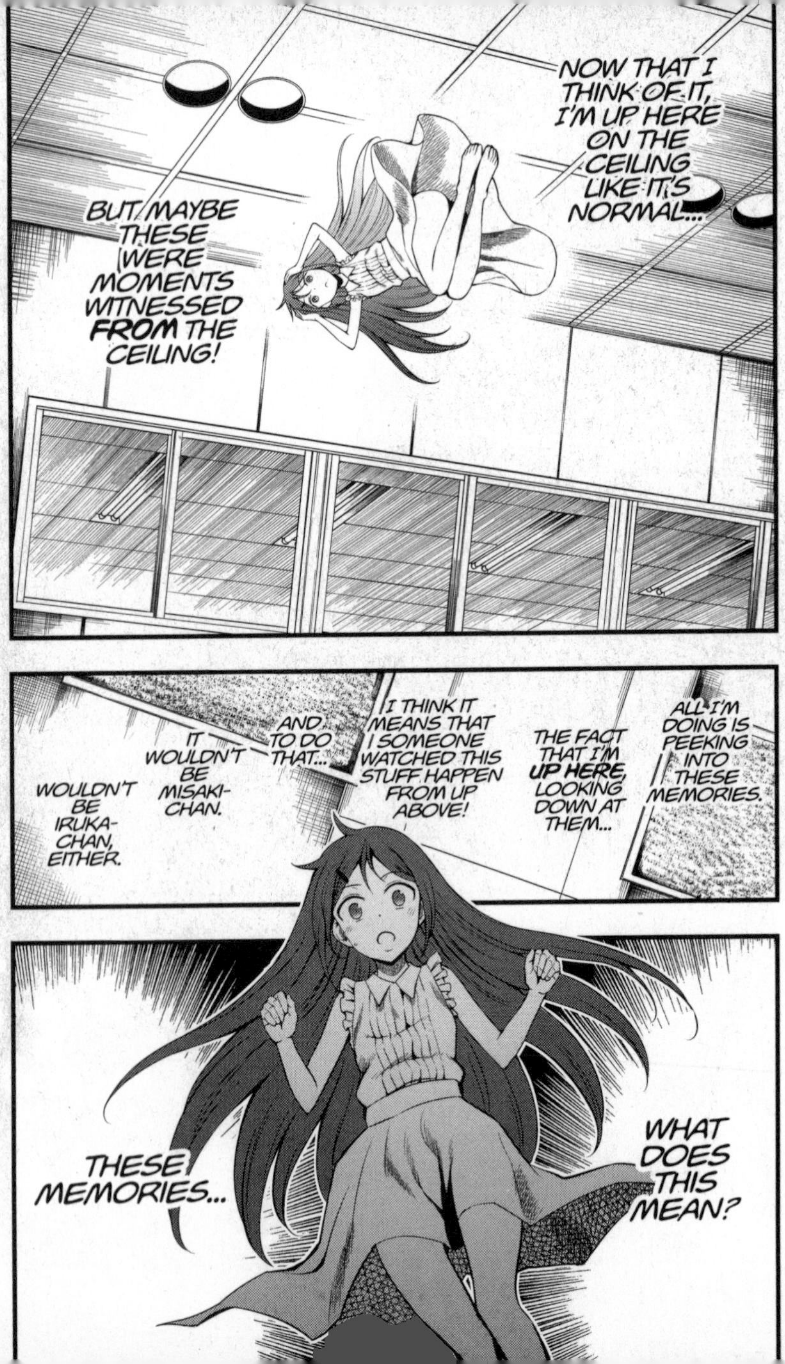
NOW THAT I THINK OF IT, I'M UP HERE ON THE CEILING LIKE IT'S NORMAL...
BUT MAYBE THESE WERE MOMENTS WITNESSED **FROM** THE CEILING!
ALL I'M DOING IS PEEKING INTO THESE MEMORIES.
THE FACT THAT I'M **UP HERE,** LOOKING DOWN AT THEM...
I THINK IT MEANS THAT SOMEONE WATCHED THIS STUFF HAPPEN FROM UP ABOVE!
AND TO DO THAT...
IT WOULDN'T BE MISAKI-CHAN.
WOULDN'T BE IRUKA-CHAN, EITHER.
WHAT DOES THIS MEAN?
THESE MEMORIES...

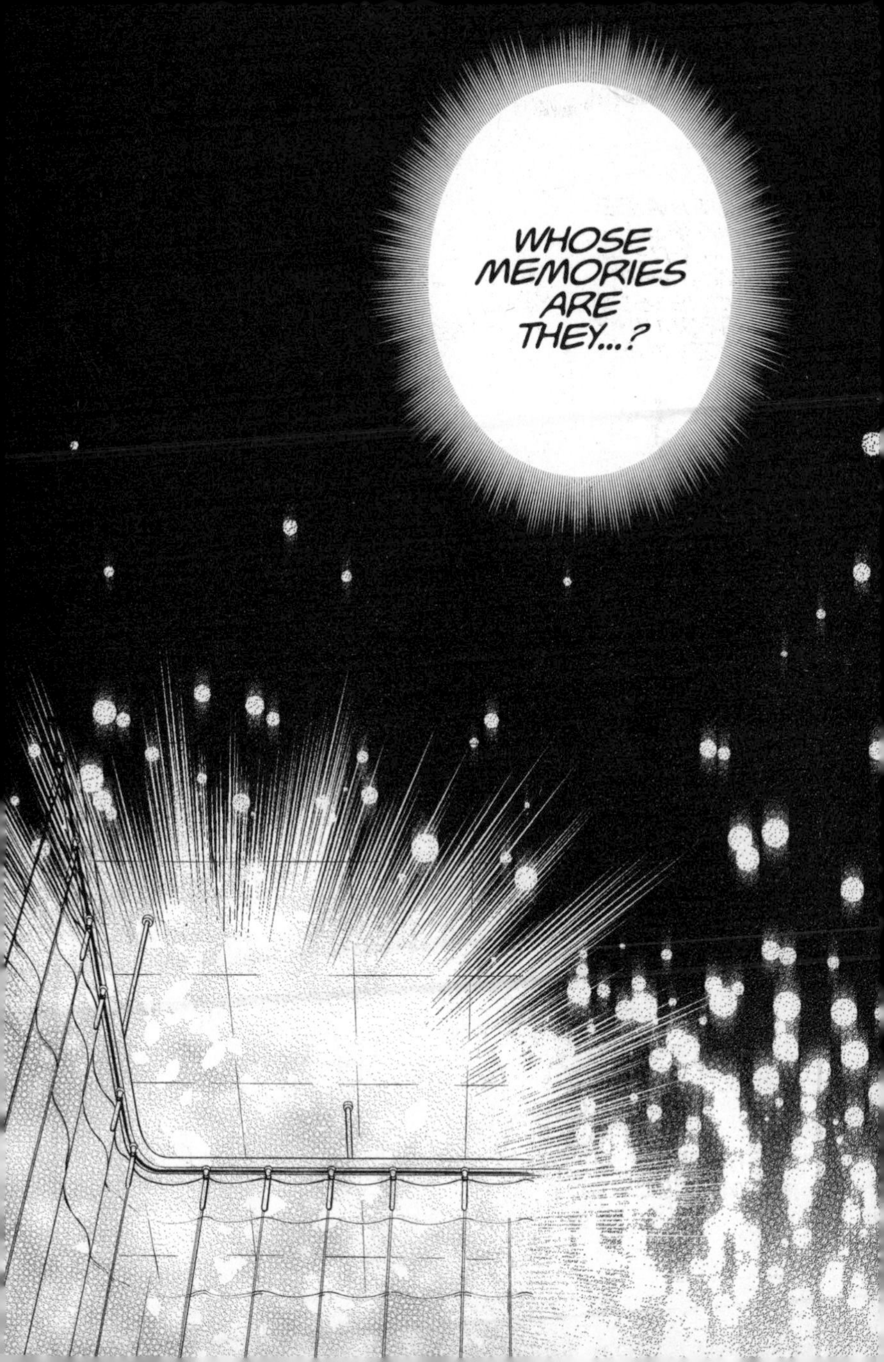
WHOSE MEMORIES ARE THEY...?

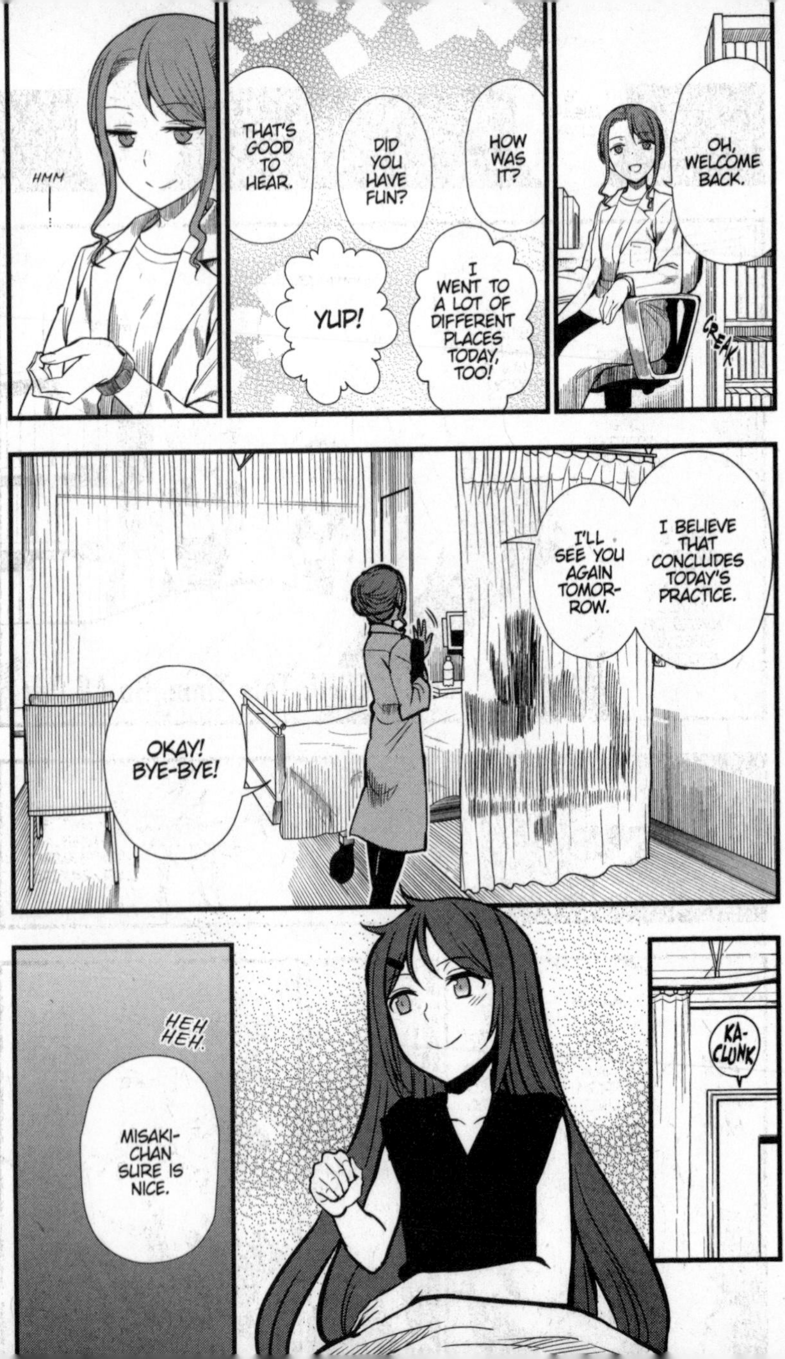
OH, WELCOME BACK.
CREAK
HOW WAS IT?
I WENT TO A LOT OF DIFFERENT PLACES TODAY, TOO!
DID YOU HAVE FUN?
YUP!
THAT'S GOOD TO HEAR.
HMM ...
I BELIEVE THAT CONCLUDES TODAY'S PRACTICE.
I'LL SEE YOU AGAIN TOMOR-ROW.
OKAY! BYE-BYE!
KA-CLUNK
HEH HEH.
MISAKI-CHAN SURE IS NICE.

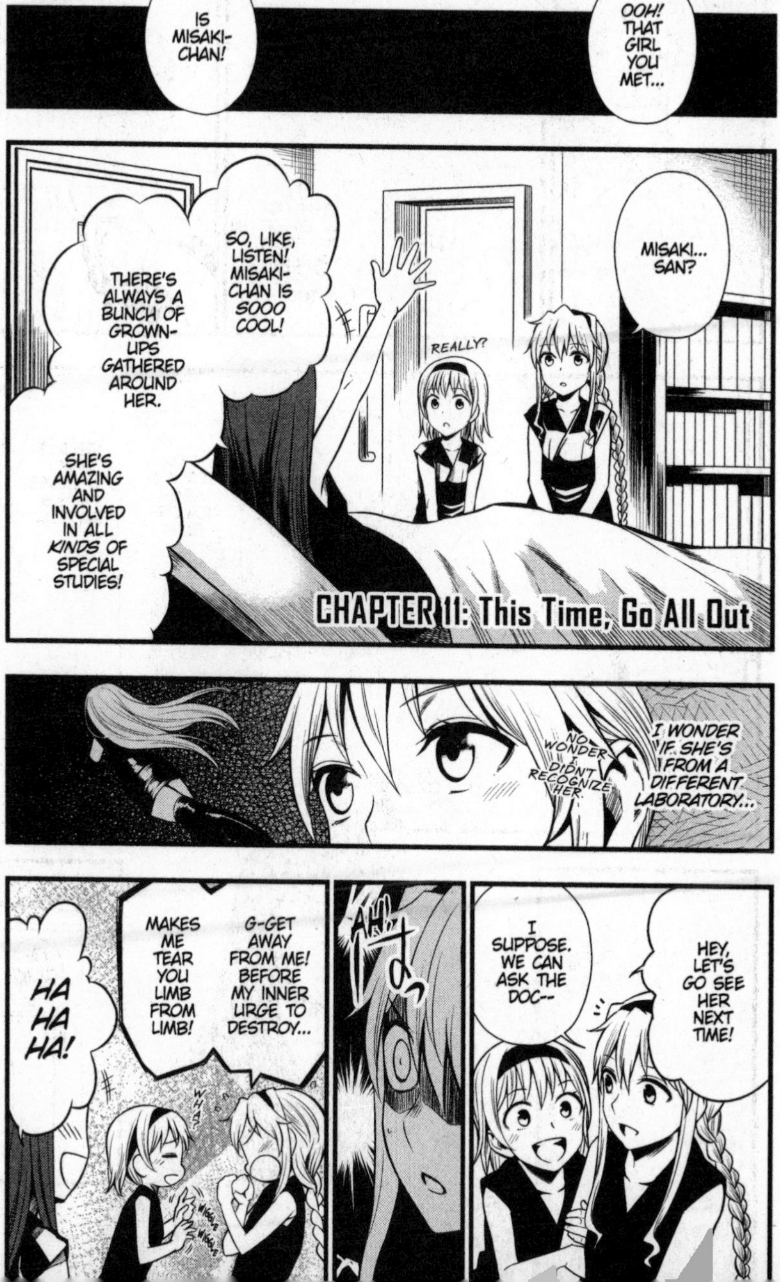
OOH! THAT GIRL YOU MET...
IS MISAKI-CHAN!
MISAKI... SAN?
REALLY?
SO, LIKE, LISTEN! MISAKI-CHAN IS SOOO COOL!
THERE'S ALWAYS A BUNCH OF GROWN-UPS GATHERED AROUND HER.
SHE'S AMAZING AND INVOLVED IN ALL KINDS OF SPECIAL STUDIES!
CHAPTER 11: This Time, Go All Out
I WONDER IF SHE'S FROM A DIFFERENT LABORATORY...
NO WONDER I DIDN'T RECOGNIZE HER.
HEY, LET'S GO SEE HER NEXT TIME!
I SUPPOSE. WE CAN ASK THE DOC--
AH!
G-GET AWAY FROM ME! BEFORE MY INNER URGE TO DESTROY...
MAKES ME TEAR YOU LIMB FROM LIMB!
WHA?
HA HA HA!
WIGGLE WIGGLE

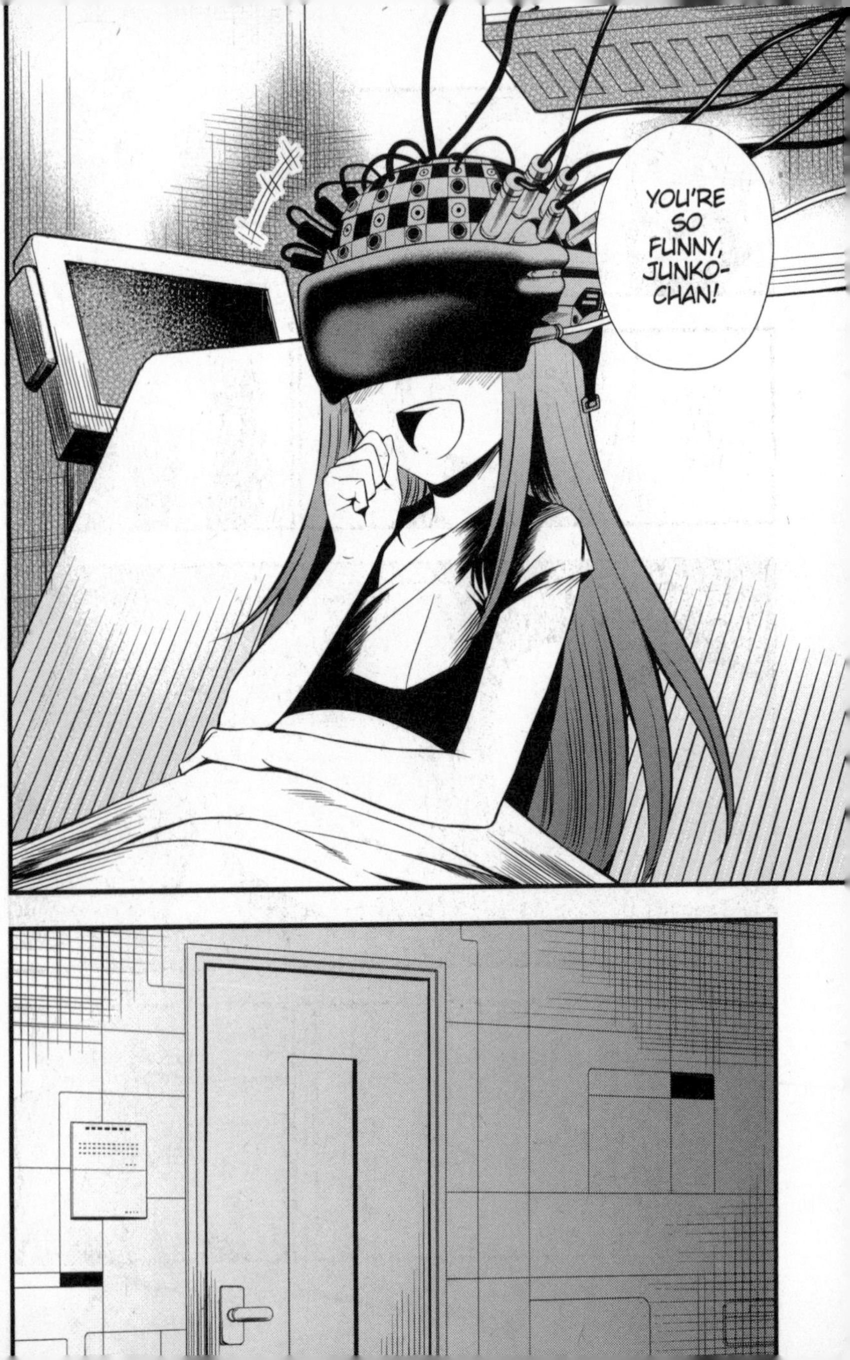
YOU'RE SO FUNNY, JUNKO-CHAN!

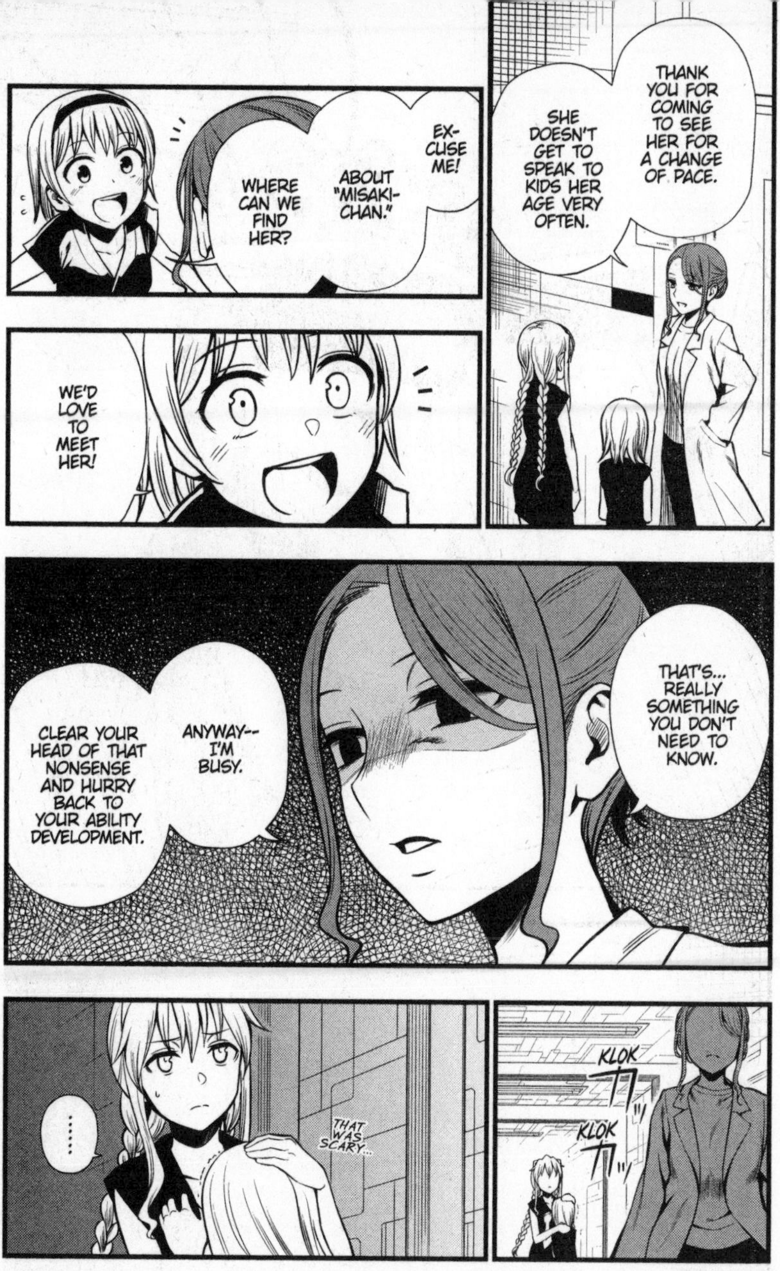
THANK YOU FOR COMING TO SEE HER FOR A CHANGE OF PACE.
SHE DOESN'T GET TO SPEAK TO KIDS HER AGE VERY OFTEN.
EX-CUSE ME!
ABOUT "MISAKI-CHAN."
WHERE CAN WE FIND HER?
WE'D LOVE TO MEET HER!
THAT'S... REALLY SOMETHING YOU DON'T NEED TO KNOW.
ANYWAY-- I'M BUSY.
CLEAR YOUR HEAD OF THAT NONSENSE AND HURRY BACK TO YOUR ABILITY DEVELOPMENT.
KLOK
KLOK
THAT WAS SCARY...
......

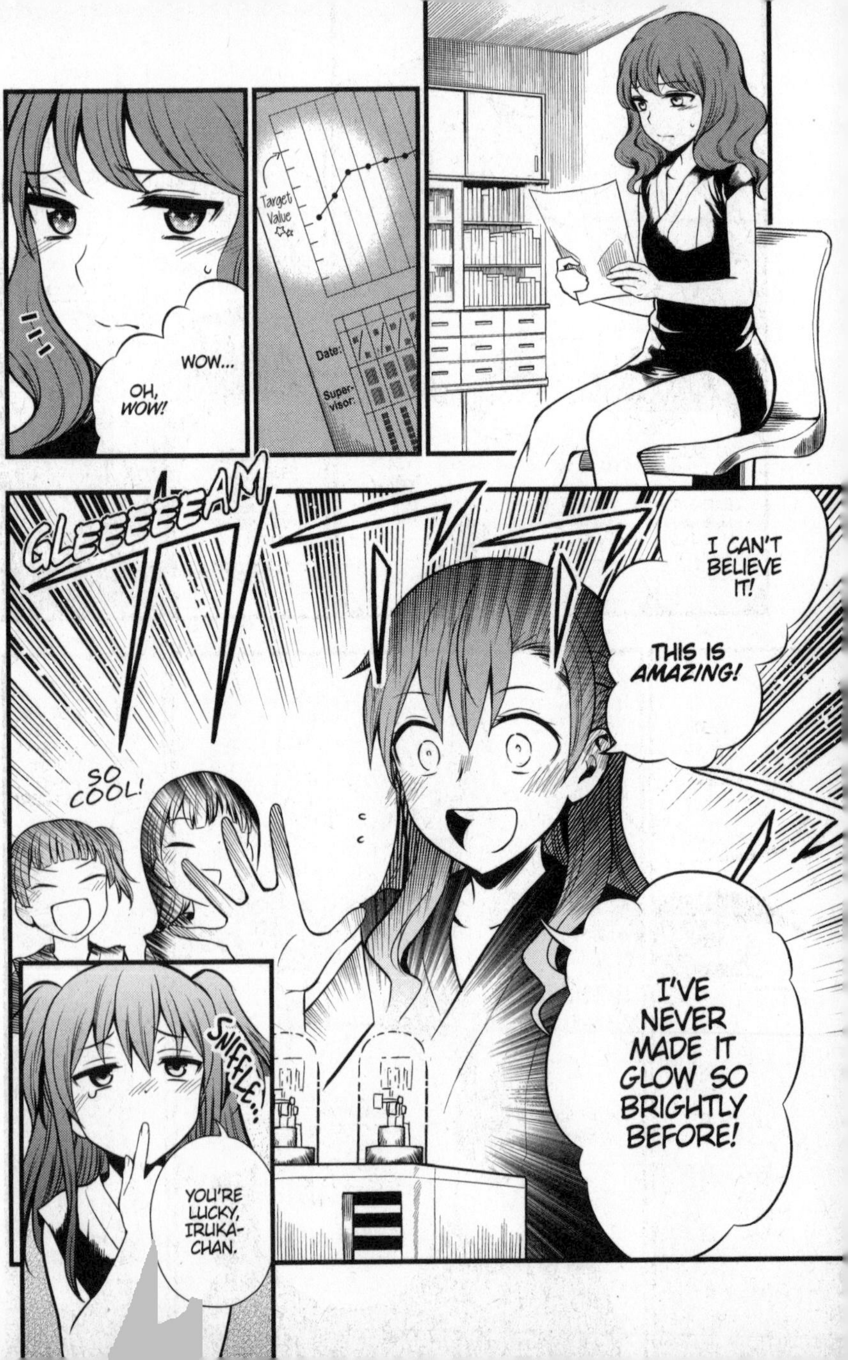
Target Value
Date:
Supervisor:
WOW...
OH, WOW!
GLEEEEEEAM
I CAN'T BELIEVE IT!
THIS IS AMAZING!
I'VE NEVER MADE IT GLOW SO BRIGHTLY BEFORE!
SO COOL!
SNIFFLE...
YOU'RE LUCKY, IRUKA-CHAN.

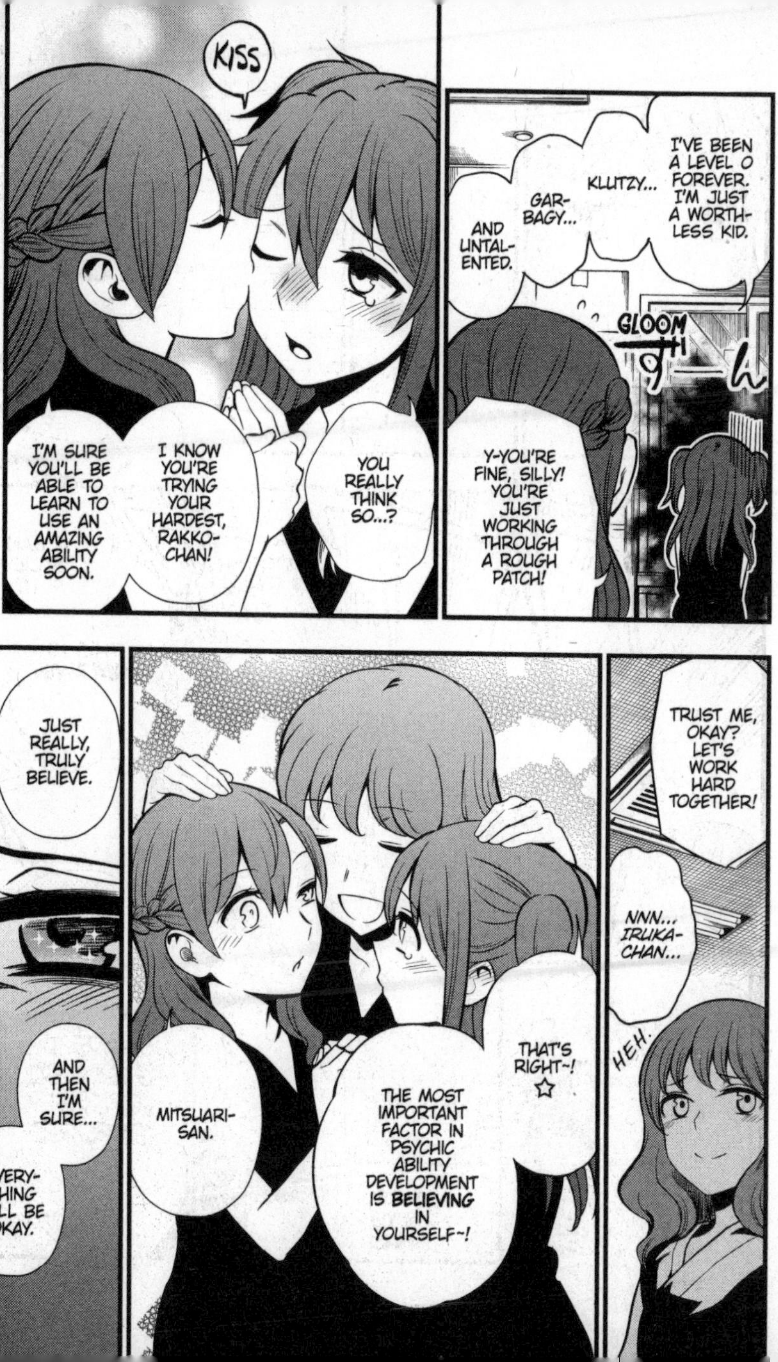
I'VE BEEN A LEVEL 0 FOREVER. I'M JUST A WORTHLESS KID.
KLUTZY...
GARBAGY...
AND UNTALENTED.
GLOOM
Y-YOU'RE FINE, SILLY! YOU'RE JUST WORKING THROUGH A ROUGH PATCH!
KISS
YOU REALLY THINK SO...?
I KNOW YOU'RE TRYING YOUR HARDEST, RAKKO-CHAN!
I'M SURE YOU'LL BE ABLE TO LEARN TO USE AN AMAZING ABILITY SOON.
TRUST ME, OKAY? LET'S WORK HARD TOGETHER!
NNN... IRUKA-CHAN...
HEH.
THAT'S RIGHT~! ☆
THE MOST IMPORTANT FACTOR IN PSYCHIC ABILITY DEVELOPMENT IS BELIEVING IN YOURSELF~!
MITSUARI-SAN.
JUST REALLY, TRULY BELIEVE.
AND THEN I'M SURE...
EVERYTHING WILL BE OKAY.

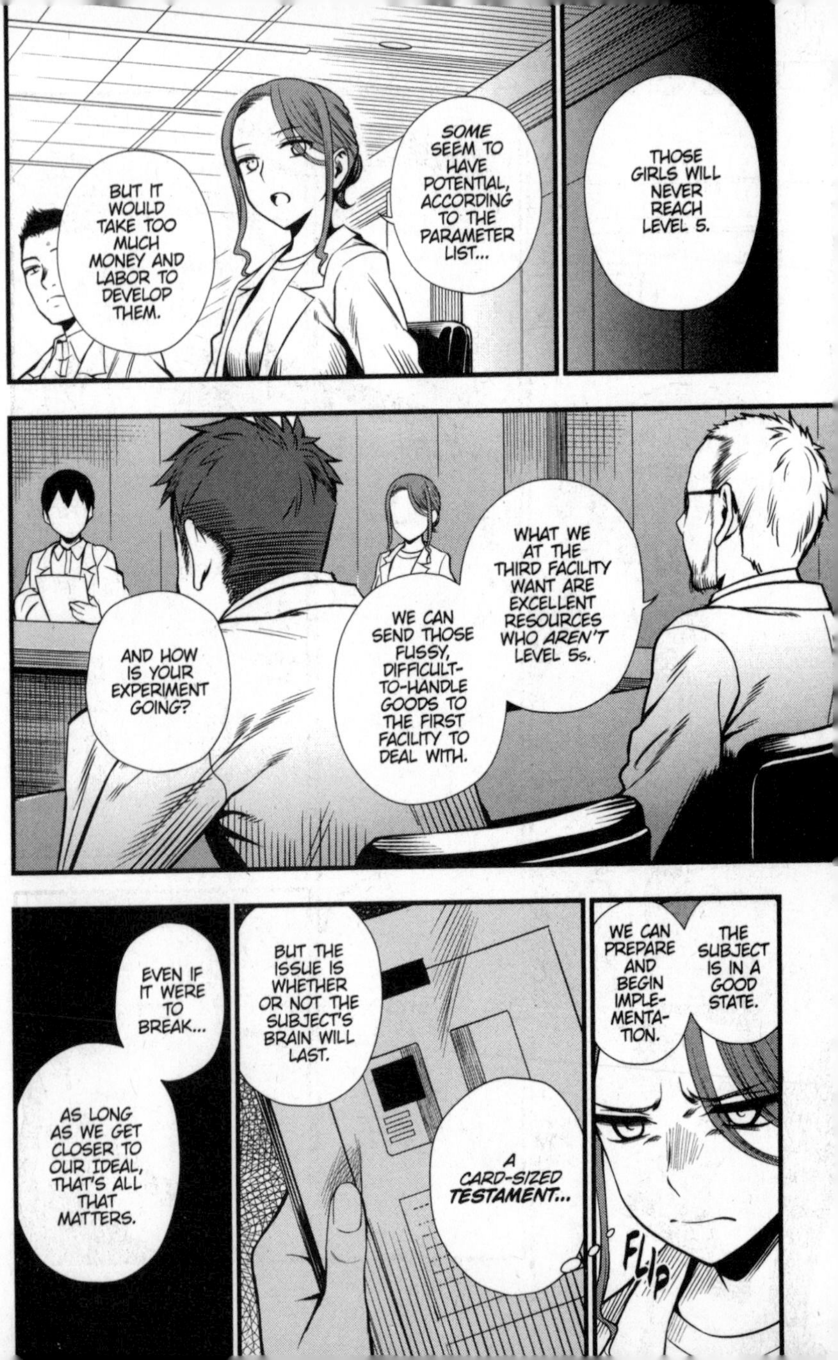
THOSE GIRLS WILL NEVER REACH LEVEL 5.
SOME SEEM TO HAVE POTENTIAL, ACCORDING TO THE PARAMETER LIST...
BUT IT WOULD TAKE TOO MUCH MONEY AND LABOR TO DEVELOP THEM.
WHAT WE AT THE THIRD FACILITY WANT ARE EXCELLENT RESOURCES WHO *AREN'T* LEVEL 5s.
WE CAN SEND THOSE FUSSY, DIFFICULT-TO-HANDLE GOODS TO THE FIRST FACILITY TO DEAL WITH.
AND HOW IS YOUR EXPERIMENT GOING?
THE SUBJECT IS IN A GOOD STATE.
WE CAN PREPARE AND BEGIN IMPLEMENTATION.
BUT THE ISSUE IS WHETHER OR NOT THE SUBJECT'S BRAIN WILL LAST.
A CARD-SIZED **TESTAMENT**...
FLIP
EVEN IF IT WERE TO BREAK...
AS LONG AS WE GET CLOSER TO OUR IDEAL, THAT'S ALL THAT MATTERS.

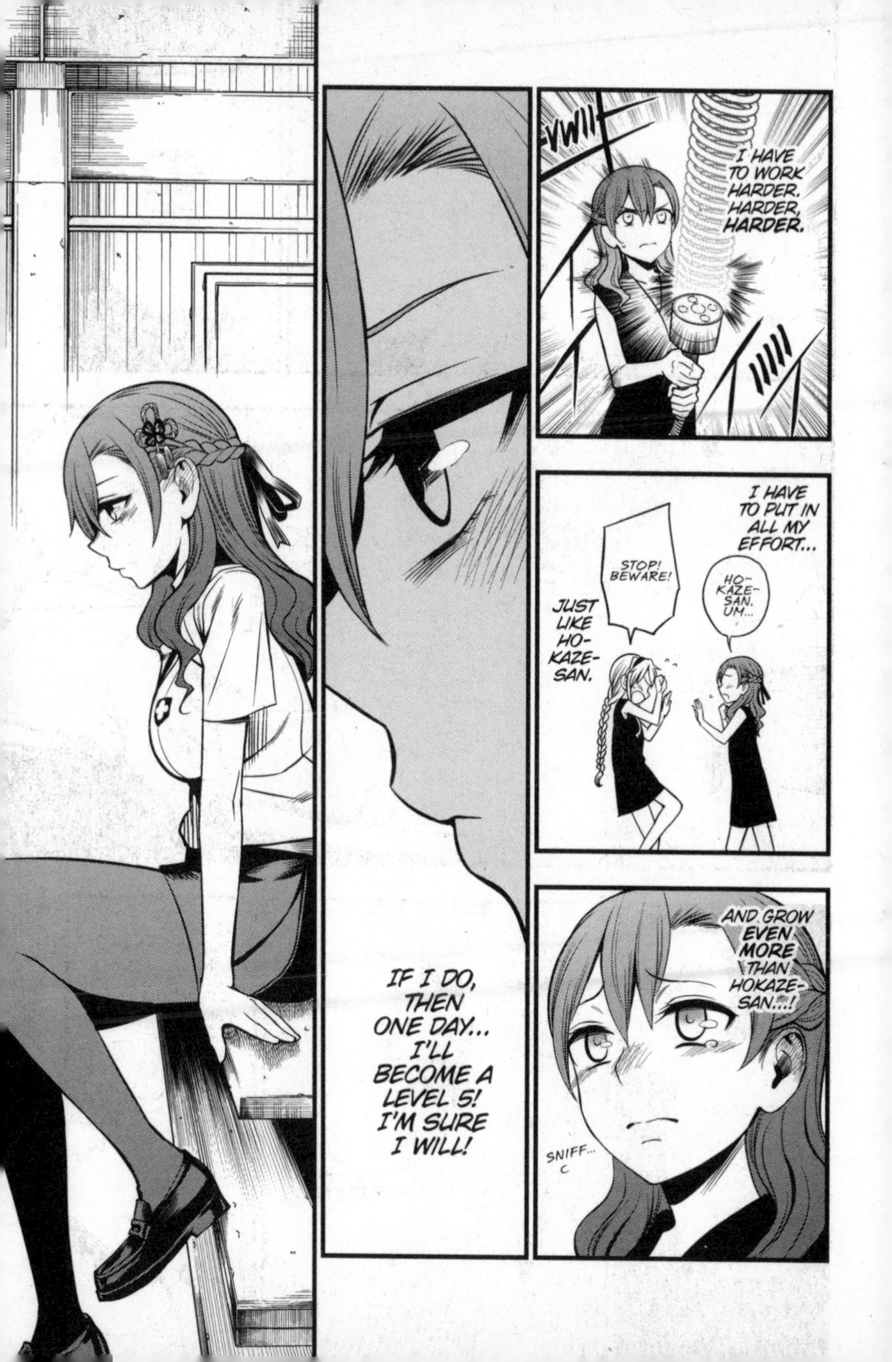
I HAVE TO WORK HARDER. HARDER, HARDER.
I HAVE TO PUT IN ALL MY EFFORT...
HO-KAZE-SAN. UM...
STOP! BEWARE!
JUST LIKE HO-KAZE-SAN.
AND GROW EVEN MORE THAN HOKAZE-SAN...!
SNIFF...
IF I DO, THEN ONE DAY... I'LL BECOME A LEVEL 5! I'M SURE I WILL!

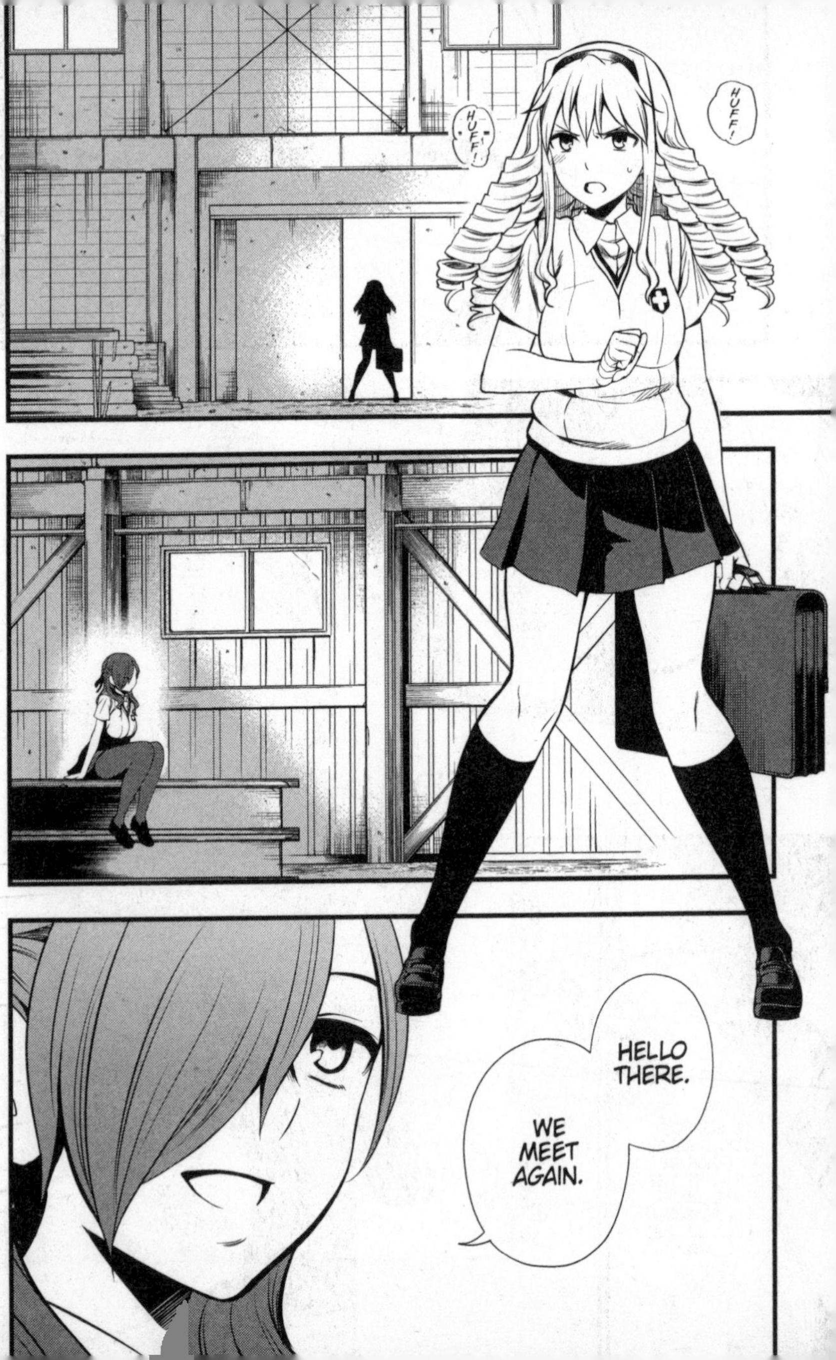
HUFF!
HUFF!
HELLO THERE.
WE MEET AGAIN.

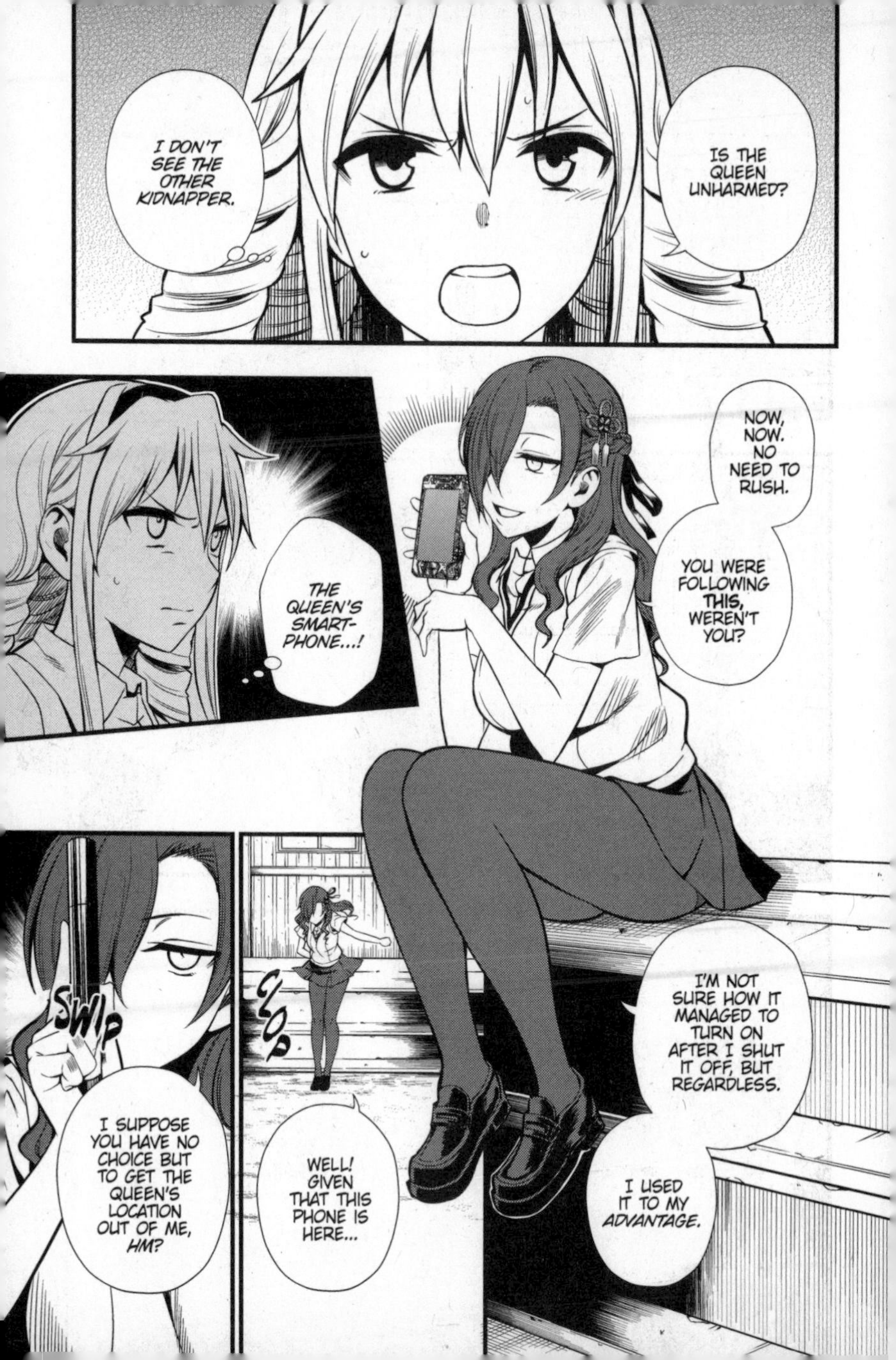
IS THE QUEEN UNHARMED?
I DON'T SEE THE OTHER KIDNAPPER.
NOW, NOW. NO NEED TO RUSH.
YOU WERE FOLLOWING THIS, WEREN'T YOU?
I'M NOT SURE HOW IT MANAGED TO TURN ON AFTER I SHUT IT OFF, BUT REGARDLESS.
I USED IT TO MY ADVANTAGE.
THE QUEEN'S SMART-PHONE...!
CLOP
WELL! GIVEN THAT THIS PHONE IS HERE...
SWIP
I SUPPOSE YOU HAVE NO CHOICE BUT TO GET THE QUEEN'S LOCATION OUT OF ME, HM?

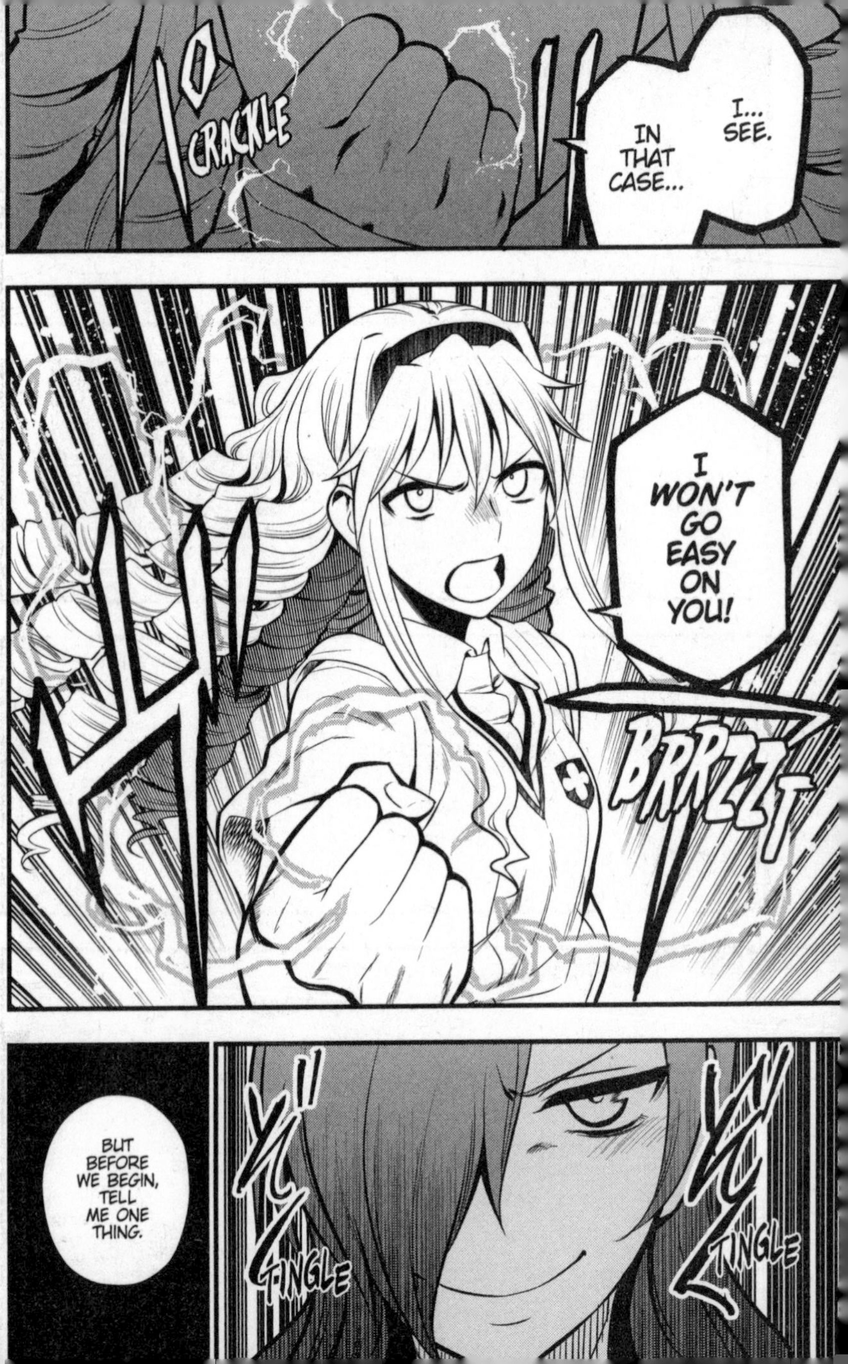
I... SEE.
IN THAT CASE...
CRACKLE
I WON'T GO EASY ON YOU!
BRRZZT
TINGLE
TINGLE
BUT BEFORE WE BEGIN, TELL ME ONE THING.

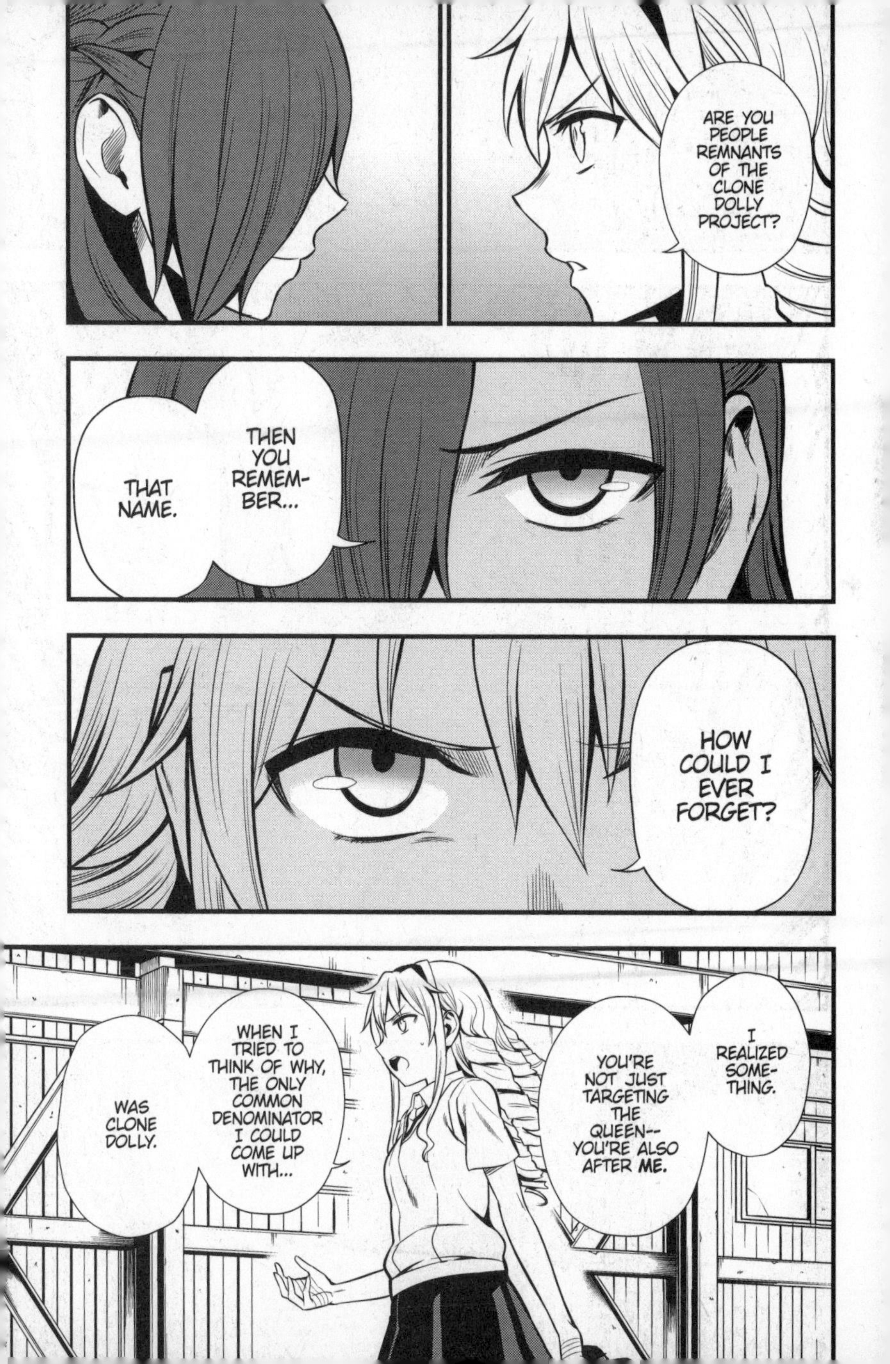
ARE YOU PEOPLE REMNANTS OF THE CLONE DOLLY PROJECT?
THEN YOU REMEMBER...
THAT NAME.
HOW COULD I EVER FORGET?
I REALIZED SOMETHING.
YOU'RE NOT JUST TARGETING THE QUEEN-- YOU'RE ALSO AFTER ME.
WHEN I TRIED TO THINK OF WHY, THE ONLY COMMON DENOMINATOR I COULD COME UP WITH...
WAS CLONE DOLLY.

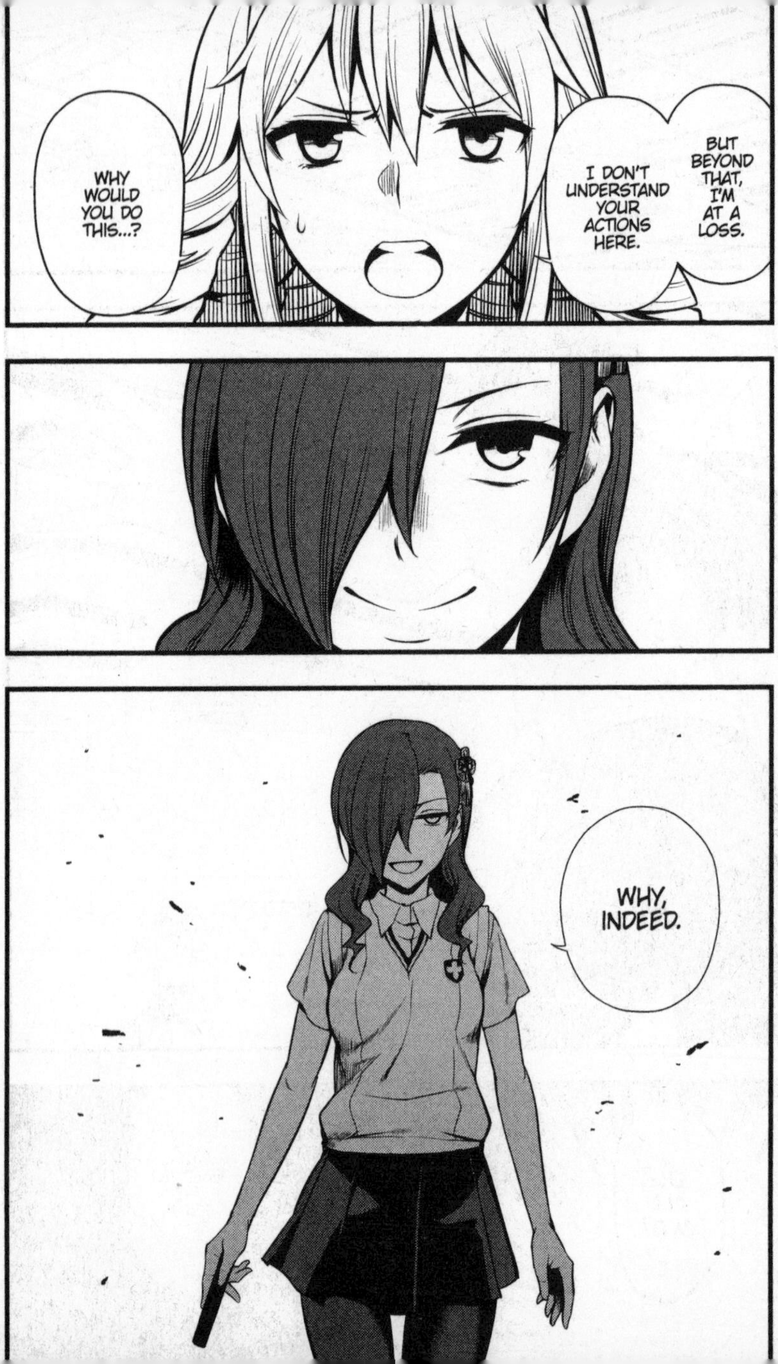
I DON'T UNDERSTAND YOUR ACTIONS HERE.
BUT BEYOND THAT, I'M AT A LOSS.
WHY WOULD YOU DO THIS...?
WHY, INDEED.

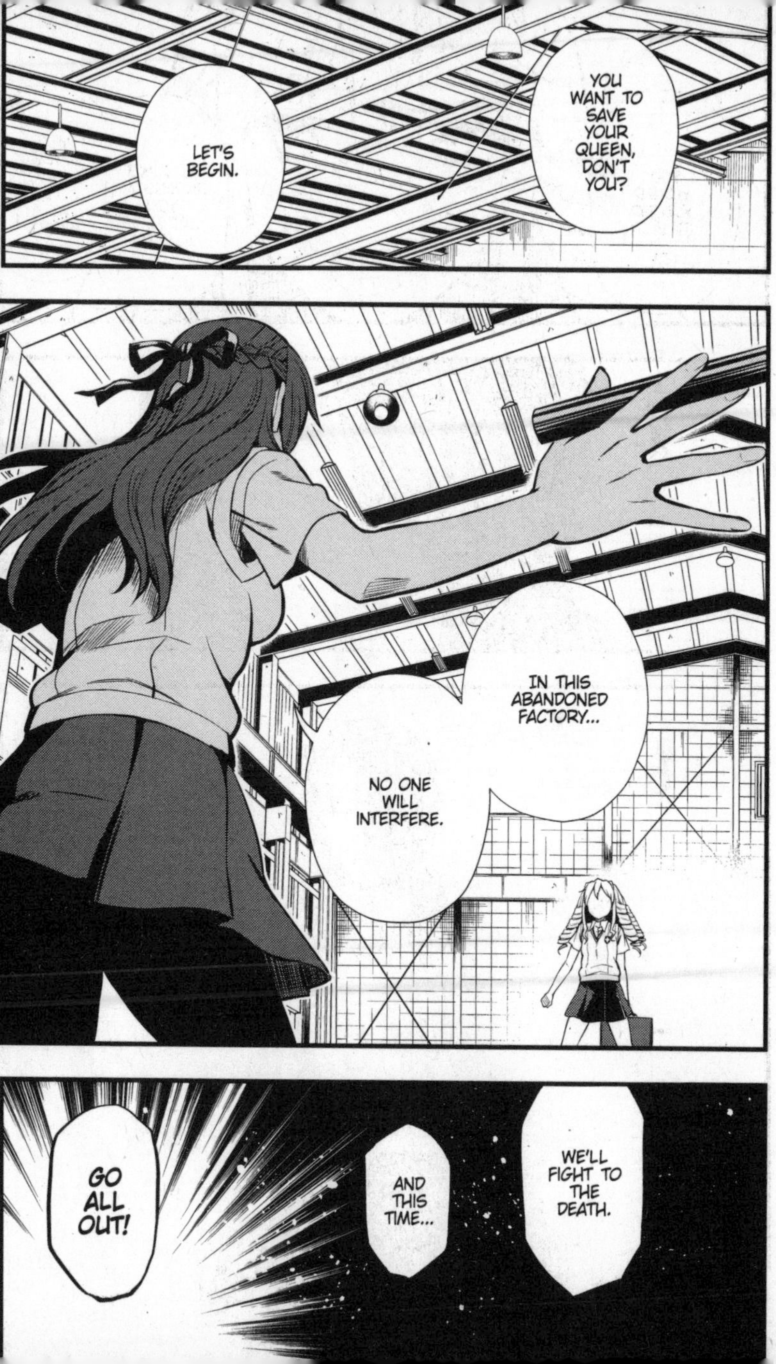
YOU WANT TO SAVE YOUR QUEEN, DON'T YOU?
LET'S BEGIN.
IN THIS ABANDONED FACTORY...
NO ONE WILL INTERFERE.
WE'LL FIGHT TO THE DEATH.
AND THIS TIME...
GO ALL OUT!

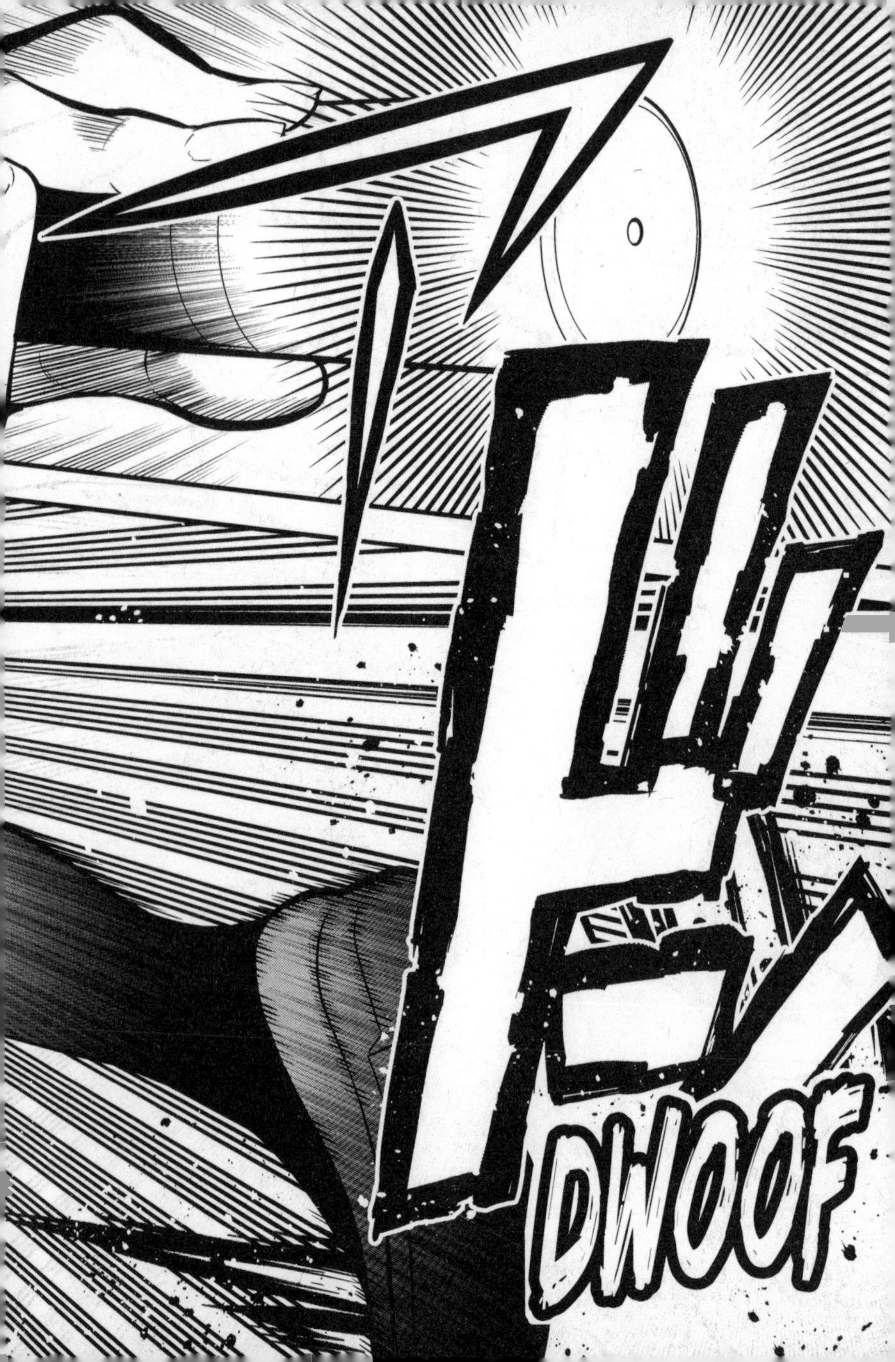
DWOOF

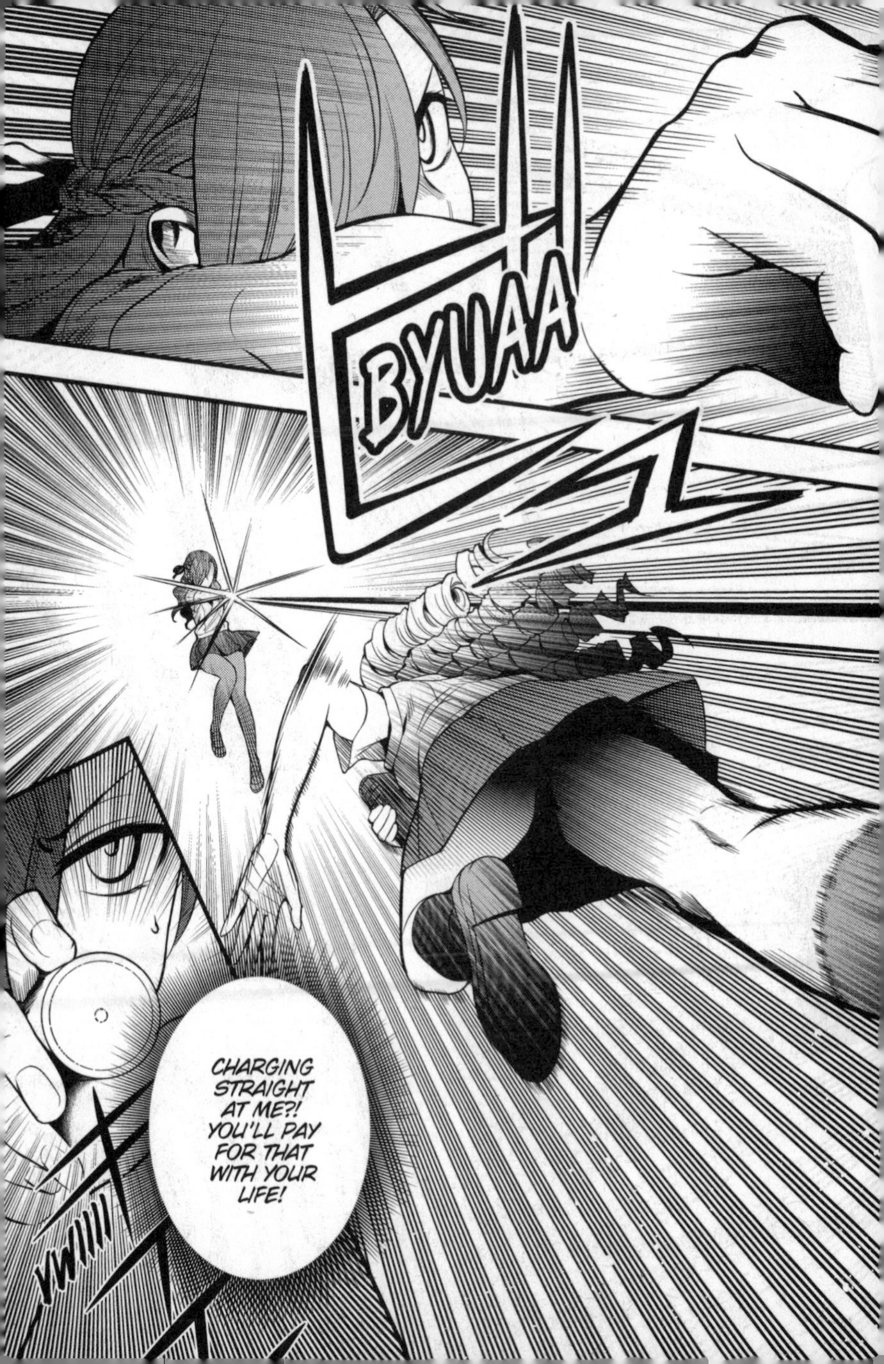
BYUAA
CHARGING STRAIGHT AT ME?! YOU'LL PAY FOR THAT WITH YOUR LIFE!
VWIIII

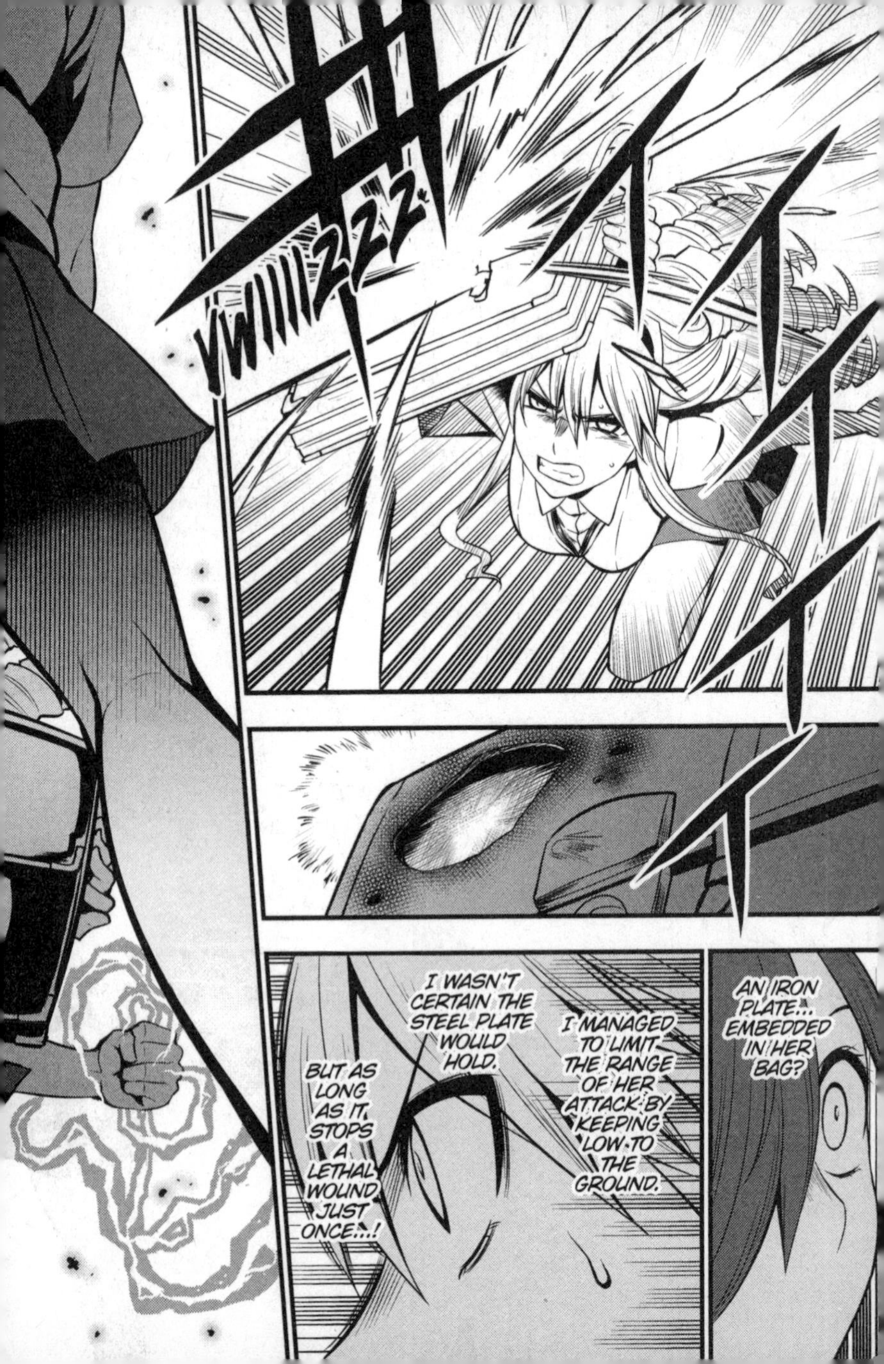
VWIIIIZZZ
AN IRON PLATE... EMBEDDED IN HER BAG?
I MANAGED TO LIMIT THE RANGE OF HER ATTACK BY KEEPING LOW TO THE GROUND.
I WASN'T CERTAIN THE STEEL PLATE WOULD HOLD.
BUT AS LONG AS IT STOPS A LETHAL WOUND JUST ONCE...!

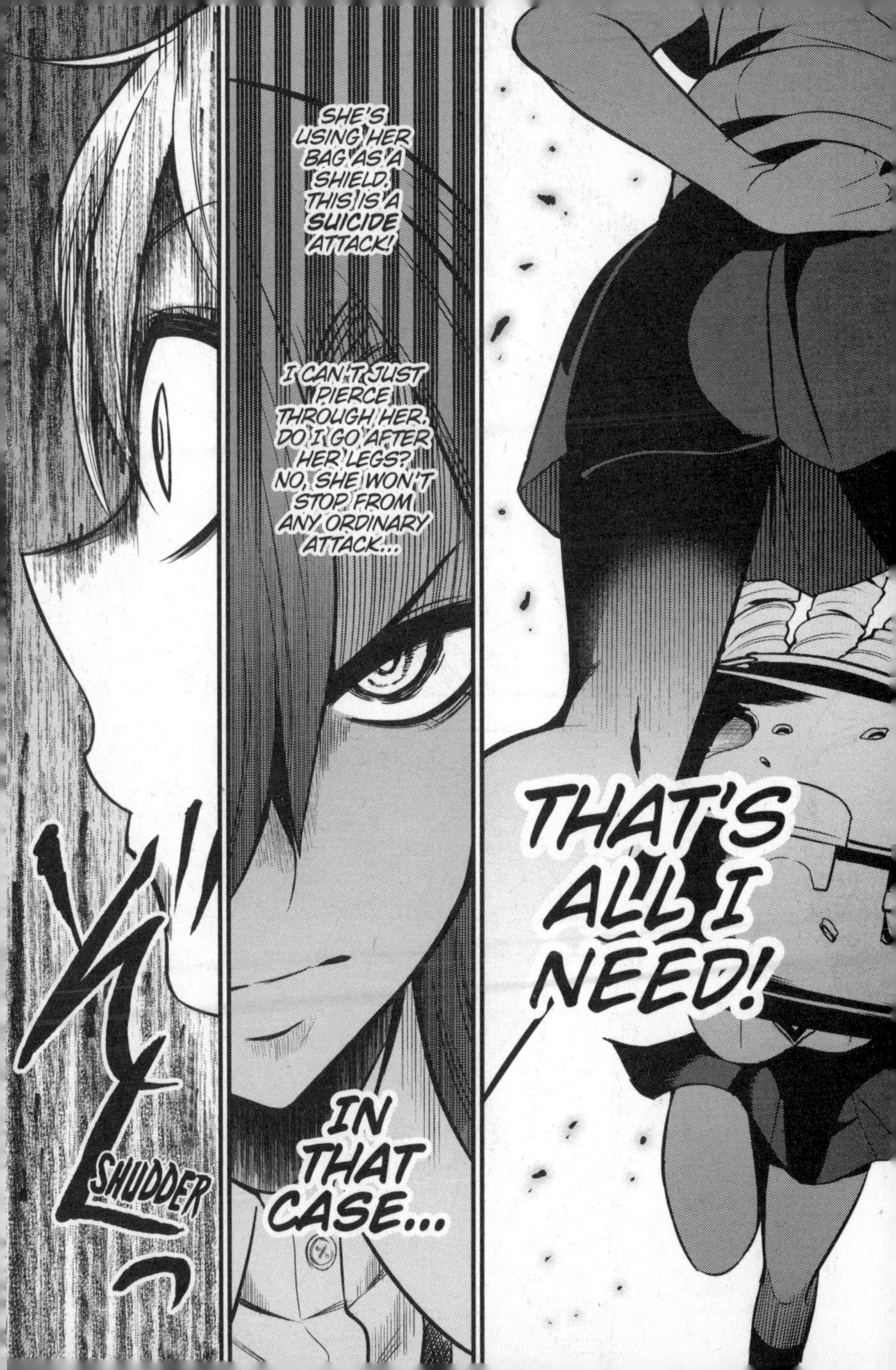
THAT'S ALL I NEED!
SHE'S USING HER BAG AS A SHIELD. THIS IS A SUICIDE ATTACK!
I CAN'T JUST PIERCE THROUGH HER. DO I GO AFTER HER LEGS? NO, SHE WON'T STOP FROM ANY ORDINARY ATTACK...
IN THAT CASE...
SHUDDER

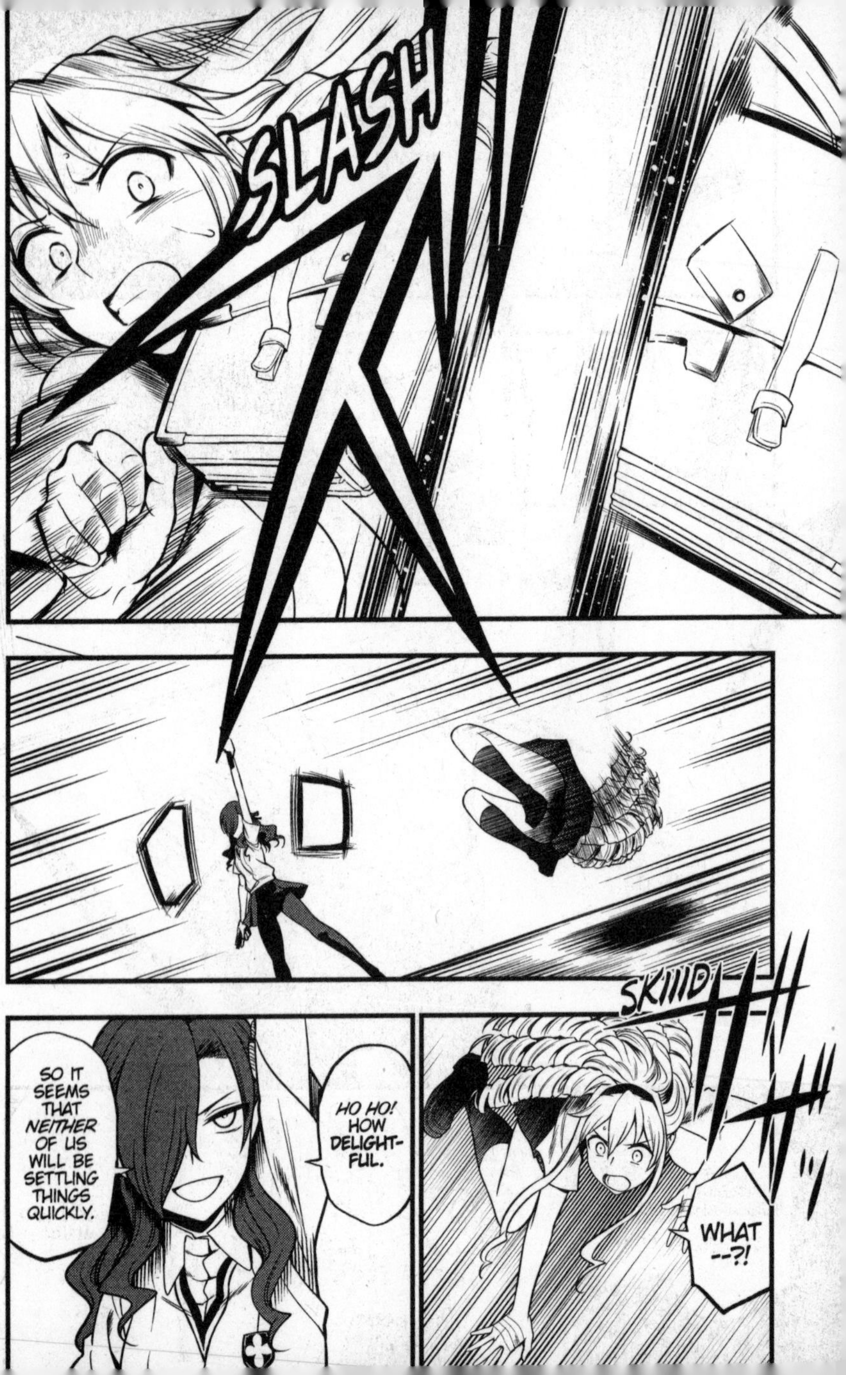
SLASH
SKIIID
WHAT--?!
HO HO! HOW DELIGHT-FUL.
SO IT SEEMS THAT *NEITHER* OF US WILL BE SETTLING THINGS QUICKLY.

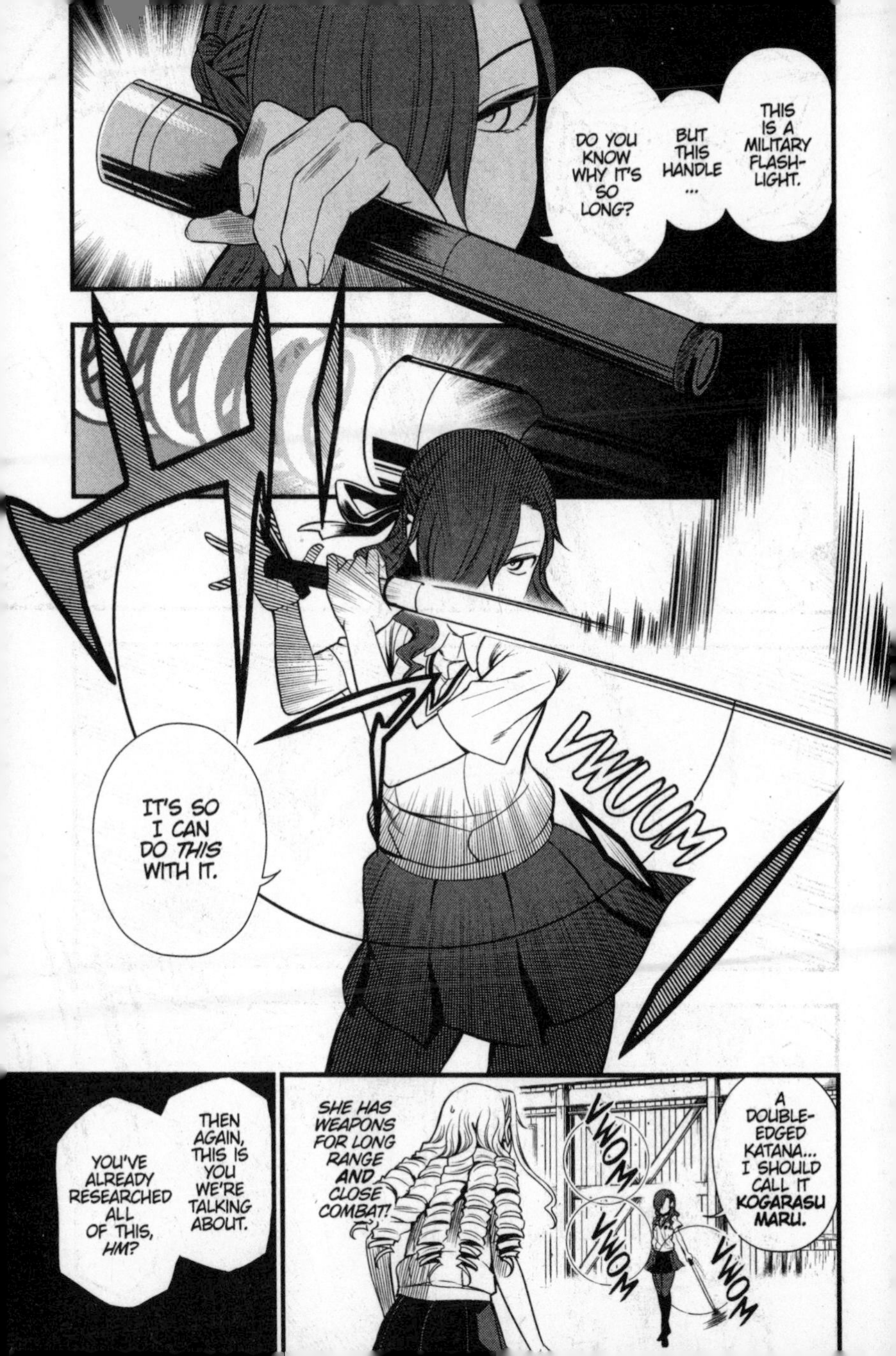
THIS IS A MILITARY FLASH-LIGHT.
BUT THIS HANDLE ...
DO YOU KNOW WHY IT'S SO LONG?
IT'S SO I CAN DO *THIS* WITH IT.
VWUUUM
A DOUBLE-EDGED KATANA... I SHOULD CALL IT **KOGARASU MARU.**
VWOM
VWOM
VWOM
SHE HAS WEAPONS FOR LONG RANGE **AND** CLOSE COMBAT!
THEN AGAIN, THIS IS YOU WE'RE TALKING ABOUT.
YOU'VE ALREADY RESEARCHED ALL OF THIS, *HM?*

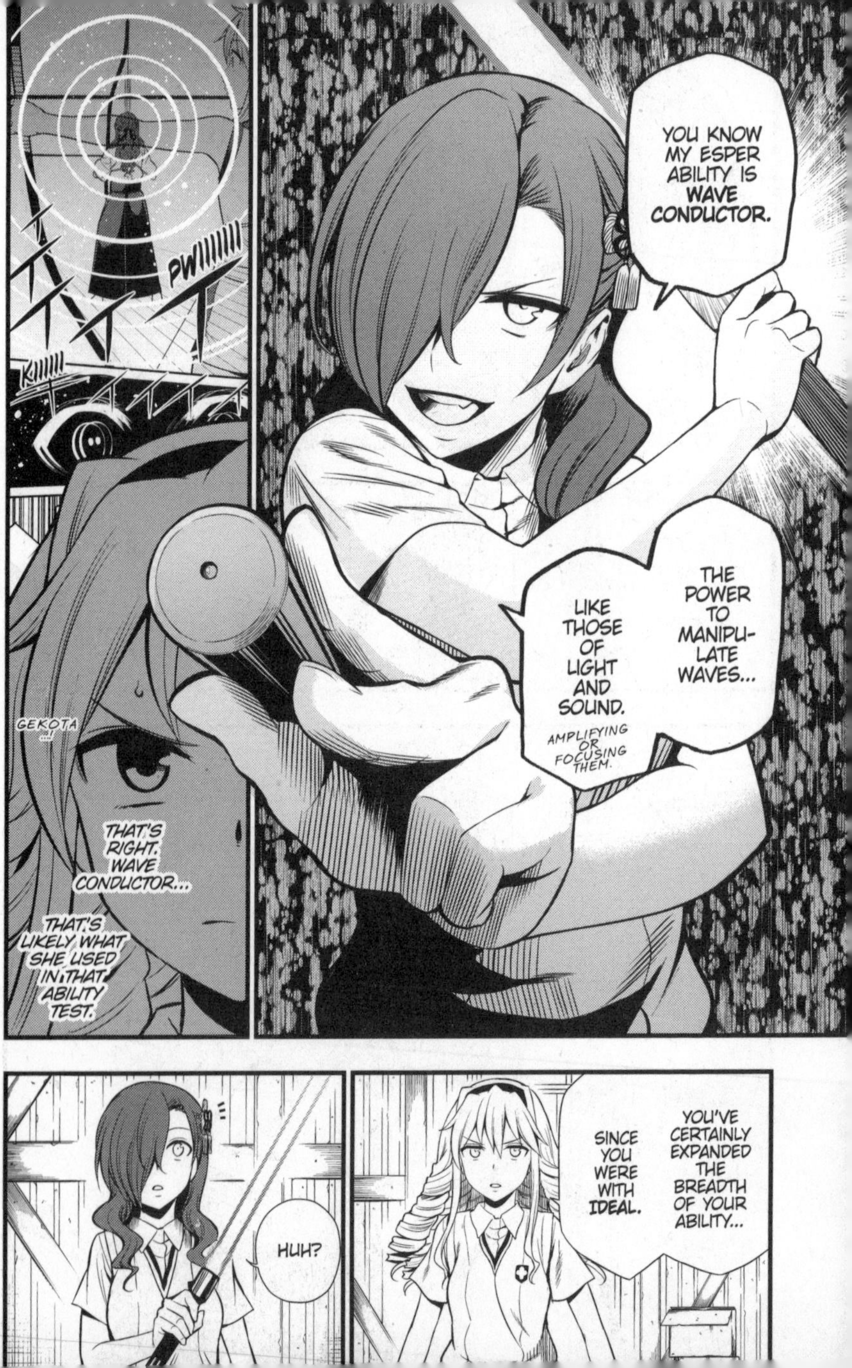
YOU KNOW MY ESPER ABILITY IS WAVE CONDUCTOR.
THE POWER TO MANIPULATE WAVES...
LIKE THOSE OF LIGHT AND SOUND.
AMPLIFYING OR FOCUSING THEM.
PWIIIIIII
KIIIII
GEKOTA ...!
THAT'S RIGHT. WAVE CONDUCTOR...
THAT'S LIKELY WHAT SHE USED IN THAT ABILITY TEST.
YOU'VE CERTAINLY EXPANDED THE BREADTH OF YOUR ABILITY...
SINCE YOU WERE WITH IDEAL.
HUH?

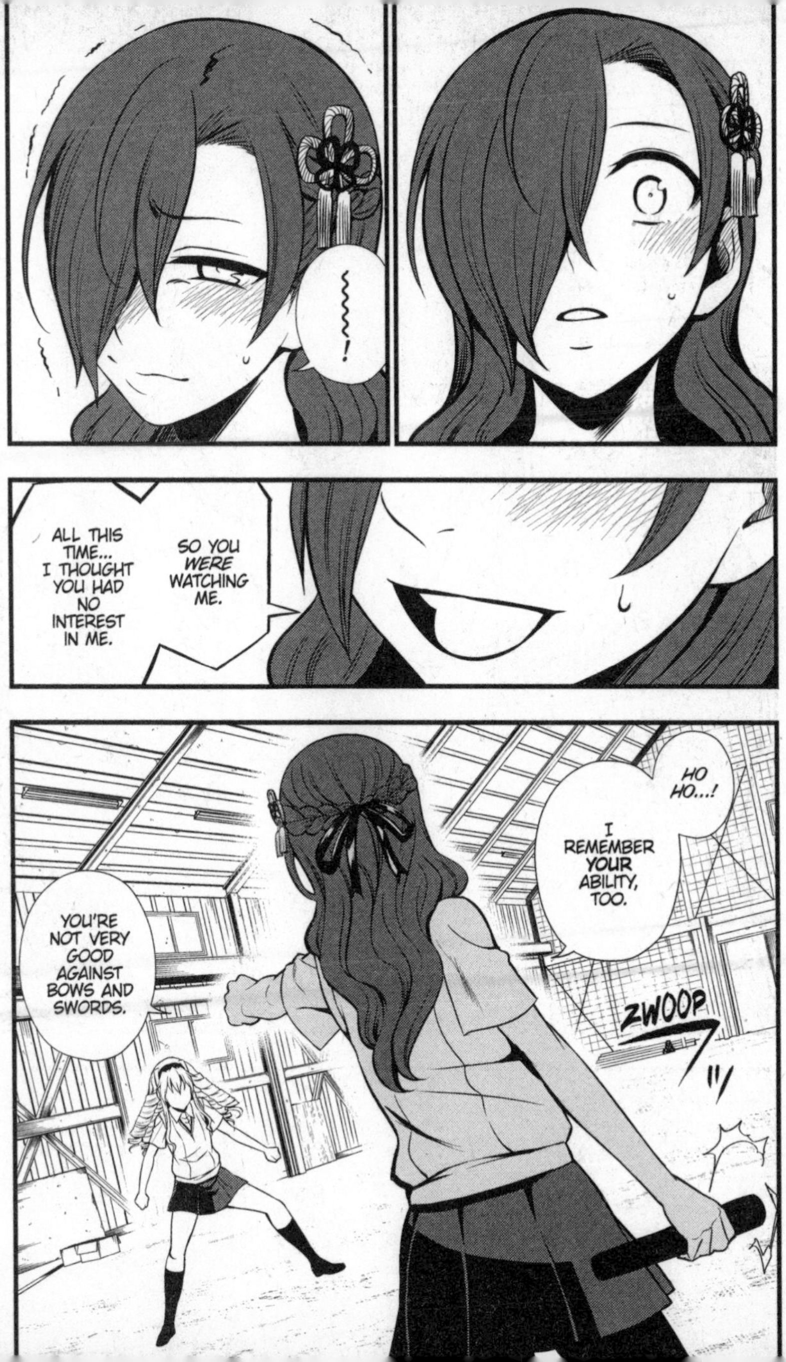

SO YOU WERE WATCHING ME.
ALL THIS TIME... I THOUGHT YOU HAD NO INTEREST IN ME.
HO HO...!
I REMEMBER YOUR ABILITY, TOO.
ZWOOP
YOU'RE NOT VERY GOOD AGAINST BOWS AND SWORDS.

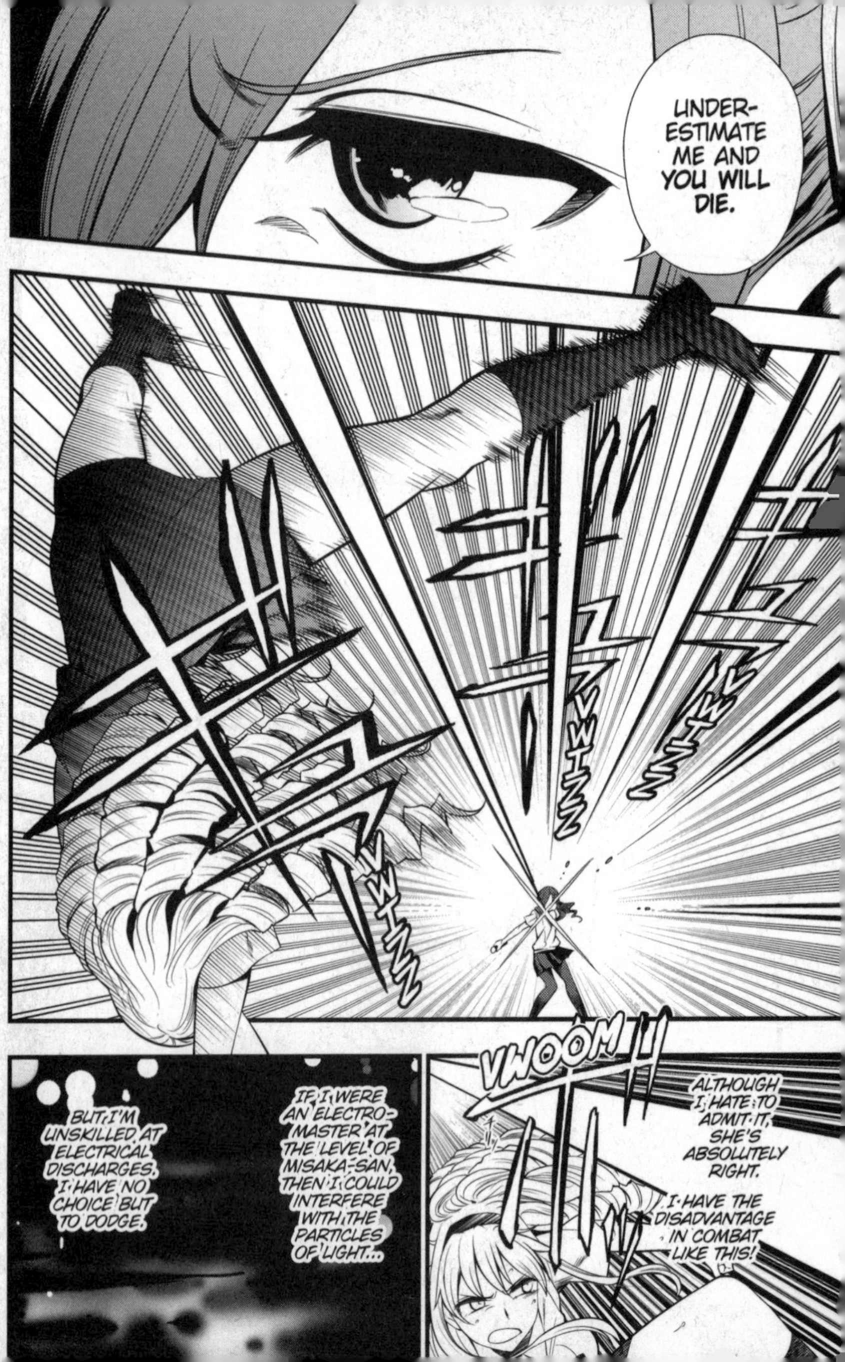
UNDER-ESTIMATE ME AND YOU WILL DIE.
VWIZZ
VWIZZ
VWINN
VWOOM!!
ALTHOUGH I HATE TO ADMIT IT, SHE'S ABSOLUTELY RIGHT.
I HAVE THE DISADVANTAGE IN COMBAT LIKE THIS!
IF I WERE AN ELECTRO-MASTER AT THE LEVEL OF MISAKA-SAN, THEN I COULD INTERFERE WITH THE PARTICLES OF LIGHT...
BUT I'M UNSKILLED AT ELECTRICAL DISCHARGES. I HAVE NO CHOICE BUT TO DODGE.

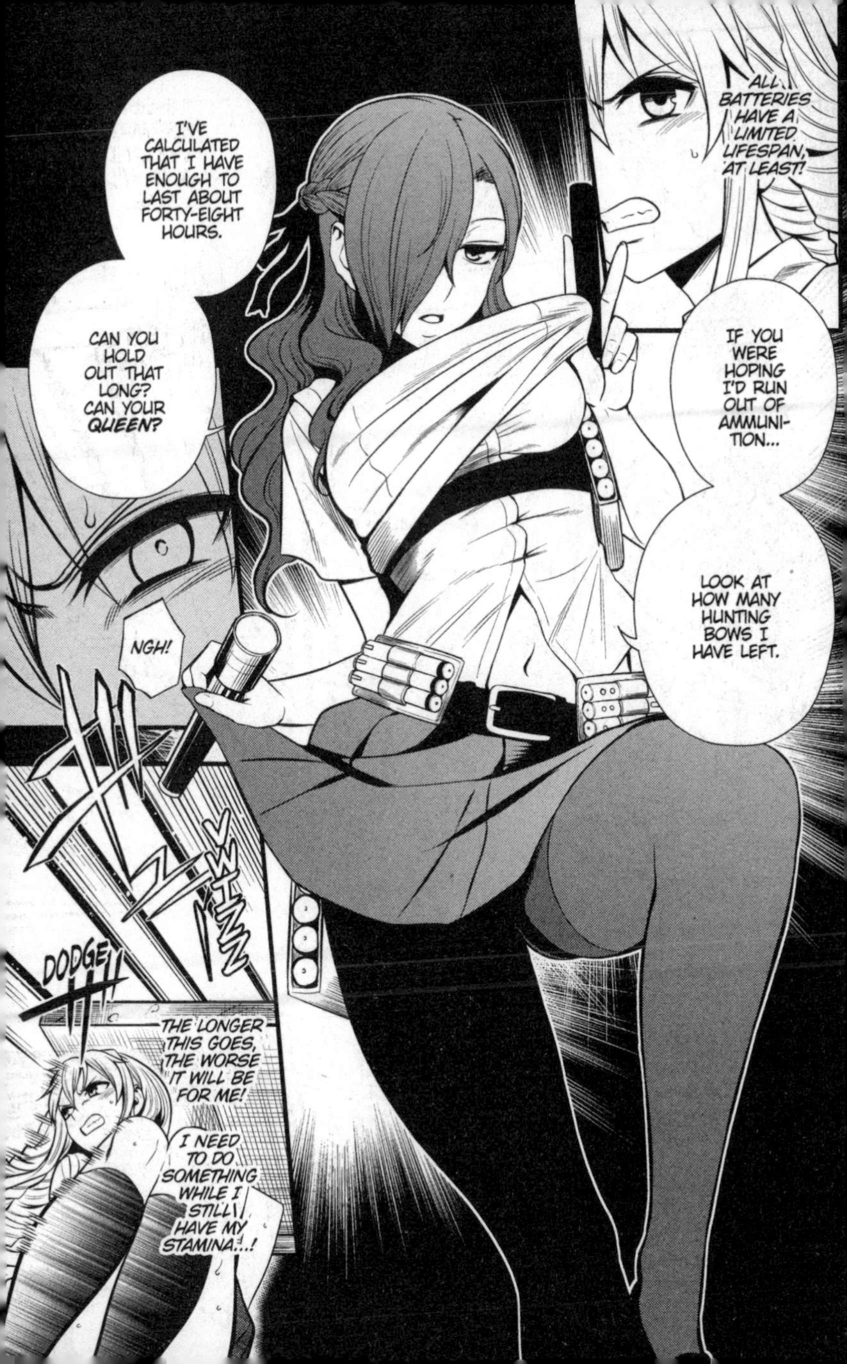
ALL BATTERIES HAVE A LIMITED LIFESPAN, AT LEAST!
IF YOU WERE HOPING I'D RUN OUT OF AMMUNITION...
LOOK AT HOW MANY HUNTING BOWS I HAVE LEFT.
I'VE CALCULATED THAT I HAVE ENOUGH TO LAST ABOUT FORTY-EIGHT HOURS.
CAN YOU HOLD OUT THAT LONG? CAN YOUR QUEEN?
NGH!
DODGE
THE LONGER THIS GOES, THE WORSE IT WILL BE FOR ME!
I NEED TO DO SOMETHING WHILE I STILL HAVE MY STAMINA...!

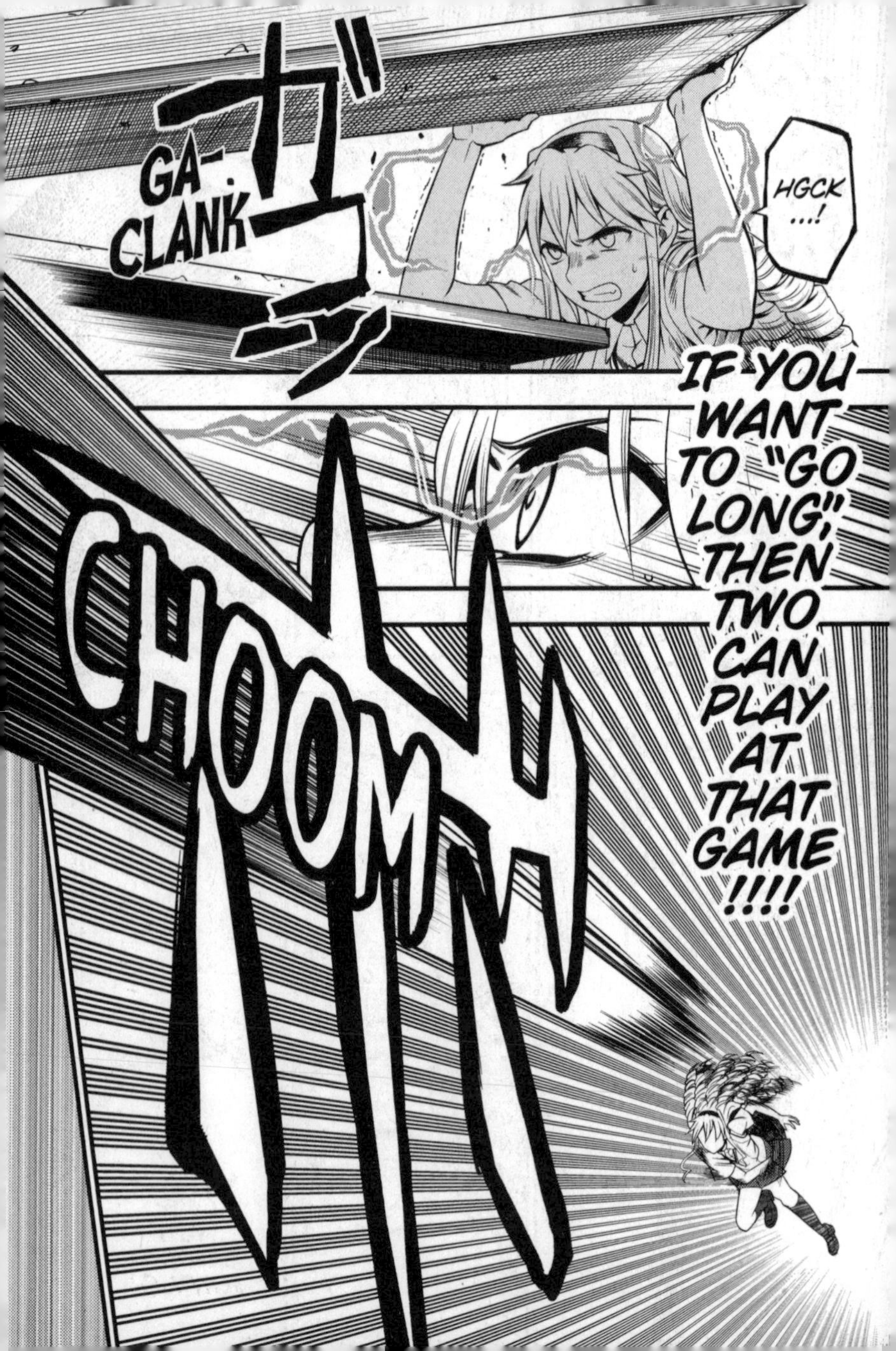
HGCK ...!
GA-CLANK
IF YOU WANT TO "GO LONG", THEN TWO CAN PLAY AT THAT GAME!!!!
CHOOM

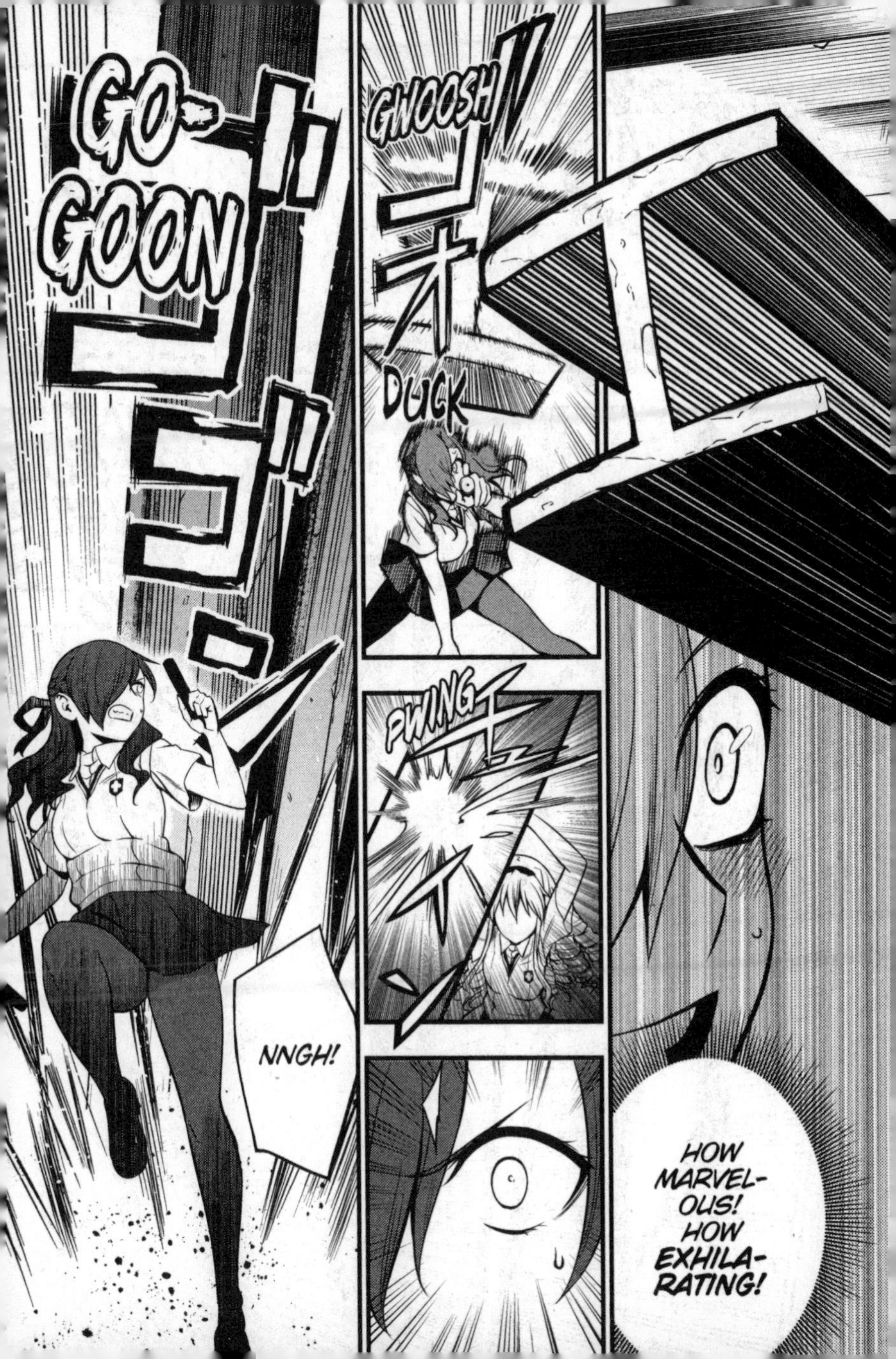
HOW MARVELOUS! HOW EXHILARATING!
GWOOSH
DUCK
PWING
GO-GOON
NNGH!

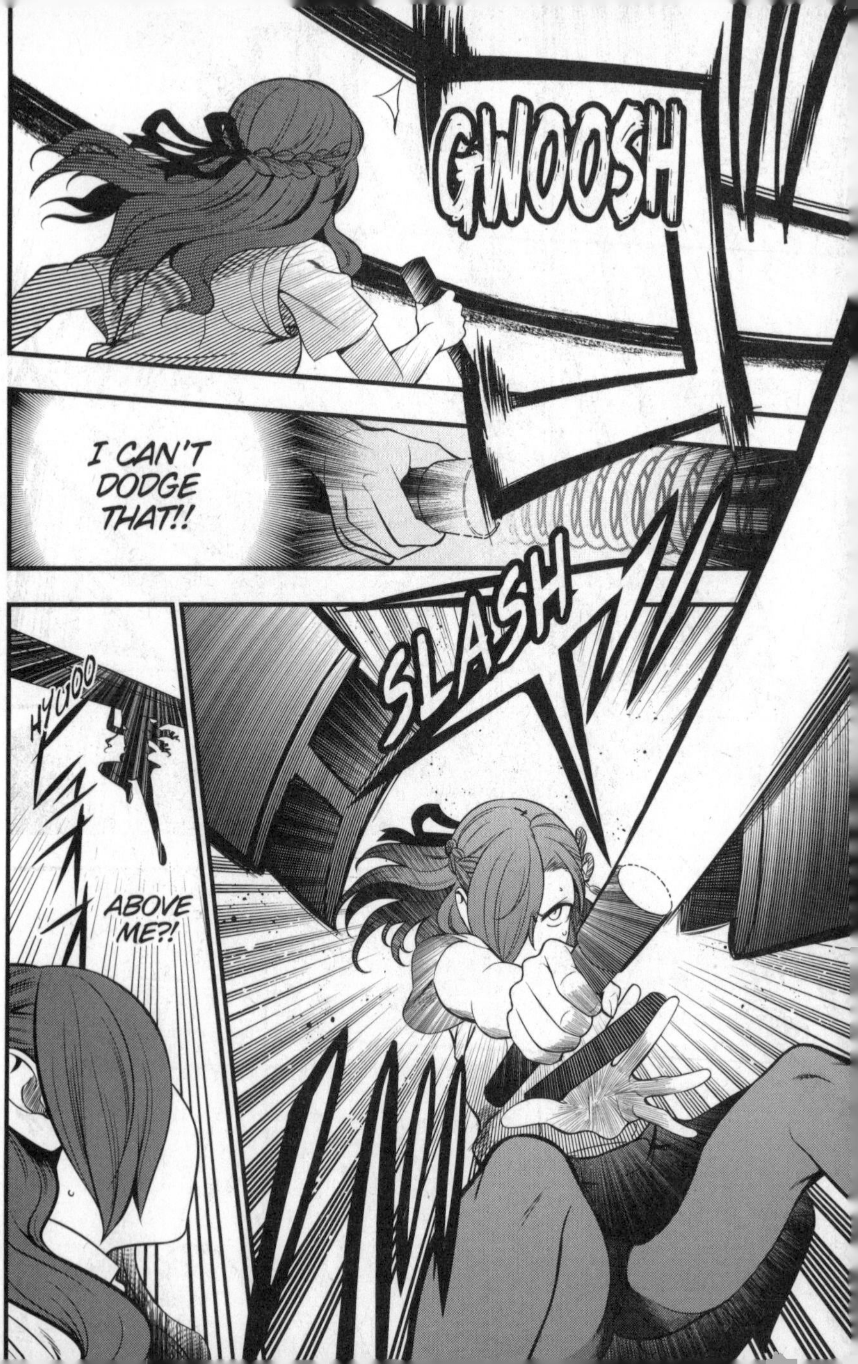
GWOOSH
I CAN'T DODGE THAT!!
SLASH
HYUOO
ABOVE ME?!

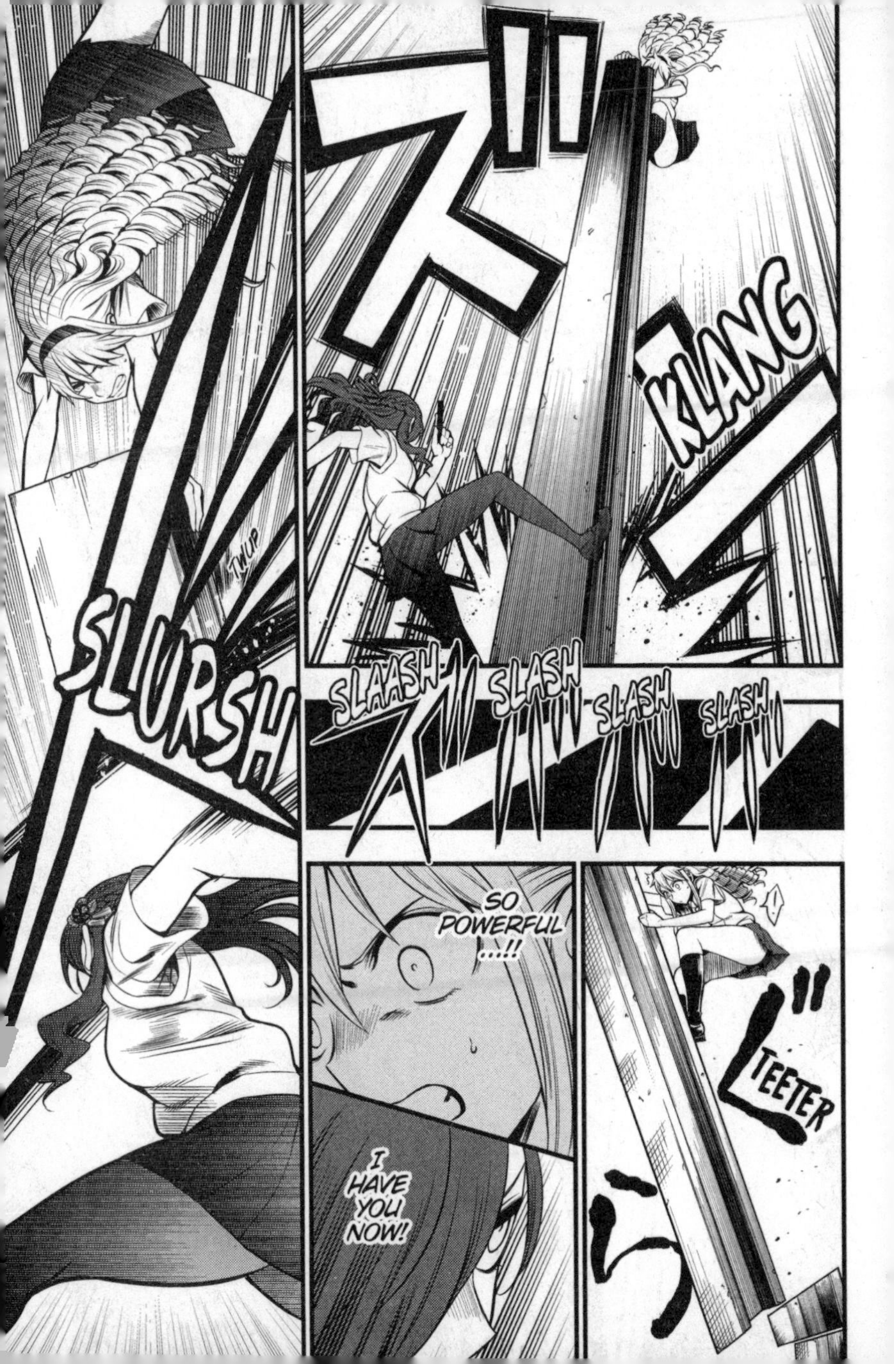
KLANG
SLAASH
SLASH
SLASH
SLASH
!
TEETER
SO POWERFUL ...!!
I HAVE YOU NOW!
THUP
SLURSH

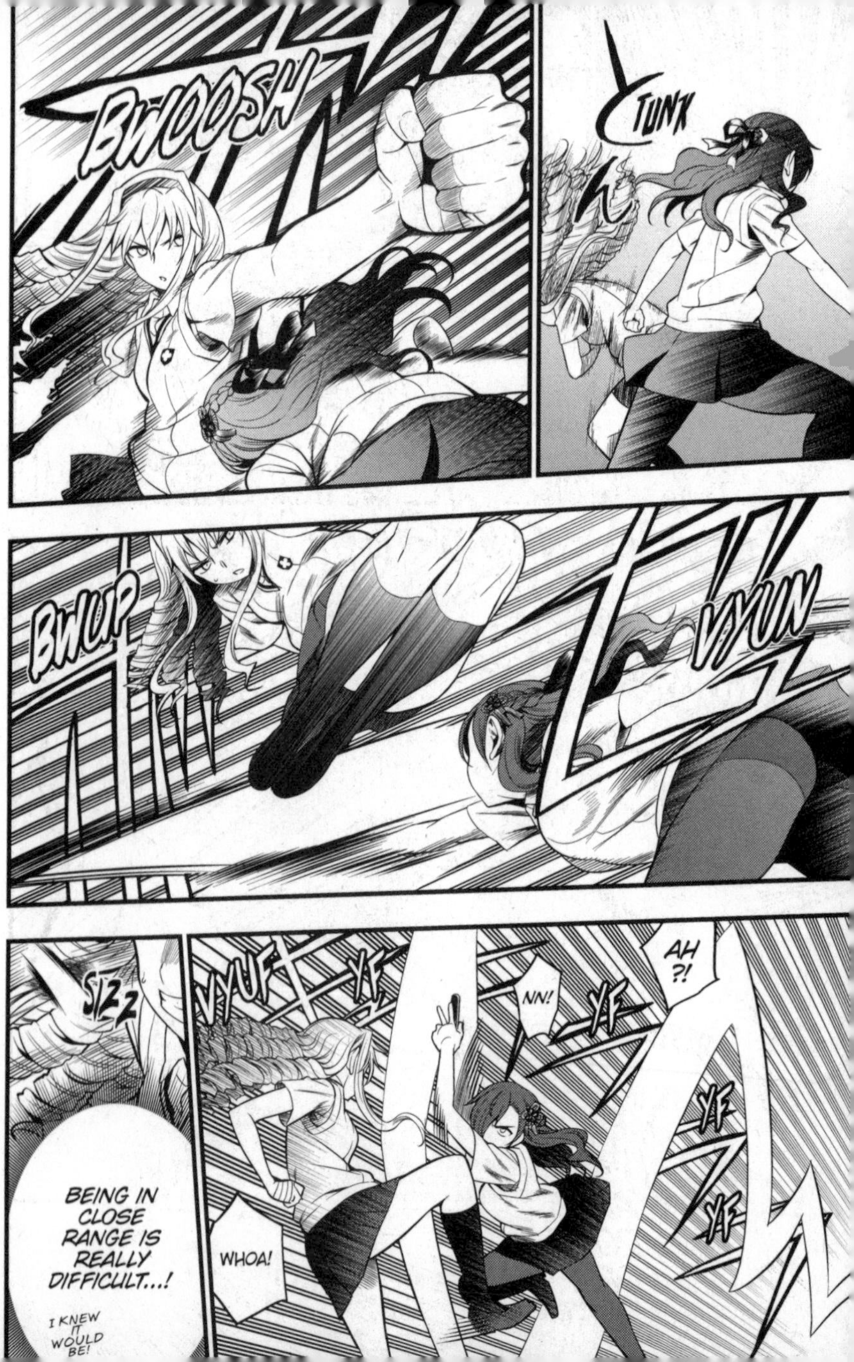
TUNK
BWOOSH
VYUN
BWUP
AH ?!
NN!
YF
YF
VYUF
YF
YF
WHOA!
SIZZ
BEING IN CLOSE RANGE IS REALLY DIFFICULT...!
I KNEW IT WOULD BE!

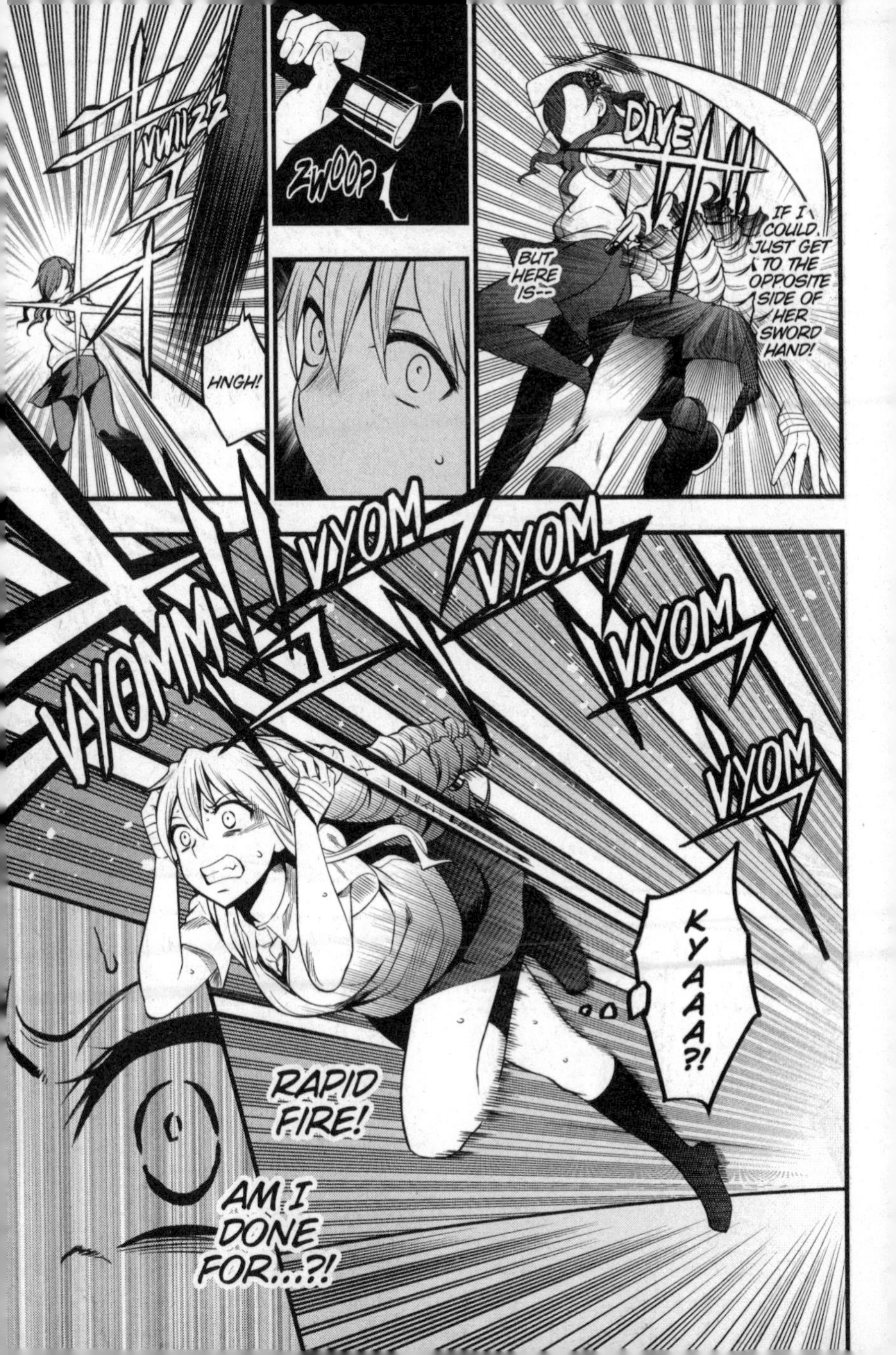

IF I COULD JUST GET TO THE OPPOSITE SIDE OF HER SWORD HAND!
DIVE
BUT HERE IS--
ZWOOP
VWIIZZ
HNGH!
VYOM
VYOM
VYOM
VYOM
VYOMM
KYAAAA?!
RAPID FIRE!
AM I DONE FOR...?!

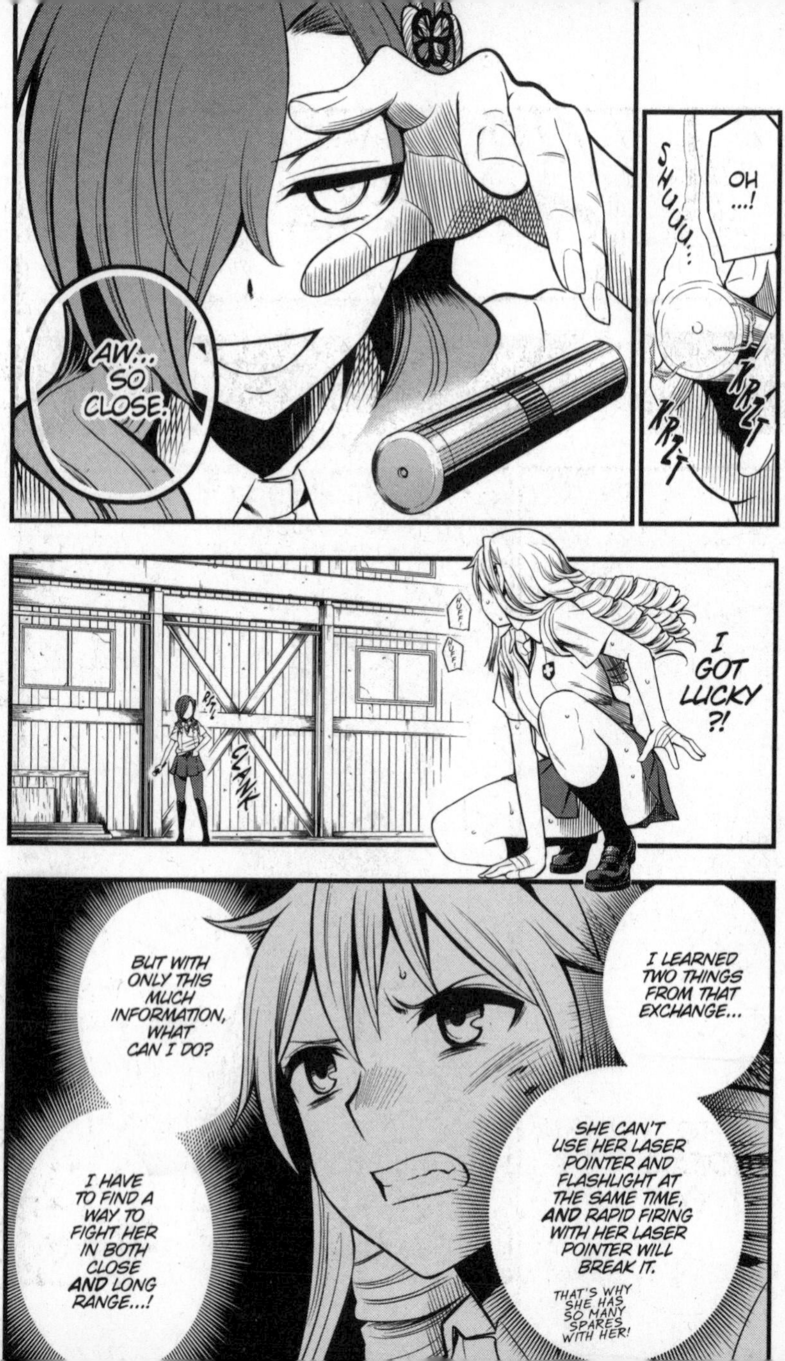
OH ...!
SHUUU...
KRZT
KRZT
AW... SO CLOSE.
I GOT LUCKY ?!
HUFF!
HUFF!
CLANK
I LEARNED TWO THINGS FROM THAT EXCHANGE...
SHE CAN'T USE HER LASER POINTER AND FLASHLIGHT AT THE SAME TIME, AND RAPID FIRING WITH HER LASER POINTER WILL BREAK IT.
THAT'S WHY SHE HAS SO MANY SPARES WITH HER!
BUT WITH ONLY THIS MUCH INFORMATION, WHAT CAN I DO?
I HAVE TO FIND A WAY TO FIGHT HER IN BOTH CLOSE AND LONG RANGE...!

CHAPTER 12: Even Though I Didn't Have the Talent

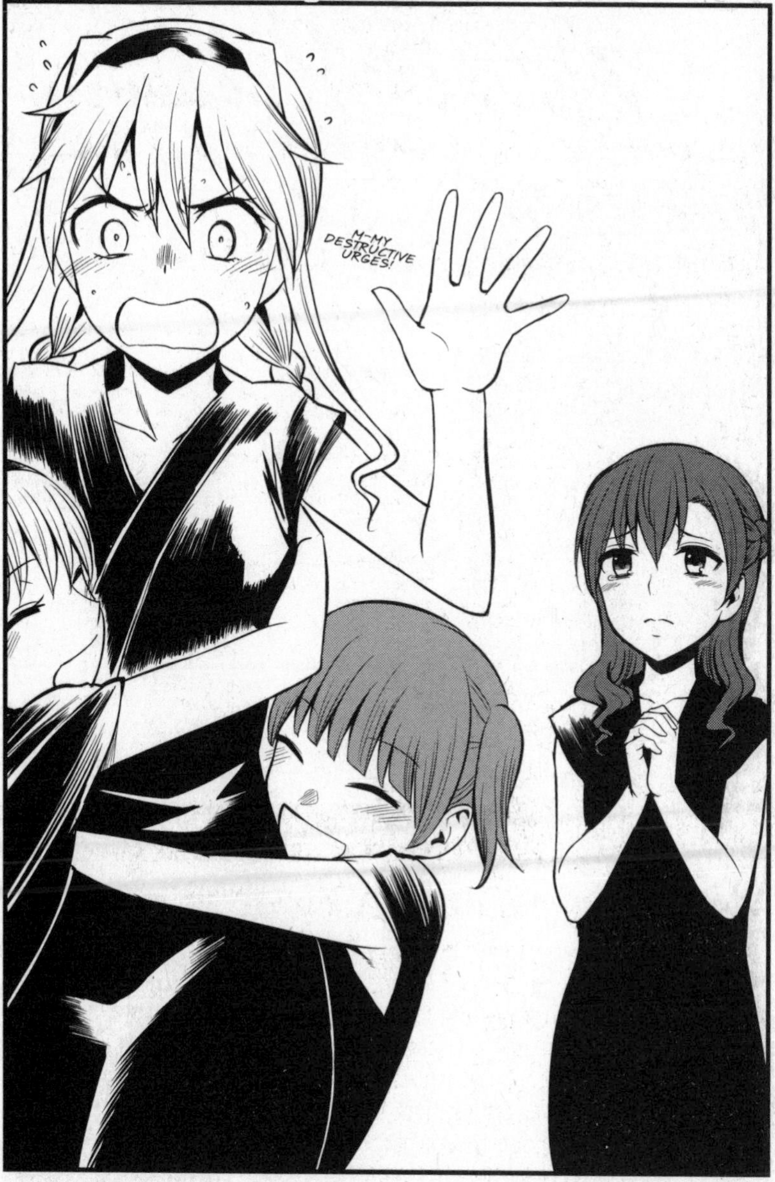
M-MY DESTRUCTIVE URGES!

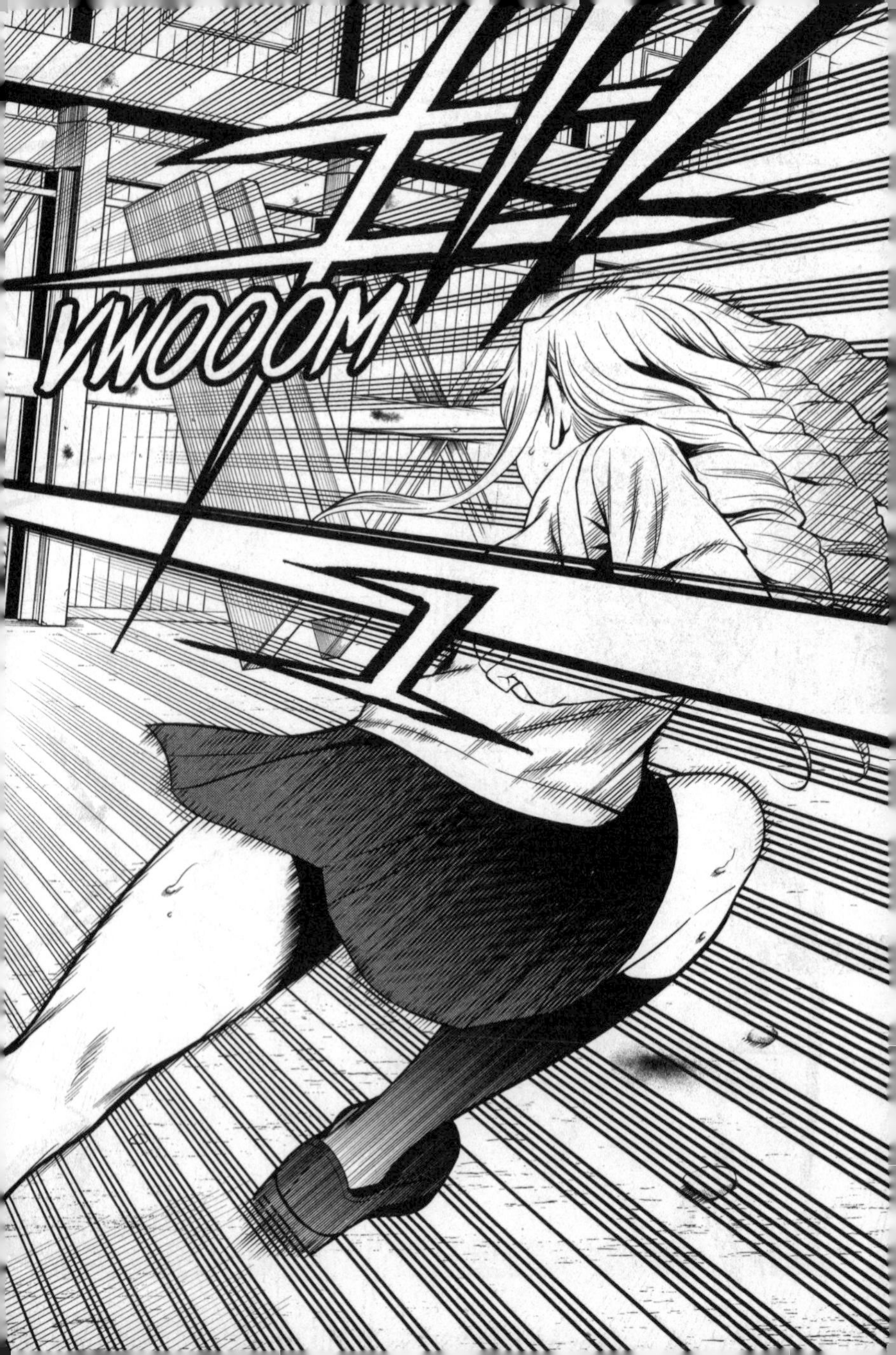
VWOOOM

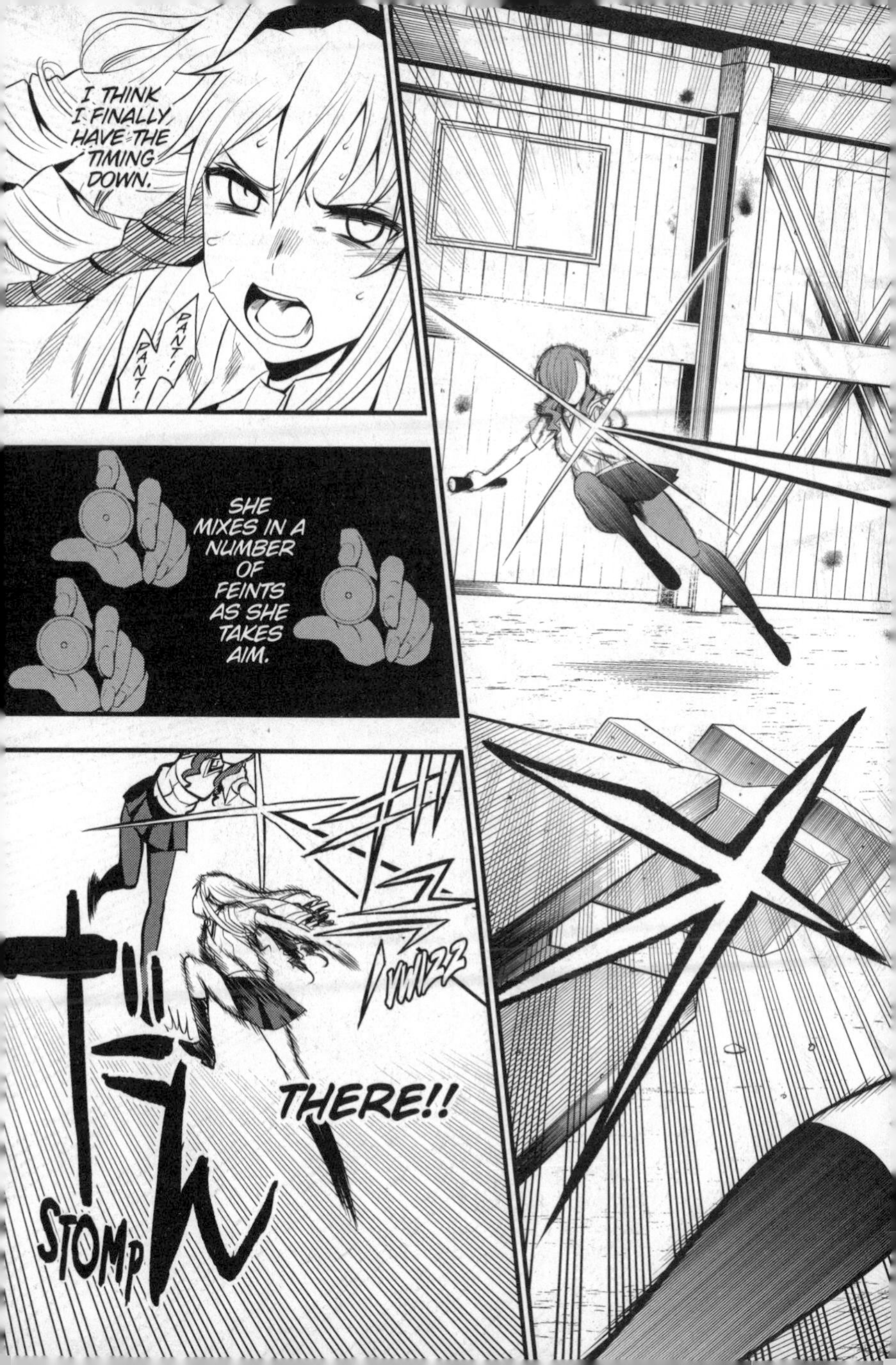
I THINK I FINALLY HAVE THE TIMING DOWN.
PANT! PANT!
SHE MIXES IN A NUMBER OF FEINTS AS SHE TAKES AIM.
VWIZZ
THERE!!
STOMP

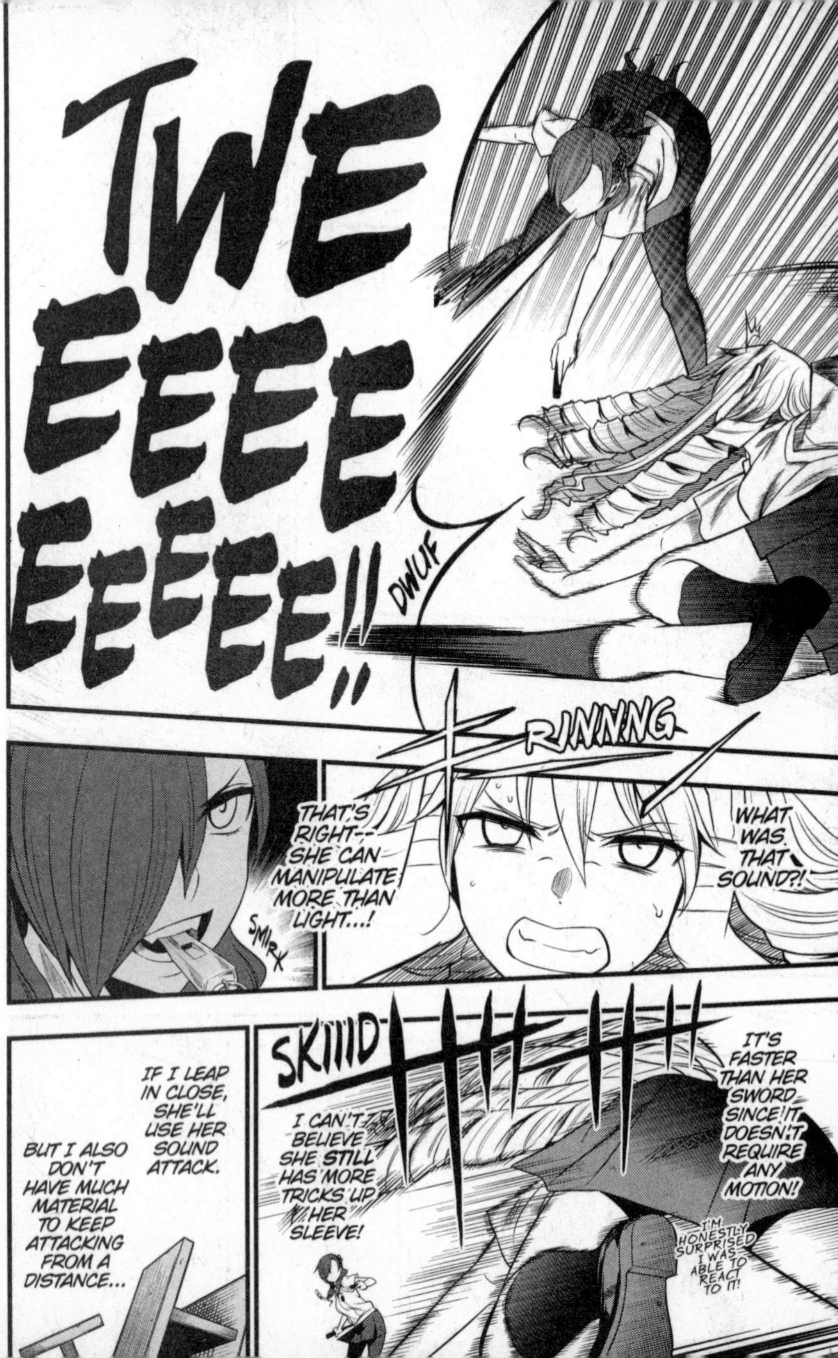
TWEEEEEEEEEE!!
DWUF
RINNNG
WHAT WAS THAT SOUND?!
THAT'S RIGHT-- SHE CAN MANIPULATE MORE THAN LIGHT...!
SMIRK
SKIIID
IT'S FASTER THAN HER SWORD SINCE IT DOESN'T REQUIRE ANY MOTION!
I CAN'T BELIEVE SHE STILL HAS MORE TRICKS UP HER SLEEVE!
I'M HONESTLY SURPRISED I WAS ABLE TO REACT TO IT!
IF I LEAP IN CLOSE, SHE'LL USE HER SOUND ATTACK.
BUT I ALSO DON'T HAVE MUCH MATERIAL TO KEEP ATTACKING FROM A DISTANCE...

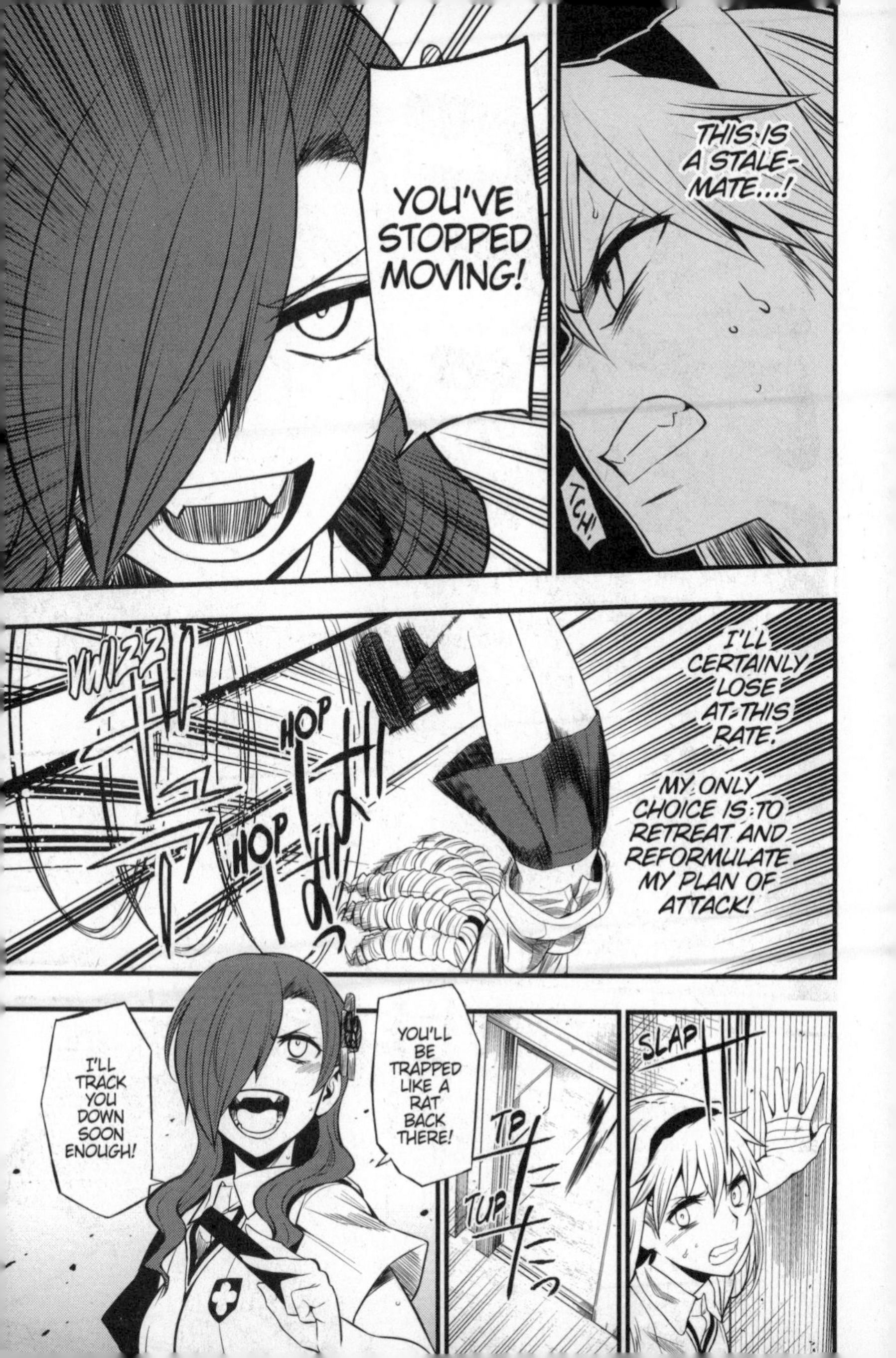

THIS IS A STALE-MATE...!
TCH!
YOU'VE STOPPED MOVING!
I'LL CERTAINLY LOSE AT THIS RATE.
MY ONLY CHOICE IS TO RETREAT AND REFORMULATE MY PLAN OF ATTACK!
HOP
HOP
VWIZZ
SLAP
TP
TUP
YOU'LL BE TRAPPED LIKE A RAT BACK THERE!
I'LL TRACK YOU DOWN SOON ENOUGH!

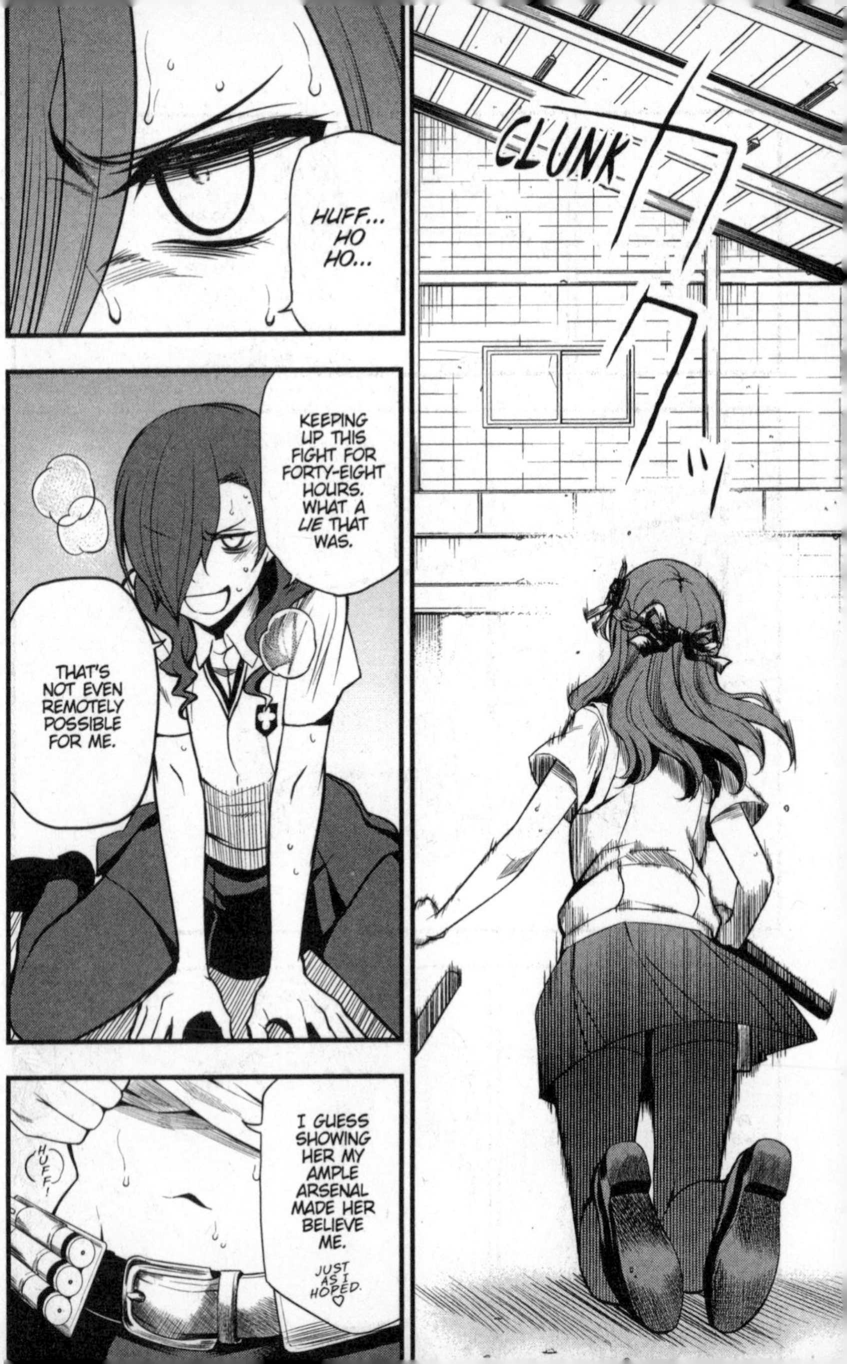
CLUNK
HUFF... HO HO...
KEEPING UP THIS FIGHT FOR FORTY-EIGHT HOURS. WHAT A LIE THAT WAS.
THAT'S NOT EVEN REMOTELY POSSIBLE FOR ME.
I GUESS SHOWING HER MY AMPLE ARSENAL MADE HER BELIEVE ME.
HUFF!
JUST AS I HOPED. ♡

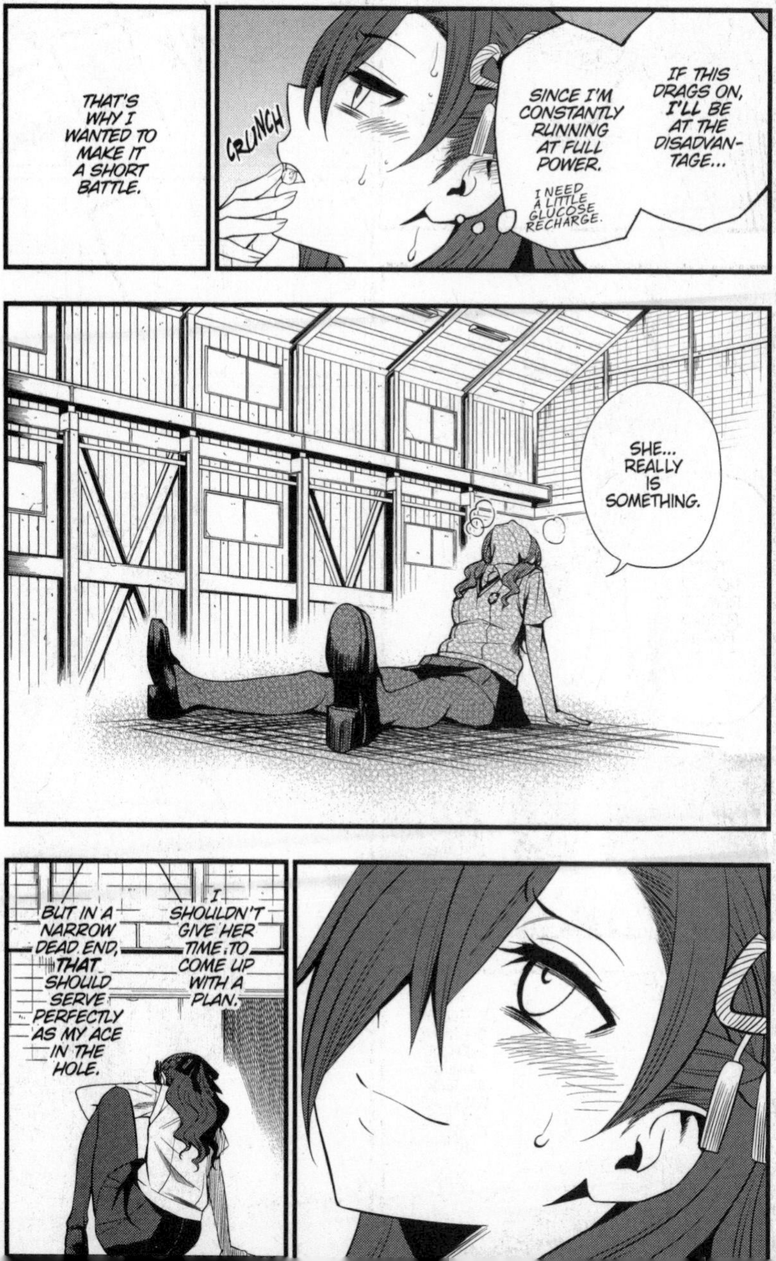
IF THIS DRAGS ON, I'LL BE AT THE DISADVANTAGE...
SINCE I'M CONSTANTLY RUNNING AT FULL POWER.
I NEED A LITTLE GLUCOSE RECHARGE.
CRUNCH
THAT'S WHY I WANTED TO MAKE IT A SHORT BATTLE.
SHE... REALLY IS SOMETHING.
I SHOULDN'T GIVE HER TIME TO COME UP WITH A PLAN.
BUT IN A NARROW DEAD END, THAT SHOULD SERVE PERFECTLY AS MY ACE IN THE HOLE.

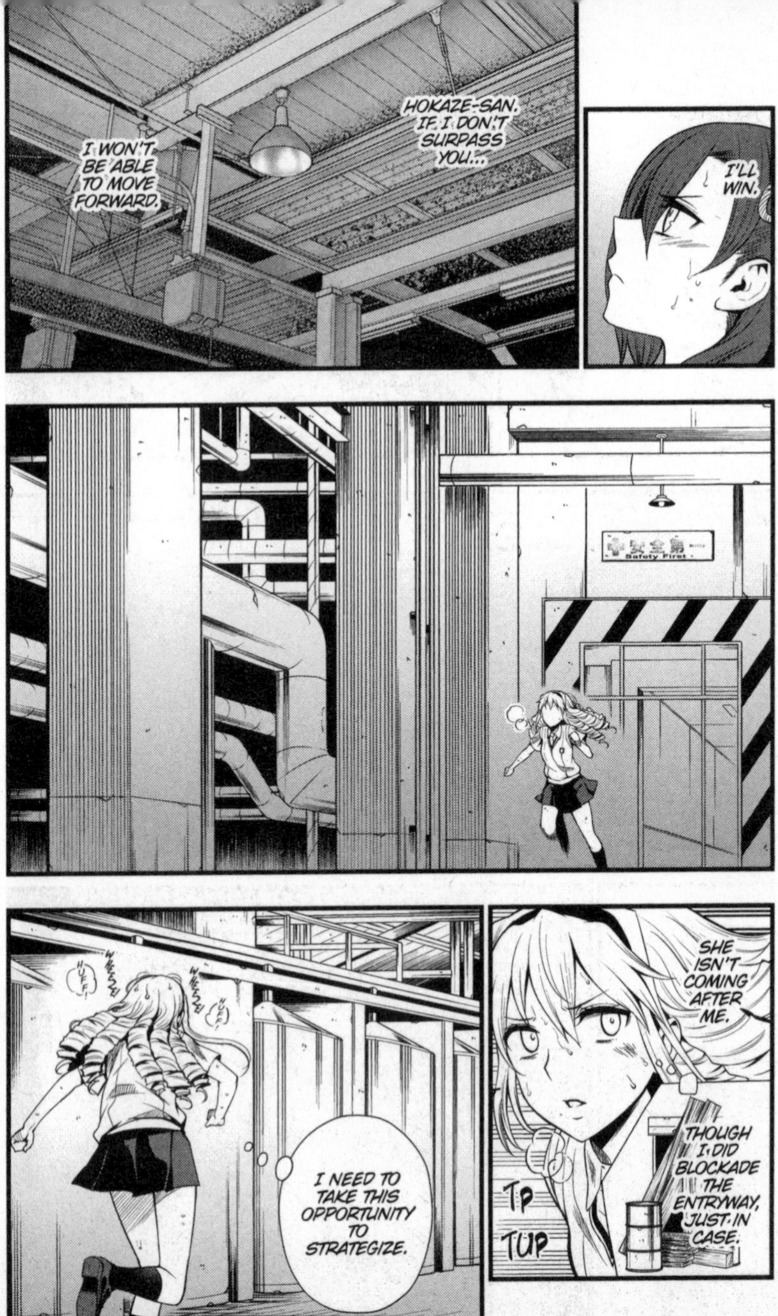
I'LL WIN.
HOKAZE-SAN, IF I DON'T SURPASS YOU...
I WON'T BE ABLE TO MOVE FORWARD.
Safety First
SHE ISN'T COMING AFTER ME.
THOUGH I DID BLOCKADE THE ENTRYWAY, JUST IN CASE.
TP
TUP
WHEEZE!
HUFF!
WHEEZE!
HUFF!
I NEED TO TAKE THIS OPPORTUNITY TO STRATEGIZE.

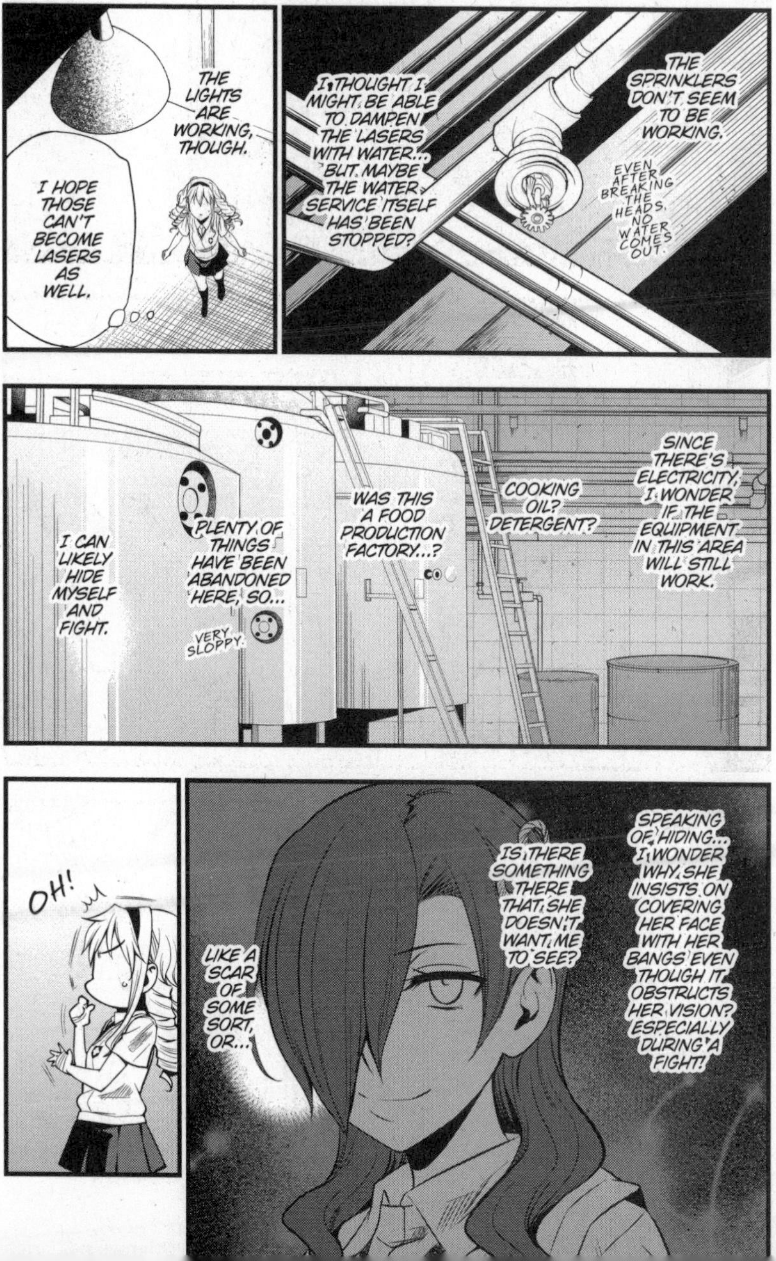
THE SPRINKLERS DON'T SEEM TO BE WORKING.
EVEN AFTER BREAKING THE HEADS, NO WATER COMES OUT.
I THOUGHT I MIGHT BE ABLE TO DAMPEN THE LASERS WITH WATER... BUT MAYBE THE WATER SERVICE ITSELF HAS BEEN STOPPED?
THE LIGHTS ARE WORKING, THOUGH.
I HOPE THOSE CAN'T BECOME LASERS AS WELL.
SINCE THERE'S ELECTRICITY, I WONDER IF THE EQUIPMENT IN THIS AREA WILL STILL WORK.
COOKING OIL? DETERGENT?
WAS THIS A FOOD PRODUCTION FACTORY...?
PLENTY OF THINGS HAVE BEEN ABANDONED HERE, SO...
VERY SLOPPY.
I CAN LIKELY HIDE MYSELF AND FIGHT.
SPEAKING OF HIDING... I WONDER WHY SHE INSISTS ON COVERING HER FACE WITH HER BANGS EVEN THOUGH IT OBSTRUCTS HER VISION? ESPECIALLY DURING A FIGHT!
IS THERE SOMETHING THERE THAT SHE DOESN'T WANT ME TO SEE?
LIKE A SCAR OF SOME SORT, OR...
OH!

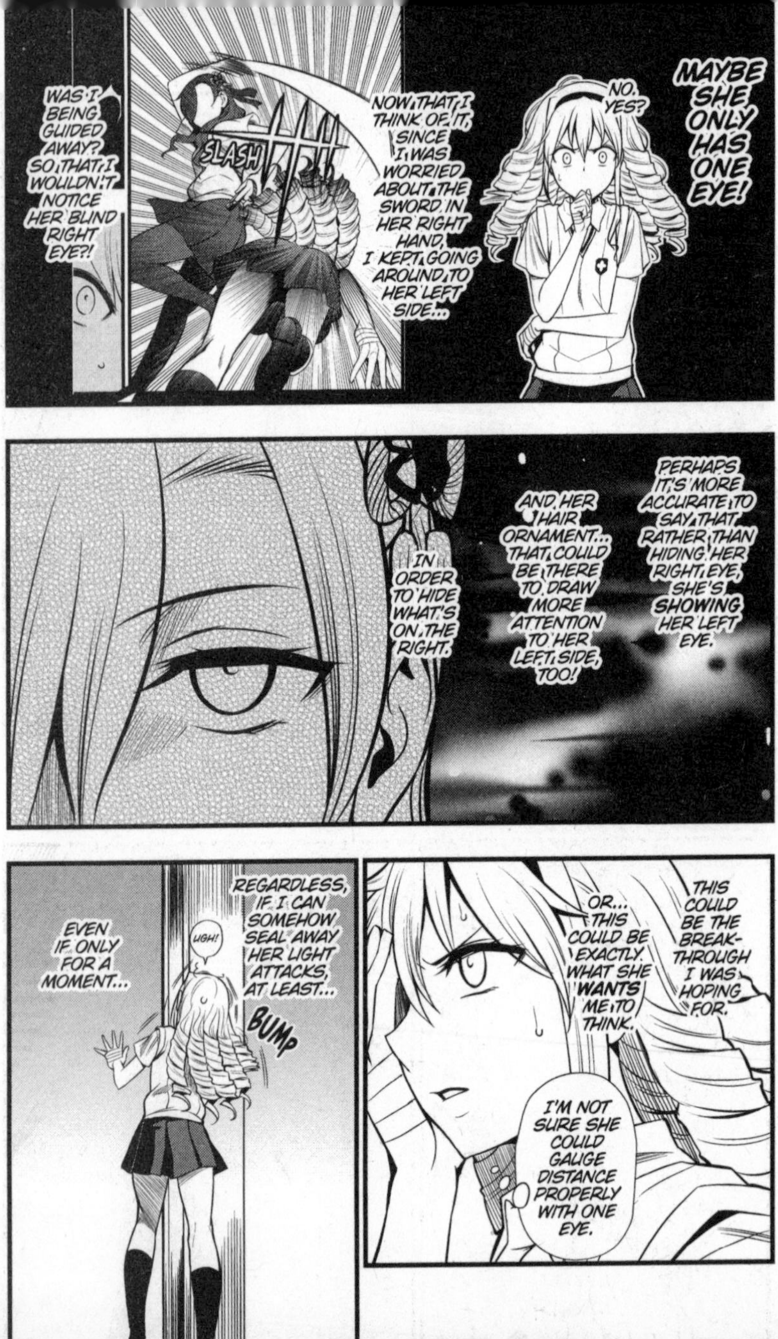
MAYBE SHE ONLY HAS ONE EYE!
NO. YES?
NOW THAT I THINK OF IT, SINCE I WAS WORRIED ABOUT THE SWORD IN HER RIGHT HAND, I KEPT GOING AROUND TO HER LEFT SIDE...
SLASH
WAS I BEING GUIDED AWAY? SO THAT I WOULDN'T NOTICE HER BLIND RIGHT EYE?!
PERHAPS IT'S MORE ACCURATE TO SAY THAT RATHER THAN HIDING HER RIGHT EYE, SHE'S **SHOWING** HER LEFT EYE.
AND HER HAIR ORNAMENT... THAT COULD BE THERE TO DRAW MORE ATTENTION TO HER LEFT SIDE, TOO!
IN ORDER TO HIDE WHAT'S ON THE RIGHT.
THIS COULD BE THE BREAK-THROUGH I WAS HOPING FOR.
OR... THIS COULD BE EXACTLY WHAT SHE **WANTS** ME TO THINK.
I'M NOT SURE SHE COULD GAUGE DISTANCE PROPERLY WITH ONE EYE.
REGARDLESS, IF I CAN SOMEHOW SEAL AWAY HER LIGHT ATTACKS, AT LEAST...
UGH!
BUMP
EVEN IF ONLY FOR A MOMENT...

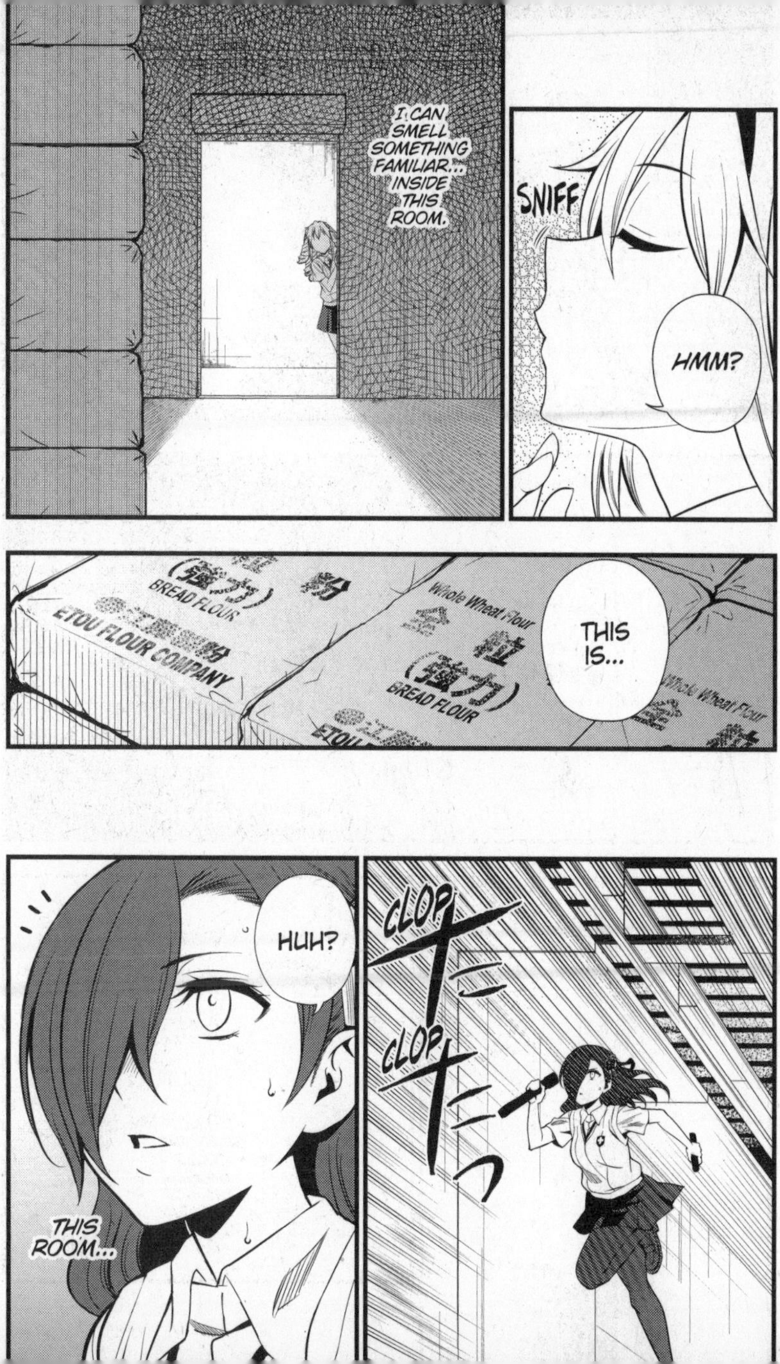
SNIFF
HMM?
I CAN SMELL SOMETHING FAMILIAR... INSIDE THIS ROOM.
THIS IS...
Whole Wheat Flour
BREAD FLOUR
BREAD FLOUR
ETOU FLOUR COMPANY
CLOP
CLOP
HUH?
THIS ROOM...

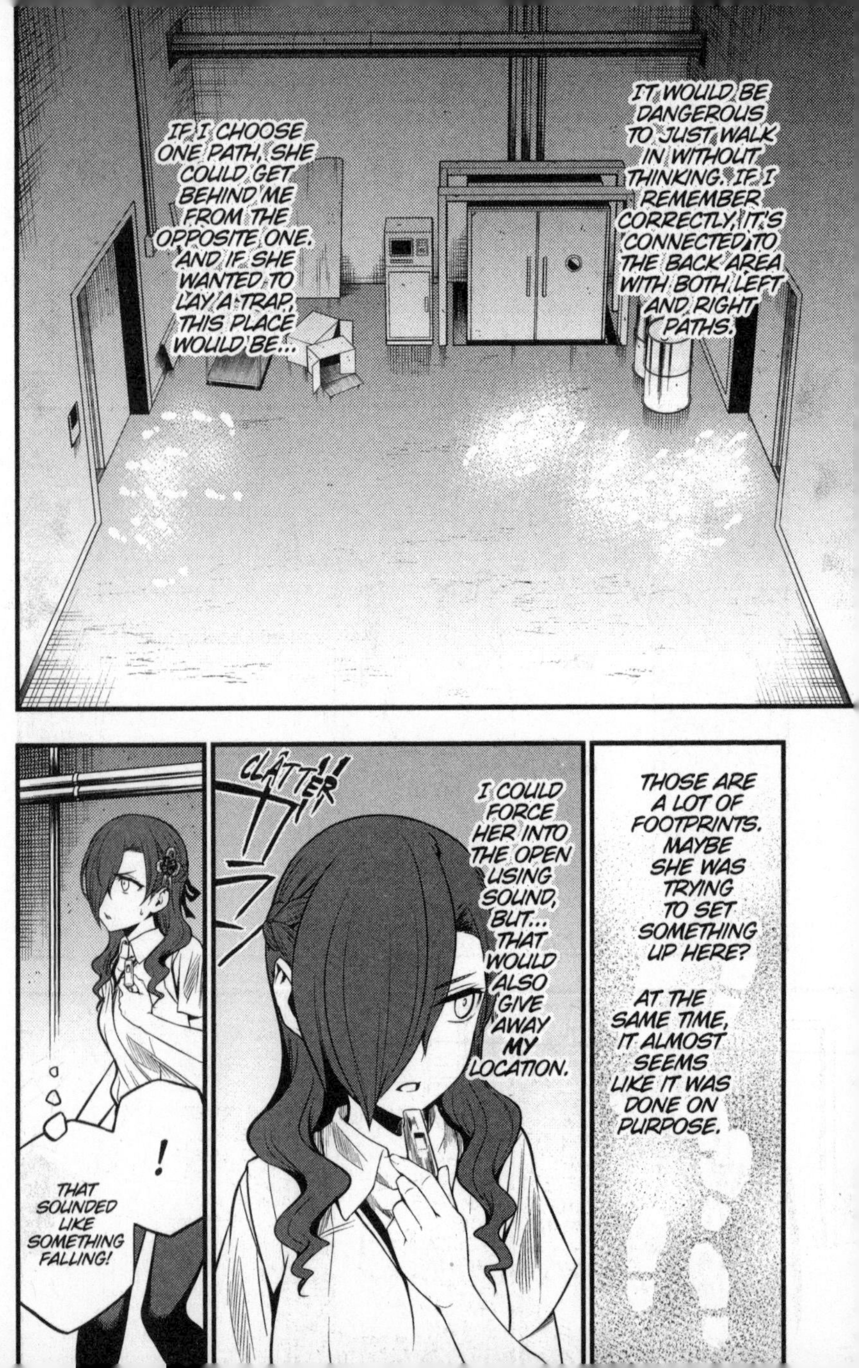
IT WOULD BE DANGEROUS TO JUST WALK IN WITHOUT THINKING. IF I REMEMBER CORRECTLY, IT'S CONNECTED TO THE BACK AREA WITH BOTH LEFT AND RIGHT PATHS.
IF I CHOOSE ONE PATH, SHE COULD GET BEHIND ME FROM THE OPPOSITE ONE. AND IF SHE WANTED TO LAY A TRAP, THIS PLACE WOULD BE...
THOSE ARE A LOT OF FOOTPRINTS. MAYBE SHE WAS TRYING TO SET SOMETHING UP HERE?
AT THE SAME TIME, IT ALMOST SEEMS LIKE IT WAS DONE ON PURPOSE.
CLATTER
I COULD FORCE HER INTO THE OPEN USING SOUND, BUT... THAT WOULD ALSO GIVE AWAY MY LOCATION.
!
THAT SOUNDED LIKE SOMETHING FALLING!

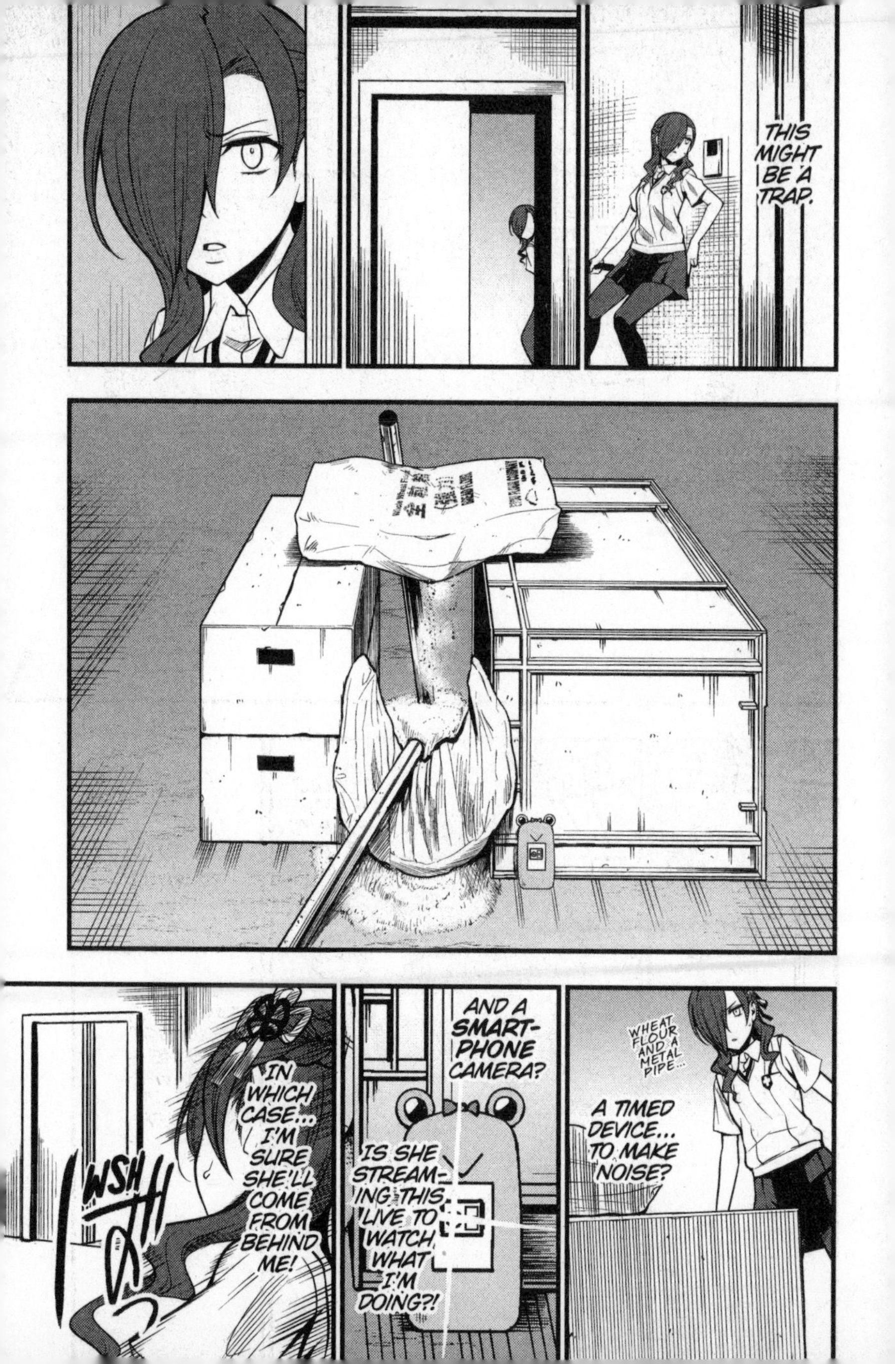
THIS MIGHT BE A TRAP.
WHEAT FLOUR AND A METAL PIPE...
A TIMED DEVICE... TO MAKE NOISE?
AND A SMART-PHONE CAMERA?
IS SHE STREAM-ING THIS LIVE TO WATCH WHAT I'M DOING?!
IN WHICH CASE... I'M SURE SHE'LL COME FROM BEHIND ME!
WSH

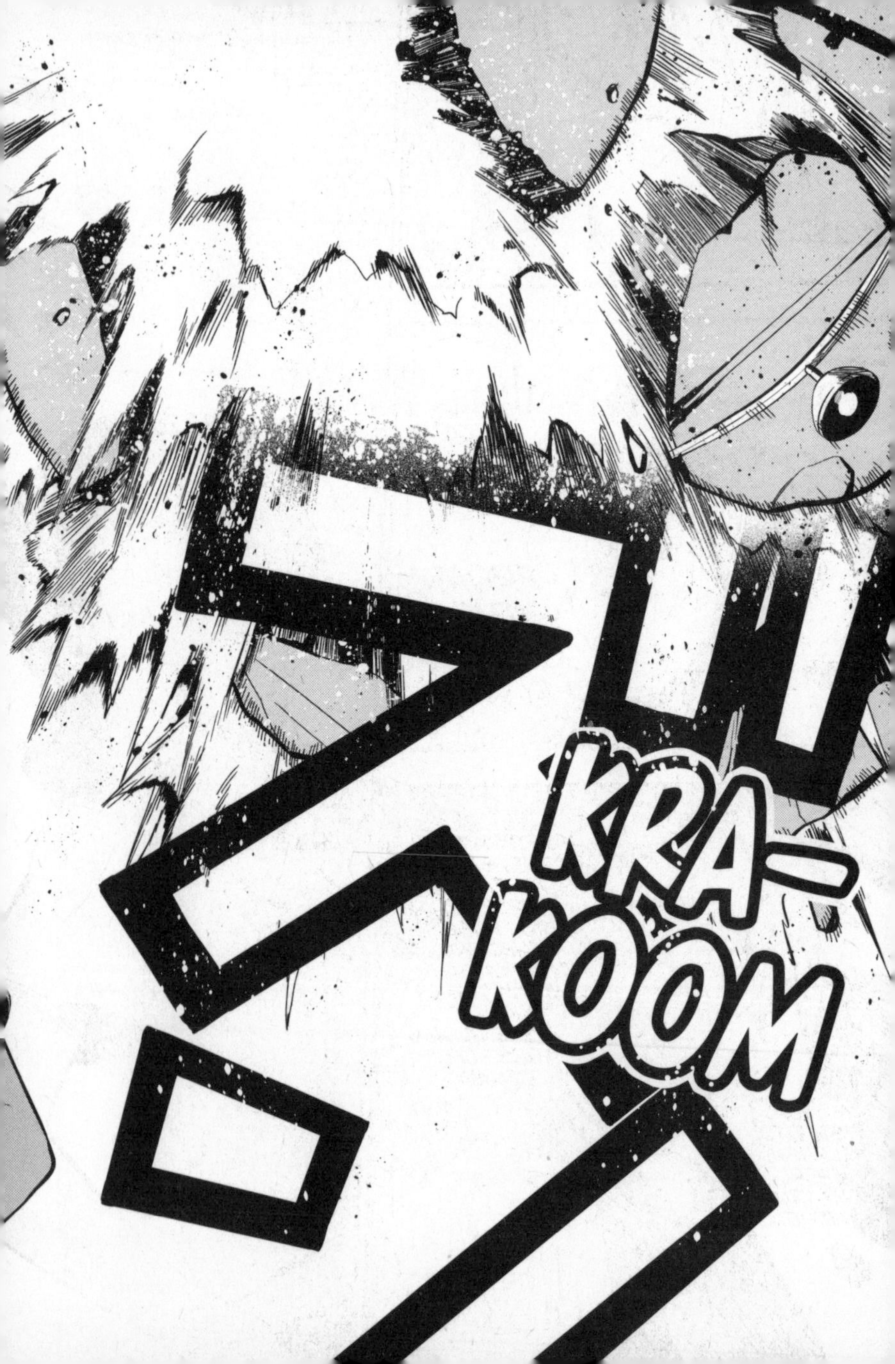
KRA-KOOM

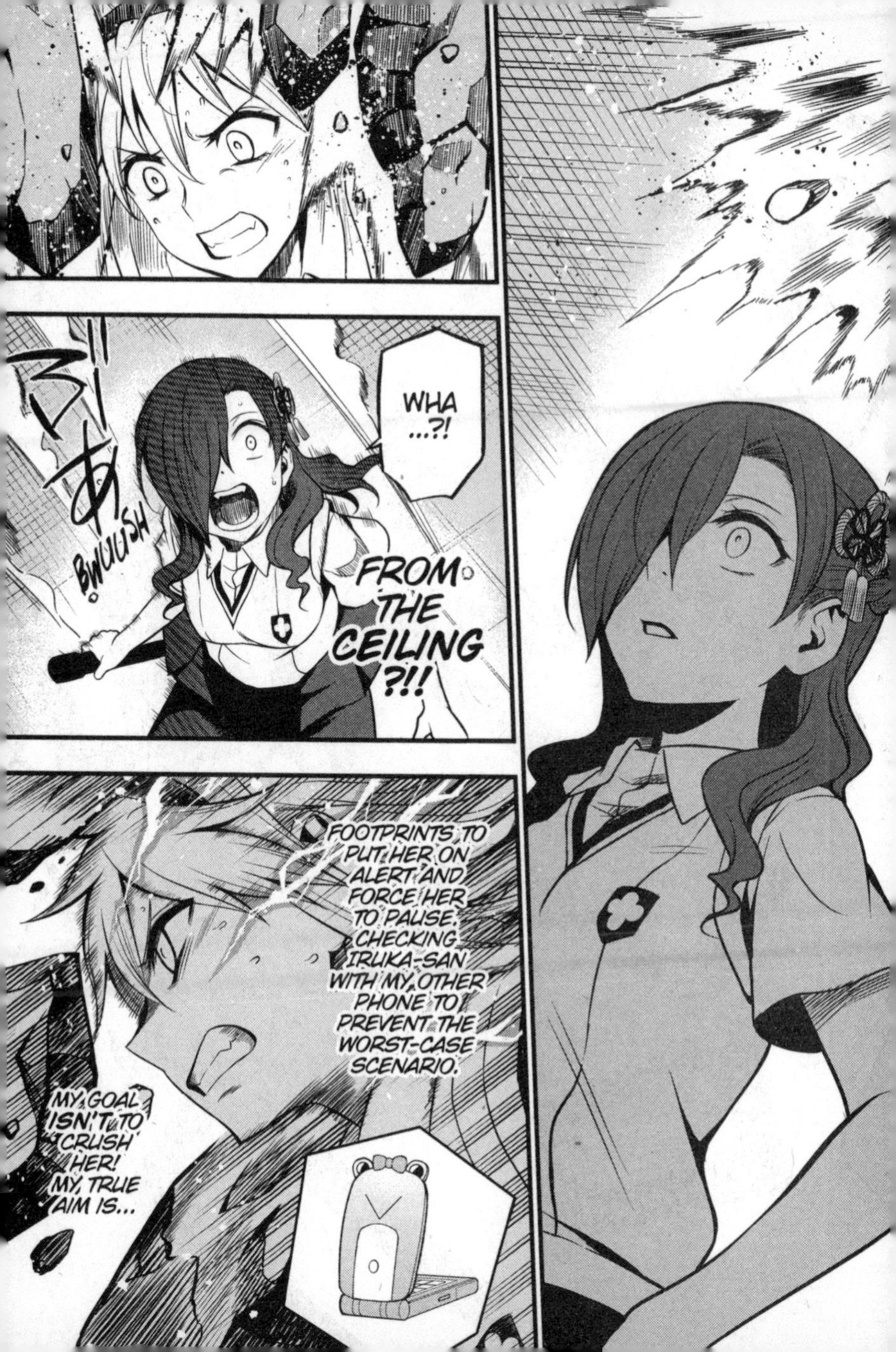
WHA ...?!
FROM THE CEILING ?!!
BWUUSH
FOOTPRINTS TO PUT HER ON ALERT AND FORCE HER TO PAUSE. CHECKING IRUKA-SAN WITH MY OTHER PHONE TO PREVENT THE WORST-CASE SCENARIO.
MY GOAL ISN'T TO CRUSH HER! MY TRUE AIM IS...

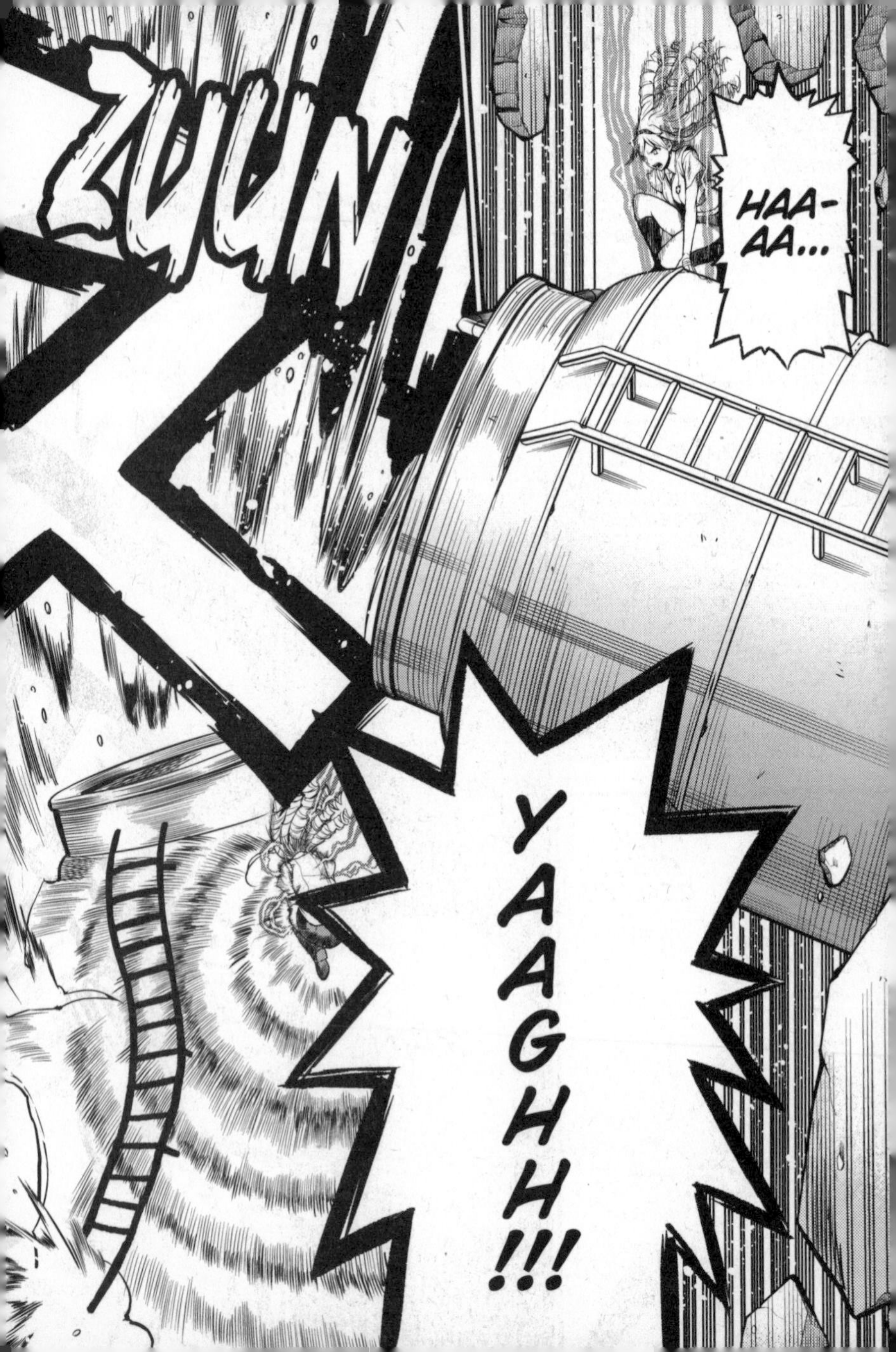
HAAA-AA...
ZUGN!
YAAGHH!!!

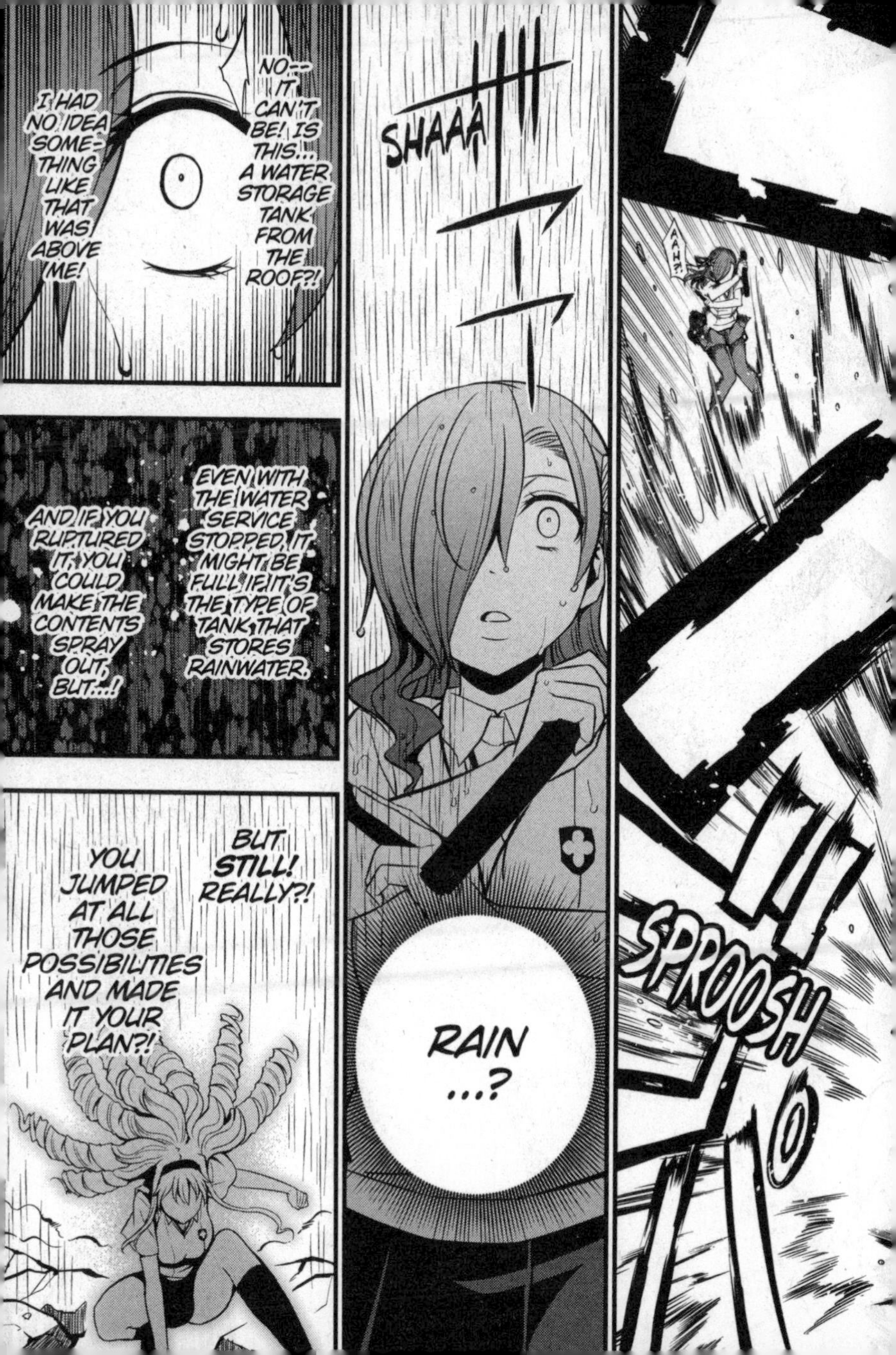
AAH?!
SPROOSH
SHAAA
RAIN...?
NO-- IT CAN'T BE! IS THIS... A WATER STORAGE TANK FROM THE ROOF?!
I HAD NO IDEA SOME-THING LIKE THAT WAS ABOVE ME!
EVEN WITH THE WATER SERVICE STOPPED, IT MIGHT BE FULL IF IT'S THE TYPE OF TANK THAT STORES RAINWATER.
AND IF YOU RUPTURED IT, YOU COULD MAKE THE CONTENTS SPRAY OUT, BUT...!
BUT STILL! REALLY?!
YOU JUMPED AT ALL THOSE POSSIBILITIES AND MADE IT YOUR PLAN?!

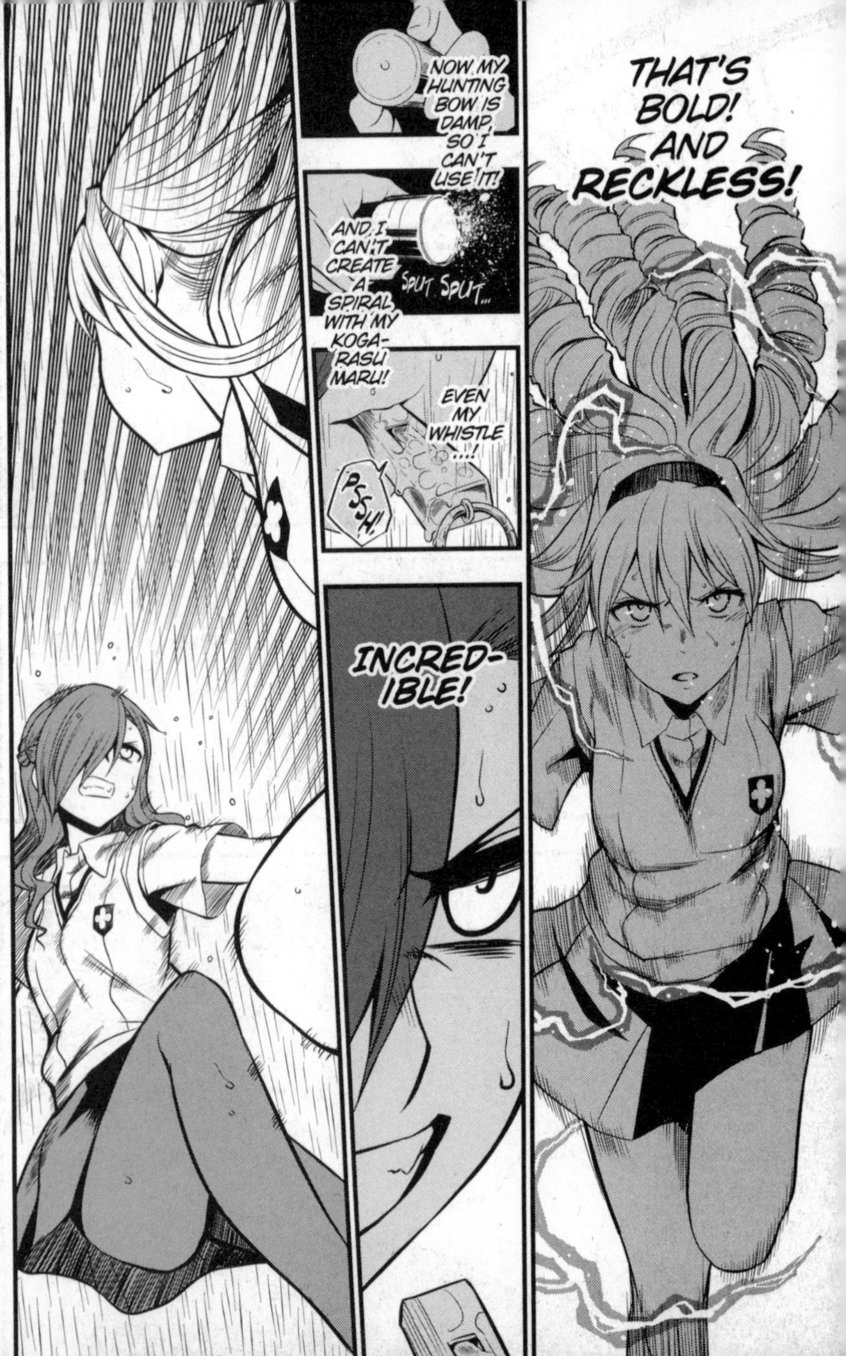

THAT'S BOLD! AND RECKLESS!
NOW MY HUNTING BOW IS DAMP, SO I CAN'T USE IT!
AND I CAN'T CREATE A SPIRAL WITH MY KOGA-RASU MARU!
SPUT SPUT...
EVEN MY WHISTLE...!
PSSH!
INCRED-IBLE!

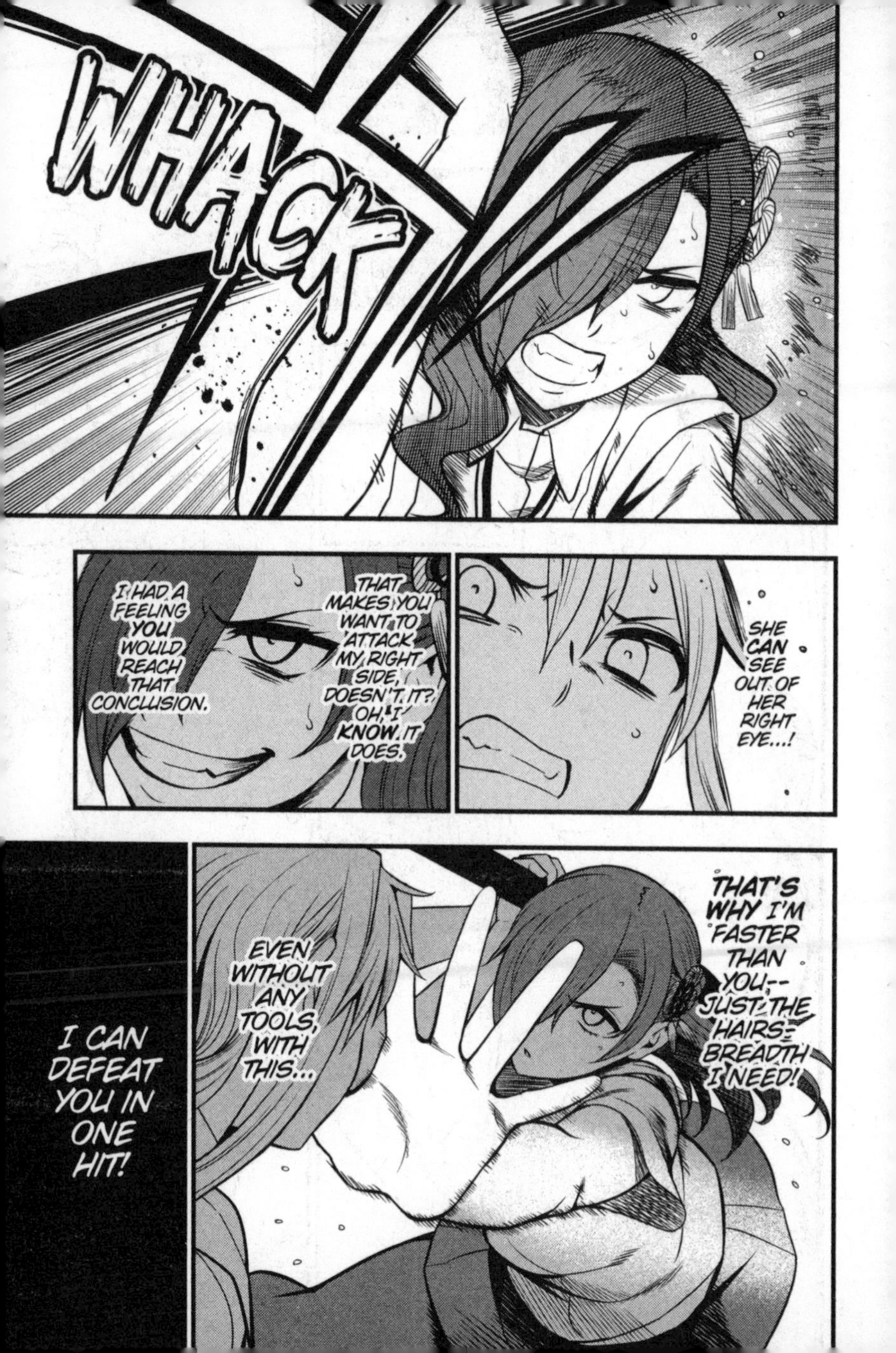
WHACK
SHE CAN SEE OUT OF HER RIGHT EYE...!
THAT MAKES YOU WANT TO ATTACK MY RIGHT SIDE, DOESN'T IT? OH, I KNOW IT DOES.
I HAD A FEELING YOU WOULD REACH THAT CONCLUSION.
THAT'S WHY I'M FASTER THAN YOU--JUST THE HAIRS-BREADTH I NEED!
EVEN WITHOUT ANY TOOLS, WITH THIS...
I CAN DEFEAT YOU IN ONE HIT!

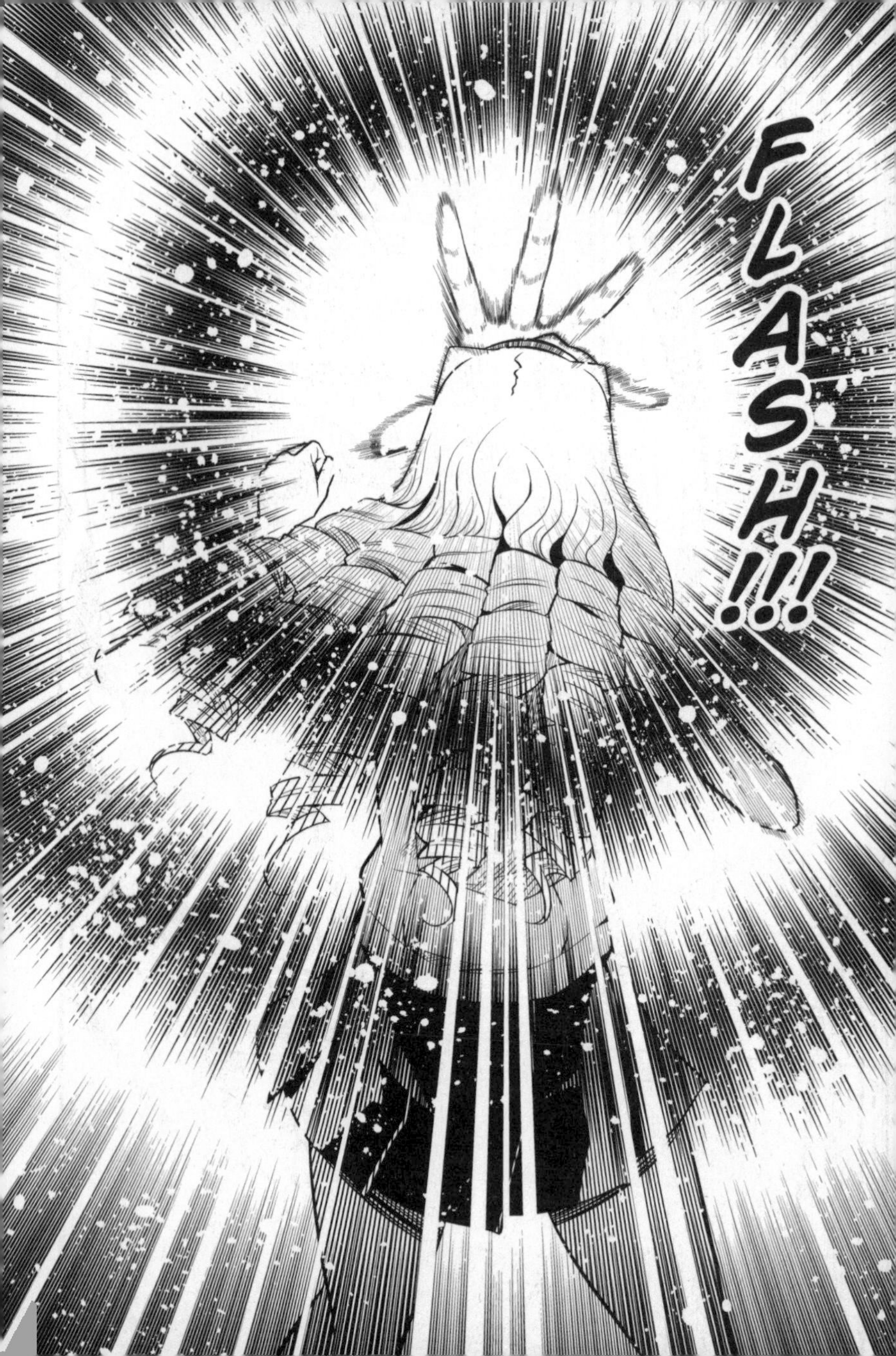
FLASH!!!

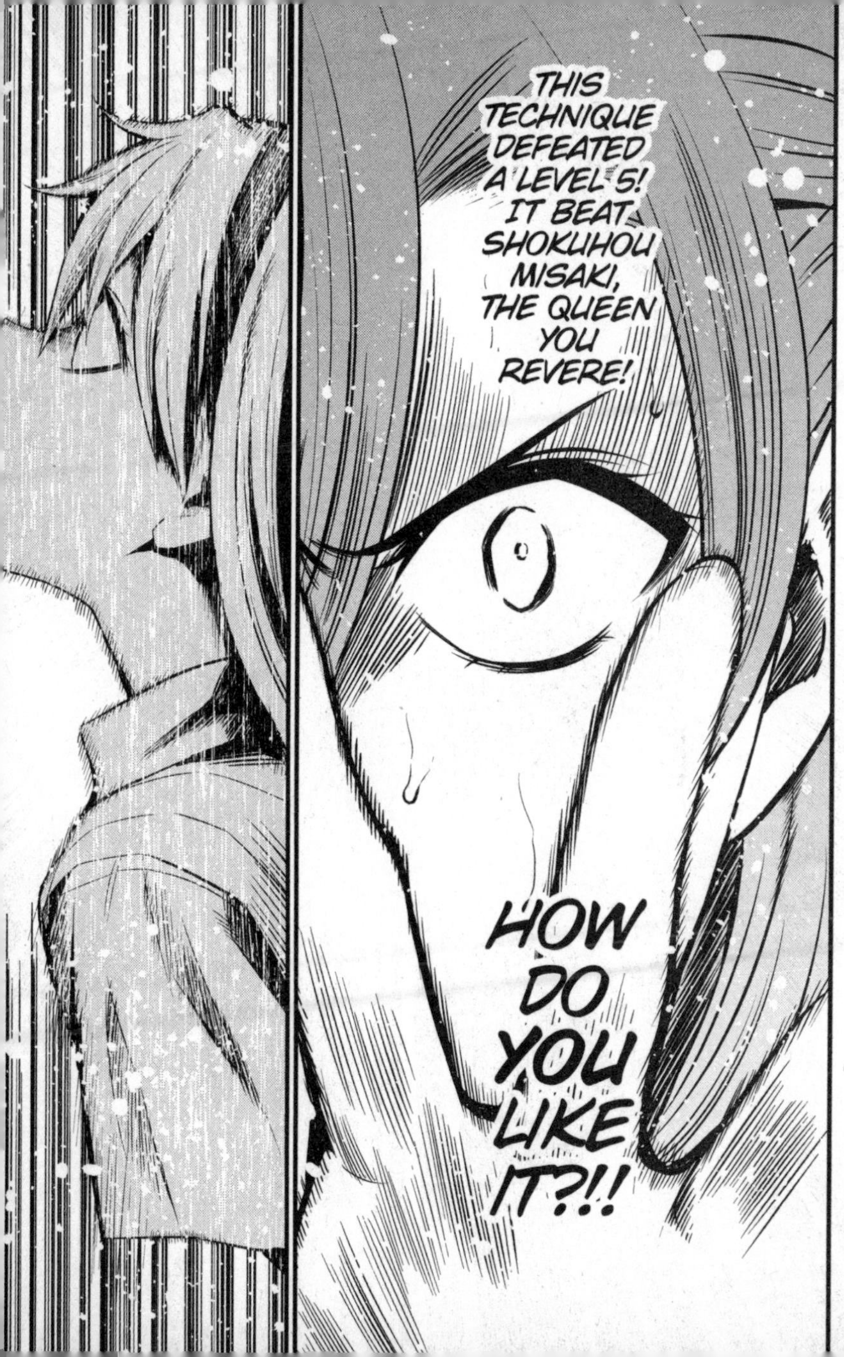
THIS TECHNIQUE DEFEATED A LEVEL 5! IT BEAT SHOKUHOU MISAKI, THE QUEEN YOU REVERE!
HOW DO YOU LIKE IT?!!

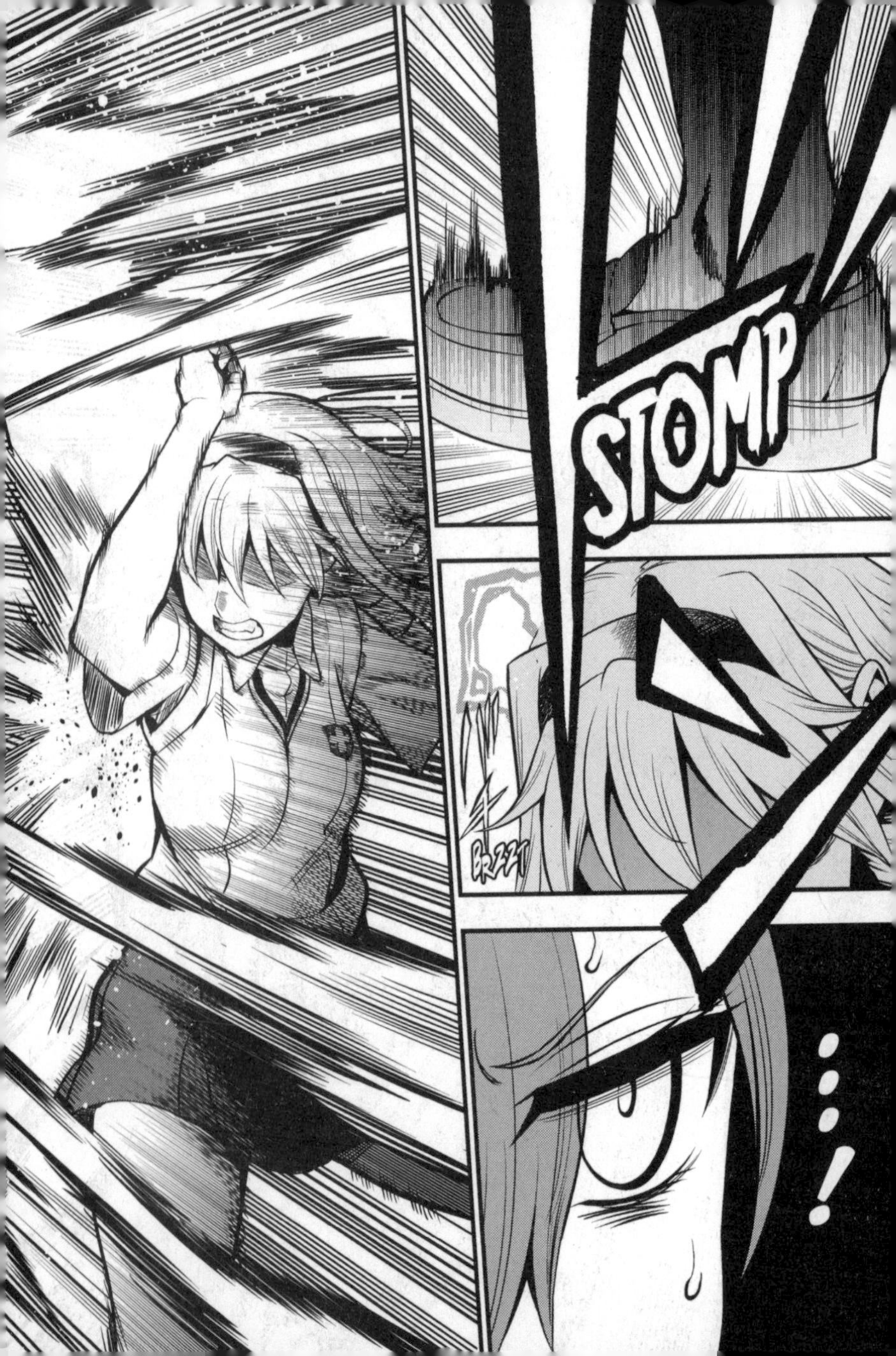

STOMP
BRZZT
...!

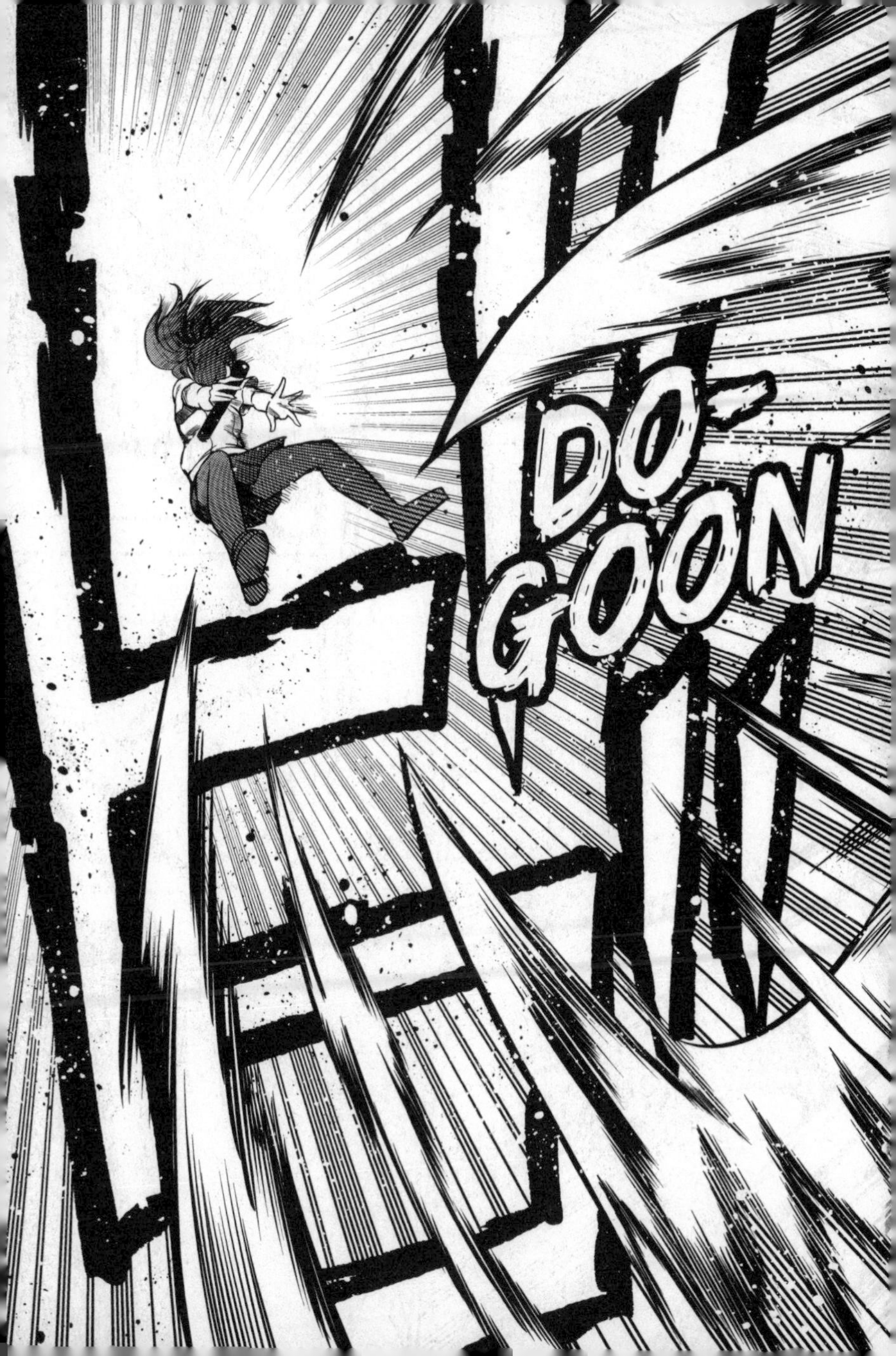
DO-GOON

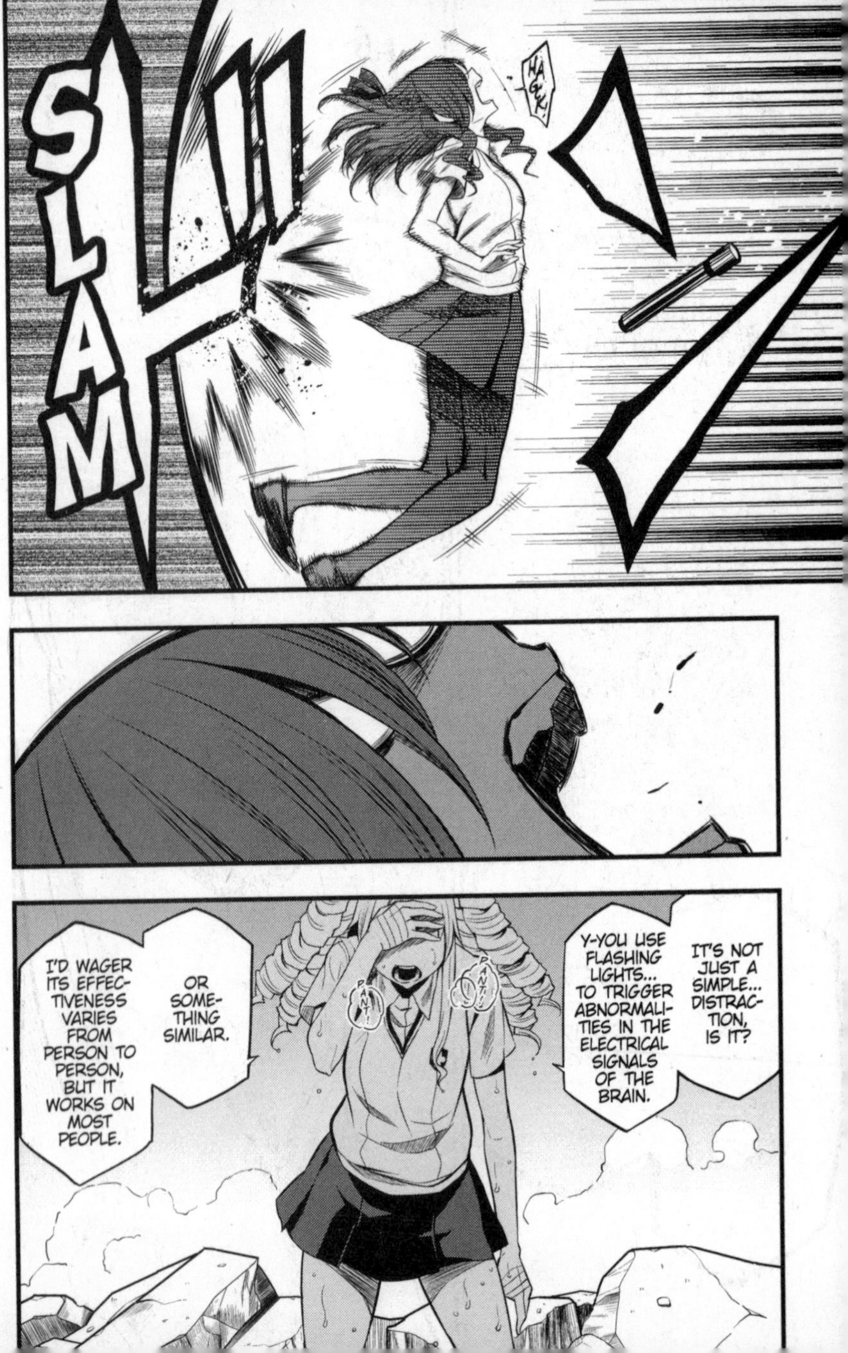
HAGK!
SLAM
IT'S NOT JUST A SIMPLE... DISTRACTION, IS IT?
Y-YOU USE FLASHING LIGHTS... TO TRIGGER ABNORMALITIES IN THE ELECTRICAL SIGNALS OF THE BRAIN.
PANT!
PANT!
OR SOMETHING SIMILAR.
I'D WAGER ITS EFFECTIVENESS VARIES FROM PERSON TO PERSON, BUT IT WORKS ON MOST PEOPLE.

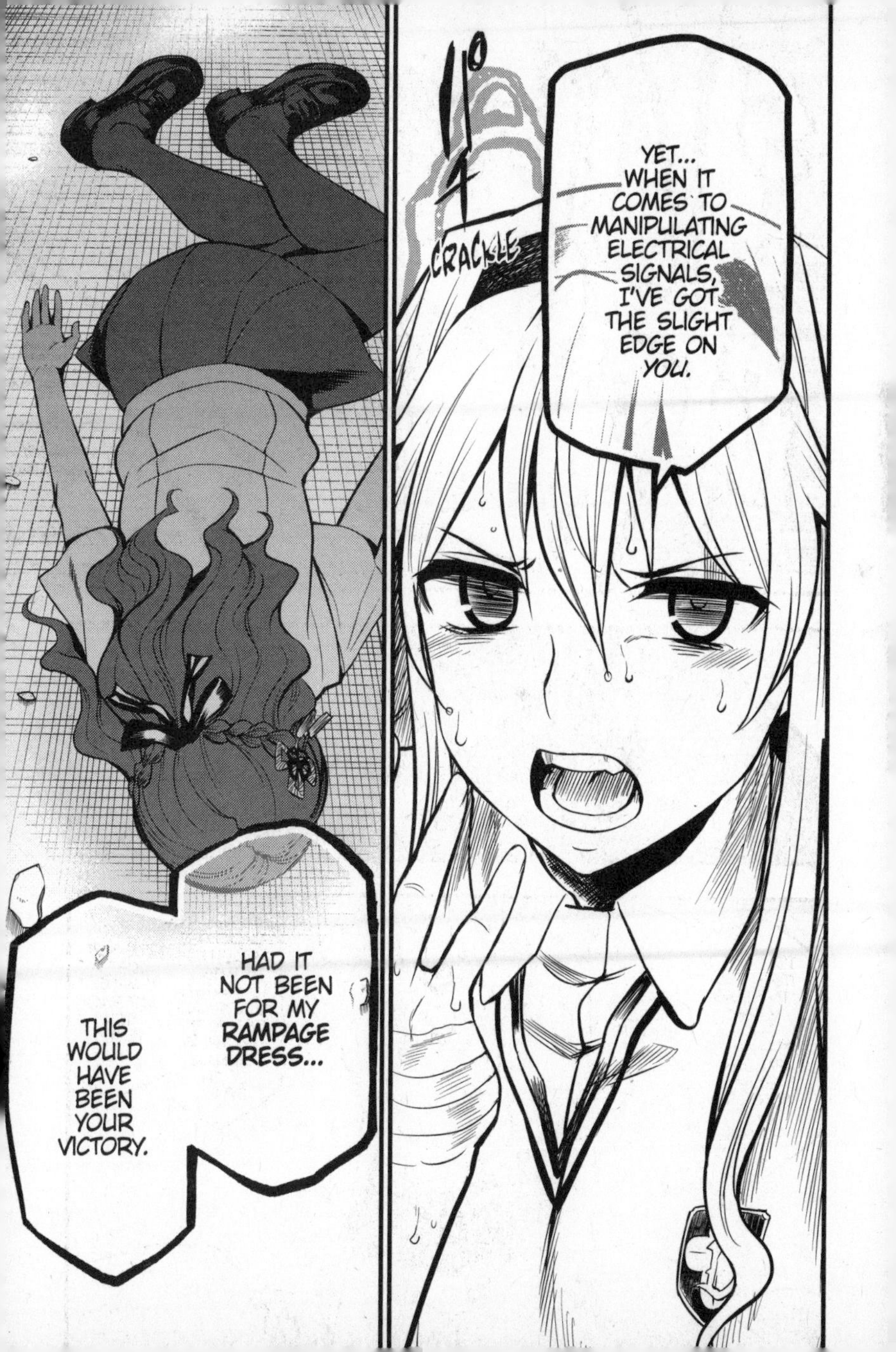
YET... WHEN IT COMES TO MANIPULATING ELECTRICAL SIGNALS, I'VE GOT THE SLIGHT EDGE ON YOU.
CRACKLE
HAD IT NOT BEEN FOR MY RAMPAGE DRESS...
THIS WOULD HAVE BEEN YOUR VICTORY.

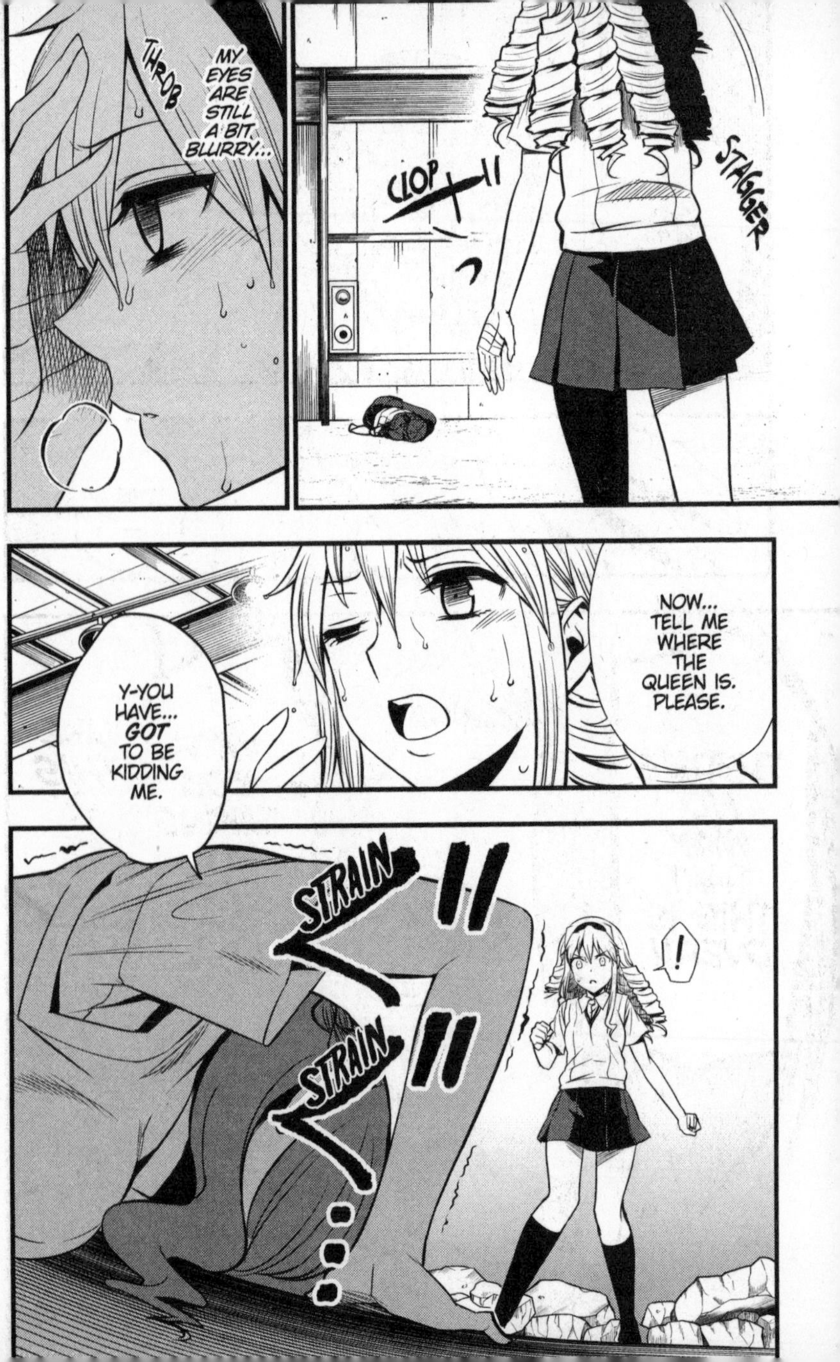
STAGGER
CLOP
THROB
MY EYES ARE STILL A BIT BLURRY...
NOW... TELL ME WHERE THE QUEEN IS. PLEASE.
Y-YOU HAVE... GOT TO BE KIDDING ME.
STRAIN
STRAIN
!
...

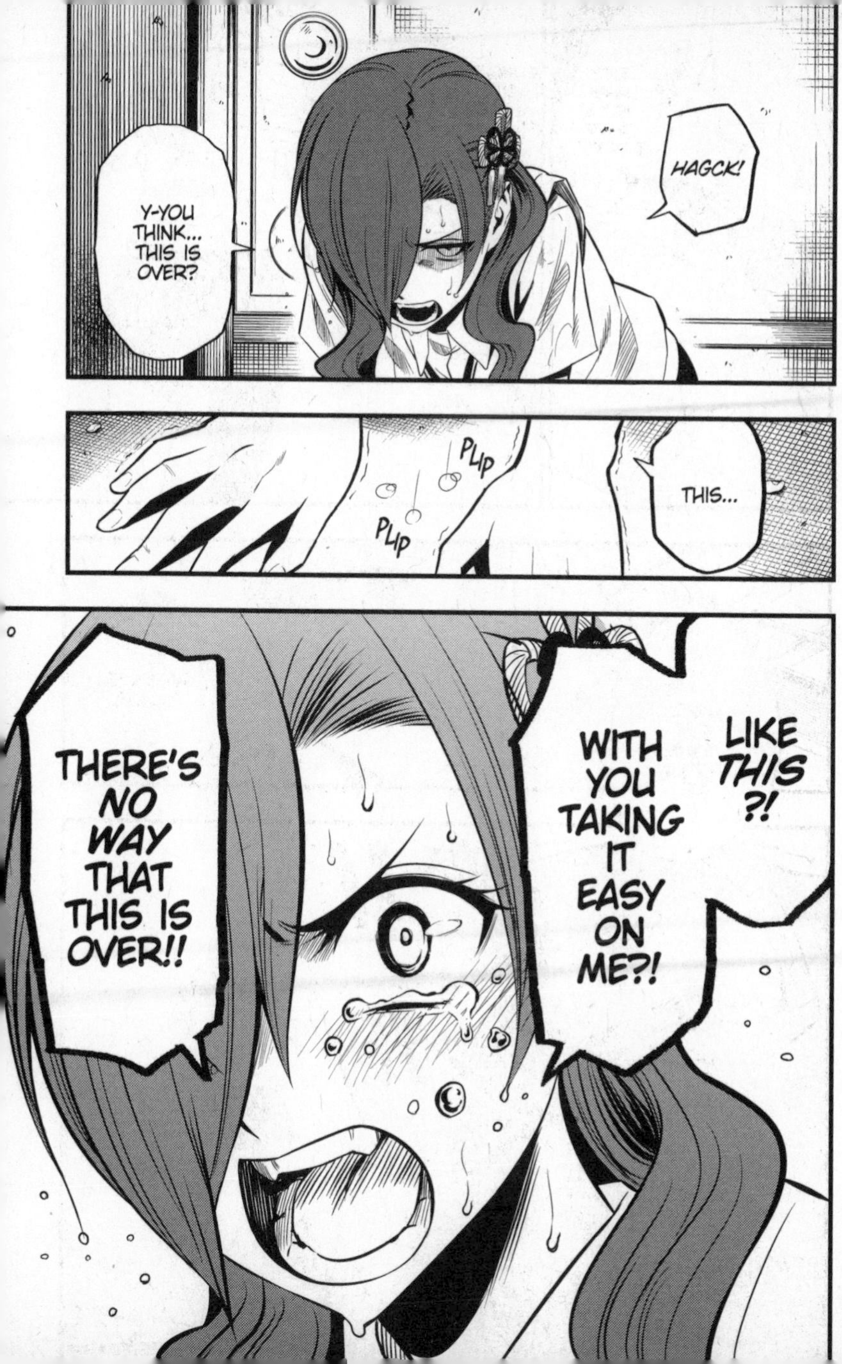
HAGCK!
Y-YOU THINK... THIS IS OVER?
THIS...
PLIP
PLIP
LIKE *THIS*?!
WITH YOU TAKING IT EASY ON ME?!
THERE'S *NO WAY* THAT THIS IS OVER!!

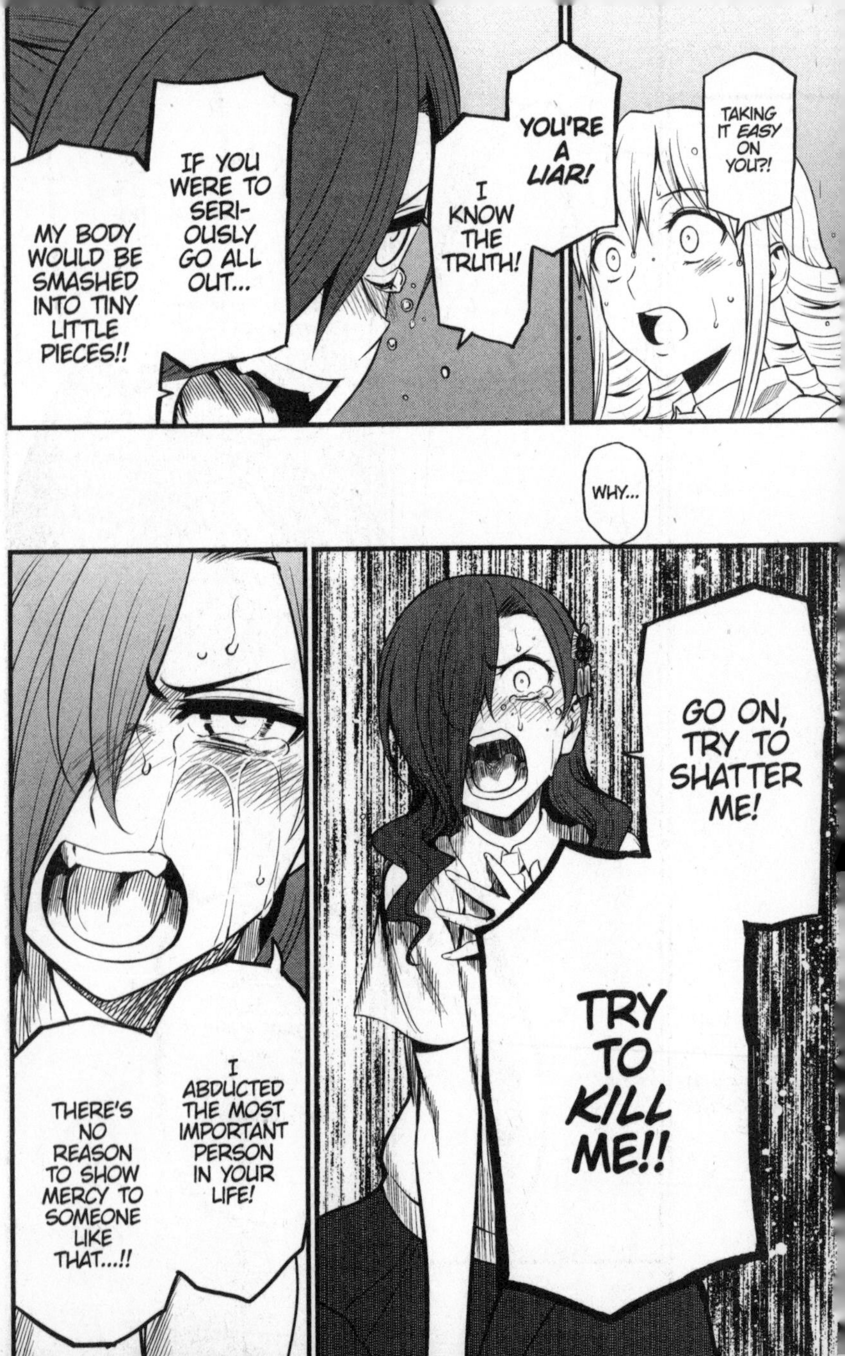
TAKING IT EASY ON YOU?!
YOU'RE A LIAR!
I KNOW THE TRUTH!
IF YOU WERE TO SERI-OUSLY GO ALL OUT...
MY BODY WOULD BE SMASHED INTO TINY LITTLE PIECES!!
WHY...
GO ON, TRY TO SHATTER ME!
TRY TO KILL ME!!
I ABDUCTED THE MOST IMPORTANT PERSON IN YOUR LIFE!
THERE'S NO REASON TO SHOW MERCY TO SOMEONE LIKE THAT...!!

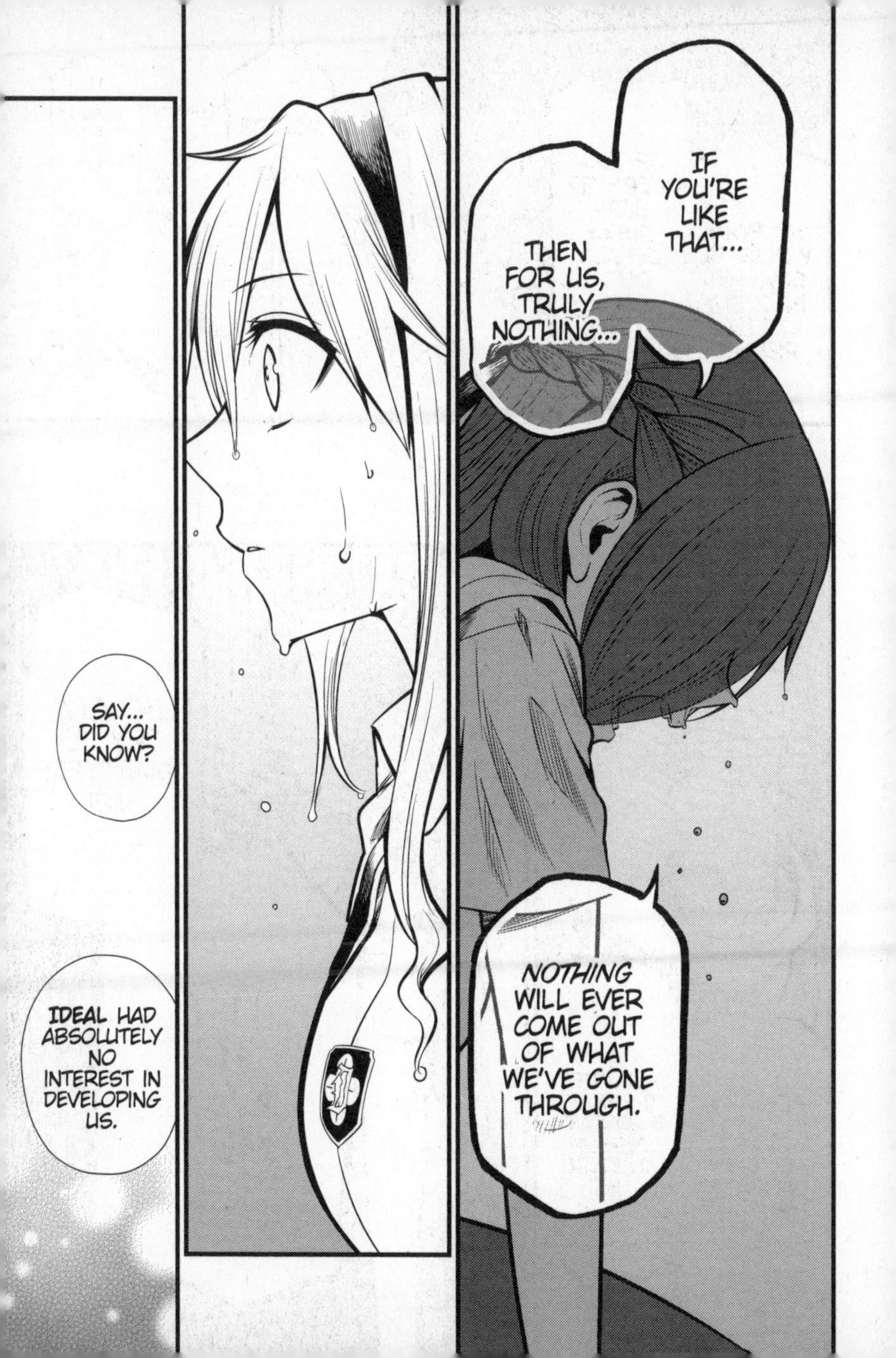
IF YOU'RE LIKE THAT...
THEN FOR US, TRULY NOTHING...
NOTHING WILL EVER COME OUT OF WHAT WE'VE GONE THROUGH.
SAY... DID YOU KNOW?
IDEAL HAD ABSOLUTELY NO INTEREST IN DEVELOPING US.

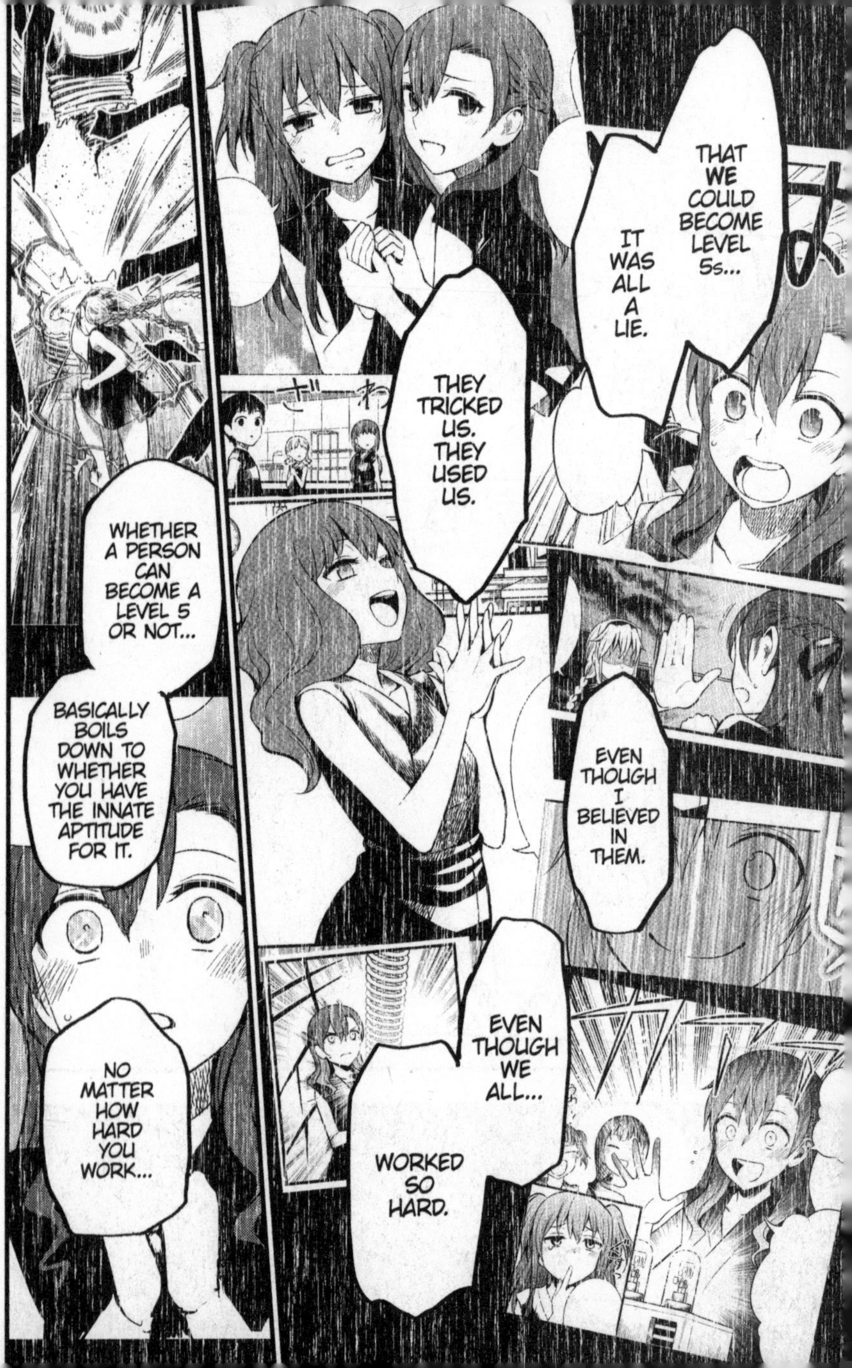

THAT WE COULD BECOME LEVEL 5s...
IT WAS ALL A LIE.
THEY TRICKED US. THEY USED US.
EVEN THOUGH I BELIEVED IN THEM.
EVEN THOUGH WE ALL...
WORKED SO HARD.
WHETHER A PERSON CAN BECOME A LEVEL 5 OR NOT...
BASICALLY BOILS DOWN TO WHETHER YOU HAVE THE INNATE APTITUDE FOR IT.
NO MATTER HOW HARD YOU WORK...

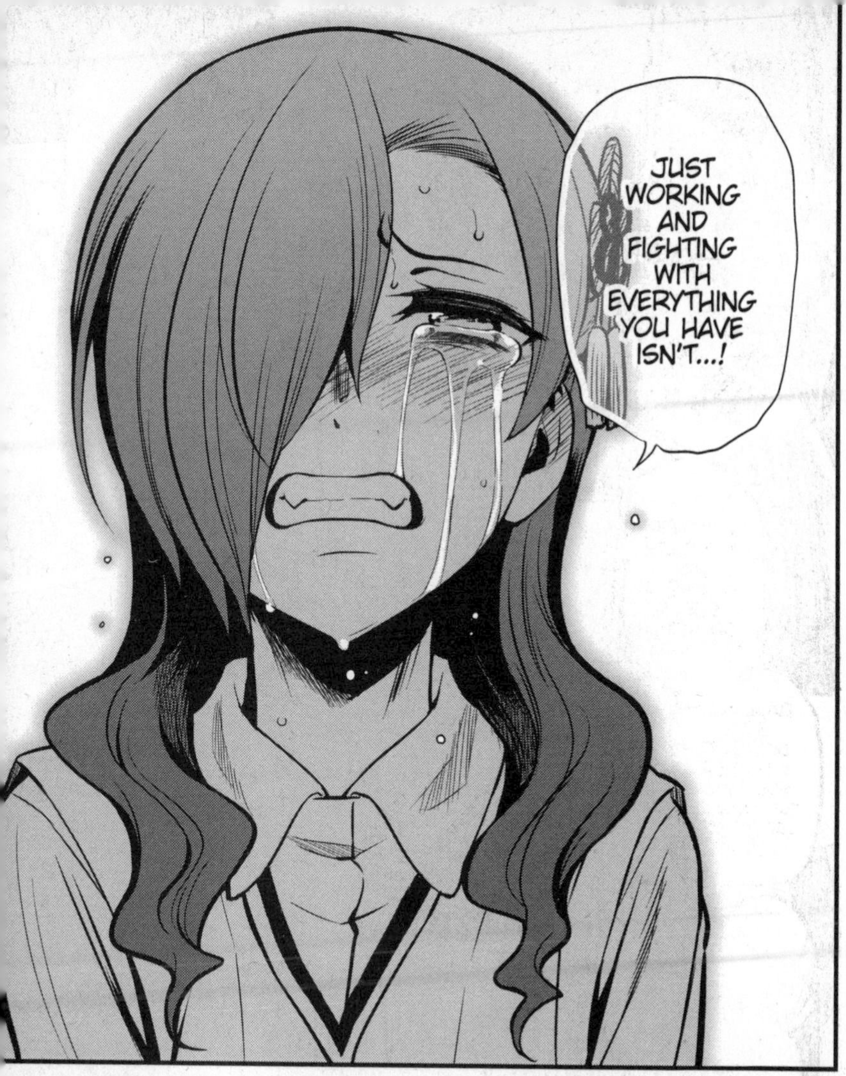
JUST WORKING AND FIGHTING WITH EVERYTHING YOU HAVE ISN'T...!

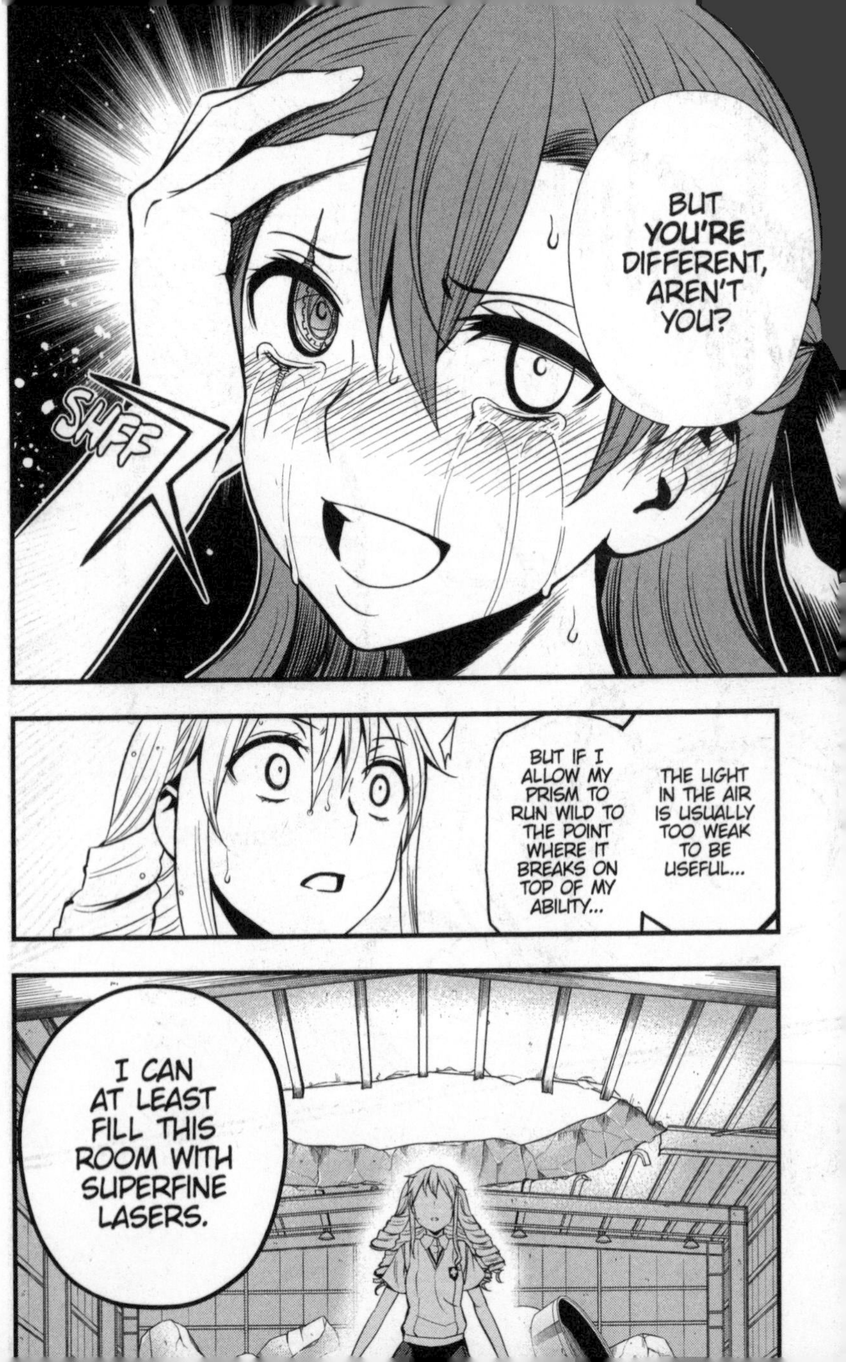

BUT YOU'RE DIFFERENT, AREN'T YOU?
SHFF
THE LIGHT IN THE AIR IS USUALLY TOO WEAK TO BE USEFUL...
BUT IF I ALLOW MY PRISM TO RUN WILD TO THE POINT WHERE IT BREAKS ON TOP OF MY ABILITY...
I CAN AT LEAST FILL THIS ROOM WITH SUPERFINE LASERS.

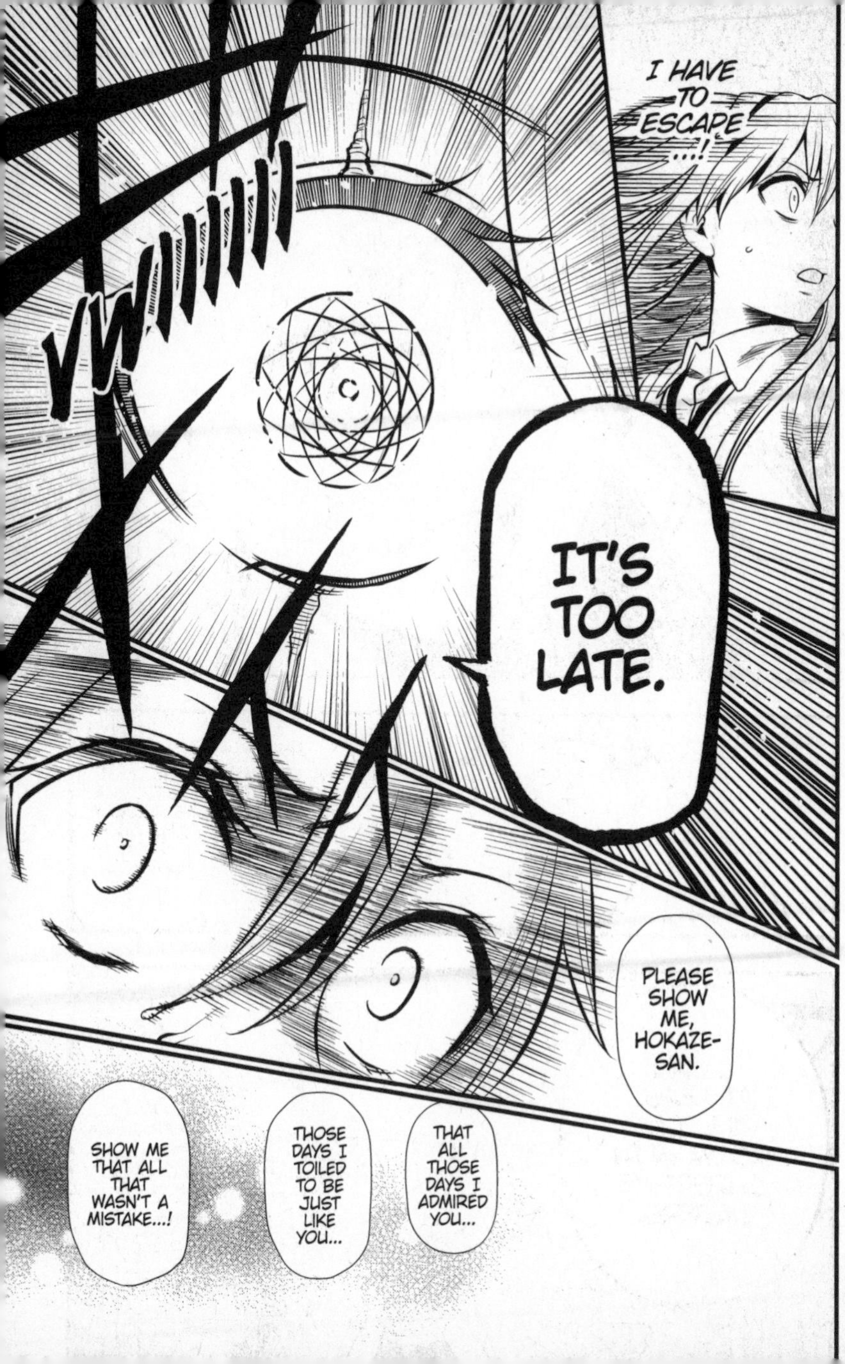
I HAVE TO ESCAPE...!
IT'S TOO LATE.
PLEASE SHOW ME, HOKAZE-SAN.
THAT ALL THOSE DAYS I ADMIRED YOU...
THOSE DAYS I TOILED TO BE JUST LIKE YOU...
SHOW ME THAT ALL THAT WASN'T A MISTAKE...!

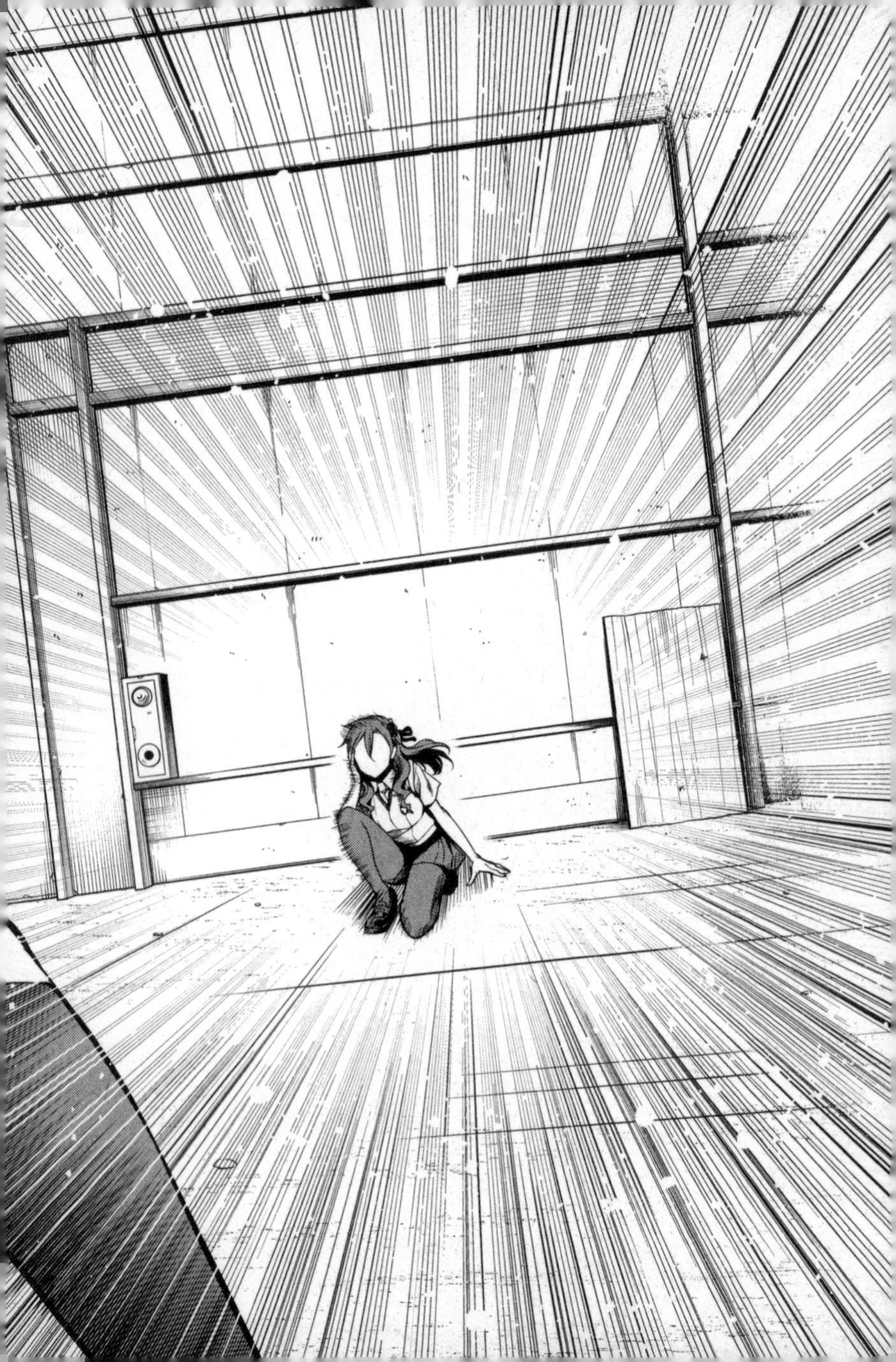

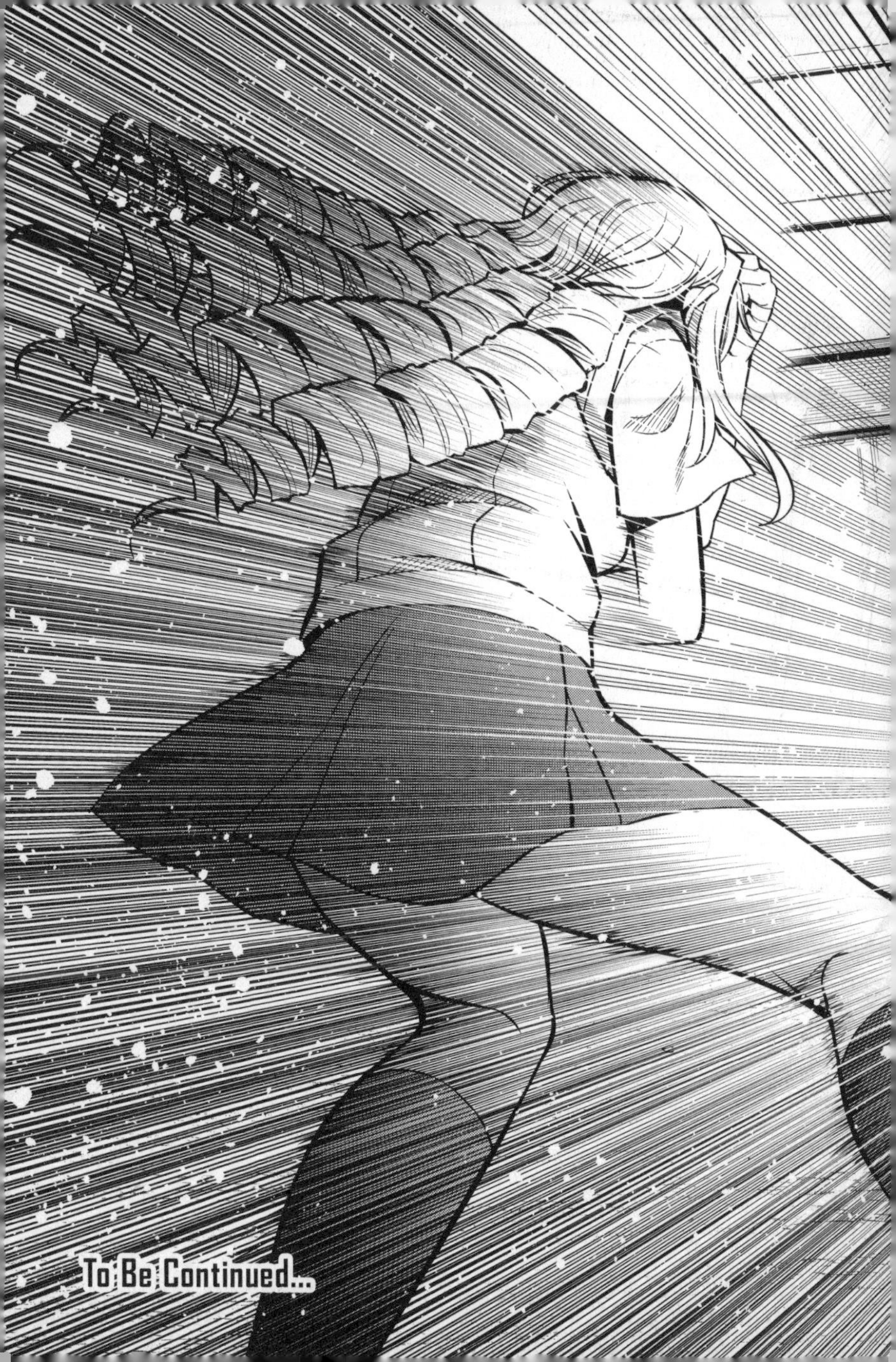
To Be Continued...

A CERTAIN SCIENTIFIC RAILGUN
Astral*Buddy

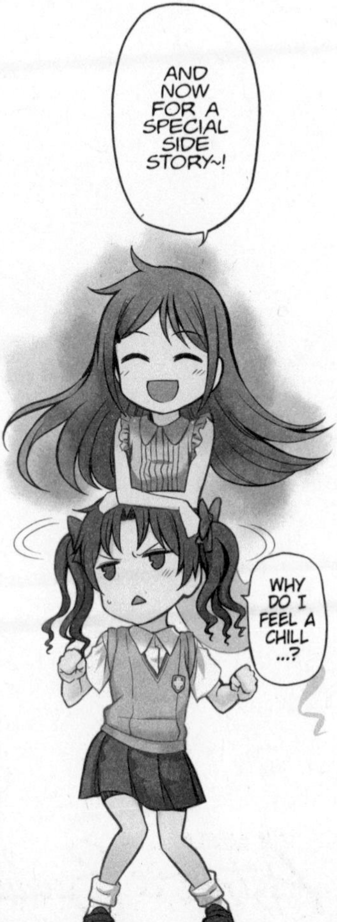
AND NOW FOR A SPECIAL SIDE STORY~!
WHY DO I FEEL A CHILL ...?

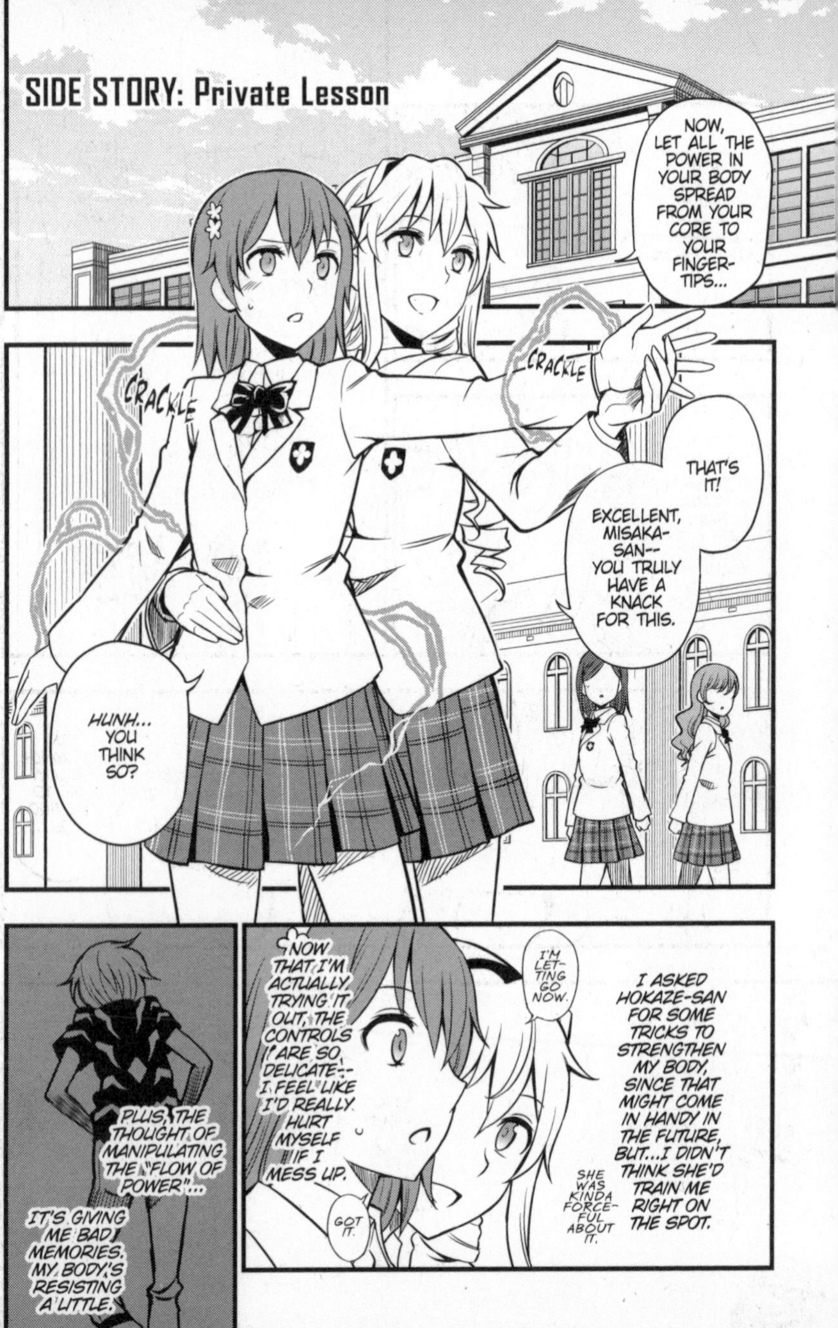
SIDE STORY: Private Lesson
NOW, LET ALL THE POWER IN YOUR BODY SPREAD FROM YOUR CORE TO YOUR FINGER-TIPS...
CRACKLE
THAT'S IT!
EXCELLENT, MISAKA-SAN-- YOU TRULY HAVE A KNACK FOR THIS.
CRACKLE
HUNH... YOU THINK SO?
I ASKED HOKAZE-SAN FOR SOME TRICKS TO STRENGTHEN MY BODY, SINCE THAT MIGHT COME IN HANDY IN THE FUTURE, BUT...I DIDN'T THINK SHE'D TRAIN ME RIGHT ON THE SPOT.
SHE WAS KINDA FORCE-FUL ABOUT IT.
I'M LET-TING GO NOW.
GOT IT.
NOW THAT I'M ACTUALLY TRYING IT OUT, THE CONTROLS ARE SO DELICATE-- I FEEL LIKE I'D REALLY HURT MYSELF IF I MESS UP.
PLUS, THE THOUGHT OF MANIPULATING THE "FLOW OF POWER"...
IT'S GIVING ME BAD MEMORIES. MY BODY'S RESISTING A LITTLE.

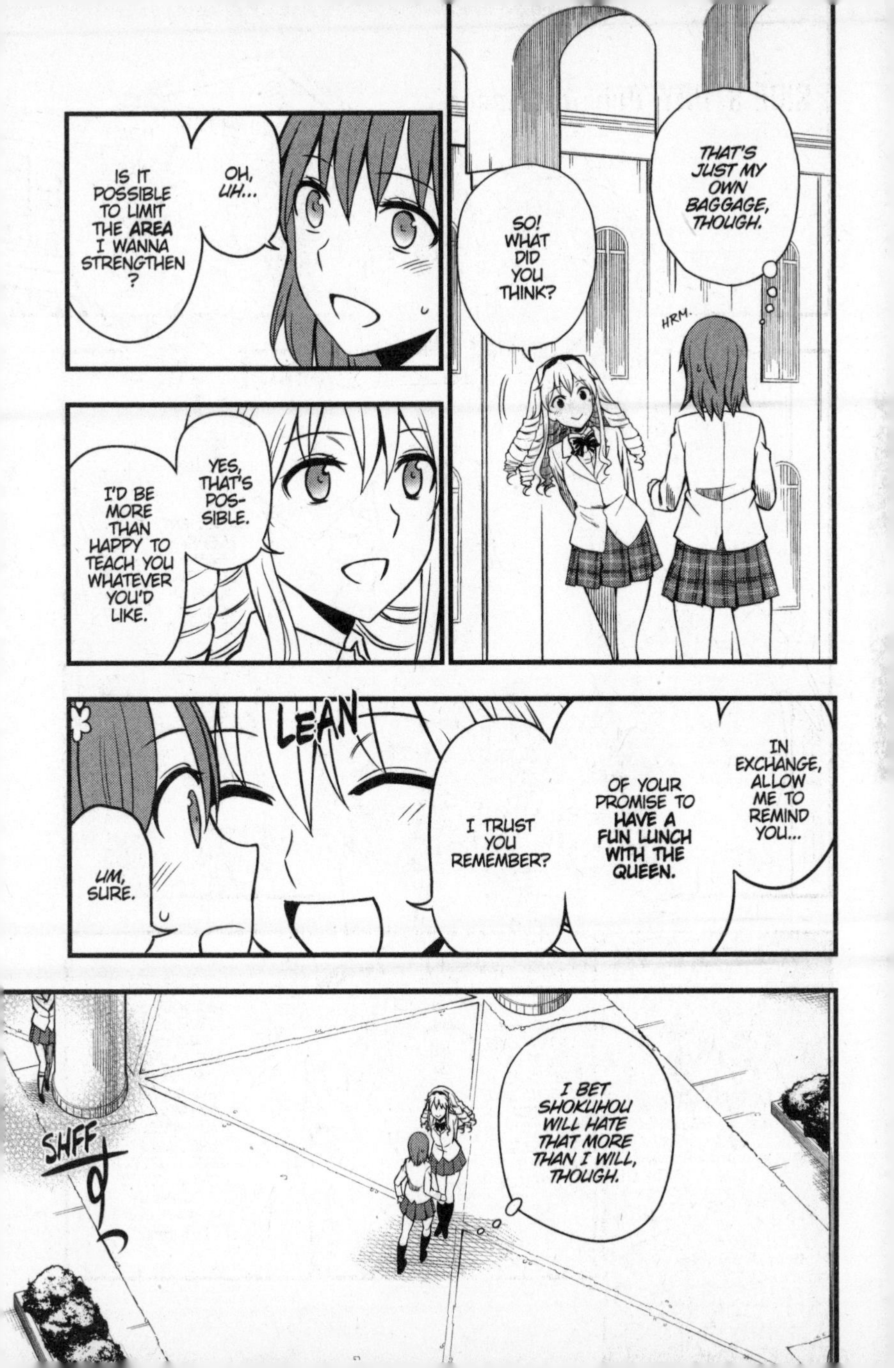

THAT'S JUST MY OWN BAGGAGE, THOUGH.
SO! WHAT DID YOU THINK?
HRM.
OH, UH...
IS IT POSSIBLE TO LIMIT THE AREA I WANNA STRENGTHEN?
YES, THAT'S POS-SIBLE.
I'D BE MORE THAN HAPPY TO TEACH YOU WHATEVER YOU'D LIKE.
IN EXCHANGE, ALLOW ME TO REMIND YOU...
OF YOUR PROMISE TO HAVE A FUN LUNCH WITH THE QUEEN.
I TRUST YOU REMEMBER?
LEAN
UM, SURE.
I BET SHOKUHOU WILL HATE THAT MORE THAN I WILL, THOUGH.
SHFF

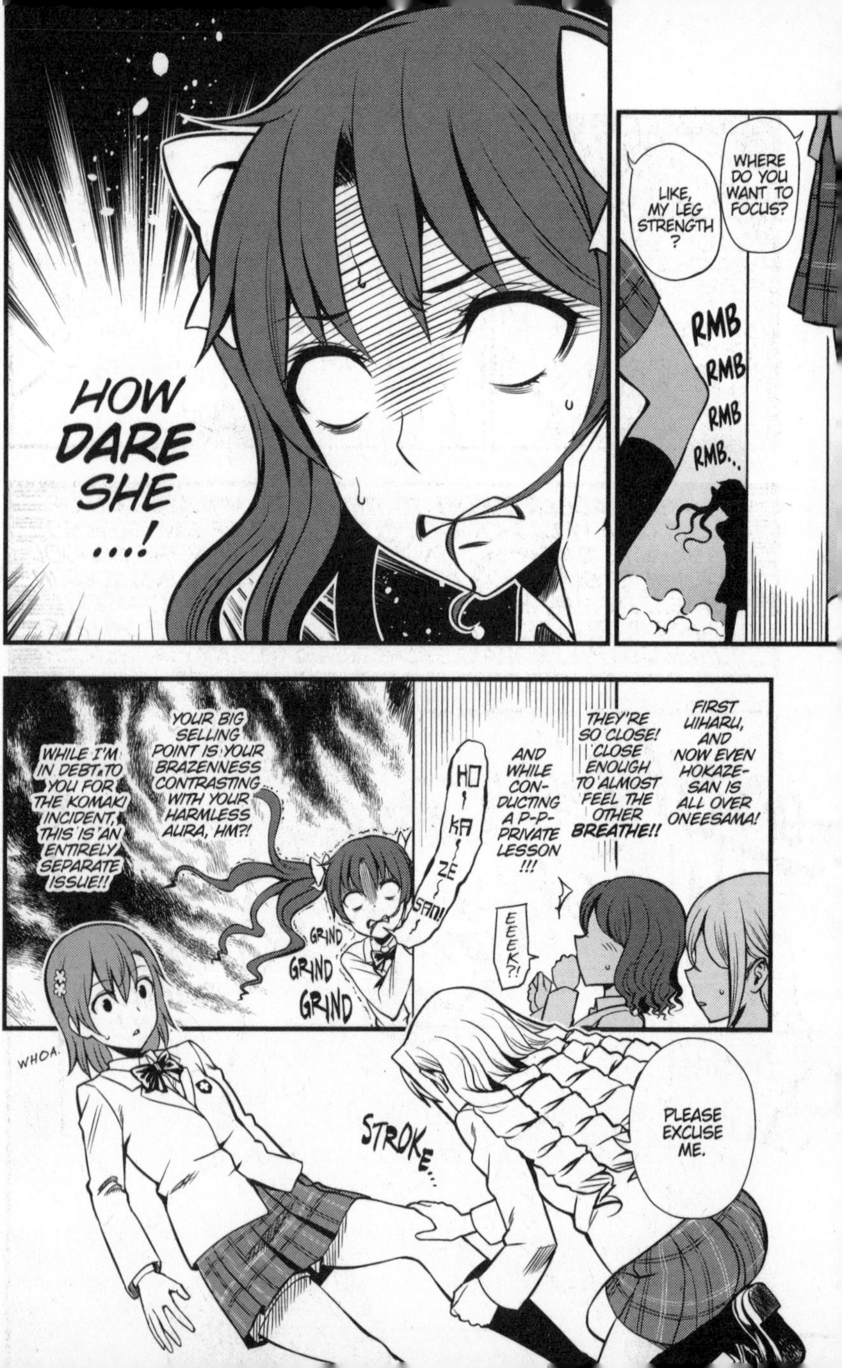
WHERE DO YOU WANT TO FOCUS?
LIKE, MY LEG STRENGTH?
RMB RMB RMB RMB...
HOW DARE SHE ...!
FIRST UIHARU, AND NOW EVEN HOKAZE-SAN IS ALL OVER ONEESAMA!
THEY'RE SO CLOSE! CLOSE ENOUGH TO ALMOST FEEL THE OTHER BREATHE!!
AND WHILE CONDUCTING A P-P-PRIVATE LESSON!!!
EEEEK?!
HO-KA-ZE~SAN!!
YOUR BIG SELLING POINT IS YOUR BRAZENNESS CONTRASTING WITH YOUR HARMLESS AURA, HM?!
WHILE I'M IN DEBT TO YOU FOR THE KOMAKI INCIDENT, THIS IS AN ENTIRELY SEPARATE ISSUE!!
GRIND GRIND GRIND
PLEASE EXCUSE ME.
STROKE...
WHOA.

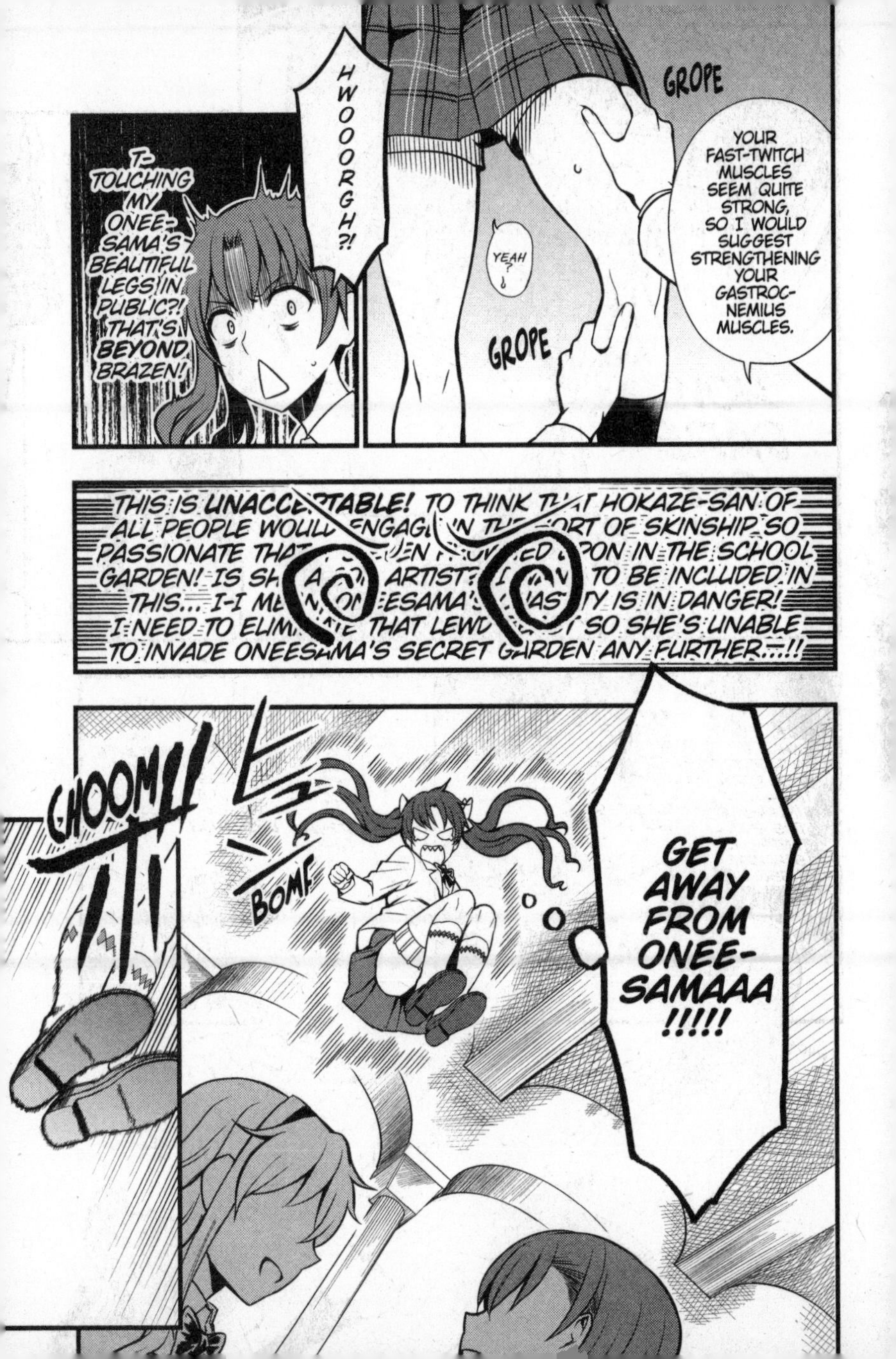
GROPE
YOUR FAST-TWITCH MUSCLES SEEM QUITE STRONG, SO I WOULD SUGGEST STRENGTHENING YOUR GASTROCNEMIUS MUSCLES.
YEAH?
GROPE
HWOOOORGH?!
T-TOUCHING MY ONEE-SAMA'S BEAUTIFUL LEGS IN PUBLIC?! THAT'S BEYOND BRAZEN!
THIS IS UNACCEPTABLE! TO THINK THAT HOKAZE-SAN OF ALL PEOPLE WOULD ENGAGE IN THE SORT OF SKINSHIP SO PASSIONATE THAT ... IN THE SCHOOL GARDEN! IS SHE A ... ARTIST? ... TO BE INCLUDED IN THIS... I-I MEAN, ONEESAMA'S CHASTITY IS IN DANGER! I NEED TO ELIMINATE THAT LEWD ... SO SHE'S UNABLE TO INVADE ONEESAMA'S SECRET GARDEN ANY FURTHER...!!
GET AWAY FROM ONEE-SAMAAA!!!!!
CHOOM!!
BOMF

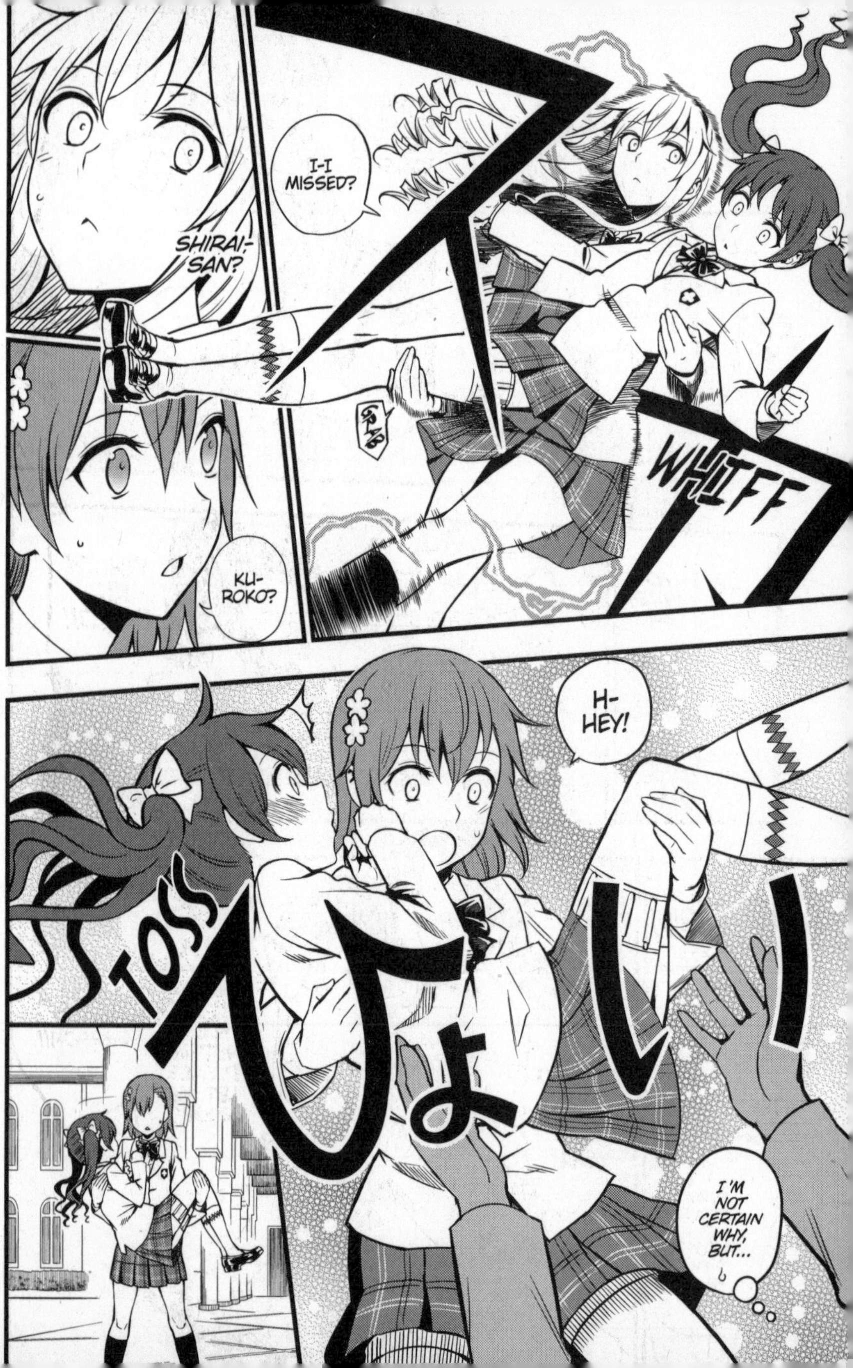

I-I MISSED?
GRAB
WHIFF
SHIRAI-SAN?
KU-ROKO?
H-HEY!
TOSS
ひょい
I'M NOT CERTAIN WHY, BUT...

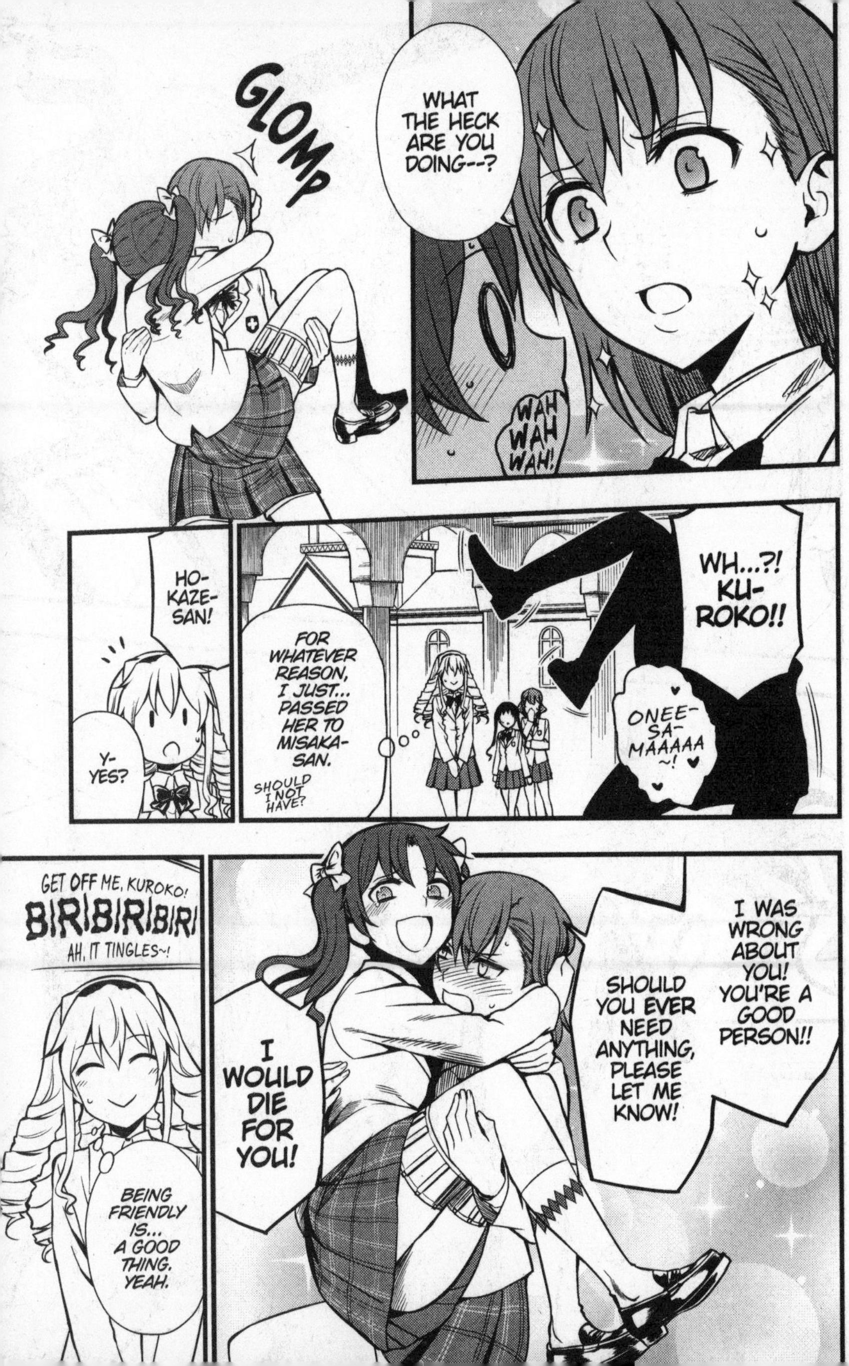
WHAT THE HECK ARE YOU DOING--?
WAH WAH WAH!
GLOMP
WH...?! KU-ROKO!!
ONEE-SA-MAAAAAA~!
FOR WHATEVER REASON, I JUST... PASSED HER TO MISAKA-SAN.
SHOULD I NOT HAVE?
HO-KAZE-SAN!
Y-YES?
I WAS WRONG ABOUT YOU! YOU'RE A GOOD PERSON!!
SHOULD YOU EVER NEED ANYTHING, PLEASE LET ME KNOW!
I WOULD DIE FOR YOU!
GET OFF ME, KUROKO!
BIRIBIRIBIRI
AH, IT TINGLES~!
BEING FRIENDLY IS... A GOOD THING. YEAH.

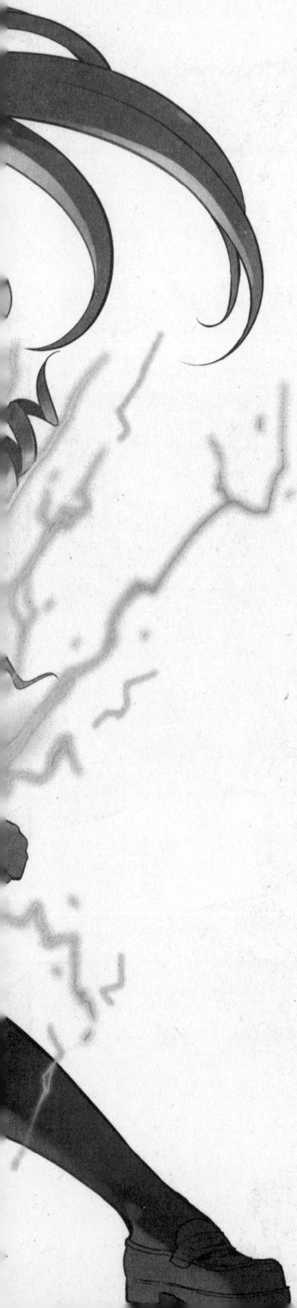

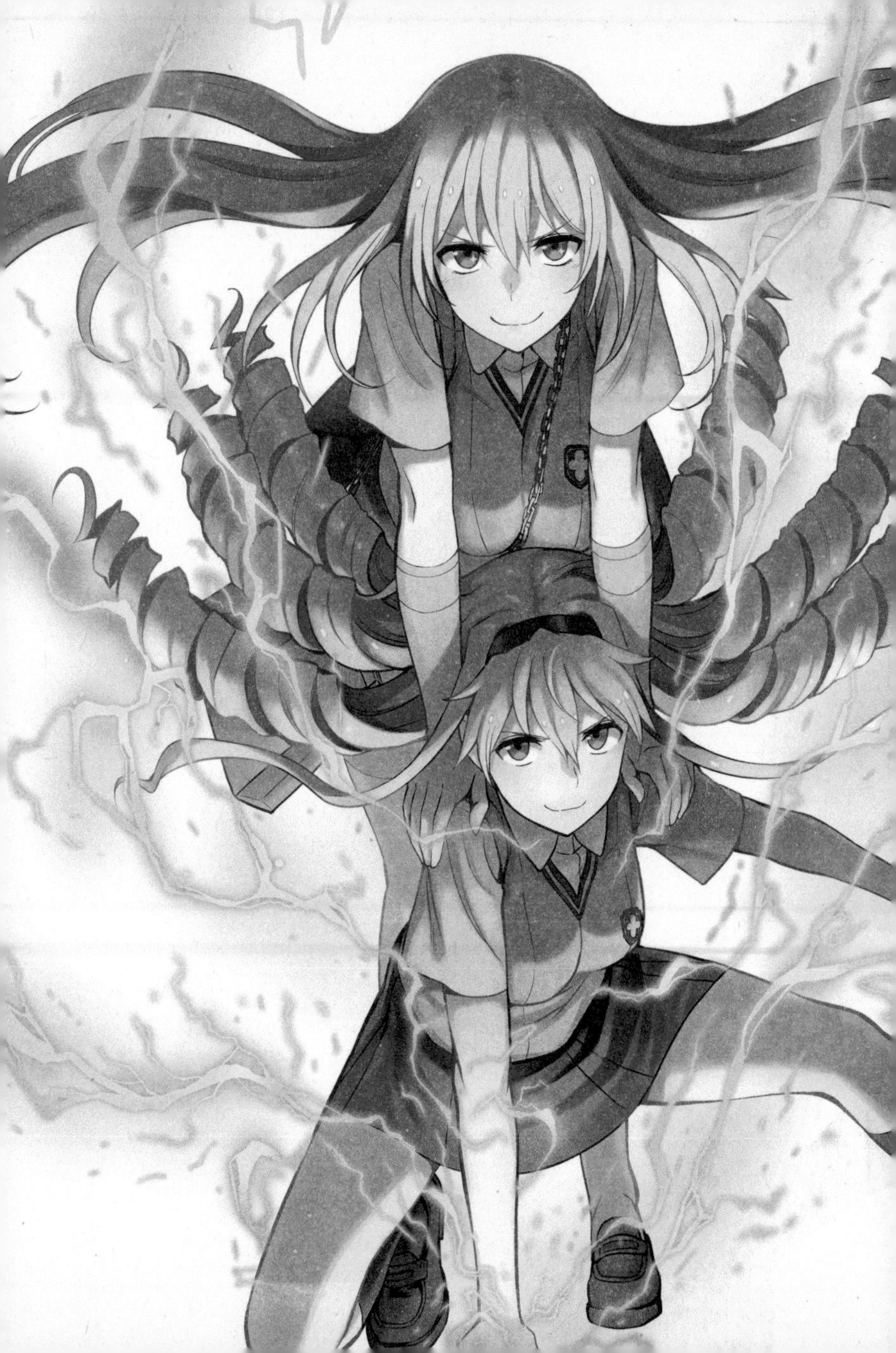

A CERTAIN SCIENTIFIC RAILGUN
Astral*Buddy

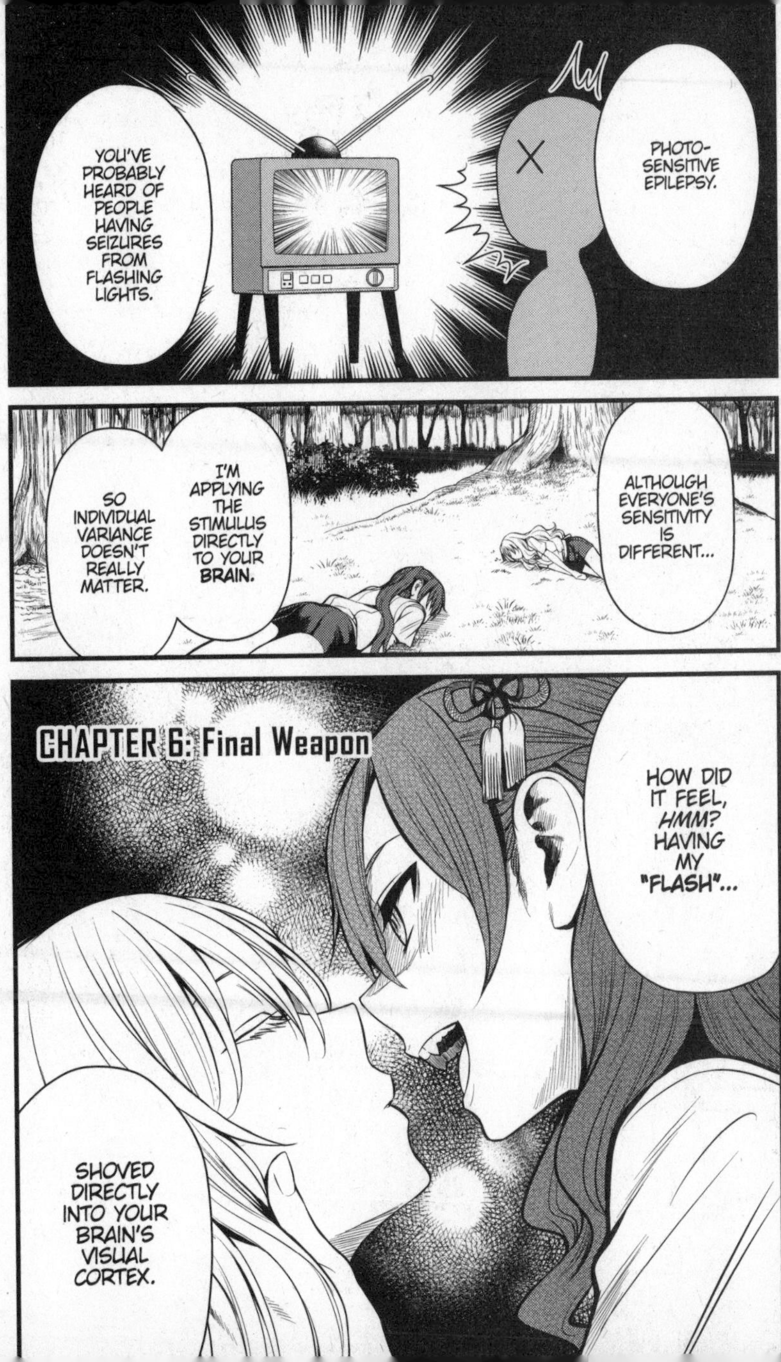
PHOTO-SENSITIVE EPILEPSY.
YOU'VE PROBABLY HEARD OF PEOPLE HAVING SEIZURES FROM FLASHING LIGHTS.
ALTHOUGH EVERYONE'S SENSITIVITY IS DIFFERENT...
I'M APPLYING THE STIMULUS DIRECTLY TO YOUR **BRAIN.**
SO INDIVIDUAL VARIANCE DOESN'T REALLY MATTER.
CHAPTER 6: Final Weapon
HOW DID IT FEEL, *HMM?* HAVING MY **"FLASH"...**
SHOVED DIRECTLY INTO YOUR BRAIN'S VISUAL CORTEX.

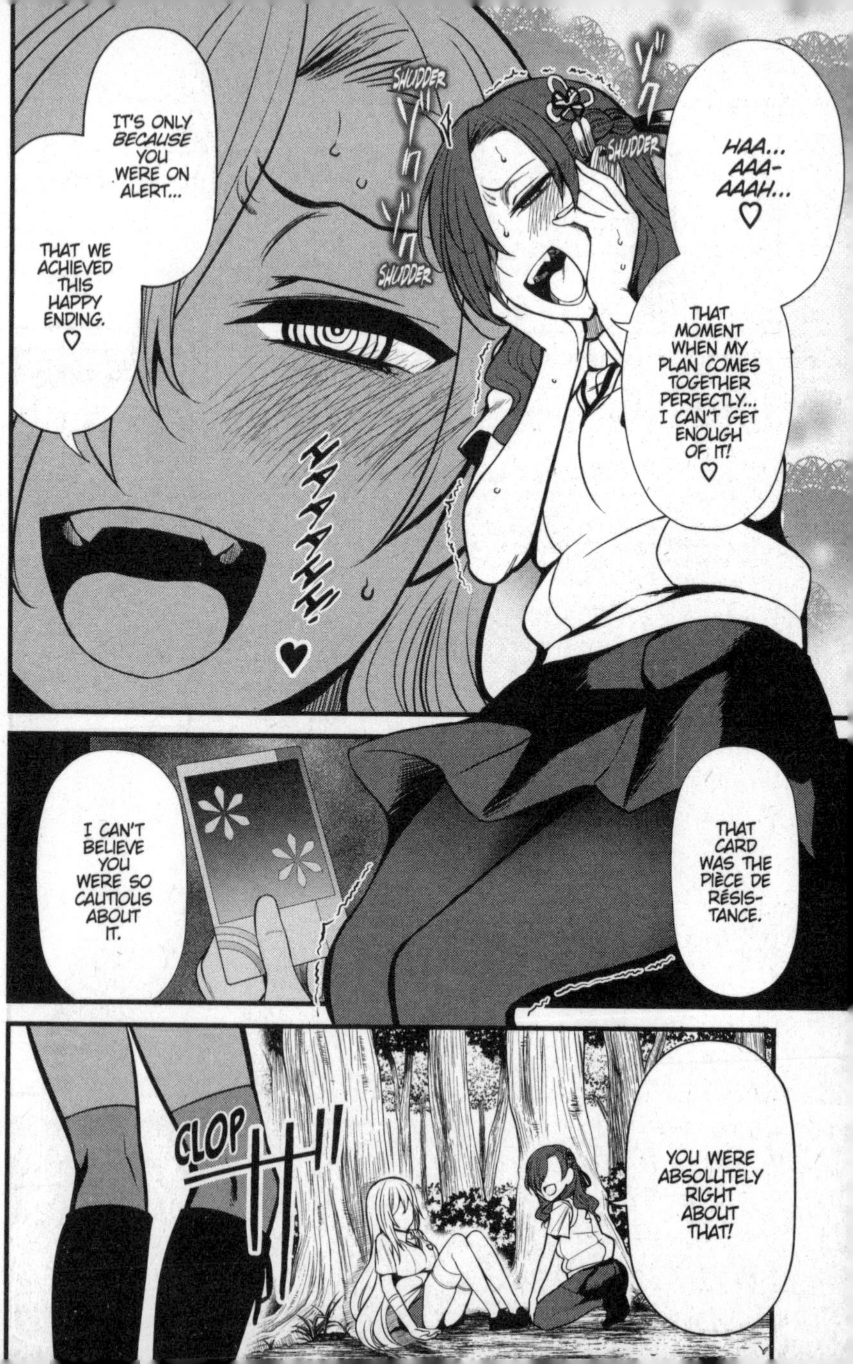
HAA... AAA-AAAH... ♡
SHUDDER
SHUDDER
SHUDDER
THAT MOMENT WHEN MY PLAN COMES TOGETHER PERFECTLY... I CAN'T GET ENOUGH OF IT! ♡
IT'S ONLY *BECAUSE* YOU WERE ON ALERT...
THAT WE ACHIEVED THIS HAPPY ENDING. ♡
HAAAAHH! ♡
THAT CARD WAS THE PIÈCE DE RÉSISTANCE.
I CAN'T BELIEVE YOU WERE SO CAUTIOUS ABOUT IT.
YOU WERE ABSOLUTELY RIGHT ABOUT THAT!
CLOP

SEVEN SEAS ENTERTAINMENT PRESENTS

A CERTAIN SCIENTIFIC RAILGUN
Astral * Buddy

ceya

story: **KAZUMA KAMACHI** / art: **YASUHITO NOGI** / character designs: **KIYOTAKA HAIMURA**   VOLUME 2

TRANSLATION
Nan Rymer

ADAPTATION
Maggie Danger

LETTERING AND RETOUCH
Roland Amago
Bambi Eloriaga-Amago

COVER DESIGN
Nicky Lim

PROOFREADER
Kurestin Armada
Janet Houck

ASSISTANT EDITOR
Shannon Fay

PRODUCTION MANAGER
Lissa Pattillo

MANAGING EDITOR
Julie Davis

EDITOR-IN-CHIEF
Adam Arnold

PUBLISHER
Jason DeAngelis

A CERTAIN SCIENTIFIC RAILGUN: ASTRAL BUDDY VOL. 2
©KAZUMA KAMACHI/YASUHITO NOGI 2018
First published in 2018 by KADOKAWA CORPORATION, Tokyo.
English translation rights arranged with KADOKAWA CORPORATION, Tokyo.

Seven Seas press and purchase enquiries can be sent to Marketing Manager Lianne Sentar at press@gomanga.com. Information regarding the distribution and purchase of digital editions is available from Digital Manager CK Russell at digital@gomanga.com.

Seven Seas and the Seven Seas logo are trademarks of Seven Seas Entertainment. All rights reserved.

ISBN: 978-1-64275-076-8

Printed in Canada

First Printing: July 2019

10 9 8 7 6 5 4 3 2 1

FOLLOW US ONLINE: www.sevenseasentertainment.com

READING DIRECTIONS

This book reads from **right to left**, Japanese style. If this is your first time reading manga, you start reading from the top right panel on each page and take it from there. If you get lost, just follow the numbered diagram here. It may seem backwards at first, but you'll get the hang of it! Have fun!!

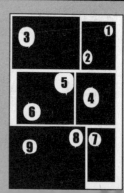